Twentieth-Century Crime Fiction

Twentieth-Century Crime Fiction

Lee Horsley
Lancaster University

OXFORD
UNIVERSITY PRESS

Great Clarendon Street, Oxford OX2 6DP

Oxford University Press is a department of the University of Oxford.
It furthers the University's objective of excellence in research, scholarship,
and education by publishing worldwide in

Oxford New York

Auckland Cape Town Dar es Salaam Hong Kong Karachi
Kuala Lumpur Madrid Melbourne Mexico City Nairobi New Delhi
Shanghai Taipei Toronto

With offices in

Argentina Austria Brazil Chile Czech Republic France Greece
Guatemala Hungary Italy Japan Poland Portugal Singapore
South Korea Switzerland Thailand Turkey Ukraine Vietnam

Oxford is a registered trade mark of Oxford University Press
in the UK and in certain other countries

Published in the United States
by Oxford University Press Inc., New York

British Library Cataloguing in Publication Data
Data available

Library of Congress Cataloging in Publication Data
Data available

ISBN 0–19–928345–1   978–0–19–928345–3
ISBN 0–19–925326–9   978–0–19–925326–5 pbk.

1 3 5 7 9 10 8 6 4 2

Typeset by RefineCatch Limited, Bungay, Suffolk
Printed in Great Britain by
Biddles Ltd., King's Lynn, Norfolk

Preface

THE aim of this book is to enhance understanding of one of the most popular forms of genre fiction by examining a wide variety of the detective and crime fiction produced in twentieth-century Britain and America. The popular market for such literature continues to expand, and the number of university courses devoted to studying the genre has been steadily increasing. This study will, it is hoped, be of interest to anyone who enjoys reading crime fiction. It is also, however, designed with the needs of academic courses in mind. In any course on genre fiction, it is important to give students a broad sense both of generic development and of the ways in which different theoretical approaches (for example, formalist, historicist, psycho-analytic, postcolonial, feminist) are of relevance to the reading of popular fiction. *Twentieth-Century Crime Fiction* is a critical text that could be used to supplement a range of crime fiction courses, whether the structure of the course brings to the fore historical con-texts, ideological shifts, the emergence of sub-genres, or the applica-tion of critical theories. Forty-seven texts are chosen for detailed discussion. These are widely available stories and novels, all of which lend themselves to detailed analysis and to the discussion of the wider issues that arise in the study of crime fiction.

In seeking to illuminate the relationship between different phases of generic development the study employs an overlapping historical framework, with sections doubling back chronologically in order to explore the extent to which successive developments have their roots within the earlier phases of crime writing, as well as responding in complex ways to the preoccupations and anxieties of their own eras. The first part of the study considers the nature and evolution of the main sub-genres of crime fiction: the classic and hard-boiled strands of detective fiction, the non-investigative crime novel (centred on transgressors or victims), and the 'mixed' form of the police pro-cedural. It looks closely at the culturally specific factors that shaped each form and at the contradictory ways of reading these traditions. So, for example, the alleged conservatism of the classic detective story is examined in the light of interpretations which stress its indeterminacy and its capacity to subvert as well as to contain; the

patriarchal fantasies of control associated with the hard-boiled tradition are set against its resistance to authoritative discourse and
the evolving representations of 'tough' masculinity. Amongst the
main writers discussed are Sir Arthur Conan Doyle, Agatha Christie,
Dorothy L. Sayers, P. D. James, Ruth Rendell, Raymond Chandler,
Dashiell Hammett, Mickey Spillane, Ed McBain, James Sallis, Jim
Thompson, Patricia Highsmith, James Ellroy, and Patricia Cornwell.

The focus in the second half of the study is on the ways in which
writers have used crime fiction as a vehicle for socio-political critique.
These chapters consider the evolution of committed, oppositional
strategies. Analysing the work of writers like Carl Hiaasen, Bret
Easton Ellis, Iain Banks, Chester Himes, Walter Mosley, Mike Phillips,
Barbara Neely, Charlotte Carter, Mary Wings, Sara Paretsky, Sue
Grafton, and Helen Zahavi, they trace the development of politicized
detective and crime fiction, from Depression-era protests against
economic injustice to more recent decades, during which the genre
has been adapted for a wide variety of purposes, with writers launch-
ing protests, for example, against a complacent conformist ethos,
commodification and commercialism, ecological crimes, racism, and
sexism. The two final chapters centre on black and feminist appropriations of a genre frequently identified with predominantly white heterosexual male values and roles. Chapter 5 asks what distinguishes
black writers' adaptations of detective fiction and the tough thriller,
which, with its depiction of character as a product of social conditions and its use of the viewpoint of the outsider as a way of exposing
the failures of the dominant society, has been readily appropriated as
a means of protest against racial oppression and exclusion. Turning to
'regendering the genre', Chapter 6 focuses on female-authored
novels, particularly those creating female protagonists. Approaching
this fiction within the context established in earlier sections of the
study, it examines the implications of texts that create female transgressor and victim protagonists; more centrally, it aims to clarify the
ways in which the figure of the detective has been reworked to bring
sexual politics to the fore, challenging patriarchal authority and
reformulating gender definitions.

Acknowledgements

THE completion of this study has been made possible by the generosity of the Arts and Humanities Research Board in giving me an award under the AHRB Research Leave Scheme. I am also grateful to the University of Lancaster for the extension of my sabbatical period, which has allowed me the time I needed to write this book. In addition, I want to thank the Department of English and Creative Writing for the strong support it has given over the last several years to those of us involved in setting up courses on popular literary forms within the department.

Having been able to mount courses at both the undergraduate and postgraduate levels, I have, for nearly a decade now, had the opportunity to discuss crime literature with some of the most enthusiastic students I have ever taught. During the past few years, the work of the best of these students has also made possible the creation of a website, www.crimeculture.com, dedicated to the academic study of crime fiction and film. Their essays on a wide range of topics are central to the site, and their lively insights have added considerably to my own enjoyment and understanding of crime fiction. Special thanks are due to three of my Ph.D. students, Jem Aziz, Sinead Boyd, and Paul Ferguson, all of whom have given me new ideas about popular literature and film. I am additionally grateful to Sinead and Paul for their willingness to read draft chapters of this study and for their many valuable suggestions. By stepping in to help with the teaching of my crime courses, they made it possible for these to run during my sabbatical year, a task to which several of my colleagues also contributed: I particularly want to thank David Law, Andrew Tate, Michael Greaney, and Jayne Steel, not just for keeping the courses going during my absence but for making my time in the Department so enjoyable when I am there.

The friendship and advice of many other colleagues, both at Lancaster and elsewhere, have helped me greatly in this project. I owe a special debt of gratitude to Richard Dutton, whose encouragement and suggestions about my research proposal were invaluable, as was the help of Patrick O'Malley and Eamonn Hughes. The advice of Fiona Kinnear, the Oxford University Press editor who commissioned this study, was of crucial importance at the planning stage. During the time I have been writing the book, I have benefited enormously from my e-friendship with Allan Guthrie, who founded www.-pulporiginals.com with me and whose knowledge of literary noir has been a constantly useful resource. I am also grateful to the far-flung group of people whose contributions to the crimeculture website have stimulated my own interest in many facets of crime fiction and film—particularly to Roger Westcombe, Philippa Gates, Vicky Munro, Stacy Gillis, and Christopher Pittard.

As always, my greatest debt is to my family: to Tony Horsley for his thoughtful and sharp-eyed reading of the book in draft form; to my sons, Daniel and Samuel, whose interest and support have sustained me; and to Katharine Horsley, co-author of three papers that contributed very directly to this study, assiduous reader of drafts, and collaborator in present and future crime literature projects. Sadly, our future collaborations will not be centred in the house we have occupied for a quarter of a century, which is scheduled to fall to developers before the end of 2005: this book is in memory of our house and all it has contained.

Portions of this book have been adapted from articles written with Katharine Horsley: '*Mères Fatales*: Maternal Guilt in the Noir Crime Novel', *Modern Fiction Studies*, 45/2, 1999: 369–402; 'Body Language: Reading the Corpse in Forensic Crime Fiction', forthcoming in *Paradoxa*; 'Learning Italian: Serial Killers Abroad in the Novels of Highsmith and Harris', forthcoming in *Murder and Mayhem in the Mare Nostrum* (University of Delaware Press). It also draws material from 'Founding Fathers: "Genealogies of Violence" in James Ellroy's L.A. Quartet', *Clues: A Journal of Detection*, 19/2, 1998: 139–61. 'Detective Story', copyright © 1966 by W. H. Auden, from *COLLECTED POEMS* by W. H. Auden. Used by permission of Random House, Inc.; and by permission of Faber and Faber Ltd.

In Memory

of Parkgate House,

1907–2005

For who is ever quite without his landscape,
The straggling village street, the house in trees . . .
A home, the centre where the three or four things
That happen to a man do happen? . . .
The little station where he meets his loves
And says good-bye continually . . .
(W. H. Auden, 'Detective Story')

Contents

Introduction

It is ... a form which has never really been licked, and those who have prophesied its decline and fall have been wrong for that exact reason. Since its form has never been perfected, it has never become fixed. The academicians have never got their dead hands on it. It is still fluid, still too various for easy classification, still putting out shoots in all directions.

(Chandler 1984: 70)

RAYMOND CHANDLER is here referring specifically to the detective or mystery novel, but he would undoubtedly have been happy to include crime fiction as well in his admonition to academics who want to get their dead hands on the genre. Since Chandler's day (he wrote these 'Casual Notes on the Mystery Novel' in 1949), there have been, of course, increasing numbers of academics who have analysed both detective and crime fiction. Inevitably many of these analyses have sought to classify the different shoots of crime writing, to find ways of fixing their characteristics. Some critics, structuralists in particular, have seen the genre itself as functioning to impose its fixed shape on whatever material is put into it (Cobley 2000: 123). Other academic studies, however, have tried to find ways of avoiding the deadening effects of 'easy classification', taking more account of the fluidity of the genre and attempting to understand the many different ways in which generic revisions have been accomplished by rereadings and rewritings of what has gone before. This line of approach, shared by the present study, recognizes loose groupings of texts—the 'classic detective tradition', say, or 'the hard-boiled tradition'—but takes what can be described as a dialogic rather than a monologic approach. Here, the chronologically overlapping sections will, it is hoped, give some idea of the complex nature of generic change in Anglo-American crime and detective fiction.

Much recent criticism has contributed to the problematizing of a monologic approach. Priestman's 'Cambridge Companion' collection of essays, *Crime Fiction* (2003), Stephen Knight's *Crime Fiction 1800–2000: Detection, Death, Diversity* (2004), Andrew Pepper's *The Contemporary American Crime Novel: Race, Ethnicity, Gender, Class* (2000), and Gill Plain's *Twentieth-Century Crime Fiction: Gender, Sexuality and the Body* (2001), amongst others, have been particularly important in stressing diversity and in developing a multi-layered as opposed to a 'unidirectional' or 'univocal' approach (Priestman 2003: 6). Those arguing for a dialogic approach have emphasized the ambiguity, or indeed the contradictoriness, of individual texts and hence the different ways of reading them. They have taken account as well of the fluidity that Chandler describes—the huge variety of detective and crime fiction loosely associated with any particular subgeneric label. One of the main underlying assumptions of such studies is that a popular work of art combines familiarity and uniqueness, producing tensions within the work itself and generating a constant process of transformation (Walton and Jones 1999: 3). The formulation of Umberto Eco in *The Role of the Reader* (1979: 173–4) sums up this process concisely, saying of the popular genre text: '1. It must achieve a dialectic between order and novelty—in other words between scheme and innovation; 2. This dialectic must be perceived by the consumer, who must not only grasp the contents of the message, but also the way in which the message transmits these contents.'

Many analytic difficulties have been caused by too ready an acceptance of what have been the standard labels, particularly by 'classic', 'golden age', and 'hard-boiled'—emotionally charged, evaluative terms which, as Stephen Knight rightly argues (2004: p. xii), can be seriously misleading. Because of the oversimplifications that have sometimes dogged the use of these traditional sub-generic labels, there have been numerous efforts to find replacement terms that are less value-laden and less burdened with earlier critical assumptions. So, for example, Priestman classifies as 'detective thrillers' those narratives that combine the elements of 'detective whodunits' and 'noir thrillers' (1998: 51); Knight substitutes 'clue-puzzle' story for 'golden age' detective fiction, recommends the abandonment of such labels as 'hard-boiled' or 'tough guy' fiction in favour of the more neutral 'private-eye' story, and suggests the coinage 'psychothrillers' for novels centred on the psychic trauma surrounding crime (2004: pp. xii–xiii,

146). All these substitutions make good sense, capturing important generic variants, though they themselves, of course, can also serve a polemical function (for example, Knight's replacement of 'hard-boiled' with 'private eye' must in part be seen in relation to his dismissal of the hard-boiled claim to a more 'realistic' agenda[1]). The general policy in the present study has been to retain the more familiar categories. What is lost by jettisoning the established labels is the sense of how writers and critics have, over the past decades, used, varied, challenged, and built on them. Part of the purpose here is to explore the values attached to these terms and the ways in which successive generations of writers have constructed their work in relation to previous categories.

The present study covers what might be called 'the long twentieth century', reaching back into the last decade of the Victorian era, to take in the seminal contribution of Arthur Conan Doyle and his contemporaries, and forward into our own century, drawing some of its examples from the fiction of the new millennium. The development of generic conventions is by no means confined to Anglo-American literature, nor did these conventions simply spring from nowhere in the 1890s. I have not had the space to include the enormous number of non-Anglophone developments that have taken place in the genre, or to analyse in any detail the development of the genre in previous centuries. A sense of origins, however, is important. Eighteenth- and nineteenth-century crime fiction has been well covered in the recent surveys brought out by Knight and Priestman, both of whom establish a broad historical context for the understanding of contemporary crime writing. The present study follows Knight and Priestman in using 'crime fiction' as the label for the genre as a whole, as well as for the large sub-genre of 'detective-less', generally transgressor-centred crime novels. This choice reflects the fact that the representation of *crime* without the reassuring presence of a detective is arguably the 'parent' tradition. 'Crime fiction' in the wider sense stretches back, for example, to Defoe's criminal-centred fiction and to the Newgate and 'sensation' novels of the nineteenth century. Equally important are the common origins of crime fiction

---

[1] Knight 2004: 111 sees Chandler's labelling of the sub-genre as one way in which he positions the American model of detective fiction as 'more truth-telling and indeed more masculine'.

and the gothic, a kinship very evident in a number of late eighteenth-century novels: for example, in Horace Walpole's *Castle of Otranto* (1764), which concerns the dark secrets of an oppressive, criminally guilty father figure; in William Godwin's *Caleb Williams* (1794), which has affinities both with detective fiction and with the gothic; and in Ann Radcliffe's gothic novels, focusing as they do on investigations into a tyrannical male's crimes by female victims (Priestman 2003: 15; Reddy 2003*b*: 191). One of the reasons for the competing, often contradictory elements in detective and crime fiction is to do with this shared history, linking crime fiction from its inception to the gothic representation of excess, violence, and transgressions of the boundaries of reason and law. As detective-centred narrative structures began to emerge in the nineteenth century, the power of the gothic in crime fiction was increasingly overshadowed by the rationalist act of detection (Knight 2004: 61), reaching its apogee in the early decades of the twentieth century. In post-Second World War crime writing, however, the presence of the gothic has reasserted itself, and it has become clear that one of the key tensions in crime fiction is between gothic excess and the solving, ordering process of detection itself—a countervailing power that often recedes or vanishes altogether in mid- to late-twentieth-century crime fiction. During this later period, the continuing influence of the gothic can be seen, for example, in the shifting perspectives of crime novels that throw the emphasis (as in the texts discussed in Chapter 3) on to the commission of the crime rather than its solution, in narratives given over to exploring the psychology of the transgressor and the traumatized body of the victim.

Some periods can be seen as unusually productive of significant generic transformations: the traumatic events of the early twentieth century stimulated the development of hard-boiled fiction and literary noir; post-Second World War social changes and innovations in the means of publication (most importantly the paperback revolution) helped to encourage much greater variation in crime and detective fiction; from the 1980s on, there has been much change generated in the main sub-genres of detective fiction by the black and female writers (discussed in Chapters 5 and 6), who have turned the genre to their own ends, using it to address issues of race and gender. But, that said, there has always been variation within the dominant sub-genres of particular periods. Throughout this study, we will see significant formal and ideological shifts, integrally related to the set of values underlying contemporary attitudes towards crime and social order. Such shifts can affect every aspect of the crime narrative: the type of crimes represented, the motives for murder and the psychological profile of the criminal, the presence or absence of a detective and, where present, the techniques of detection, and the character of the detective (whether male or female, rational or intuitive, cerebral or physical, morally admirable or semi-criminal). The use that writers make of these elements is often very self-reflexive. Aware of the need for a dialectic between familiarity and novelty, writers often show themselves to be particularly attuned to the way in which revisions of this basic framework will be interpreted by readers *in relation to* the generic traits with which they are familiar. Ray Browne says, discussing Ross Macdonald, that the most powerful genre fiction is that which 'develops through the conventional by use of the inventional, then folds back upon itself and consciously reuses the formulas and conventions to create a new power of convention and formula' (1990: 103). This interplay between a known form and the constant variation of that form is what vitalizes genre fiction, sometimes transforming an existing pattern sufficiently to create what then comes to be classed as a new sub-genre, as, say, when earlier forms of investigative fiction spawned the police procedural; it also challenges expectations by combining the elements of different sub-genres—when the police procedural is merged, for example, with the transgressor-centred narrative of the crime novel, as it is in Thomas Harris's Hannibal Lecter trilogy.

Generic variations are sometimes primarily formal, particularly in classic detective fiction, which, as we will see in Chapter 1, was repeatedly transformed as a result of the highly sophisticated game that writers played with their readers, renewing the sub-genre by producing surprising innovations whilst still at least partially adhering to a widely understood set of rules for the construction of a satisfying mystery story. Generic change can also, however, be integrally related to shifting socio-political circumstances and to the dominant anxieties and preoccupations of different periods. As Carl D. Malmgren argues, being intertwined with the codes and conventions of society, generic codes and conventions are a particularly effective context for the investigation of such issues as race and gender (2001: 8–10). Chapters 4–6 of this study focus on texts that exploit the potential of the genre for critiquing society. Crime fiction has qualities that make it well-suited to the tasks of critique and protest: it deals with acts of violence, with devious methods of securing the subordination of others, and with the process of subduing them to your will; its plots turn on the revelation of hidden criminality; its protagonists are marginalized, outsiders forced into awareness of the failings of established power structures; in some of the most popular generic variants, the alienated protagonists are also capable of effective agency, enabling them to act against the corrupt and powerful. The hardboiled tradition in particular was from the outset directed towards the contemporary scene, focusing on social and economic corruption in American cities, the economic effects of the American Depression, endemic violence, and the remoteness of institutionalized law from any broader concept of justice. The underlying assumption—that crime fiction did say something about contemporary society and did have a role to play in socio-political critique—has been taken up by successive generations of crime writers with very different agendas.

The message embedded in the crime fiction medium can be transformed in numerous ways. Amongst the most obvious is for writers to disrupt what they take to be the 'known' form of the genre, playing against what an audience might expect, and locating the values they oppose in some earlier version of the genre they are revisioning. Often it is the contradictions that later writers uncover in their predecessors that function to create space for oppositional critiques, for subverting, parodying, or playfully reconfiguring previous ways of writing about crime. This process of defining a new text in relation to the existing codes and conventions generally involves some oversimplification of what has gone before. Writers who commit themselves to rethinking the genre tend to construct themselves in opposition to a somewhat narrowly conceived prior tradition. That is, generic changes may well be premised on an assertion that the previous variant of the genre was fixed, whereas their 'subversion' has broken through this generic rigidity. As Andrew Pepper notes, we have in recent years in particular seen, not infrequently, the bland assumption that, say, black or feminist crime fiction is inherently more 'radical' than white male detective fiction, with critics building on this—so, for example, paying 'lip service to the concept of genre as fluid in its construction and constantly shifting in its parameters, whilst conflating the whole spectrum of crime fiction into simple categorizations that deny its fluidity' (2000: 12–13). A number of

writers have dedicated themselves to creating a 'distinct countertradi-
tion' whilst still labelling the genre itself as 'basically monologic'. This
is, Ian Bell and Graham Daldry suggest, a form of 'covert devalu-
ation', a move that almost invariably involves ignoring the actual
diversity of the existing traditions (1990: p. x).

It is not only recent minority writers, however, who have succumbed
to the temptation to caricature their predecessors. In fact, successive
generations of writers have sought to 'fix' the nature and meaning of
a sub-genre as practised by earlier writers, each self-consciously new
departure in an evolving tradition taking as a starting point a reductive characterization of the preceding form of the genre. So, for
example, Doyle, in *Study in Scarlet* (chapter 2), gestures towards nineteenth-century parent texts in Holmes's mock-denigration of his
predecessors:

Sherlock Holmes rose and lit his pipe. 'No doubt you think that you are
complimenting me in comparing me to Dupin,' he observed. 'Now, in my
opinion, Dupin was a very inferior fellow . . . He had some analytical genius,
no doubt; but he was by no means such a phenomenon as Poe appeared to
imagine.'

'Have you read Gaboriau's works?' I asked. 'Does Lecoq come up to your
idea of a detective?'

Sherlock Holmes sniffed sardonically. 'Lecoq was a miserable bungler.'

Doyle's successors, from turn-of-the-century story writers to golden
age novelists like Christie and Sayers, teasingly refer back to the image
of the great Holmesian detective. Chandler, in his lively defence of
hard-boiled fiction, sets up the straw woman of the cosy, artificial,
Christie-style feminized tradition. Transgressor-centred fiction often
refers back wryly to an oversimplified image of the all-solving private
eye (the totally imperceptive detective encountered by Tom Ripley in
Patricia Highsmith's *The Talented Mr Ripley*). The overarching myths
of binary oppositions (like that, for example, conventionally taken to
exist between classic and hard-boiled detective fiction) are thus sustained by a widespread habit of acting 'as if' the previous conventions
cohered as a limited and unified tradition 'which they can then
disrupt' (Rowland 2001: 18).

The readers of detective and crime fiction are, of course, expected
to grasp the implications of these transformations of perceived categories. In *The Role of the Reader*, Umberto Eco, as we have seen, draws
attention to the importance of readers' recognition of the generic

structures and strategies exploited by the text they are reading: the effect of the text will depend upon their understanding the implications of a writer's play with convention, and they must themselves take an active part in constructing meanings. The underlying insight here is that meanings are not fixed or inherent in the nature of the genre itself but are at least in part dependent on the way in which an individual text is read. This participation of the reader in the construction of meaning is another key factor cutting against fixed constructions of popular texts. The process by which readers construct politically or culturally transgressive meanings by way of their own interaction with the text and the world is illuminated by several recent critical texts, such as Scott McCracken's *Pulp* (1998) and Priscilla L. Walton's and Manina Jones's *Detective Agency: Women Rewriting the Hard-Boiled Tradition* (1999). Walton and Jones put the argument concisely: 'Far from the limited view that such readers will tolerate only those works which "correctly" conform to the rules of formation of their favored genres, the proliferation and development of popular fictional genres suggests that playing off and even violating norms of genres are essential aspects of reader enjoyment' (1999: 147–8). Recent cultural studies analyses have given considerable thought to the problems of mediating between text-based and audience-based criticism, relying particularly on Christine Gledhill's articulation of the idea of 'negotiation': that is, that meaning 'is neither imposed, nor passively imbibed, but arises out of a struggle or negotiation between competing frames of reference, motivation and experience' (1988: 68). The reading, like the writing of crime fiction is very dependent on which elements are brought to the fore, and the same text will therefore have contradictory meanings to different readers. So, for example, a crucial question is whether the audience is reading for the sense of resolution or whether their responses are more complex than that: do we perhaps interest ourselves more in the ambiguities than in the restoration of order offered by formal closure? McCracken (1998: 50) argues that we read detective fiction as much for the uncertainties provoked by our encounter with the unknown as for the reassurances of conventional endings, and that this is a more compelling factor than any security given by the conclusion.

The critical debate about the crime and detective fiction of any given period is bound to reflect this sort of schism in reading practices. Conflicting interpretations are produced by reading for closure as opposed to reading for the more 'progressive' elements in a text, or by seeking out socio-political meanings as opposed to turning away from historically specific meanings (as structuralist and Freudian critics, say, tend to do). As we will see in Chapter 1, variant readings of classic detective fiction have been very much bound up with the question of which elements in the texts critics decide to regard as the 'most important'. They might, for example, place their strongest emphasis on the neat closure of the 'classic' ending and the control exercised at the end of the novel by the solving detective. Alternatively, a deconstructive reading (such as Pierre Bayard offers in his critique of Christie) emphasizes the way in which a superabundance of clues destabilizes the meaning of the novel as a whole. Other readings of classic detective fiction concentrate instead on the implications of the type of crimes represented: Alison Light's *Forever England* (1991), for example, argues that the sources of criminality in Agatha Christie's novels reflect what is basically a critical and unsettling view of inter-war British society. Or critics might pursue the psychoanalytic implications of the investigator's discovery of the clues to a midnight murder, comparable, Geraldine Pederson-Krag contends (Most and Stowe 1983: 13–20), to the child's encounter with the primal scene.

Hard-boiled detective fiction, discussed in Chapter 2, has been even more subject to critical dispute. Within its own period, early hard-boiled fiction is most helpfully seen in relation to classic liberalism. This connection has been explored by Sean McCann, whose *Gumshoe America* (2000) provides a painstaking historical contextualization demonstrating that the sub-genre was centrally concerned with that fundamental principle of liberal theory, the rule of law. In recent decades, however, it is the charge of conservatism (as understood from our own political perspective) that has dominated critical controversy. Debate has centred on the question of whether the hard-boiled sub-genre possesses genuinely radical potential or is, in late twentieth-century terms, inherently conservative, imposing in the end a resolution that makes the private eye the instrument of a repressive political order. The answers readers give to this question depends very much on the *way* they read individual hard-boiled novels, on whether they are attuned to the ambiguity of individual texts. It also depends on whether they have experienced the actual diversity of the range of hard-boiled writing, which as we will see contains a huge number of texts that do not conform to a model of a genre in which there is always an underwriting of the dominant order. A number of critics of the 1980s—for example, Stephen Knight (1980), Dennis Porter (1981), Franco Moretti (1983)—identified the detective novel, both the English and the American variants, as a form so committed to the restoration of the status quo that it can only be seen as being in thrall to the existing social order. Other, more recent critics, however, including Andrew Pepper, Jim Collins, Ralph Willett, and Woody Haut, have challenged this, emphasizing the alienation of the private eye, the moral ambiguity of the resolutions, and the ultimate intractability of the socio-political problems represented. In such readings, far from being conservative and integrative, hard-boiled writing is seen as disrupting reassuring views of the world and as showing justice to be 'provisional, incomplete and virtually unenforceable by a State incapable of understanding its complexity' (Collins 1989: 55–60; Pepper 2000: 10–11).

Critical analyses that bring to the fore different elements in the texts considered have in time fed back into the readings that are enacted by the authors of subsequent crime fiction. Individual writers create transgressive meanings that respond to critical dissections of the ideological content of crime fiction. They may, like the black and feminist writers considered later in this study, create detective figures who embody the oppositional values articulated in existing genre criticism, or who challenge the assumptions about race and gender that are seen as ingrained in earlier detective fiction. They sometimes produce, in addition, highly politicized rewritings of earlier texts, asking readers to return with an altered sensibility to their conception of the original. Walter Mosley, for example, does this in *Devil in a Blue Dress*, which recasts Chandler's *Farewell, My Lovely*; P. D. James creates her own kind of double perspective by basing *An Unsuitable Job for a Woman* on Dorothy Sayers's *Gaudy Night*. Ways of reading become ways of writing, and the genre, as Chandler says, is 'still putting out shoots in all directions'.

An introductory warning: multiple spoilers ahead

In November 2003, IMDb (the Internet Movie Database) ran the following as its daily poll:

What now-infamous spoiler do you think shouldn't be considered a spoiler anymore? (Warning: Multiple, innumerable spoilers ahead!)

The Sixth Sense—He's really dead!

The Others—They're all dead!

Citizen Kane—It's a sled!

The Crying Game—She's a he!

The Usual Suspects—Verbal Kint *is* Keyser Soze!

Psycho—Mother Bates is dead, and he's the killer!

The Empire Strikes Back—Darth Vader is Luke's dad!

Fight Club—They're both the same guy!

Seven—It's her head in the box!

Basic Instinct—She *is* the killer!

Jagged Edge—He *is* the killer!

What Lies Beneath—Her husband's the bad guy!

Planet of the Apes—They did it! They blew it up! Damn them all to hell![2]

A book on crime fiction, particularly one that includes a fair amount on classic detective fiction, might be expected to respect the wishes of readers with regard to the preservation of the mystery. To anyone who comes to this study with such expectations, I can only say—please finish reading the stories themselves before you turn to the following chapters. As Robin Winks writes in *Modus Operandi*, 'For—yes, if one is to discuss mystery fiction seriously, one must "give away the plot" ' (1982: 11).

---

[2] *Online*, http://uk.imdb.com.

1

Classic Detective Fiction

JOHN DICKSON CARR's *The Hollow Man* (1935) candidly draws attention to its own fictionality:

'But, if you're going to analyze impossible situations,' interrupted Pettis, 'why discuss detective fiction?'

'Because,' said the doctor frankly, 'we're in a detective story, and we don't fool the reader by pretending we're not. Let's not invent elaborate excuses to drag in a discussion of detective stories. Let's candidly glory in the noblest pursuits possible to characters in a book.' ([1935] 2002: 152)

The Hollow Man is not a novel that seeks to destabilize our sense of the outside world. Although the admission that 'we're in a detective story' might strike us as distinctly postmodern, it is unlikely that readers of the mid-1930s would have seen Carr's mischievous metafictional move as a challenge to their expectations about the genre they were reading. This sort of deconstructive play is very much a part of the highly contrived and self-referential world of 'classic detective fiction'. The other labels for this tradition (analytic detective fiction, the 'whodunit', the mystery story, the clue-puzzle story) all refer in one way or another to the basic structure of the sub-genre—to its characteristic pattern of death–detection–explanation. It is a tradition of crime writing in which the reader's attention is focused on the process by which a brilliant or at least uncommonly perceptive detective solves a case so intricate and puzzling that ordinary minds are baffled. The detective's solution brings a satisfying sense of completion and closure. Sherlock Holmes is, of course, the tradition's best-known father figure, and he has a vast number of descendants, each giving his or her name to a different series of stories—the Father Brown stories, the Hercule Poirot or Lord Peter Wimsey novels.

Writers of classic detective fiction address us, above all, as *readers*, and they very often, like Carr, offer light-hearted reminders that they are producing a work of fiction. As the tradition develops, they increasingly write in the expectation that most of their readers will have read many other books belonging to this hugely popular sub-genre of detective fiction; they create characters who themselves are avid readers of their own genre; and they ensure that at least one of these characters, the detective, will ultimately succeed in reading his fellow characters 'like a book'. It is often said that a detective story will sustain only a single reading. This seems a questionable prop-osition, but whether it is true or not, it is undeniable that these are novels very much about acts of *rereading*. Within the narrative, pro-gress towards a resolution is through a series of rereadings of a single text (the interpretation of clues); as readers/critics of a detective story, we, too, are engaged in an interpretative quest, and our clues to mean-ing consist both of the details embedded in the narrative and (as we become more experienced interpreters) of our readings of earlier examples of classic detective fiction.

The texts discussed in this chapter were all published before 1970. Beginning with Sir Arthur Conan Doyle and his contemporaries, we will follow the development of the tradition through the 'golden age' of British detective fiction, which produced such writers as Agatha Christie, Dorothy L. Sayers, and Margery Allingham.[1] We will round off by looking at two mid-1960s novels by P. D. James and Ruth Rendell, who are, at the time of this analysis, still producing novels centred on their series detectives, Superintendent Adam Dalgliesh and Chief Inspector Wexford. It has been said that the tradition of classic detective fiction begins to die out in the 1960s. It would be truer to say that the evolution of the genre has led to the abandon-ment of some, but by no means all, of the generic rules established in the early twentieth century. Writers like James and Rendell (and more recent writers such as BarbaraNeely[2]) have revitalized the tradition with both formal and ideological transformations. These heirs of

---

[1] John Dickson Carr was an American writer but can easily be mistaken for British, having set many of his best-known novels in England and in fact having lived in England for many years.

[2] BarbaraNeely chooses to have no space between her first and last name—as Stephen Knight suggests, resembling bell hooks in her disruption of patriarchal tradition 'at the level of the signifier' (2004: 189).

Sherlock Holmes are still hugely popular, and still recognizably in the same line. Why, one might ask, has so unashamedly artificial a genre had such enduring popular appeal? One answer might be that this reassuring object (a well-known kind of text) is also an invitation to playful readers to participate, challenging them to put a fictional world in order by the act of being, simply, a 'good reader'. Such a person will judge the writer as 'good' partly because he or she manages to delay an appreciative audience's recognition of the 'true' narrative. Seen in this way, the classic detective story combines the comforting familiarity of a repeated pattern with the surprising turns of a well-played game. These ludic (playful, game-like) qualities will be central to our discussion of classic detective fiction.

The values implicit in this game are often associated with such quintessentially English qualities as fair play and the sporting spirit, adjusted to the smaller playing field of the armchair. And classic detection is in important respects a very 'English' tradition. It is, as Stephen Knight has demonstrated, misleading to see the development of detective fiction in terms of a strict British–American bifurcation. But the classic and hard-boiled sub-genres did 'take special root in the different countries' (Knight 2004: 132), and it is probably fair to argue that the fiction of American mystery writers (including that of John Dickson Carr) was largely imitative rather than innovatory, modelled on what they themselves perceived as a very British phenomenon.[3] Though an American, Edgar Allan Poe, is the writer most often credited with 'inventing' the classic detective story (and 'Murders in the Rue Morgue', published in 1841, remains one of the most frequently discussed of all detective stories[4]), it was the British tradition inaugurated by Doyle that established the defining features of analytic detective fiction.

In the inter-war period, the flourishing of golden age crime fiction, epitomized by Christie and Sayers, coincided with the emergence of

---

[3] A number of American authors enjoyed success writing classic detective novels from the late 1920s on—the most popular amongst them being, in addition to Carr, Willard Huntingdon Wright (who wrote under the name S. S. Van Dine) and the two cousins Frederic Dannay and Manfred B. Lee, who combined their talents under the name Ellery Queen. The more identifiably American contribution to detective fiction was made by their contemporaries, 'the *Black Mask* boys', discussed in Ch. 2.

[4] See e.g. the entire collection of essays devoted to psychoanalytic readings of Poe: Muller and Richardson 1988.

another favourite British game, the cryptic crossword. The cryptic crossword, it should be emphasized, differs from the variety of word puzzle which is solved by filling in famous names, general knowledge, or words that fit dictionary definitions. Rather, it consists of complicated wordplay (puns, anagrams, etc.), with completion of the puzzle involving a battle of wits between clue-setter and solver.[5] Although the early cryptic crossword was somewhat anarchic, it soon became established that all good setters must abide by the fundamental principle of fair play. One of the best-known setters, Afrit, offered the dictum, 'I need not mean what I say, but I must say what I mean.'[6] This would, I think, serve equally for any good detective story writer. Both games mirror the nature of civilized discourse in their careful ironies, their nuances and clever evasions, and their attentiveness to the exact meanings of words (a particular skill, for example, of Christie's Hercule Poirot). The correct answer should be accessible to the solver, but must be cleverly hidden, in such a manner that, once enlightened, he or she will 'see that the solution had, in a sense, been staring him in the face'. Both mysteries and cryptic crosswords use a variety of devices to prevent the reader from grasping the solution too quickly. In detective fiction, what we see is a constant tension between formal innovation and readers' expectations about the form as they know it. There are not infrequent allegations that one famous detective story writer or another has not 'played fair'. So, for example, Dorothy Sayers objected that Doyle did not always 'play fair', although

---

[5] So, for example, a 'straight' clue would be 'Intelligent (6) = brainy', whereas the cryptic clue for 'brainy' might be: 'Intelligent female supporter one takes to New York', with the answer present once as a synonym ('intelligent') and once in the form of wordplay (here, 'bra' is a 'female supporter', 'i' is another way of writing 'one' and 'ny' is the abbreviation of New York). Coming 'cold' to this clue, one would be in the position, of course (as in a mystery story), of not knowing which part was the 'real meaning' and which part was tricky and misleading. Example taken from Francois Greeff, *The Code of Cryptic Crosswords*. Slough: Foulsham, 2003: 18.

[6] A. F. Ritchie took as his pseudonym 'afrit', which, aside from being the first five letters of his name, means 'a sort of demon' (Brian Greer, *How to Do the Times Crossword*. London: Times Books, 2001: 6); D. S. Macnutt, *On the Art of Crossword* (1966). Claverley, Shropshire: Swallowtail Books, 2001: 9. Knight 2004: 105 mentions E. R. Punshon's *Crossword Mystery* (1934), a detective story that exploits the similarities between crosswords and mysteries. Colin Dexter also gestures towards parallels between the mystery story and the cryptic crossword in *The Silent World of Nicholas Quinn* (1977), which involves Inspector Morse with a suspect who is a crossword-setter called Daedalus.

she defended Christie's trick in *The Murder of Roger Ackroyd* (which Van Dine thought 'hardly legitimate' (Symons [1972] 1992: 86–7; 121)). The general principle at work is perhaps most famously summed up in the subtitle of Stephen Potter's comic guide to success in games, *The Theory and Practice of Gamesmanship: The Art of Winning Games without Actually Cheating* (1947). A devotion to what Potter calls gamesmanship, to bending the rules without 'actually cheating', is one of the most important reasons for both the durability and the rapid transformations of classic detective fiction.

Almost all of the texts analysed in this chapter violate the 'rules of the game' in significant ways, altering what is widely seen as the basic formula (a formula playfully adumbrated by Ronald Knox and S. S. Van Dine in the 1920s and 1930s). The 'violations' discussed include the creation of apparent victims who are in fact the villains ('Silver Blaze', *Peril at End House*), a narrator who is not to be trusted (in *The Murder of Roger Ackroyd*), a detective who is unscrupulous and morally dubious (Morrison's Dorrington stories), and a detective who has a love interest in the murderer being tried (Sayers, *Strong Poison*); they even include the revelation of 'whodunit' at the very beginning, before the description of the investigation (Freeman's 'inverted' detective stories). The structuralist analysis of detective fiction, which we will examine in some detail in the following section, offers effective ways of identifying similarities. One might argue, however, that *difference* accounts for the larger part of the reader's enjoyment. The process of revitalizing the tradition has relied most of all on a constant process of reinventing generic conventions. This creates a simultaneous sense of similarity and dissimilarity, a text that is recognizably part of a tradition but also one that reinvents itself in unexpected ways.

The primacy of intertextual play and gamesmanship in our discussion so far arguably suggests that we are looking at a sub-genre of crime fiction that has very little connection with 'life as we know it'. Indeed, it can be argued that an attachment to classic detective fiction reflects a tendency to deceive oneself about the nature of reality. In *Anatomy of Murder*, for example, Carl D. Malmgren suggests that the generic preoccupation with textuality reveals 'a subconscious desire to treat the world as if it were a book', that is, to endow the world itself with such book-like traits as readability, decipherability, intelligibility (2001: 47). Not too surprisingly, this has been one of the topics most regularly canvassed in analyses of classic detective fiction. Raymond Chandler, as we will see in the following chapter, saw hard-boiled detective fiction as a much-needed antidote to the triviality and the contrived nature of the British tradition, with its elaborately formal presentation of cunning tricks and intricate solutions. In the decades since Chandler wrote 'The Simple Art of Murder' (1944), much other criticism has accused the classic detective tradition of lacking 'realism', in both its selection of material and its underlying view of the socio-political context within which it is written. The most frequently levied ideological charge involves the very circumscribed way in which the 'world' of the classic detective novel is constituted. This kind of limitation is particularly evident in the golden age fiction set in the archetypal country house, but even the Holmes stories, though they are primarily set in London, can be accused of leaving out a great deal of contemporary experience—as is suggested by the occasion on which Watson, asked by Holmes about whether the papers contain anything of interest, infers that 'by anything of interest, Holmes meant anything of criminal interest. There was the news of a revolution, of a possible war, and of an impending change of government; but these did not come within the horizon of my companion.'[7] Stephen Knight points out that, although there was plenty of 'real crime' in Victorian London, Doyle, particularly in the early stories, tended to focus on 'disorders in the respectable, bourgeois family', rather than on the most common forms of criminality to be found in the new conurbations ([1981] 1994: 370–1). The Holmes stories have indeed been seen as a form of escapism analogous to Holmes's own cocaine taking, functioning as 'our cocaine, our diversion from contemporary reality' (Thomas 1999: 2). As a genre, then, classic detective fiction has often been defined *in terms of* its limitations: Symons, for example, quotes Freeman's 'The Art of the Detective Story' as saying that things like characterization and setting must be 'secondary and subordinate to the intellectual interest, to which they must be, if necessary, sacrificed'.[8]

---

[7] Arthur Conan Doyle, *His Last Bow* (1917), in *The Complete Sherlock Holmes*. Garden City, NY: Doubleday, 1930: 913, discussed by Roth 1995: 27–8.

[8] R. Austin Freeman (1924), 'The Art of the Detective Story', reprinted online at http://gaslight.mtroyal.ab.ca. See also Symons [1972] 1992: 14–15, referring to W. H. Auden and Howard Haycraft, *Murder for Pleasure* (1942). Haycraft, for example, wrote that 'The crime in a detective story is only the means to an end which is—detection.'

The argument here is twofold: the remoteness of this 'exclusionary discourse' from the actual content and crises of its socio-political context prevents it from engaging with the troublesome realities of its own time; and the narrowing of its sphere of concern makes the containment of crime and the restoration of order far too unproblematic (Porter 1981: 189–90). Reluctance to comment on contemporary affairs is in itself, of course, an ideologically loaded decision, and it is important to emphasize that classic detective fiction, in spite of its apparent insularity, does nevertheless *implicitly* have a great deal to say about social power and contemporary concerns. It can be seen, in Porter's terms, to be 'making ideologies visible', revealing much about conceptions of virtue and heroism, national identity and 'otherness', the ideal of masculinity (its alliance with reason and science), class assumptions and gender (1981: 127–8). As Symons says, detective stories 'pure and simple' don't exist ([1972] 1992: 16).

The ideologies made visible by classic detective fiction have undeniably been seen as in the main conservative, and even the techniques of accurate detection can be seen as faithfully supporting the socio-political assumptions embodied in setting, characterization, and selection of material. This harmonious coupling appears in miniature, for example, in the wonderfully symbolic clocks described towards the end of *The Hollow Man*. Here, an orderly, correct English clock epitomizing concord between church and state (the church bells and Big Ben sound the hour simultaneously) is set alongside a trumpery foreign clock, the slovenly inaccuracy of which has very nearly prevented the rational understanding of the sequence of events that is essential to a precise narrative of the crime ([1935] 2002: 190). The *techniques* of solving the crimes are in themselves potent analogies for a wider process at work, converting the body to 'a text to be read' and to be subjected to categorization within the body politic.

The 'conservative' label, however, cannot stand without qualification. In its own historical context, detective fiction is closely bound up with classic liberalism. From our contemporary perspective, this liberal ethos can be categorized as a conservative mythologizing of individualism, but this is a significant shift in political vocabulary: in his own time, Doyle, for example, can be seen as fashioning 'a myth of liberal society', as celebrating the ideals of personal freedom and the rule of law, as well as responding to the urban problems that were, by the turn of the century, providing a serious challenge to the tenets of liberal theory (McCann 2000: 15–16). The issue can also be approached with reading strategies in mind. Some recent critics have suggested that the charge of conservatism is based on a misapprehension about the way in which we read detective fiction. Is it really true, they ask, that we read primarily for the *ending*? There has been a tendency (especially amongst structuralist critics) to stress the finality of the closure reached at the end of the investigation as opposed to its 'critical, speculative aspects'. It is, however, a whole process of investigation, which cannot simply be (as Moretti argues) 'negated' by the narrative resolution (McCracken 1998: 56; Rowland 2001: 39). Those who see the sub-genre as less rigidly conservative will realize that the reader's experience contains more questions than answers, and it is arguable that this process of disruption is what readers of the genre find most compelling.

This line of argument has been reinforced by 'less conservative' interpretations of some of the novels most closely identified with the kind of closure that shuts out any troubling forms of incertitude. Many golden age texts, upon closer inspection, reveal the hidden tensions beneath the surface of genteel English society, exhibiting its insularity, its greed, the instability of identity, its obsession with the hierarchies of class and gender. Rereading classic detective fiction in this way, it becomes clear that the convoluted crimes central to the tradition are not just a formal requirement (permitting the exercise of the detective's solving intelligence) but a way of probing the elaborate deceptions of a sophisticated society. The nature of the crimes themselves is a metaphor for the lengths to which such a society is willing to go in the interests of hypocritical concealment. Individual contrivances undertaken to prevent detection are an index of the multiple lies and deceits of a whole society. It is not just the murderer who conceals but, typically, a range of other characters as well. In contrast to hard-boiled fiction, classic detective fiction may not launch a sweeping attack on brutal and corrupt cops and politicians or on capitalist exploitation. Within its microcosmic domestic sphere, however, it does expose abuses of power and callous greed.

Critics like Alison Light (1991) and Susan Rowland (2001) remind us that detective fiction is, after all, a form of *crime* fiction, and that we are perhaps drawn to read crime stories not by our need for the reassurance that comes with a restoration of order but by our suspicion that there is always 'more to it' than institutionalized accounts acknowledge: 'Perhaps the appetite for crime fiction is driven by the desire generated by a sense of cultural excess to the operations of the law' (Rowland 2001: 17). Do readers really turn to such fiction just for confirmation of their existing beliefs? Porter, drawing on Stanley Fish, suggests that the activity is more to do with the 'primitive' pleasure of experiencing loss and recovery, danger and return from danger after a protracted period of tension and fear. Only the most 'ratiocinative' works of classic detective fiction do not involve this 'exposure to a form of danger' and the subversive enjoyment of stepping outside the law.[9]

The turn of the century: Sherlock Holmes and his contemporaries

Sir Arthur Conan Doyle *The Adventures of Sherlock Holmes* (1892) and *The Memoirs of Sherlock Holmes* (1894); Arthur Morrison, *The Dorrington Deed-Box* (1897); G. K. Chesterton, *The Innocence of Father Brown* (1911); R. Austin Freeman, *The Singing Bone* (1912)

The first appearances of Sherlock Holmes were in two novels, *A Study in Scarlet* (which, after some difficulty in finding a publisher, appeared in *Beeton's Christmas Annual* for 1887) and *The Sign of Four*, published in 1890. Neither, however, achieved the huge success of the short stories which were to follow, starting in July 1891 with 'A Scandal in Bohemia', the first of the six stories Doyle was commissioned to write by the owner of the *Strand Magazine*: 'It had struck me,' Doyle wrote, 'that a single character running through a series, if it only engaged the attention of the reader, would bind that reader to that particular magazine'.[10] This was a crucial insight into the power

---

[9] Porter 1981: 235–6. Porter adds that: 'In short, the reading experience itself suggests that the affirmation of rationality with which the detective story traditionally ends overlays irrational notional premises and that the relief provided by the former depends largely on a responsiveness to the latter.'

[10] Doyle, *Memories and Adventures*. London: Hodder and Stoughton, 1924: 95, discussed by Priestman 1998: 14.

of the short-story formula (with its convention of a twist at the end) combined with serial publication. The circulation of the *Strand Magazine* immediately rose,[11] and the fifty-six Holmes stories published over the next decades (the last appearing in 1927) established with a very wide audience one of the most recognizable figures in popular fiction, his appearance fixed by the famous Holmes illustrator, Sidney Paget. Doyle did, of course, have important predecessors. The most obvious of these was Poe, who wrote his Dupin tales in the 1840s, but there has been much work done on the numerous other texts that can be seen as early models of the disciplinary detective: glimmerings of 'rational inquiry leading to the containment of crime' in the eighteenth-century compilations of criminal lives, *The Newgate Calendar* (or *Malefactor's Bloody Register*); William Godwin's *Caleb Williams* (1794); the *Mémoires* (1829) of François Eugène Vidocq (an ex-criminal who became the first head of the Parisian Sûreté); the novels of Charles Dickens, such as *Oliver Twist* (1838) and *Martin Chuzzlewit* (1844); Émile Gaboriau's *Monsieur Lecoq* (1868); Wilkie Collins's *The Moonstone* (1868); the detective figure (Robert Audley) in a 'sensation novel' like Mary Elizabeth Braddon's *Lady Audley's Secret* (1862); and many others.[12] None of these texts, however, crystallized the role of the detective and the nature of the detective story in the way that the Holmes stories did.

In considering the question of why the 1890s were propitious to the emergence of Holmes, critics generally take account of the fact that the stories contain a core of bourgeois values, combining an attachment to fair play with an appeal to the growing belief in individualism and addressing widespread anxieties about the presence in late Victorian society of potentially disruptive forces. Martin Priestman suggests that much of what Holmes accomplishes as a detective can be summed up as the 'individuation' of particular facts and particular

[11] Chris Willis, 'The Story of the *Strand*' (*Online Publishing*, www.strandmag.com), notes that 'Conan Doyle was to prove one of the *Strand's* most popular (and prolific) contributors. From mid-1891 until his death in 1930, there was scarcely an issue which did not contain at least one of his stories or articles. The serialization of *The Hound of the Baskervilles* in 1901–2 was estimated to have increased the magazine's circulation by 30,000.'

[12] Pykett 2003: 19–29; Knight 2004: 9–21; Priestman 1998: 14–15; Symons [1972] 1992: 87; Christopher Pittard, 'Victorian Detective Fiction—An Introduction', *Online Publishing*, www.crimeculture.com.

people; Julian Symons that he was 'the great protector of bourgeois society [. . .] made more attractive by the fact that his personal life in some respects outraged bourgeois standards' (Priestman 1998: 10–17; Symons [1972] 1992: 24). Even more importantly, perhaps, Holmes can be seen as an exemplar of the scientific way of thinking that was gaining ground in the late nineteenth century. Doyle was explicit in urging the detective story writer's reliance on a scientific method-ology—the collection of evidence, the analysis of information, the construction of a legal case—as opposed to depending on happy accident.

This mastery of the scientific means of investigation comes together with an urge to explain the unknown and to fix identities that can be seen in relation to the emergence of a modern police force, under-pinning the development of the modern bureaucratic state. There was a contemporary sense that threats to property and the body could be dealt with by disciplinary detection—a manifestation of the anxiety to bring under control the possible sources of disorder, attendant, for example, on rapid urban growth and democratic reform (Knight 2004: 62–3; Thomas 1999: 3–4). There had been rudimentary investigative machinery in existence since the time of the Bow Street Runners. During the course of the nineteenth century, however, detection itself gained much greater credibility. As Foucault writes in *Discipline and Punish*, rather than accounts of the torture and confession of the criminal, we see 'the slow process of discovery'; our attention is focused not on the execution but on the investiga-tion, 'the intellectual struggle between criminal and investigator' ([1975] 1991: 68–9). Whereas the eighteenth century had regarded the 'thief-taker' with suspicion, the late nineteenth century was much more favourable to the activity of criminal detection, the figure of the detective becoming increasingly respectable from the early nineteenth century on. The French Sûreté was formed in 1812; the Metropolitan Police Force was established in London in the following decade when Sir Robert Peel's 'New Police' came into being.[13] Investigative crime fiction, then, developed during a period in which the process of the identification and legal conviction of the criminal was being consoli-dated. Street-level law enforcement was beginning to function as a

---

[13] See e.g. Ousby 1997: 15–24; Priestman 1998: 10; and Knight 2004: 30–63 on 'The Development of Detection'. The Metropolitan Police Force was created in 1829.

cornerstone of the modern state. The figure of the detective can be seen both as a mediator (his investigations involving him in the socio-legal contradictions of the time) and as himself an embodiment of 'the contradictory nature of the disciplined, modern self' (McCracken 1998: 51).

The centrality of the investigator's role creates the characteristic 'backward' construction of analytic detective fiction, which throws emphasis on the task of explaining what has happened at some earlier point in time.[14] This produces a dual structure, the 'double logic' seen by structuralist critics as deserving of special attention. The structuralist approach is a useful point of departure in considering the formula established by Doyle. It provides an explanatory frame, which can be used to disentangle the two separate stories constituting the classic detective narrative: that of the crime and that of the investigation, the 'first story' ending before the second begins. The 'first story' is what the Russian formalist critic Victor Shklovsky called the *fabula*, the story, or the events 'as they happened'. The 'second story', the way the events are narrated, he called the *sjuzet*. The model was elaborated by Tzvetan Todorov, who used it to create a typology for the various forms of crime story. Detective fiction, he argued, differed from the thriller and the suspense novel in making both *fabula* and *sjuzet* present, putting them 'side by side' (Todorov 1977: 46). As we will see (in looking, for example, at Christie's *Peril at End House*), one of the main spaces within the detective story for generic play is in fact created by a temporal overlapping of two stories (bringing the narrative closer in structure to the thriller and the suspense story). But in the 'purest form' of detective fiction, the two stories (as in 'Silver Blaze') have no point in common. They come together only as the detective puts the pieces of the puzzle in place and reveals the guilty party, in the process explaining both the nature of his own reasoning and the manner in which the crime was committed. The dual structure helps to account for other distinguishing traits of the detective story: its linear, end-oriented nature; its characteristic proliferation of detail; and its prioritizing of hermeneutic code over character (McCracken 1998: 50). With the detective's investigative efforts shaping the plot, we feel impelled to read towards a definitive solution, but we also see as we read a multiplication of possible mysteries,

[14] See Porter 1981: 25–52 on 'Backward Construction and the Art of Suspense'.

necessary to the creation of a sufficiently complex sphere of investigation. The responsibility of the detective is gradually to transform the indeterminacy of the beginning into a determinate meaning, closing down the possibilities at the end of the story and punishing the criminal for his creation of unintelligibility (Malmgren 2001: 19–25). The Holmesian method (though often simply labelled as deductive reasoning) is in fact both inductive and deductive, or, as Holmes himself says at the beginning of *The Sign of Four* (in the chapter called 'The Science of Deduction'), it must add 'the power of observation to that of deduction'. The inductive part of this procedure (the drawing of inferences from observed facts and particulars) is a potential cause of indeterminacy (there are innumerable 'particulars'). Holmes has, however, the ability to form a theory rapidly about the way in which facts are connected and to construct a chain of reasoning that leads from this theory to his conclusion. It is this deductive process that delimits his inspection of particulars and that in the end produces 'determinate meaning'.

'Silver Blaze' (1892, included in *The Memoirs of Sherlock Holmes*) offers a particularly good example of Holmes's detective methodology. His solving powers are tested here by a deviation from the (by now) established pattern: the apparent victim is in fact the villain. This means that the story's key revelation is that the victim himself was the creator of unintelligibility, his 'clever contrivance' having been interrupted by an event—his own death—that he clearly did not foresee. It also means that 'Silver Blaze' is not, in fact, the murder story it at first appears to be (characteristically of the early Holmes stories, it is another crime against property, the property in this case being Silver Blaze himself). The *fabula*, the sequence of events in the first story, is: (1) a horse trainer (Straker), encumbered with an expensive mistress, plans to bet against his own horse, Silver Blaze; (2) to prepare himself for the disabling of the horse, he practises nicking the tendons of sheep; (3) on the night the stable boy is fed curried mutton, Straker puts opium in his dinner; (4) having led the horse to a hollow, he makes his attempt, but the frightened horse lashes out with his hooves, killing Straker; (5) the horse bolts and is found running loose by a neighbour, who, having his own horse in the upcoming race, hides Silver Blaze, concealing his distinctive markings.

The mystery of 'Silver Blaze' is resolved during a London-bound train journey, in which Holmes explains all to Dr Watson and to the horse's owner, Colonel Ross. What Holmes says is both an account (chronological) of his process of arriving at a solution and a reconstruction of the first story, not chronologically ordered but revealed piece by piece, with each link in the 'chain of reasoning' determining the sequence. Thus, he begins with his crucial insights (relating to 3 above) into the significance of the curried mutton (whoever planned drugging the stable boy knew what he would be having for dinner) and of the dog that didn't bark at the 'midnight visitor' (it was someone he knew). The next link in Holmes's reasoning, he recounts, involved the close inspection of the items found in Straker's possession: these included some things (a 'singular knife', a candle, and matches) that he intended to use in event 4, and another item that supplies the motive of the crime (1 above), a bill that provides evidence of the expensive mistress. We then learn of Holmes's 'final shot [. . .] a very long one', his guess (2 above) that the culprit had practised on three sheep, now lame. The reader's role at this stage is a sort of second-order version of the Holmesian process: we connect each link in his chain of reasoning to an earlier fact concerning the part of the investigation that we have witnessed and we also reconstruct for ourselves the chronology of the first story. It is our participation in this reconstructive process that is so compelling, with everything 'falling into place' as Holmes *reorders* events to bring them into line with his carefully constructed interpretative model.

It is the *sjuzet*, the manner of telling the story, which ensures our involvement with the process of investigation. In 'Silver Blaze', for example, this begins with an extended account of why Holmes is interesting himself in the case. He gives an impromptu disquisition on the art of detection, which consists in the 'sifting of details' (of paramount importance in the present case, since many details have already been discovered and reported on) and 'the acquiring of fresh evidence'. It is a process in which 'undeniable' and 'essential' facts have to be detached from a 'plethora of surmise, conjecture and hypothesis' in order to find 'the special points upon which the whole mystery turns'. In terms of our experience of reading the story, the process Holmes is describing can clearly be seen in relation to what we might call the digressive and progressive elements in the narrative. 'Silver Blaze' provides a fine example of the ways in which Doyle teasingly, indeed mischievously, draws out the final answers in the interest of a theatrical and unexpected 'exposure' scene at the end.

This delaying of resolution is crucial to the nature of a genre in which it is particularly true that the art of narrative is the art of misleading. One of the main means of achieving retardation of the plot is, of course, the inclusion of various possible culprits; the mistaken speculations of the police are generally very helpful in this aspect of plot retardation, as is the suspicious behaviour of other characters. In 'Silver Blaze' we have two stock examples of this: the 'obvious suspect', Fitzroy Simpson, the man who has been 'promptly found and arrested' by the competent but woefully unimaginative Inspector Gregory; and some suspicious outsiders, the 'party of gypsies' known to be camping on Dartmoor. The suspected guilt of Simpson, in particular, generates alternative narratives—his own story of what he was doing at the stable, Inspector Gregory's narrative of his guilt, Holmes's explanation of why he does not suspect Simpson. The plot is also opened up by the presence of a plethora of potential clues: thus, in the pockets of the dead trainer, for example, there are five coins, five papers (a letter and some accounts), and seven other items; of these seventeen items, only four are of significance, and (this being a short story) Holmes's sifting process only delays matters for a short time.

But however efficiently it is dealt with, this plenitude is crucial, and is closely related to the nature of the clues examined in the second story's reading of the first story. In considering Holmes's inspection of signs, we see what Marty Roth calls 'the paradox of the obvious'—that is, the assumption that 'open and shut' cases must be more difficult to solve, given that the 'obvious' suspect cannot be guilty and that all readily available signs are bound to be either false or misleading. A key contrast here is that between 'evidence' and 'clues', *evidence* consisting of 'obvious signs', *clues* of signs that are overlooked or dismissed as irrelevant by others (1995: 179–80, 187–8). Thus, in 'Silver Blaze', Inspector Gregory maintains that he has several pieces of 'evidence' against Fitzroy Simpson (for example, his cravat was in the dead man's hand); Holmes, on the other hand, dismisses or reinterprets the obvious evidence, and, with what seems to a sober policeman a violation of common sense, he instead fixes his attention on clues that remain unregarded by others. This apparently perverse inversion is (in 'Silver Blaze' as in the other Holmes stories) decisive in his solution to the mystery, involving (again, as in other stories) a list of items or facts, which seem unconnected to the non-Holmesian eye (a milliner's account, a wax vesta, three lame sheep, and, most famously, the dog that 'did nothing in the night-time'). The Holmesian detective rejects the notion of the meaningless or accidental fact, acting instead on an underlying faith 'that all signs in a bounded space must be relatable'.[15]

Throughout, then, the detective controls the narrative structure of the *sjuzet*. As we have seen in our discussion of the two stories of 'Silver Blaze', his reordering activities are central to our experience of reading the classic mystery story, from the chronological reordering (in which investigative order is substituted for chronological event order) to the moral reordering that takes place after the detective has sorted everything out. As a *metonymic structure*, it is in crucial respects *his* narrative. The detective himself, however, is part of the *metaphoric structure* of the classic detective story, and here it is the reader/critic who poses the questions. Having entered into the game of asking and ultimately, with the detective's assistance, answering the questions about the crime committed (who? how? etc.), we might now want to ask other questions. What is it that we find compelling about the detective himself? What is it in modern experience that he represents and appeals to? What are the hidden elements in his own character? What is the nature of his relationship to his society? What anxieties are embodied in the crimes he investigates and the criminals he pursues? What aspects of his society are brought to the fore in his narrative? And, to use the term Holmes uses in 'Silver Blaze', what has he 'sifted' out? When we read with this sort of question in mind, the fixed roles of classic detective fiction (centrally, detective, victim, and criminal; peripherally, helper, witness) can all be seen as having metaphoric significance: so, most obviously, the detective can be seen as the modern self, the criminal as a source of contemporary anxiety.[16]

---

[15] This relatedness of all things within a bounded space is one of the things that differentiates classic detective fiction from hard-boiled detective fiction, which dispenses with the device of a bounded space and, Roth argues, 'suppresses relatedness' (Roth 1995: 185–9).

[16] McCracken 1998: 59–61. McCracken (p. 60) provides a concise explanation of the ways in which metonymic and metaphoric structures function in detective stories: 'A comparison of the metonymic and metaphoric structures of the detective narrative show how each metonymic narrative function corresponds to an interpretable metaphoric structure which gives it meaning in the world.'

Two of the most important metaphoric threads running through classic detective fiction are order and identity, related, respectively, to *closure* and *disclosure*, identified by Catherine Belsey as two of the basic predicates of classic realist fiction (Malmgren 2001: 25–6). Mystery fiction exemplifies, in a particularly transparent form, this double movement, with a story's or novel's closed ending following on from the disclosure of a hidden truth. Its 'meaning in the world' emerges from this twofold resolution, feeding a generic preoccupation with destabilization, disguise, and social pretence. In 'Silver Blaze', for example, the disclosure essential to the resolution of the mystery is the fact that Straker is 'someone else in town' (it is his town life that disrupts and disorders his place in the rural hierarchy). The ending of this story also involves Holmes's disclosure of the real Silver Blaze under the disguise applied to him by the neighbouring stable owner, and this double revelation underscores the emphasis on identity as a central part of the story's metaphoric structure. The horse, of course, though he is 'the murderer', is innocent, whereas Straker, the victim, is revealed as a wrongdoer whom we might think of as deserving of his end. Whereas Silver Blaze, however disguised, remains himself (he still runs perfectly), the trainer's doubleness of identity signifies more fundamental sources of anxiety in contemporary life (characteristically of the early Holmes stories, apparently respectable lives are disordered by personal greed and duplicity). This is not simply a matter of disclosing Straker's 'true' identity under a false one; it functions more widely as a symptom of the breakdown of confidence in the whole idea of the stable, knowable self. The identity *revealed* is in fact a false identity, not an exposure of the 'real man'; and what this discovery demonstrates is the theatricality or falsity of both of the identities he is known by. This erosion of the sense of self is part of the disorder of contemporary society that the detective combats, as he negotiates between conceptions of civilized life and fears of chaos lurking beneath the surface. The classic detective is less implicated in (and less threatened by) the underlying disorder than is the hard-boiled private eye, but the position he occupies can none the less be a liminal one. For in order to restore order, he must enter into the disturbed criminal mind. He has to have the capacity to understand the darker reality covered by the civilized veneer, and this capacity in itself destabilizes the detective's identity. It links him to the metaphoric darkness associated with the impenetrability and disorder of the urban scene (Roth 1995: 221–5).

It is in the metaphoric structure of a story like 'Silver Blaze', then, that we most obviously see the underlying socio-political implications. In the Holmes stories, London is one of the main sites of disorder, containing as it does a destabilizing proliferation of identities. Although the London scenes in 'Silver Blaze' take place off-stage, it is the place of Straker's undoing. It can be argued that the London axis of the Holmes stories, coupled with their seriality, is one of the main things preventing them from providing an essentially reassuring demonstration of the investigator's capacity for restoring order, and that this constitutes another key element in their metaphoric structure. Martin Priestman identifies the two 'axes' of the detective story as, on the one hand, indeterminacy, anonymity, generality, a mass of data and mass of men; and, on the other, determinacy, identity (or identification), singularity, interpreted clue, and individual client or culprit. He argues that what can be called the 'indefinite' axis of the story might be thought of as 'imaginatively coterminous with London itself, the sprawling anonymous city perceived as virtually unknowable'. The second story may act to allay anxiety and clarify confusion, but the pull of the first story is towards dissolution (Priestman [1990] 1994: 315–16). The seriality of the stories means that the reader is repeatedly returned to the city, to see in it, as Holmes does at the beginning of 'A Case of Identity' (1891), 'the queer things which are going on, the strange coincidences, the plannings, the cross-purposes, the wonderful chains of events, working through generations, and leading to the most outré results.'

There is an aesthetic pleasure involved in perceiving with the detective the 'hidden structure' that is there even when the city seems most random and disconnected (the 'wonderful chains of events'). But there is also, contained within this opening passage of 'A Case of Identity', the implication that there is an endless succession of disturbances taking place underneath or behind the apparent order of city streets, ordinarily hidden from view inside the civilized structures of the houses themselves. This inner reality of the city goes on impervious to local restorations of order, a skein of cross-purposes, cruelties, and crimes that are all the time being generated by 'ordinary life'. It is a city that in many ways is very like London as seen by Joseph Conrad, except that in the Conan Doyle stories one has Holmes himself, more than ever in this passage a Superman figure—capable of an imaginative fly-over ('If we could fly out of that window . . .') in which he is a sort of gentle, all-seeing, detached guardian who is able to penetrate the truths that are stranger than fiction, is able to make known the hidden connections—and so is finally able to restore comfortable ordinariness. Holmes's repeated resolutions in successive stories are required, however, by the repetitiveness of disorder itself. As readers and critics, our interpretation of this pattern will depend upon whether we focus our attention on the order-conferring activities of the detective or on the representations of disorder itself—the violence and greed, the class tensions and individual weaknesses that constantly threaten to undermine the presumptions of civilized society.[17]

The detective capable of penetrating these dark recesses of the modern city is a contradictory figure, and is himself the source of some of the instabilities that critics find in Doyle's stories. A scientific investigator and restorer of order might on the face of it be thought of as a stable construct. He is the embodiment of the Law of the Father, a disciplinarian who punishes the wayward, the embodiment of rationality in an age of 'widespread optimism [. . .] concerning the comprehensive power of positivist science'.[18] Readers are often, however, struck by the extent to which the detective himself is divided, his identity unsettled by mood swings and inconsistencies of character. This can be viewed as part of the historical development of the character of the detective, since Doyle seems to subsume within the character of Holmes many of the qualities of his diverse predecessors, making his protagonist an 'apotheosis' of such figures, aloof like Dupin, characterized by the 'active urban dedication' of Lecoq, but also by the *fin de siècle* bohemianism to be found in *Lady Audley's Secret*, and so on (Knight 2004: 55–7). Another way of reading Holmes's divided character is to relate it to the subsequent evolution of detective fiction during the course of the twentieth century. Might the great detective be said to embody the disorder and division within the modern identity? Viewed in this way, he can be seen

---

[17] As McCann 2000: 11–14 argues, it is important to recognize that such a detective figure signified not oppressively disciplinarian surveillance, but a commitment to the preservation of civil society.

[18] Knight 2004: 383; see also Rowland 2001: 45–7 and Munt 1998: 133–45.

as standing at the start of a tradition in which the figure of the detective is used to explore a variety of subversive identities—the different facets of contemporary anxiety and the variety of selves that can be contained within the modern individual (McCracken 1998: 53–4). In the case of Holmes, conflicting tendencies are apparent, for example, in the way his methods of detection combine the artistic and the scientific, the intuitive and the rational. He is a melancholy, drug-taking bohemian aesthete but also an energetic exemplar of intellectual power and rational penetration. Critics who probe the metaphoric structure of the stories also find various forms of doubling, for example, of Holmes and the 'false beggar' in 'The Man with the Twisted Lip' (1892).[19] More famously, Holmes encounters his dark double in the form of Professor Moriarty, introduced for the purpose of killing off Holmes in a story entitled 'The Final Problem' (December 1893) and brought back in the later series of stories in which Holmes was revived (starting in 1903 with 'The Empty House'). Moriarty can be regarded as a simplification of the causes of crime but a complication of the character of the detective— a particularly striking example of the generic tendency to double detective with criminal mastermind.

The almost uncontainable contradictions in Holmes's character can be taken to suggest what Scott McCracken calls the 'surplus or excess' of the genre, soon to be productive both of subversive transformations of the genre's 'fixed' structure and of new detective identities (1998: 50–3). This diversification of the detective figure gained momentum during the course of the twentieth century, but almost as soon as the classic form was created it started to generate imitations, variations, spoofs, and a wide variety of alternative sleuths. The unprecedented success of the Holmes stories very quickly prompted others, writing for the *Strand Magazine* or for other popular British magazines of the day, to deploy some recognizable features of Doyle's stories but at the same time to put their own stamp on the genre. There was a proliferation of new series, the best-known of which are

---

[19] See Audrey Jaffe's analysis of this story, Jaffe ([1990] 1994: 402–27, a new historicist reading that finds analogies between the eponymous man and Sherlock Holmes: Jaffe argues that class anxieties are apparent in this story of the transformation of identity, with Holmes himself (who is in a disreputable disguise in an opium den at the beginning of the story) presented as analogous to the 'false beggar', St Clair disguised as Hugh Boone.

those written by Arthur Morrison, G. K. Chesterton, and R. Austin Freeman. Their revisions of plot structure and their transformations of the character of the detective are crucially to do with the kind of knowledge required on the part of the detective *and* the reader, and also reveal how closely the investigator's persona is connected to the metaphoric meanings of the story.

Within a few months of 'The Final Problem', Arthur Morrison had introduced his series detective, Martin Hewitt, in 'The Lenton Croft Robberies', also in the *Strand Magazine* (March 1894). Like the Doyle stories, these were illustrated by Sidney Paget. Morrison's first solution to the complicated process of both 'following' the Holmes stories and differentiating himself from them was to introduce a central character as unremarkable as Holmes is remarkable. An ordinary man, occupying the role of a 'detective adviser' for a number of London banks and insurance offices, Martin Hewitt has a large store of technical and statistical knowledge and well-developed deductive abilities, but is otherwise unremarkable: he is stout and of average height, with a round, cheerful face, decidedly not, in Symons's terms, one of the 'Supermen of detection'. Morrison's more subversive creation, however, was Horace Dorrington, protagonist of a group of stories collected together as *The Dorrington Deed-Box* in 1897. In writing his Dorrington stories Morrison drew to some extent on the adventure stories of the Rogue school (tales about thieves and swindlers popular at the end of the nineteenth century) and the ironic anti-heroes popular at the time, in particular Ernest William Hornung's creation, the 'amateur cracksman' A. J. Raffles.[20] Having grown up in poverty, Morrison wrote (also in the 1890s) notable 'slum novels', and in a sense his work looks forward to American hard-boiled detective fiction (his *Tales of Mean Street*, published in 1894, can arguably be seen as the source for Chandler's famous description of the archetypal hard-boiled milieu, the 'mean streets' down which a man must go who is 'not himself mean' ([1944] 1988: 18)). Dorrington, though, is a rather less moral being than the average American private eye. As described in 'The Narrative of Mr James Rigby' (*Windsor Magazine*,

[20] The 'Rogue school', which includes such writers as Guy N. Boothby, Max Pemberton, Maurice Leblanc, and E. W. Hornung, wrote tales (light in tone) about dextrous thieves and clever swindlers. For a detailed account see the 'Rogue fiction writers' page on the Classic Mystery and Detection site, http://members.aol.com/MG4273/rogue.htm; see also Knight 2004: 70–1.

1897), he is a 'private inquiry agent' who has done 'much *bona fide* business', but who is utterly unscrupulous, willing to murder, steal, and defraud without compunction. Rigby, who narrates the stories, acquires the records of cases contained in 'Dorrington's deed-box' after narrowly escaping when Dorrington tries to murder him in order to steal his property. The other narratives reconstructed by Rigby move not towards the just punishment of offenders or the restoration of conventional order but towards affirmations of the total depravity of Dorrington's own moral universe. In 'The Case of Janissary' (*Windsor Magazine*, 1897), for example, Dorrington's thwarting of an intended murder ends in his 'talk[ing] business' with the would-be killers, explaining that he will not hand them over to the police but will instead take them into his service, making them his accomplices: 'I may as well tell you that I'm a bit of a scoundrel myself.'

At the opposite moral pole, we find Chesterton's Father Brown, who first appeared in the *Storyteller* magazine in 1910. His début, 'The Blue Cross', was followed by five more stories, later published by Cassell as *The Innocence of Father Brown*. Chesterton wrote five collections of Father Brown stories in all, and they provide some of the classic examples of the puzzle plot, 'impossible crime' stories that are generally seen as having been a major influence on such later clue-puzzle novelists as Agatha Christie and John Dickson Carr. Like Morrison's Hewitt, Father Brown can be classed as in many respects perfectly 'ordinary': he is another round, dumpy contrast to Holmes's angular, impressive figure. But he also possesses a kerygmatic 'one and only' quality that places him amongst the 'Supermen' (Roth 1995: 59–60; Symons [1972] 1992: 94). Like Holmes, he is gifted with the power of noticing what no one else can see, or at least, not see so clearly, but he is, as Chesterton himself suggested, a kind of 'transcendental' Sherlock Holmes and is not reliant on the scientific logic of Doyle's situational observer. Whereas Holmes turns to the minute inspection of the scene of a crime (in 'Silver Blaze', for example, lying on the muddy ground, examining it closely for tiny pieces of physical evidence), Father Brown need not even visit the scene. Though he has an admirably logical mind, what he specializes in is a knowledge of people comparable to that of the later 'feminized' detectives such as Christie's Poirot or Sayers's Lord Peter Wimsey— or, of course, to that of Miss Marple, another sleuth whose intuitions can make it possible for her to solve a crime without leaving her cottage.[21]

What is most distinctive about Chesterton's stories is the moral universe inhabited by Father Brown, a reflection of Chesterton's 'own ideal of humble, intelligent populist Catholicism' (Knight 2004: 75). He uses his protagonist to demonstrate repeatedly that crime fiction (in contrast to supernatural or gothic stories) deals only with 'the possible', with what is ultimately explicable in terms of common sense: Father Brown champions the soul, but the 'mysteries' he solves are to be understood entirely in human terms. One must, he insists, 'reckon on the unforeseen' and understand 'the limits of reason', but, although his powers of perception often strike his companions as miraculous, they are invariably based on insights into very ordinary facets of human thought, perception, and action. In 'The Invisible Man' (*Cassell's*, 1911), for example, he realizes that the mystery is not to do with any supernatural powers of movement but with the very human fact that people often fail to see someone because they are 'mentally invisible'. The nature of his authority as an investigator is reflected in endings that move towards a quite different kind of closure than is to be found in the work of his contemporaries. Father Brown's human ordinariness means that he is no more exempt from human flaws than others, and his detection characteristically terminates not in summoning the police (and certainly not in a Holmes-like beating with a hunting crop) but in a good long talk. These chats are not, of course, a Dorrington-style talk leading to a criminal alliance but an inducement to confession and repentance. 'The Invisible Man', for example, ends with a conversation the substance of which lies outside the secular bounds of the detective story: 'Father Brown walked those snow-covered hills under the stars for many hours with a murderer, and what they said to each other will never be known.' The murderers in some of the other stories give themselves up to the law as a gesture of reconciliation (for example, 'The Hammer of God' and 'The Wrong Shape' (*Storyteller*, 1910; 1911)) or may simply be

---

[21] In 'Oracle of the Dog' (*Nash's Magazine*, 1923), for example, Father Brown solves a case 'without ever having been near the place or the people'. I am indebted to Sinead Boyd for the example of Miss Marple's remote solving of a crime in *4.50 from Paddington* (1957). See Plain 2001: 25–6 on Poirot in relation to the feminizing of the tradition.

allowed to escape. In either case, more emphasis is placed on divine than on human order.

Chesterton's near-contemporary, R. Austin Freeman, created a detective who is more to be seen as a competitor with Holmes than as a contrast. Dr Thorndyke, who features in dozens of stories and novels, is the archetypal scientific investigator. Other writers of the time also amplified the rational, scientific side of the Holmes investigative technique, most notably the American writer Jacques Futrelle, who created the near-sighted, large-headed Professor Augustus S. F. X. Van Dusen, protagonist of *The Thinking Machine* (1907) and *The Thinking Machine on the Case* (1908). It was Freeman, however, who provided the most memorable stories of scientific detection. Both a physician and a lawyer, Thorndyke calls himself a medical jurist, and carries his expertise to a level of specialism that clearly distinguishes him from Holmes. Thorndyke is well equipped with scientific instruments: he is armed for travel with a square green box, a 'portable laboratory' containing materials essential for use in the detection of crime. At home he has an assistant and all the facilities in his well-equipped laboratory for such things as chemical and microscopic analysis, photography, radiography, and fingerprinting. Freeman's protagonist, preoccupied as he is with detailed physical investigation, can in fact be regarded as one of the earliest examples of the detective as a forensic scientist. Though in contrast to more recent forensic pathologists he is not intimately involved in the grisly details of autopsies, Thorndyke is a figure whose methods reflect the medicalization of crime, valorizing the work of the expert diagnostician, using scientific methods to illuminate the pathology of crime, converting the body and the scene of the crime into a text to be studied.[22]

So committed was Freeman to the fascination of the investigative activity itself that he could afford to make what is generally regarded as a major formal innovation in the analytic detective story, inventing the 'inverted' detective story, employed in the stories collected as *The Singing Bone* (published in 1912). The inverted structure starts with an account of the actual crime. That is, it gives us what the structuralists call the 'first story' *first*, so that we already know the identity of

---

[22] Knight 2004: 175–6; Thomas 1999: 3–4. See also Daryll Anderson, 'Physicians as detectives in detective fiction of the 20th Century', *Southern Medical Journal*, 1/10/2002, online at www.highbeam.com.

the criminal and have read in some detail about the commission of the crime before we witness Thorndyke's investigation of it. The effect is to eliminate the major element of mystery and to throw all of the emphasis on to Thorndyke's methods of solution. Knowing as much as we do, we are, of course, a more informed and appreciative audience than we would have been if we had not witnessed the crime. The first of these stories, 'The Case of Oscar Brodski' (1910, republished as the first story in *The Singing Bone*), was constructed in two parts: 'The Mechanism of Crime' and 'The Mechanism of Detection'. By Freeman's own account (in 'The Art of the Detective Story'), it was an experiment premised on the belief that, no matter how minute a description of the crime was given in the first part ('setting forth the antecedents, motives, and all attendant circumstances'), the reader 'would be so occupied with the crime that he would overlook the evidence. And so it turned out.' Freeman's aim was to produce a type of story that would yield genuine intellectual satisfaction to the reader by completely establishing all data and by creating 'an orderly train of reasoning', excluding all fallacies and leading to a conclusion that is 'the only possible conclusion'. Such a story leaves the competent reader 'in no doubt as to its unimpeachable truth'.

This is the type of detective story that aspires to the ultimate in detached rationalism. It is a model which seeks to close down all ambiguities and which might be said to support the contention that readers turn to detective fiction to escape, as Marjorie Nicolson said, from literature to objectivity. But there is another aspect of the inverted story that is of some interest to readers of later crime fiction: it begins by placing the criminal's own narrative at the centre of our attention. Although Freeman himself was clearly preoccupied with the details of the investigation, readers may well, as he charges, be very much 'occupied with the crime'—with the transgressor's thoughts, plans, actions, and efforts to prevent the discovery of his guilt. In rather a different way than the scurrilous Dorrington stories, then, Freeman's inverted tales put the criminal at the centre of our consciousness, and this reversal, as we will see in what follows, is one of the major sources of generic change during the course of the twentieth century.

Classic detection in the inter-war years

Agatha Christie, *The Murder of Roger Ackroyd* (1926) and *Peril at End House* (1932); Dorothy L. Sayers, *Strong Poison* (1930)

The English detective fiction produced in the inter-war period is easily reducible to its clichéd components, imitated so often and so badly, Raymond Chandler charged in 'The Simple Art of Murder', that the novels became farcical and self-parodying, with their invariable reliance on ludicrously complex methods of murder and 'the same careful grouping of suspects' ([1944] 1988: 10). Ronald Knox, a writer as well as an avid reader of classic detective fiction, observed rather more affectionately: 'If I walked into the detective-story house, I believe I should be able to find my way about it perfectly; it is always more or less the same design' (Ousby 1997: 77). This was the great age of the country house mystery story, or, should the scene shift to London, of crime within the restricted milieu of fashionable society. In either case, it took place in an *exclusive* setting. The enclosed community itself was the source of tensions, deceptions, betrayals, and death—this being the period during which murder came to be an essential part of the detective story (in contrast to the early Holmes stories, for example, which tend to focus on fraud and crimes against property). It was also the period during which the methods employed for intriguing the reader became ever more intricate. With its carefully assembled group of possible suspects, all conceivably hostile to a victim of some social standing, and its teasing array of clues, this was a form of mystery story that required an exceptional degree of cleverness on the part of both murderer and detective. More productive of novels than of the short stories associated with the genre at the turn of the century, this 'golden age' of English detective fiction began to emerge in the 1920s, some three decades after the Holmes stories were originally serialized. It is exemplified by the work of writers such as Agatha Christie, Dorothy L. Sayers, Marjorie Allingham, Josephine Tey, and Ngaio Marsh. American writers between the wars also contributed in substantial ways to the development of the 'clue-puzzle' formula (Stephen Knight, for example, emphasizes the work of Carolyn Wells, whose discussion of the techniques of the mystery story arguably influenced Agatha Christie's conception of the form), but the tradition was predominantly English. The golden age label carries romantic connotations, as well as 'an aura of static harmony' (Knight 2004: 84–94). A period of highly stylized crime writing, it has also been labelled 'cosy', reflecting the preference for plots in which a comfortably recognizable pattern (a highly wrought version of the death–detection–explanation model) is acted out in a familiar domestic setting, with the restoration of reassuring orderliness guaranteed.

Readers return compulsively to the intimately known, ultimately reassuring dining rooms and libraries of the detective-story house. Upon arrival, however, they expect surprise, a turning in the corridor they had not previously guessed to be there. In trying to fulfil this need, detective story writers invented ever-more convoluted plots and ingenious methods of murder. At their best, however, they also developed more interesting variations of the form, changing the too-familiar design in fundamental ways. This tension between consoling uniformity and energizing revision is one of the most interesting aspects of the work of Agatha Christie and Dorothy L. Sayers.

Numerous male writers contributed to the golden age (Anthony Berkeley [A. B. Cox], who also wrote as Francis Iles, A. E. W. Mason, Michael Innes, and Nicholas Blake, for example, together with American imitators like John Dickson Carr, S. S. Van Dine, and Ellery Queen), and the detective figures themselves remain predominantly male. This is, however, generally thought of as a period during which detective fiction became feminized. What we particularly notice are such things as the domestic scale of the action, the politeness of the language, the effeteness of many of the detective protagonists, and their frequent association with kinds of knowledge traditionally considered to be feminine (for example, Poirot's intuitiveness). These are characteristics that signal a shift in the nature of crime writing analogous to that seen in other popular fiction of the time, symptomatic of a post-First World War trend towards the publication of novels that catered to a growing female readership. Golden age detective fiction exerted its appeal in part because of its *containment* of violence. Its settings function to remove the story from a wider sociopolitical sphere, and this isolated context reinforces the formal closure of the narrative and symbolizes what many later writers and critics have felt to be a constricting intellectual and emotional retreat from uncomfortable realities, the diversion of an insular community turning its back on much that was of importance in inter-war society. It could easily be accused of being, as Chandler complained in 'Simple Art', 'too little aware of what goes on in the world' ([1944] 1988: 11) We would never guess, immersed in the world of golden age detection, that we were reading about a period of history during which there was, for example, rapidly increasing unemployment, the General Strike of 1926, the Great Depression of the 1930s, and the rise of the European dictatorships. The majority of those who wrote detective fiction during these decades are associated with right-wing socio-political views—views summed up in the title of Colin Watson's 1971 study, *Snobbery with Violence* (Symons [1972] 1992: 117–18).

A frequent critical judgement of both Christie and Sayers, then, has been that they are conservative in style, setting, characterization, subject matter, and socio-political views—purveyors of 'a typifying vision of British society as a whole strikingly at odds with many insistent realities of the interwar years' (Priestman 1998: 21–2). The detective-figures operating within this narrow environment can be seen as closely identified with the privileged classes, and the crimes they solve are no more than ripples on the surface of an otherwise comprehensible, largely benevolent universe—not, for example, the acts of deranged psychopaths wreaking havoc, but crimes characterized by intentionality, premeditation, and rational self-interest, serving entirely comprehensible private ends.

The image conjured by the phrase 'golden age' is, however, belied by the nature of the traumas and anxieties that require the solving power of the detective. Is it right to see the whole body of this fiction simply as evidence of English middle-class arrogance and national complacency? The standard view of the uniformly insular and snobbish character of inter-war detective fiction is effectively challenged, for example, by Alison Light in *Forever England*. For a start, she reminds us that in the wake of the First World War, the need for reassurance, for a consoling pattern, is a wholly understandable impulse. The setting—whether country house or the Oxbridge college—signifies a safer world; the preference for dandyish, 'bloodless' detectives can be said to embody a 'bearable masculinity'. Hercule Poirot and Lord Peter Wimsey are appropriate protagonists for a 'literature of convalescence', which was reacting against the martial atmosphere and carnage of an exceptionally destructive war (1991: 74–5). Furthermore, these are novels that can be seen as encoding disturbing issues that, although not directly articulated, are inescapably present. Thus, Light argues, if we look more closely at the anxieties expressed by texts themselves we might find them to be less unproblematically conservative than we first imagined. In particular she seeks to counter the critical tendency to patronize Christie, whose views she distinguishes from those, for example, of Sayers. Instead of giving her readers a reassuring, defensive fiction or nostalgia for the aristocracy, Christie creates plots that are symptomatic of instability. She focuses on the disruption of family life from within, reworking Victorian transgression in plots that turn on masks, mistaken identity, hidden madness. She portrays a society of *strangers* in which all social exchange is theatrical and she structures her narratives to reveal sources of menace that seem inextricably bound up with the traditional social hierarchies she represents. In this reading, 'containment' of crime is double-edged: it allows reassuring closure but also implies that the class represented is preying on itself, and that it contains the seeds of its own destruction.

If we turn to the allied charge of formal conservatism, it is not hard to find, in the 1920s and 1930s, evidence of an obsession with the fixed elements of the form and with constructing a well-defined subgeneric identity. The rule-bound nature of classic detective fiction is epitomized in the tendency of golden age mystery writers to entertain themselves by drawing up tongue-in-cheek lists of 'commandments'. These are presented most famously in the 'Ten Commandments of Detection' laid down by Ronald Knox in 1928: his codification included the requirement that the criminal must be mentioned in the early part of the story, and, in the manner of commandments, a list of 'thou shalt nots'. For example, there were to be no supernatural explanations, no secret passages, undiscovered poisons, accidents, twin brothers, or Chinamen. More importantly, the writer must on no account allow concealment of clues by the detective or concealment of thoughts by 'the stupid friend of the detective' who tells the story. The London-based 'Detection Club', formed towards the end of the 1920s, included amongst its rituals an oath, administered by 'The Ruler', or club president, with members required to promise that they would abide by rules similar to those laid down by Knox. S. S. Van Dine set out an even more comprehensive set of requirements in his 'Twenty Rules for Writing Detective stories', published in 1936. This proliferation of rules is often taken as evidence that golden age writers had confined themselves within a rigidly formulaic sub-genre susceptible to little variation. The rules themselves, however, with their prohibitions against using clichéd devices, are also indicative of a heightened awareness of writers' interactions with their audience and of the need to involve the reader as a participant. Their purpose was to aid in the creation of ingenious puzzles, formally intricate crimes presented in ways that would keep readers guessing until the final elucidation of the events, when the multiple connections between the story's separate parts have all been revealed and everything has been reordered, thus ensuring the final readability of the text. Ever-more ingenious methods of murder produced much of this surprising variation, but, as we have suggested, the inherent playfulness of the game was also a constant inducement to bend the rules without breaking them. Both Christie and Sayers wrote novels that contain all of the key identifying features of golden age detective fiction. However, being self-referential in the extreme, they also turned their preoccupation with form to more deconstructive ends, Christie in particular overturning many of the tradition's formulaic elements. As Robin Winks (1982: 10) says, 'before she died, rich in age, books, and cash, [Christie] systematically broke every one of Knox's commandments, though she waited for a posthumous publication to smash the seventh one' (the rule is that 'the detective must not himself commit the crime', and the novel is *Curtain: Poirot's Last Case*, published in 1975).

One of the most obvious ways in which writers could vary the formula was to disrupt such apparently predictable elements as the reliable narrator and the reliably 'fixed' triangle of characters—detective, victim, criminal. The stories discussed in the previous section had already begun to destabilize key roles, but the process is taken further in some of the most interesting novels of the golden age. Anthony Berkeley, for example, writing as Francis Iles, brought the story of the murderer to the fore, somewhat in the manner of Freeman's inverted detective stories, but developing the idea much more subtly and with quite different effect, in *Malice Aforethought* (1931) and *Before the Fact* (1932), which were, as Dorothy Sayers said, 'studies in murder rather than detective stories'.[23] In contrast to

---

[23] Another early writer mentioned in this connection is Marie Belloc Lowndes, whose novel *The Lodger* (1913), about a Jack the Ripper-style murderer, was adapted by Hitchcock in the mid-1920s. See Knight 2004: 126; and Symons [1972] 1992: 149–51.

Berkeley/Iles, Christie and Sayers did not abandon the mystery structure: we still must read to the end to discover 'whodunit'. They did,
however, play in various ways with readers' expectations and generic
conventions relating to the functions of different characters—most
famously in Christie's *The Murder of Roger Ackroyd*, but also in the
other novels discussed in this section. Both writers play with the
victim/murderer relationship, Christie in *Peril at End House* and Sayers in *Strong Poison*. In the latter, Sayers also created a detective writer
within the story who moves through all of the main types of role,
researching poisons in a detective-like manner, standing trial for
murder, and finally being revealed as a victim whose life must be saved
by Lord Peter. As Susan Rowlands argues, by manipulating formal
expectations in this way writers like Christie and Sayers critiqued the
idea of a stable, knowable self in modern society (2001: 39–42).

Another important element in the flexible use of the formula—in
its 'transformability'—is to do with overlap between the 'two stories'
of classic detective fiction. In the structuralist model, as we have seen,
the two stories, that of the crime (the *fabula*) and that of the investigation (the *sjuzet*), do not overlap but only come together at the end.
In practice, however, writers often create space for varying the formula by constructing stories that are temporally overlapping and
interpenetrating. When we look more closely at even quite conventional golden age fiction, we see that the chronologically ordered
narrative not only contains the crime and the events leading up to it
but also the aftermath of the crime, a period during which the criminal tries (ultimately unsuccessfully) to conceal his part in the crime.
There is, then, an ongoing process of deception, often practised directly on the detective; the criminal can, in fact, at this stage in the
narrative be viewed as a competing narrator, trying to ensure that the
events are narrated in the way that he would wish. At the same time,
the detective, who is ultimately successful in controlling 'the way
the story is narrated', can at this point be quite closely involved
with the criminal. They are alike not just as fellow narrators, but also
as tricksters (deceiving people for their own purposes) and as
arrangers of scenes (the villain stages the scene of the crime, the
detective stages the final scene of exposure). As is often pointed out,
they are also twinned as murderers: having solved the case, the detective—not invariably but as a general rule—commits the perfect murder, whether by handing over the murderer to the legal system or, say,

by letting him go off to commit suicide. This overlapping of the two stories and of the central antagonists is crucial to the evolution of the detective story, and is one of the main things that frees the genre from the conservative straightjacket of a rigid two-story structure. What we will see in looking at Christie and Sayers is that it is very often in this shifting 'interzone' that changes are most marked. There is just such an increased interpenetration of the first and second stories, for example, in *Peril at End House*: since Poirot is investigating an *anticipated* murder for three-quarters of the novel, he is on the scene virtually from the planning stages of the crime, and the destabilizing questions that the reader asks arise out of the relationship that the detective develops with the person ultimately revealed to be the culprit (Poirot is working to help the person who turns out to be the murderer).

When *The Murder of Roger Ackroyd* was published in 1926, Christie had already written five mystery stories. It was this book, however, that really established her reputation, because it was here that she most flagrantly violated the expectations of her readers whilst at the same time demonstrating her technical brilliance in handling the clue-puzzle plot. It is a novel that at first glance appears to conform in every particular to the familiar pattern, set in a small village, containing a body in the study, several promising suspects, and Poirot conveniently at hand to solve the crime. The deception of the reader, however, is carried further than usual, in violation of Knox's ninth commandment (which requires that the 'stupid Watson' figure who narrates the tale must not conceal his thoughts from the reader), and Christie is at full stretch to stay within the conventions whilst, by means of a very deft sleight of hand, tricking the reader more outrageously than usual. It is this devious play with the conventions that made Christie's sixth whodunit an ideal text for the deconstructive criticism of the French critic Pierre Bayard. In *Who Killed Roger Ackroyd?*, Bayard analyses in detail the way in which the reader interprets and acts to produce meaning in a text.

There has been much discussion of classic detective novels as, using Barthes's terms (*S/Z*, 1970), *lisible* (readerly) as opposed to *scriptible* (writerly) texts. The former, conventional and conservative, produce what Barthes calls an irreversibility in their narrative momentum; they have a stable, singular meaning; they may contain disorder in the sense of including it, but will also ultimately *contain* disorder in the sense of controlling or checking it. Writerly texts, on the other hand, refuse this kind of narrative logic, presenting the reader with a proliferation of meanings. What Bayard does is to counter the conception of Christie's novels as the very embodiment of 'readerly' texts, instead encouraging the sense that her readers *are* involved as active participants in the production of meaning. Analogous to the detective rather than in thrall to him, the reader is invited to interpret, to exercise intellectual acuity rather than just passively submitting to a conventional and endlessly repeated, always predictable ritual. Whereas critics stressing the inflexibility of the formula tend to regard such fiction as unaware of 'its own silences or of its continual repetition' (Porter 1981: 189–90), Bayard's analysis suggests that it is precisely an acute awareness of all the various forms of repetition and silence that characterizes the good detective writer, contributing to a heightened sense of how readers actually play the game—of the expectations they bring to any text on the basis of their encounter with repeated examples of the same form, and of the way in which an astute reader will fill in the silences, the ellipses.

Bayard's discussion, then, offers lively insights into the claim that detective fiction is an essentially conservative literary art, resting upon the privileging of 'closure' over 'process' in story-telling (since closure brings the subsequent restoration of social order). Bayard's point of departure is Van Dine's formulation of generic rules, the most important of which, he suggests, are the two rules of the 'disguise principle': (1) 'the truth must be hidden throughout the book'; and (2) 'while being hidden, this truth must be accessible to the reader, even in plain view.' This second rule (the fifteenth in Van Dine's list) means that, if the reader were to reread a detective novel, he would 'see that the solution had, in a sense, been staring him in the face' ([1998] 2000: 19–40).

Christie, Bayard says, 'seems to have perfected' the 'disguise principle', and as a result her fiction allows us to explore in great detail the 'wealth of the modalities of blindness and of the production of meaning'. She mines the 'Freudian question of psychic blindness', asking why we repeatedly fail to see things, and she shows her ingenuity by inventing various devices to prevent her readers from grasping the truth. Christie's exceptionally rigorous methods of hiding what is in plain view involve, Bayard says, three main techniques: disguise, distraction, and exhibition. The classic technique of misleading the reader is simply to disguise the murder itself (for example, as a natural death or suicide) or to disguise the nature or function of the murderer (perhaps playing on our assumptions about the public image that he or she projects). Another technique is to distract the reader with red herrings, multiplying suspicious clues or characters (this is 'a kind of negative disguise'). Additionally (one of the paradoxical aspects of classic detective fiction) the truth can be hidden by making it 'apparent everywhere', rendering it so absurdly obvious that it will not be considered as a solution to the crime. These modes of concealing the truth can often be employed simultaneously, or can be 'doubled' (as when, for example, a murderer is given a respected status and *also* made to seem a victim). The application of these modes of concealment produces what Bayard sees as another central paradox in the genre. That is, detective fiction works by complicating events, which requires the proliferation of signs (if not, there would be no plot, no point in reading it). If we consider the way this lengthy process of creating confusion leaves a residue of doubt in the reader's mind, a kind of inbuilt generic *lack* of closure is apparent, even though we are finally asked to accept that there is in fact one truth, that all signs are determinate. What most interests Bayard here is the difficulty of arresting meaning: he argues that Christie's work ends by generating 'a model of polysemy', raising the question of whether such a multiplicity of possible hypotheses 'finally generates undecidability', thus undermining the model of readability underpinned by the codification of rules.

In *The Murder of Roger Ackroyd*, the main technique used is that of disguise (Dr Sheppard masquerades as someone unlikely to be a murderer), but this is 'doubled' by the fact that the murderer is concealed in the narration itself, since the first-person narrator is conventionally the mouthpiece for the truth. This effect is augmented by two other closely related methods that are key to the production of illusion: double-edged discourse and the 'lie by omission'. Double-edged discourse entails the use of statements that can signify two completely contrary things. By means of such ambiguous formulations, Sheppard 'manages to tell us nothing but the truth'. It requires a second reading for us to read them 'correctly'. This is a novel that would seem to be written to be reread. So, for example, there is a complicated series of such devices at the end of Chapter 4, the key period following the murder, where a gap in the representation of time is crucial: 'The letter had been brought in at twenty minutes to nine. It was just on ten minutes to nine when I left him, the letter still unread. I hesitated with my hand on the door handle, looking back and wondering if there was anything I had left undone' (Christie [1926] 1993: 41). Here and elsewhere, this kind of discourse involves words that are carefully chosen to be vague enough for us to fill with different meanings. Sheppard may tell 'nothing but the truth', but he does not tell the *whole* truth: his account is full of ellipses between one statement and another, into which we retrospectively have to insert things that the narrator has suppressed. Dr Sheppard emulates Poirot's usual narrating friend, Hastings, in producing a written account of the novel's events, which he in fact gives to the detective to read (pp. 209 ff.). Poirot's comments are themselves nice examples of double-edged discourse, his commendation couched in terms that on a second reading clearly indicate his knowledge of Sheppard's guilt: ' "Eh bien," he said, "I congratulate you [. . .] on your reticence" ' (p. 210). As the novel moves towards its resolution, Poirot's own 'counter narrative' is set against that of his narrator, with 'two facts and a little discrepancy in time', and a concomitant shift in (visual) perspective revealing a gap created by the movement of a chair (p. 224). The solution of murder cases often turns on these 'little discrepancies': our whole reading of detective stories involves our ultimately filling, with the help of the detective, the little gaps in an earlier narrative. But of course, as Bayard points out, it is never *really* possible to fill all gaps.

Poirot gives Sheppard the standard way out, suggesting an overdose, recommending that he first finish his manuscript, ' "but abandoning your former reticence" ' (p. 232). We thus have a third narrative. As Bayard asks, however, why, given the multiplication of narratives so far, need one stop at three? Sheppard does indeed 'tie it all together for us', explaining with some self-congratulation the gaps in his first account, but what guarantee have we that he is not again concealing things? Might he, for example, be constructing an altruistic narrative in order to exculpate the real killer, his sister, who could equally have committed the crime? As a text like Doyle's 'Silver Blaze' suggests, detective stories have conventionally created such gaps: for example, Holmes's crucial 'off-stage' twenty-minute conversation with Silas Brown is an explicit gap that draws attention to itself, a physical absence, an answer known but deliberately withheld. In Christie's writing, though, the gaps are so deftly managed that we often do not realize until a second reading the exact point at which the gap has occurred. One consequence of this, particularly in *The Murder of Roger Ackroyd*, is that once we realize the nature of the deception practised on us we recognize the unreliability of narrative itself, the existence of gaps *where we do not recognize them:* 'We see how this opens a door that will be difficult to close' (Bayard [1998] 2000: 40).

The conclusions that Bayard draws from his analysis are primarily formal, but it is also the case that Christie's formal play creates a strong example of her characteristic preoccupations with social deceits, pretence, and theatricality. *The Murder of Roger Ackroyd*, Susan Rowland argues, 'is a comedy in which the self-conscious artifice derives both from cultural stereotypes and from crime fiction'. The formal play and self-referentiality also carry metaphoric meanings, extending the exposure of social pretence and arguably undermining narrative reliability in a way that requires us to adopt a more 'feminine' method of reading. That is, we are prompted to read without the expectation of secure and confident closure, but instead to see the text as more open to interpretation: 'Such a "learning to read differently" must be seen as a gendering strategy in the novel because it is explicitly said to work against the assumptions of a heroic male model' (Rowland 2001: 28).

Although *The Murder of Roger Ackroyd* is rightly acknowledged to be her most 'radical' treatment of the form (Rowland 2001: 27), Christie is constantly experimenting with the limits of the genre. *Peril at End House* is another very self-reflexive novel, with Poirot discussing the 'least likely' convention with Hastings, for example, and telling him he reads too many detective stories (Christie [1932] 1995: 100). *Peril* also obeys many of the rules whilst simultaneously violating and calling attention to them. Here the key convention that Christie manipulates is the innocence of the victim. Poirot's reflections on the solution to the crime have an alphabetic structure: there is a sheet of paper on which he has written a list of possible suspects, A to J, and his eventual resolution of the crime depends upon his sudden recognition that there is something missing, an 'unknown', the letter K. '[T]he person—K' is in fact the 'other self' of the young woman who has throughout appeared to be the intended victim of a murder plot; it stands for her own 'secret chamber' of obsession and grim determination (pp. 184–5, 208). Poirot's alphabetic list, then, provides a repeated sense of logic and progression whilst also reserving a place for the 'unknown'. What he identifies as the missing factor is of course there all the time if viewed from a different angle. Such shifts in perspective, routinely required in classic detective fiction, are necessary if Poirot is to recontain the irrational elements of the gothic that in *Peril at End House* seem more than usually threatening.

As we have seen, traditional detective fiction ultimately acts as a repudiation of the gothic (eschewing supernatural explanations, throwing light into dark recesses). It may also, however, play extensively with it, as here, not just by searching for the 'originating moment' of gothic fears but also by sustaining (if not too seriously) a gothic atmosphere, feeding the reader's suspicion that there is something uncanny going on. In *Peril*, space for such a suspicion is created by the substantial overlap Christie allows between the 'two stories' of the classic form: the anticipated murder has not yet taken place when Poirot becomes involved, and this creates for him a role far less detached than is usually the case. He fears the worst, he tentatively explores like 'a little child in the dark', and he moves towards a solution that is concealed in the kind of secret chamber beloved of gothic novelists, contained within an 'eerie and imposing' house, standing 'by itself far from anything' (pp. 176–7, 14). The role of Hastings reinforces this atmosphere, since, being in a malarial fever, he perceives all as though in a nightmare, seeing Poirot as a kind of 'fantastic clown' and glimpsing a 'dreadful face' peering in at the window (p. 188).

The victim/murderer, Nick, has a dark mysteriousness about her, with her 'haunting and arresting' eyes (p. 15). She is not, of course, the gothic heroine playfully suggested by Poirot (' "Me, I was picturing you in a dark mysterious mansion, haunted by a family curse" ' (p. 14)). But what Poirot calls his own 'melodramatic mind' (p. 33) is given free rein in this novel, right up to the seance he organizes at the end. And it is an ending in which we find that Nick has indeed been haunted by an ancestral curse, the overwhelming desire to keep possession of family property. She has 'feverishly' (p. 212) tried to acquire the money that would enable her to retain her ownership of the 'end house' of a family line that has been passed down by an ancestor unscrupulous enough to be suspected of a pact with the devil ('Old Nick', the grandfather from whom she gets her 'nickname'). Nick in fact is doubled by name with two characters—her devilish grandfather and her innocent cousin Maggie, with whom she shares her actual Christian name (Magdala) and whom she murders. These doubles correspond to her dual role within the novel (actual transgressor but pretended victim) and also embody, respectively, an old order clinging to its 'rights' set against a youthful possibility of social mobility.

This image of an established class protecting its privileges with violence, heir not just to fine country houses but to murderous desires, is a recurrent one in Christie's novels, and supports the contention that Christie's work cannot unreservedly be judged as conservative. Dorothy L. Sayers is arguably less easily defended and more easily caricatured, with her effete, aristocratic protagonist, Lord Peter Wimsey. Second son of the Duke of Denver, Lord Peter was conceived, as Julian Symons says, with 'an immensely snobbish, loving seriousness' and was regarded by his creator with 'an adoring eye' ([1972] 1992: 123–4). Less adoring readers, however, have increased in number over the years, and even in Sayers's own time Lord Peter was an obvious target for parody (skilfully parodied in the 1930s, for example, by both Anthony Berkeley and, in 'Greedy Night', by E. C. Bentley). But Sayers was also a subtle practitioner of her craft, entirely capable of problematizing in various ways the role of the aristocrat-detective 'as redeeming hero' (Rowland 2001: 43–6), of challenging class values and of playing with the conventions of the genre—and indeed of having her hero parody himself. The tensions between the snobbish, conservative Sayers and a less conventional self are very apparent in *Strong Poison*.

There is little doubt that Sayers thinks of class and hierarchy as basically right and necessary, part of the indispensable fence against barbaric acts. When Lord Peter feels briefly tempted to shatter decorum with a rash act, he is restrained by his adherence to the system of small niceties, routine, hierarchical responsibility, and carefully preserved façades that stands between violence and civilized balance:

He snatched up a heavy bronze from the mantelpiece—a beautiful thing [. . .] and the impulse seized him to smash the mirror and smash the face—to break out into great animal howls and gestures. Silly! One could not do that. The inherited inhibitions of twenty civilized centuries tied one hand and foot in bonds of ridicule. What if he did smash the mirror? Nothing would happen. Bunter would come in, unmoved and unsurprised, would sweep up the debris in a dust-pan. (p. 126)

His submitting himself to the constraints of the society he lives in and of the aristocratic history that is always at the front of his mind is a constant aspect of Lord Peter's persona. But at the same time, as Susan Rowlands argues, Sayers's conservatism is moderated, for example, by her representation of a degree of desirable class fluidity and of a process of relegitimizing class 'by prescribing a moral dimension and a duty of consideration towards aspirants from below' (2001: 40–1). Although he will never be less than an exemplary part of the establishment, we do see Lord Peter on the last page, in his announcement of the marriage plans for himself and his sister, pushing towards a less repressive, restrictive kind of social hierarchy than the Duke would wish. Class barriers are permeable—though this in itself, of course, acts to validate the basic notion of hierarchy.

The construction of gender in *Strong Poison* is also in many respects fluid, and indeed one of the things that helps to moderate the implied approval of a repressive class structure in *Strong Poison* is Lord Peter's marked feminization. When he considers the act of impetuous violence mentioned above, it is not, of course, violence along the lines of the self-assertion of an American hard-boiled hero, but the smashing of a mirror with a fine bronze, and Lord Peter restrains himself with the thought that his 'man' would be along straight away to pick up the pieces. He is a protagonist who is part of a well-established social fabric, able to fit into a range of social relationships with consummate ease, and this, of course, is a resource he uses in his work of detection. But it is also something that sets him considerably apart from the more individualistic protagonists who tend to dominate the masculine tradition, and there is more than social dependence and obligation hampering him in *Strong Poison*: there is the fact that he falls in love with Harriet Vane, which has the effect of unmanning him as a detective, reducing his investigative self to impotence. It is an attachment that is 'forbidden' not just socially but generically (a flagrant transgression against the third rule formulated a few years later by S. S. Van Dine—'The detective should not have a love interest'). The effect of his involvement in a romance plot is unquestionably that he loses some of his masculine self-sufficiency as a detective—'For the first time, too, he doubted his own power to carry through what he had undertaken [. . .] He was fumbling— grasping [. . .] He asked questions at random, doubtful of his object' (Sayers [1930] 2004: 71). He is still, of course, characterized by key moments of standard detective insight ('those bursts of illumination which come suddenly when two unrelated facts make contact in the mind' (p. 89)). But when he emulates Holmes it is in a decidedly parodic manner—'Give me the statutory dressing-gown and ounce of shag' (p. 89). In many ways the antithesis of the super-masculine, rational, and omni-competent Sherlock Holmes, Lord Peter, even apart from his debilitating infatuation with Harriet, is shown as lacking the force of the traditional detective.

The secrets that must be uncovered to resolve the plot lie in recesses that he cannot himself penetrate, and this means that in *Strong Poison*, as so often in the post-Second World War novels discussed in the following section, there is considerable dispersal of the investigative activities which had conventionally rested entirely on the shoulders of the heroic detective. To answer the crucial questions with which he is faced, Lord Peter requires Miss Climpson's spinsters, the women 'of the class unkindly known as "superfluous" ' (pp. 40–1) who in fact take on the major investigative roles in the novel. Lord Peter's investigating women are still, of course, 'his' women (part of his 'Cattery'). They clearly remain subordinate, and do not step out of their social places any more than his man Bunter would do (even though Bunter himself is virtually as quick as Lord Peter in arriving at the final answer needed to solve the crime). But their roles are active and admirable, whereas the detective figure—who recognizes the need for and holds together this necessary if unequal alliance—has lost much of his solving power, and we are in a sense left with an image of a class structure in which it is actually the men and women of the lower orders who accomplish what needs to be done.

For all of her innate conservatism, then, one might argue that Sayers did in effect develop the genre in ways that accomplished a weakening of its male-dominated character, putting the real work of detection in the hands of women and (although most modern feminists would presumably find Harriet's romantic preferences a little curious) putting on the scene a female detective story writer whose desires become a driving force in the series. The 'first story' of *Strong Poison*, leading to Harriet's arrest and trial for a crime she did not commit, is more unequivocally feminist than the 'second story' of Lord Peter's investigation, in which, for all his debilitating weaknesses, he remains the controlling figure. In the first story, on the other hand, Harriet is juxtaposed with men whose misogyny is made more apparent by the presence of a heroine who is, in essential respects, the representative of the author herself. *The Murder of Roger Ackroyd*, in Bayard's analysis, can be shown by a certain amount of critical ingenuity to contain strong traces of the author (as Caroline Sheppard); *Strong Poison*, by comparison, does not force us to hunt around too much for this sort of identification. Harriet, the judge at her trial says, ' "is also [that is, like Boyes—but also like Sayers] a novelist by profession, and it is very important to remember that she is a writer of so-called "mystery" or "detective" stories, such as deal with various ingenious methods of committing murder and other crimes" ' (p. 7). As the Dowager reflects, ' "I wonder whether, if she didn't do it, she has spotted the murderer herself?" ' (p. 27). The similarities between the author and her heroine here are too strong to be contested: Harriet as a fictional author is even writing a novel that is in effect the story of this novel; she debates, in a key scene with Lord Peter, the possible plot developments in a novel such as *Strong Poison*; and, of course, she is in love with the detective-protagonist, though not quite admitting this openly. As the accused, Harriet is subject to the kind of masculine prejudice that nearly makes her the victim of a miscarriage of justice, and she has put herself beyond the pale not merely by living in sin with Boyes but by carrying out her very practical detective work on poisons. Associated with Boyes by scandal, she is also set against him, a popular female author opposed to an unpleasant exemplar of high modernism, whose novels, essays, and articles were all 'of what is sometimes called an "advanced" type' (pp. 6–7). His misogyny is abundantly apparent—not the sort of man who would make friends with a woman, but who demanded devotion. It is also, however, in filling out the Harriet–Boyes relationship that Sayers most signals her conservative resistance to the kind of literary transgressiveness represented by modernism itself, the detective story being claimed (if light-heartedly) for the forces of more traditional morality, its resolution confirming order and virtue (p. 99): when another friend suggests, ' "From all accounts she was just as bad as he was" ', Wimsey responds, ' "[Y]ou can't think that, Helen. Damn it, she writes detective stories and in detective stories virtue is always triumphant. They're the purest literature we have" ' (p. 99).

Transforming the tradition in the 1950s and 1960s

Margery Allingham, *Tiger in the Smoke* (1952), P. D. James, *A Mind to Murder* (1963), Ruth Rendell, *Wolf to the Slaughter* (1967)

In Margery Allingham's *Tiger in the Smoke*, one of the characters wryly observes, ' "Values are so relative. I thought that when I was trussed up, listening to that bunch of crazy thugs. Hitler wanted the modern world. Well, I mean to say, Campion, look at the modern world!" ' (Allingham [1952] 1992: 173). Post-Second World War, the most notable heirs to the traditions of classic detective fiction have given readers the sense that they are very self-consciously responding to a modern world in which criminality is less easily contained than it was in the world of the country house murder mystery. With 'Dear Old Agatha', P. D. James says, 'the peace of that mythical little village is totally restored once the murder is solved. But with my novels, everybody who comes in touch with that very contaminating crime is changed. You don't get things back to what they were.'[24] 'Dear Old Agatha', as we have seen, was perhaps not quite so blithely unaware of the 'contaminating' nature of crime as James implies (we have here another example of the way in which generic shifts tend to be contextualized by oversimplified representations of the 'old guard'). But the post-Second World War writers are unquestionably more concerned to engage directly with the conditions of contemporary society: ceasing to 'get things back to what they were' implies both a scepticism about the possibility of achieving optimistic closure and a stronger impulse to comment on the state of things as they now are. The very taken-for-grantedness of key elements in the tradition—the social hierarchies, the logic of detection—makes it ripe for disruption. In the work of Allingham, James, and Rendell, we see how each writer re-examines what she perceives as the ordered world of classic detective fiction, entering into a dialogue with the assumptions stereotypically associated with it. There were occasional hints of an

---

[24] P. D. James in interview with Mel Gussow, 'Savoring Old Murders, Spinning Tales of New Ones', *New York Times*, 10/1/2004, online at www.nytimes.com.

explicit moral or socio-political agenda in the work of earlier detective story writers (Chesterton, for example, and E. C. Bentley), but
we now see such elements playing a much more central part in the
structure of the plot and the explanation of the murder. The 'death–
detection–explanation' model is retained, but is now explicitly linked
to contemporary reality. So, in Allingham's *Tiger in the Smoke*, for
example, the quest at the centre of the story has a back story that is set
at the time of the war, which is itself represented throughout the novel
as a kind of crucible out of which comes much that *is* the modern
world; and the villain of the piece, who wants to 'have' the modern
world, is emblematic of the contemporary prioritizing of material
over spiritual and aesthetic values. P. D. James and Ruth Rendell, who
started writing over three decades after Allingham published her first
mystery novels (in the late 1920s), broaden their aims even more to
address what they see as serious moral and social issues. The police
detectives created by James and Rendell are in many respects simply
updated versions of the heroic detective, but they occupy roles
embedded in an official investigative structure that confronts them
with crimes that derive from a wide range of contemporary issues
(for example, class conflict, race, mental illness, paedophilia, abortion,
euthanasia, drug addiction, the environment).

This thematic adventurousness goes with considerable experimentation with the form of the mystery story. Whereas Sayers signals her
attitude by having Lord Peter reject the idea of links with modernist
writing—firmly asserting that the 'purity' of detective fiction is proof
against the corrupting effects of literary modernism—modernist
influences can be discerned in the work of all three of the writers
discussed in this section. Whilst still retaining key characteristics of
classic detective fiction (meticulous plotting, a complicated mystery, a
detailed investigation, and important revelations reserved until the
end of the novel), they also found means of breaking out of the more
enclosed world of the golden age tradition, most importantly, perhaps, by giving over sections of their texts to the criminals, shifting
the centre of attention away from the investigators. There are
accompanying changes that affect the nature of both the criminal and
the investigator. With the emergence of psychopathic characters,
criminality becomes less rational and more alarming; at the same
time, investigators appear to be lacking in the kerygmatic qualities of
earlier sleuths (Roth 1995: 61–3) and (even more than Lord Peter in

Strong Poison) to be losing the capacity to single-handedly solve a case. Although we are still some way from the world of the fully professionalized police procedural, the police force is no longer filled with officers who are invariably stupid or incompetent. The investigator now sometimes simply assists policemen who are themselves forceful and astute (in Allingham's *Tiger in the Smoke*) or are actually (in the series novels of James and Rendell) members of the force themselves. James and Rendell have also produced highly successful non-investigative, non-series novels (Rendell under the name Barbara Vine), but they clearly have had a long-term commitment to their Superintendent Adam Dalgliesh and Chief Inspector Wexford series. Symons, in *Bloody Murder*, raises the question of why writers like James and Rendell have continued to work within the form, given their changing agendas, their more modernist approach, and their more transgressive subject matter. The answer, he suggests, is that both see advantages in the very limitations of the form. He quotes James as saying that, although she at first thought of genre fiction only as a kind of apprenticeship for writing 'serious' literature, she later saw it quite differently: 'after I had done three or four [detective] novels, I realized that in fact the restriction . . . could almost help by imposing a discipline, and that you could be a serious novelist within it' ([1972] 1992: 221–4).

Their strong connection with the existing tradition also enables Allingham, James, and Rendell to enter into a dialogue with the forms and assumptions of golden age crime fiction. In Allingham's *Tiger in the Smoke*, for example, this dialogue centres on the meaning of 'mystery': she to a degree abandons the formal requirement ruling out anything 'supernatural or preternatural' (Knox's second rule), modifying generic expectations as a way of advancing a critique of a materialistic society that has lost its capacity to understand mystery in a deeper sense. James's *A Mind to Murder* asks detective story readers to think again about the requisite skills of the investigator, about the relative importance of precise investigative techniques as opposed to self-knowledge, to 'looking within'; and Rendell, in *Wolf to the Slaughter*, takes as her main theme the order/disorder binary that is at the heart of traditional detective fiction, suggesting the numerous ways in which such a binary in reality breaks down.

Allingham's series protagonist, Albert Campion, is in many ways a very conventional example of the classic detective—aristocratic (though he does not use his title), tall but slight, kindly, unemotional, unassuming, 'misleadingly vacant of face and gentle of manner' (pp. 14–15)—a near relation to the dandy-ish golden age investigators. By the time of *Tiger in the Smoke* an 'old-fashioned primness' (p. 118) seems to be growing on him and he is losing some of his more youthful brio; he still has sound insights and an investigator's impressive store of knowledge but he is becoming increasingly marginalized (a screen adaptation of *Tiger in the Smoke* was in fact filmed to eliminate Allingham's detective). When the distinctly unbalanced Havoc escapes from his hideout before Campion can get his hands on him, Campion reflects, 'I was most relieved. The days when little Albert charged into battle single-handed have gone for good. Havoc is police work, good hefty police work, with medals and promotions at the end of it' (p. 164). There is, in fact, a proliferation of other investigators, each of whom has his virtues, making *Tiger in the Smoke* almost a compendium of the various kinds of detective narrative that flourished in the early twentieth century: a young man called Geoffrey Levett puts himself into extreme danger by trying to investigate the man who has impersonated his wife-to-be's previous husband, and so has clear similarities with the American investigator whose life is constantly at risk; Chief Inspector Charlie Luke, with his physical dynamism, also has affinities with the American private eye; Campion has a pivotal insight (finding the hideout, arrived at by a classic sort of clue) but is marginalized in comparison to Luke on the one hand and the Canon on the other; the Canon, with his moments of synthesizing insight 'standing alone in the dark' (p. 195), representing a Chestertonian sort of detection, though more lacking worldly wiseness than any series detective could afford to be. The Canon is, however, almost killed, and is an 'old-fashioned' figure throughout, whereas Luke is explicitly represented as a man on his way to legendary status. In the contrast between Campion and Luke, we perhaps see—exactly at mid-century—an acknowledgement of the sidelining of the effete amateurs (Campion) or unworldly founts of intuition (the Canon), to be replaced ultimately by a more professional, more vigorous kind of investigator.

The police themselves function in harmony with the series investigator, and he is indeed only a helper in their efficient enterprise, 'the whole beautiful mechanism of detection', working tirelessly, examining every false report and sifting 'every piece of incoherent evidence'

(p. 164). The qualities ascribed to Chief Inspector Luke are even more striking: a powerful man capable of unpredictable force and sudden savagery, 'vivid and more than life-size'. Campion sees him as set to become 'one of the great policemen', possessing 'that utter persistence which only derives from an almost unnatural interest' (pp. 24, 175). Hunting the villain with passionate devotion, he is also repeatedly compared to his quarry ('personal magnetism' glowing in both of them (p. 131))—the doubling these two extreme men being much more central to the novel than the somewhat neurasthenic presence of Campion himself.

Allingham gives what at the time was an unusual amount of space to the perspectives of the criminal elements. Chief amongst the novel's wrongdoers there is a symbolically named multiple murderer, Havoc, who comes close to sharing the qualities of later crime fiction psychopaths—though, very explicitly, he is not categorized in that way, since Allingham clearly wants to associate him with a kind of radical evil that cannot be diminished by psychologizing it away. Although a grotesque band of street musicians/ex-soldiers is responsible for the first murder of the novel, these men are only a pathetic echo of the violence embodied by Havoc. Coming into their midst, 'the Gaffer' exudes menace as he drops on them from above, taking command of them 'as if they had been a crowd of impressionable girls' (p. 134). Even the Assistant Commissioner, who is very much against turning criminals into legends, perceives Havoc as an embodiment of evil whose 'atmosphere' marks him out—'an extraordinarily vital animal. He's got force' (pp. 116–17). If the name Havoc suggests wreaking wanton destruction, his other name, 'Cash', points to the rational motive of greed rather than lunacy, and the distinction ensures that his presence in the novel signifies not the disruptiveness of mental aberration but the devastating materialism that Allingham perceives in post-war society.

The 'smoke' in which this tiger prowls is, of course, London itself, and in making such extensive use of her urban setting Allingham establishes a strong polarity between the threatening, unstable modern city with its capitalistic ethos and the traditional sheltered locus of classic detective fiction: the post-war condition is exemplified in a movement away from the kind of small closed community presided over by the Canon into a place that is volatile, unpredictable, violent, disordered, and that of course also intrudes on the world of the

Canon. The atmosphere and inhabitants of the metropolis are repeatedly figured in terms of cacophony and lack of distinction ('the evil smell of fog [. . .] the distinctive noise of the irritable, half-blinded city' (p. 25)), a malign, impenetrable urban jungle that is set against another kind of impenetrability, and one that offers potential salvation—the unfathomable mystery.

At first the novel, in a chapter called 'Ghosts', acts in the usual detective story manner to discredit the suspicion of anything super-natural. But as the quest is pursued to its end something more genu-inely mysterious is found. In comparison to more traditional detective fiction, mystery in Allingham's novel comes near to 'mystery' in the Canon's sense of larger powers at work, of human actors just being part of something ultimately beyond their control. A quest motif and a romance structure can obviously be used without such implications (as, for example, in Hammett's *Maltese Falcon*, in which the object of the quest is ultimately discovered to be nothing but a hollow signi-fier). In Allingham's novel, the fabulous object pursued is also one that fails to contain the riches greedily sought, but the twist here is of a quite different kind, the object being not a sham but 'real' in a sense that Havoc is simply unable to comprehend, possessing a spiritual and aesthetic value. Too 'fragile' to be touched by rough hands, it is something that must remain in the keeping of those who have had the ancient privilege of caring for it. It is an ending in which we can clearly read a profoundly conservative message, signifying the inaccessibility of all that is truly worthwhile to the Cashes of the world, who would simply break them apart in a vain search for what-ever vulgar and debased kind of value they could 'lay their hands on'.

In the novels of P. D. James we encounter a not dissimilar tendency to import a theological dimension into the detective novel—a sense of divine design that is working to counter modern realities that are being critiqued, conveyed by inserting mysteries of a kind not nor-mally admitted to the secular crime novel (as, for example, in James's 1986 novel, *A Taste for Death*). For James, one of the most conserva-tive of British crime writers, individual evil would seem to be a con-sequence of the growing secularization and fragmentation of modern society: she refuses 'to find an earthly home to match her moral vision' (Rowland 2001: 13), and her high-church Anglicanism is joined politically to Thatcherite Conservatism. Her nostalgia for what she has come to regard as largely a lost cause makes her a more pessimistic writer than, for example, Sayers and Christie, whose delusory belief in the possibility of a unified culture produced fiction that exhibits a kind of cultural confidence—a belief in a world in which crime is the exception rather than the rule and in which the restoration of order seems a real possibility. However one qualifies this view of the earlier tradition of classic detective fiction, it is clearly the case that the evils depicted by P. D. James are darker and more irremediable: 'James creates a fictional realm, by contrast, that is rife with the horror and blood and grief largely absent from her predecessors.'[25]

One of the ways in which James brings readers closer to the disturbing nature of the criminality she explores is by giving them access to minds of actual and possible murderers. Allingham, in *Tiger in the Smoke*, spends time in the milieu of her transgressors and gives us some insight into their view of the world, but what both James and Rendell do is subtler and more unsettling, using close third-person narration to bring us into contact with criminal acts and motives. *A Mind to Murder*, James's second novel (1963), is not one of her darker stories, containing only hints of the gothic atmosphere and tragic sense emanating from such later novels as *Original Sin* (1994) and *A Certain Justice* (1997). It does, however, offer a very good example of the way she sets about revising the traditional form to make room for a more complex analysis of contemporary society. The traditional elements of detective fiction are clearly, sometimes parodically, present, with a concentration in the early part of the text, for example, on establishing exact time and place. Although the novel is set in a London psychiatric out-patient clinic, this location is, for the purposes of the commission and solution of a crime, very closely related to the country house, in its provision of a small community, several members of whom might be possible suspects, enclosed in ways that make the intrusion of a murderous outsider an unlikely possibility. The staff of the clinic are so knowledgeable about the nature of the conventional murder scene that they make sure no one touches the body, allow no one to leave or enter, and even offer a psychological profile of the killer: 'They've read all the best detective fiction' (James

---

[25] Ralph C. Wood, 'Deep Mysteries: Christian Liberalism in the Works of P. D. James', *Christian Century*, 27/9/2000, online at www.highbeam.com. Wood adds, 'James looks back, rather wistfully, to the time when throne and altar were still united in a national church that symbolized England's "moral and religious aspirations", its "generally accepted values, [its] common tradition, history and culture".'

[1963] 1985: 15–16). Much attention is given over to trying to map everyone's exact location at the approximate time of the murder and to creating for the reader the layout of the clinic, but within this solid structure of investigative detail James leaves herself room to inhabit the minds of those suspected of and affected by the murder—a cast of characters belonging to a variety of different social worlds within the larger city.

In spite of being set in the Steen Psychiatric Clinic, *A Mind to Murder* contains little suggestion of seriously aberrant psychology. It does, however, direct our attention inwards, towards the effects of varieties of human diminishment. Here as elsewhere, James interests herself in the many ways in which the mind can come to lack any moral centre, and a narrative method that allows her to occupy different minds in turn facilitates her exploration of the causes of psychic distortion, taking us on a tour of the effects of the crime in the consciousnesses of various main characters, connected by a clinic that deals in the repressed elements in 'polite' society. With careful phrasing (making use of modes of concealing the truth not unlike those Christie employs to such effect in *The Murder of Roger Ackroyd*), James is able to combine this inner exploration with a fairly traditional whodunit structure, preserving a concluding twist in spite of the fact that we could well believe we are witnessing a final confrontation between Dalgliesh and the murderer.

Though this suspected killer, Nagle, has, we find, only attempted rather than committed murder, his mind is, morally and psychologically, the murkiest vantage point James can provide for us, and she uses it to create a showdown in which we experience the terror of a man who, at this stage, believes himself to be a murderer. The disorienting urban street scene where the encounter takes place is perceived by Nagle as 'a confused whirl of noise and blinding lights' (p. 216). The fact that the images and sensations are presented to us as from Nagle's own point of view means that we experience very directly the dryness of his mouth, his helplessness, his feelings of horror and panic as he moves automaton-like towards the looming silhouette of the law, only able to guess 'how he looked in that fierce light: a death's head, the mouth agape with fright, the eyes staring' (p. 216). Martin Priestman argues that it is really only in the 1980s and 1990s that we see the emergence of the truly 'split-level' crime novel in which the perspective of the investigative figures of the police procedural alternates with a narrative of the killer's own thoughts and actions (1998: 30–1), and it is certainly the case that it would be hard to imagine Nagle emerging as a compelling narrative centre in the way that, say, Hannibal Lecter does. Nevertheless, what James does here is a significant step in the direction of the split-level narrative, and one that brings the tensions of the confrontation and the reader's uncertainties much more to the fore than they would be in, say, the usual Agatha Christie denouement.

The scene also has the effect of deferring Dalgliesh's exercise of the detective's explanatory powers: his error in the solution of the crime prevents him from speaking at this point in the assured voice of his predecessors in the tradition of classical detection. He has offered his own reconstruction of events before the encounter with Nagle, and thus, in this climactic confrontation, Nagle is able to seize the possibility of challenging the authority of the 'great detective's' narrative: ' "You've worked it all out very cleverly, haven t you? You've been too clever by half, you bloody supercilious copper!" ' (pp. 218–19). It is therefore the novel's most culpable transgressor, not the murderer sought but a scoundrel and a near-murderer, who stage-manages the end, producing with a flourish the conclusive evidence that Dalgliesh has been wrong. There is, of course, another shift in power to follow this, with Dalgliesh again in control, a stronger man because he is able to look within himself and recognize the sources of his mistakes—in this case, the sense of proud singularity associated with the 'great detective', who sees himself competing with the traditional 'worthy adversary' and who has therefore dismissed the actual killer as beneath his notice. In the end, he lectures himself on the need for humility. He has employed with admirable precision and cleverness all of the techniques of detection but has failed to plumb his own motivation (his worries about his own 'mastery') and has overlooked the obvious—a demonstration of the limitation of method alone, and a reinforcement of the injunction (a moral constant in the work of P. D. James) to 'look within'.

In the work of Ruth Rendell, we see many of the same modifications of the traditional form that characterize the novels of James. In Rendell's novels, however, these changes serve ends that are (in a political sense) liberal rather than conservative; whereas James views with suspicion explanations that attribute crime to environmental influences, Rendell uses the capacity of the crime novel to explore the complex social causes of criminal behaviour. There is a very trad-itional economic motive behind the crime committed in *A Mind to Murder* (poor relations and an inheritance), but it would be hard to read into this a critique of social injustice. In Rendell's novels, on the other hand, coercive class structures, social pressures, prejudice, and deprivation are themselves her subject, most obviously in a non-series novel like *A Judgement in Stone* (1977) and in the powerful literary noir she writes as Barbara Vine (for example, *A Dark-Adapted Eye* (1986) and *A Fatal Inversion* (1987)), but also in Rendell's Wexford novels. A restoration of the established social order, as in the reso-lution to the traditional country house murder, would not address the problem of crime because these inherited structures are them-selves part of the problem; and her aim seems always to work towards a more complex understanding of the nature of disorder itself—of its dangers and its attractions.[26]

Rendell's *Wolf to the Slaughter* (1967), her third Chief Inspector Wexford novel, uses the series's usual setting (Wexford's Sussex town, the imaginary Kingsmarkham) as a site of conflict between the opposing impulses—to order and to disorder—that conventionally structure classic detective fiction. Here, however, in place of the sim-ple dynamic of the traditional mystery (an intrusion of disorder fol-lowed by a restoration of order) Rendell explores the treacherousness both of compulsive ordering and of the many varieties of disorder. *Wolf to the Slaughter* is very much about putting houses in order—a complicated, often comic, compulsive activity that prompts readers to reconsider both the central motif of the country house mystery—the house restored to order—and the role of the detective-as-housecleaner. As part of her metaphoric structure, Rendell uses an artist figure (Rendell [1967] 1990: 21–2), Margolis, whose paintings, *Dawn of Nothing* and *Painting of Dirt*, are manifestations, according to the art critics, of a fascination with the 'marvellous, multifarious textures of matter in the wrong place'. His work is an analogue for all of the intractably messy realities that do fascinate as well as repel, causing random damage but also obscurely attractive, drawing in

---

[26] As Rowland writes, 'Conservatism is thereby indicted as oppressive because it provokes criminal desire. Apprehending the criminal does not restore moral and social order; first because the criminal is in part a victim, but particularly because the conservative societal codes implicated in the crime are still operating' (2001: 39–40).

susceptible people from more 'ordered' levels of society (as Ann Anstey is drawn in by a beautiful sado-masochistic mechanic, and Drayton, the most compulsively orderly of the police investigators, by the equally beautiful Grover girl). Although there are suggestions of 'craziness', the painter's emphatic denial of this possibility in a way applies to the rest of the narrative as well: the people involved have some serious psychological flaws but none of them (including the mildly sadistic supposed killer/actual murderee) constitutes 'craziness'. Much more, it is simply the mess and irresponsibility endemic to so many portrayed that lead both to the commission of the crime and to the sundry confusions surrounding its solution—from Margolis and his newspapers to the grubby chaos of the paper shop that turns out to have been central. Mess of this kind is so apparently insignificant that the police fail to see what it contains, even when they are looking directly at it from the station (pp. 179, 166–7).

The initial 'seamy disorder' (pp. 25–9) described in the Margolis household after the loss of his sister Ann is so random that the police do not even consider trying to sort through the papers that litter the yard (in amongst which, we eventually learn, Margolis would have thrown out her note of explanation). The literal mess that so disturbs Drayton and Burden suggests to them lives that are not only untidy but immoral—the presumption here in favour of order being stereotypical ('The woman was thoroughly immoral too. Decent women had clean tidy homes' (p. 43)). The paper shop is likewise, in a less bohemian though no less disgusting way, a scene of dispiriting disorder, within which the Grover girl has an incongruous loveliness. And Drayton, a man of compulsive tidiness, succumbing to her attractions, is ironically being tempted in by the girl because she means him to 'clean up' her father's car, which contains the messy reality of a corpse. The novel's mystery is sustained by an untidy detail (the missing body), and the motif of disordering and 'cleaning up' runs through the novel, with comic and aggressive tidying as the *reductio ad absurdum* of the investigator's role.[27]

The reader's entry into *Wolf to the Slaughter* is via an opening scene that goes considerably beyond the other novels so far discussed in its immersion of the reader in what we assume to be the actual

[27] Knight describes both Poirot and Miss Marple as representing a 'heightened version of female domestic knowledge as a weapon against fictional disorder' (2004: 91).

commission of a criminal act. Rendell gives us a close-up of the criminal event itself, seen from the shared perspective of the young man and woman involved in something that goes 'hideously wrong' (pp. 10–11). We cannot see this event quite clearly enough to know who is actually stabbed, however, and this gap in our knowledge is also the gap in the knowledge of the investigators: a body is missing, and this absence is what makes it possible to sustain the mystery. It also facilitates Christie-like, intertextual play with the conventions of the genre: the suspected murderer (the man seen stumbling 'drunkenly' along with a young woman who is assumed to be the murder victim (p. 67)) turns out himself to be the victim; the woman, the murderer. This opening scene, then, framing the moment of the stabbing itself, both conceals and reveals, obscuring what has in fact happened but giving readers the sense that they are in possession of *more* information than the struggling police investigators, even though they have difficulty ordering their confused impressions. The mistaken speculation about the identity of the missing body is ironically appropriate to the victim's own tendency in life to masquerade as someone else, hence setting in motion one of the trains of misunderstanding that have to be cleared up before the end.

Rendell's handling of this scene is an excellent example of the way in which she simultaneously plays with the form and adheres to its conventions. So, for example, the main physical clues are all introduced in the first scene—a lighter and its inscription, a car, a flick knife—and are things that keep coming back for further inspection during the course of the narrative. The discovery and conferring of meaning on these clues is complicated by the division of investigative responsibilities. Rendell's close third-person narration, here as elsewhere, does not just enable her to establish a much fuller sense of several actors in the drama but facilitates a shift away from the central, controlling persona of the classic detective and his methods of investigating the clues that present themselves. Although one cannot entirely imagine this without Wexford, he is more a world-weary resister of false narratives than the one person in control of the master narrative, and we in fact see very little of the story through his ultimate piecing together of what happened. In contrast to the traditional detective, although Wexford has personal authority and is responsible for some important breakthroughs, he does not lay any claim to uniqueness or superhumanity. This dispersal of investigative effort is entirely appropriate to the nature of the crime investigated. *Wolf to the Slaughter* contains an intricate assortment of clues. It is a messy and totally unintended crime, and the casual disorder of many of the lives portrayed is reflected in the unpremeditated, accidental, haphazard nature of the murder itself. Quotations scattered through the text from the *Rubaiyat of Omar Khayyam*, offering images of capricious destiny and children stumbling in the dark, reinforce our impression of a criminal event the antithesis of the cunningly contrived crime that is stereotypically seen as the essence of analytic detective fiction.

2

Hard-Boiled Detective Fiction

HAVING made fun of detective stories with titles like *The Triple Petunia Murder Case* and *Death Wears Yellow Garters*, Raymond Chandler's 'The Simple Art of Murder' (1944) sets out its famous defence of a group of writers 'who wrote or aimed to write realistic mystery fiction' ([1944] 1988: 3, 13)—an identifiably American, 'hard-boiled' variety of detective fiction, of which Dashiell Hammett and Chandler himself are generally taken to be the progenitors:

Hammett took murder out of the Venetian vase and dropped it into the alley; it doesn't have to stay there for ever, but it looked like a good idea to get as far as possible from Emily Post's idea of how a well-bred débutante gnaws a chicken wing.

Hammett wrote at first (and almost to the end) for people with a sharp, aggressive attitude to life. They were not afraid of the seamy side of things; they lived there. Violence did not dismay them; it was right down their street. Hammett gave murder back to the kind of people that commit it for reasons, not just to provide a corpse; and with the means at hand, not with hand-wrought duelling pistols, curare, and tropical fish. He put these people down on paper as they were, and he made them talk and think in the language they customarily used for these purposes.

He had style, but his audience didn't know it, because it was in a language not supposed to be capable of such refinements. (pp. 14–15)

Chandler brings together here all of the aspects of crime writing that he sees as undergoing a contemporary transformation: setting, language and gesture, plot structure, attitudes towards violence, the methods and motives of the murderer, the relationship between fiction and contemporary reality. His objective is to delineate a distinct form of detective fiction that he thinks capable of capturing American experience in the early part of the twentieth century.

In mocking the British tradition and its American imitators, he is assuming a close relationship between style and moral content. The decorous prose that would never describe a well-bred débutante as 'gnawing' her chicken wing is of a piece with what Chandler sees as the false moral coherence and the bland reassurances of the classic tradition. Nothing short of a radical revision of the genre, he argues, can make it 'belong to' an altered set of historical circumstances, a society in which violent rupture is not routinely healed by a re-establishment of life's reassuring patterns. He puts the case that only a new language can reveal the truth about corrupt and criminal city administrations, dishonest judges and policemen, moral coward-ice—about what is 'not a fragrant world, but . . . the world you live in' (p. 17). Plots that turn on solutions to intricate and improbable murders, he implies, are incapable of illuminating such a society. They are not the stuff of 'important writing'. In contrast, Hammett's 'spare' and 'frugal' use of 'the American language' and his lack of interest in the 'formal and exact problem' of the classic detective story are inseparable from his realism. The fiction he created is, like all fiction, 'made up', but it is 'made up out of real things' (pp. 14–15, 17). In the tradition that begins in the 1920s with Hammett's contri-butions to *Black Mask* magazine, the investigator is no longer detached and immune from danger. The hard-boiled private eye's self-conscious toughness and his aggressive involvement in his city's criminal milieu give him a very direct investment in the world he investigates.

As the champion of a new paradigm, Chandler naturally wants his readers to recognize the limitations of the 'soft-boiled', feminized mysteries of the British tradition. He caricatures their clichéd puzzles, their repeated exploitation of 'the same utterly incomprehensible trick of how some body stabbed Mrs Pottington Postlethwaite III with the solid platinum poniard just as she flatted on the top note of the "Bell Song" from *Lakmé* in the presence of fifteen ill-assorted guests' (p. 10). This sort of polemic can help to consolidate any sig-nificant departure within an established genre, and American hard-boiled detective fiction was unquestionably a major transformation. But equally one has to acknowledge the oversimplifications that sup-port this kind of foundational binarism. In making his case Chandler exaggerated the contrasts between golden age convention and hard-boiled innovation, and his effectively articulated counter-aesthetic became a defining myth of the development of detective fiction. It is a myth that has generated a conception of hard-boiled writing itself as a unified phenomenon, when the truth of the matter is that neither hard-boiled nor classic detective fiction can be contained in these overly schematic generalizations.

The notion of a stark contrast between 'rival' traditions has been reinforced by the critical habit of choosing representative writers, as Chandler himself does in 'The Simple Art'. When later critics wanted to compare British and American detective fiction as it developed in the inter-war period, Christie and Chandler seemed to be obvious choices. This line of argument, however, not only oversimplifies a complex generic relationship but is based on a reductive reading of both writers. Christie and Chandler do not, in fact, conveniently conform to a binary opposition between conservative feminine and ground-breaking masculine. As Gill Plain has argued, there are actually some striking thematic and structural parallels between the two authors, calling for a more 'multidimensional reading' (Plain 2001: 30–1). In critiques that generalize about hard-boiled writing on the basis of Chandler's work, it is common to take Philip Marlowe as the exemplar of tough masculinity, exaggerating his typicality. In this chapter we will focus on the investigative figures of hard-boiled fiction, and Marlowe himself will be of central importance. But one has to bear in mind that 'tough guy writing' contains many other types of protagonist. In addition to private eyes of all descriptions, its central characters include downtrodden victims, 'wrong men', small-time crooks, outlaws, psychopathic lawmen, and other killers. It is a hugely diverse tradition. Indeed, this diversity is itself one of the effects of the agenda Chandler set out for American crime fiction in 'The Simple Art'.

One of the main reasons for the readily transformable nature of the hard-boiled tradition is that, as Chandler suggests, it aims to represent 'the world you live in'. Whereas the golden age writers can be said to have created detective fiction that *encodes* the socio-political anxieties of their time, hard-boiled writers addressed the problems of their society explicitly. Classic detective fiction is, as we have seen, nowhere near as static as its critics often imply, but in the inter-war period the generic changes that did occur were primarily formal. Successive developments were not without thematic implications, but they were seen primarily as moves in an ever-evolving game played with readers whose interest could be kept alive by the ingenious modification of existing conventions. It is, as Van Dine's nineteenth rule suggests, a game that deliberately excludes the larger concerns of politics and government, with motives for crimes restricted to the personal. Whatever the exaggerations of Chandler's 'Simple Art', his condemnation of this limited sphere of interest signalled a shift that did in fact constitute an opening out of the genre, a new responsiveness to altered socio-political circumstances. One consequence of this is that hard-boiled fiction came to be a natural generic home for many different kinds of protest writing.[1] As the world changed, so did hard-boiled fiction. The class-based assumptions and economic determinism of the inter-war years were supplanted by other preoccupations during later decades, when Cold War paranoia, say, or racism, or Reaganomics and rampant consumerism emerged as central concerns.

Chandler's hard-boiled manifesto also makes much more explicit the relationship between form and ethos. One of his leading objections to classic detective fiction is to what he sees as the socio-political implications of its closed form. Disruptions in the fabric of society are invariably produced by individual violations; if one assumes that every crime is a manifestation of such temporary aberrations, it follows that the detective has the capacity to restore a community ruled by law. This consolatory, potentially redemptive myth no longer seems viable within a complex urban, industrialized society, and hard-boiled fiction reflects this by structuring its narratives in ways that avoid neatly optimistic closure. Sean McCann, in *Gumshoe America*, argues that crime fiction in this period, like liberalism itself, was moving from an emphasis on the centrality of the individual towards a broader emphasis on the sources of corruption and dishonesty, economic injustice and exploitation, creating 'a pulp version of the populist jeremiad'.[2] Hard-boiled detective fiction was born in a period of political and economic changes for which people were wholly unprepared: the stock market crash of 1929; the Great Depression; Prohibition and its attendant gangsterism; the growing evidence of

---

[1] The capacity of hard-boiled crime fiction to develop a radical critique is discussed more fully in Chs. 4–6.

[2] McCann 2000: 18–19. McCann (2000: 39–86), very fully explores the relationship between this anti-élitist fiction and 'nativist populism' (e.g. Ku Klux Klan propaganda).

illicit connections between crime, business, and politics in rapidly expanding American cities. All of these upheavals and injustices find their way into the detective fiction of the time, as causes of crime that seem incapable of real improvement. A little local order might be restored, but none of the rooted sources of despair are removed. As McCann argues, the tough guy writers, in re-imagining the genre for a new time and country, were representing problems that seemed in many ways irremediable, the 'central, unresolved problem' being 'how to imagine a decent society in a country that had few compelling sources of solidarity and only the most rudimentary language of mutual obligation' (2000: 85).

As we have seen, one of Chandler's underlying assumptions is that hard-boiled fiction was bringing a new realism to bear in its representation of this turbulent society. It is a claim that has not gone unchallenged, and one that unquestionably requires some modification. The hard-boiled novel, in making a *judgement* of contemporary society, often couples harsh realism with the fantastic and the symbolic. Another of Chandler's well-known assertions of the importance of speaking to the discontents of one's own time, in the Introduction to *Fingerman*, describes characters who 'lived in a world gone wrong, a world in which, long before the atom bomb, civilization had created the machinery for its own destruction and was learning to use it with all the moronic delight of a gangster trying out his first machine-gun. The law was something to be manipulated for profit and power. The streets were dark with something more than night.'[3] What is striking here is that Chandler stresses political realities—a world in crisis, destabilized by international war, urban crime, and the corrupt exercise of power—but at the same time uses highly metaphoric language to pass judgement on these very real threats. The technique is also characteristic of hard-boiled crime novels: their *method* of more overtly responding to contemporary reality is just such a mixture, presenting a solidly realized but metaphorically heightened cityscape, with violence itself often taking on symbolic force in scenes of grotesque, sometimes surreal destruction and viciousness. As David Madden argues in *Tough Guy Writers of the Thirties*, these are novels that provide 'stylized exaggeration of very real traits in the American

---

[3] Chandler, Introduction to *Fingerman* (1950). London: Ace, 1960: 5.

character [. . .] the nightmare version of the American Dream' (1968: pp. xxv–xxvi).

Whether closer to reality or symbol, the cityscape itself is generally taken to be one of the defining features of the hard-boiled novel. Though hard-boiled fiction is by no means invariably urban, it is the big city that most regularly threatens a protagonist's sense of a discrete self, his powers of understanding, and his physical safety. Chandler's juxtaposition of the 'Venetian vase' of the classic tradition with the alley into which Hammett 'dropped' the detective story clearly refers to more than just a change of scene. It is a contrast between the containment possible in the classic form and the dark open-endedness of the alleyway, a location never conducive to the confident act of bringing forth order from confusion. Just as importantly, the emphasis on *scene itself* constitutes one of the key developments in the American tradition. The contention that scene has supplanted plot in importance is central to Chandler's *Fingerman* Introduction. Celebrating *Black Mask*'s break with the 'standard detective story', Chandler writes: 'The technical basis of the *Black Mask* type of story [. . .] was that the scene outranked the plot, in the sense that a good plot was one which made good scenes. The ideal mystery was one you would read if the end was missing' ([1950] 1960: 6, 8). The narrative of the classic detective story was, strictly speaking, meant to contain no extraneous elements. Its plenitude of detail was simply included for the purpose of delaying the solution of the mystery.[4] But the metaphoric dark alleyway and the associated geography of the labyrinthine big city are not just a tidy source of clues. Much less comprehensible than Holmes's London, this is an intractable, uncontainable, ultimately unknowable terrain, to be grasped only in a fragmentary way. The detective possesses heightened powers in negotiating this difficult territory, but there is no possibility of imposing his will on it. The Conradian sense of the city as a jungle ('This, too, has been one of the dark places of the earth') often informs

---

[4] So Van Dine, for example, includes as his sixteenth rule, 'A detective novel should contain no long descriptive passages, no literary dallying with side-issues, no subtly worked-out character analyses, no "atmospheric" preoccupations. Such matters have no vital place in a record of crime and deduction. They hold up the action and introduce issues irrelevant to the main purpose, which is to state a problem, analyze it, and bring it to a successful conclusion.' See Forter 2000: 12 on the 'non-teleological narrative elements that are strictly absent from the analytic detective story'.

the metaphoric structure of the hard-boiled novel. As McCann points out, there are affinities with the settings of the exotic adventure stories that flourished during the same period as the early hard-boiled novel, which might be said to have relocated the alien landscape, re-imagining it in the interior of American society, creating an under-world scene that had 'its own language, customs, and mysterious affiliations' (2000: 68).

Confronted with the urban nightmare and the 'world gone wrong', hard-boiled private eyes are not, on the whole, reluctant to draw their guns. In Hammett's 'The Tenth Clew' (*Black Mask*, January 1924) the Continental Op dismisses nine red herrings (false 'clues' constructed to mislead him) and instead immerses himself in the physically demanding action by means of which protagonists of the hard-boiled tradition conventionally reach resolutions (Knight 2004: 114). Chandler was only partly jesting when he wrote that the main principle of construction in the tough thriller was 'When in doubt, have a man come through a door with a gun in his hand' (*Fingerman*, 1960: 6). Whatever way one modifies the stereotyping of the reso-lutely masculinist American detective, it is probably not unfair to associate him (at least in the first half of the twentieth century) with a readiness to resort to violence. Not too surprisingly, feminist criti-cism in particular tends to interpret this physical aggression as a misogynistic form of self-definition that depends on triumphing over a threatening feminine principle. If we accept such an interpretation, then we will see hard-boiled crime fiction as inviting readers to iden-tify with a larger-than-life embodiment of male power. Challenging this reading, some critics probing the construction of the tough guy protagonist have stressed another of the traits separating him from the classic detective: his vulnerability. When he 'finds no way out', the detective 'is slugged, shot at, choked, doped, yet he survives because it is in his nature to survive' (Ruhm 1977: p. xiv). The hard-boiled thriller, in terms of Todorov's typology, suppresses the 'first story', so that 'the narrative coincides with the action'. This vitalizes the 'second story', the dangerous and problematic quest, which has the effect of undermining the protagonist's potential for confident mastery of the situation. Instead, the central figure is integrated into 'the universe of the other characters', and it is during this process of assimilation that he loses his immunity to physical harm. The punishments he rou-tinely suffers arguably create their own dynamic: Greg Forter, for example, suggests the fundamental importance of the masochistic enjoyment of traumatic violation. Since the scene of the crime is not 'mastered', as it is in classic detective fiction, we might regard it instead as 'a scene to whose trauma we're invited to submit'. It is not just the origin of a quest that will validate the detective's masculine prowess but an initiation into the limitations of his own agency, leading him towards 'an opportunity to let the mind play over death as one's ownmost destiny'. Interpreted in this way, the hard-boiled detective, courting violence and death, undergoes trials which in fact subvert the stereotypical image of male mastery. Upon analysis, his tough image seems more like a reflex of fear, or even a thinly disguised desire for 'repeated submission to the pleasures of masochistic pain' (Forter 2000: 11–12). The danger the detective faces, as Marty Roth argues, can be viewed as part of a masochistic erotics inherent in the hard-boiled form: the detective's 'dares and challenges and his wisecracks' are in actuality an invitation to the infliction of pain (1995: 68–87).

The typical image of the private eye is constituted by those resources he marshals in order to defend himself against a hostile environment. Part of his attraction as a character lies in the fact that these qualities are not superhuman intellectual skills but are available to 'everyman'—toughness and tenacity, of course, but also a distinctive kind of verbal combativeness. Voice is crucial to hard-boiled fiction, and the verbal armoury of the private eye—slang and tough talk, the laconic wit of the wisecrack, the hard-boiled simile—affords him an aura of mastery, however illusory his control might be. The private eye is, in his most familiar incarnations, aging, bruised, booze-sodden, and betrayed, but his gift for streetwise slang enables him to project a coherent self in the face of the chaos that threatens to engulf him, and in defiance of his own manifest weaknesses.

Hard-boiled language, the sign of or the substitute for phallic potency, is also a signifier of 'the neglected popular virtues' (Forter 2000: 24–5; McCann 2000: 147). At the end of 'Simple Art', Chandler declares that the detective must be a 'common man' ([1944] 1988: 18). The fact that he talks like one means that the language of the pulps can also be seen as an assertion of the detective's democratic credentials. Hammett's *style*, Chandler argues, is not seen as 'style' because it employs language 'not supposed to be capable of such refinements'. The foregrounding of a highly recognizable form of vernacular speech is, then, another quality which distinguishes the hard-boiled form from classic detective fiction, setting the tone of the narrative but also establishing a masculine ethos. It might even be said that, in its playfulness and excess, tough talk so far exceeds 'the simple inscription of male power' that it in fact acts as a reminder of the constructedness—the theatricality—of tough masculinity.[5]

The private eye's characteristic competence is closely associated with the qualities of American individualism: as Dennis Porter suggests, the label 'private eye' in itself connotes solitariness, 'a non-organization man's eye, like the frontier scout's or the cowboy's; an eye that trusts no other' (Porter 2003: 95). The American image of heroic manhood has a long tradition, and the private eye, as has often been observed, is 'the cowboy adapted to life on the city streets' (Rzepka 2000: 699–700; Porter 2003: 95–7), an updated, cynical version of the frontier scout or lawman, patrolling the border between civilization and savagery. Under his tough façade, he also can be said to possess a core of romantic yearning for a lost ideal. As this suggests, the literary antecedents of the hard-boiled novel include the dime-novel, the Western, the frontier romance—the work of such writers as Bret Harte, Jack London, and James Fenimore Cooper. The genre's frontier heritage can be related to what are often seen as marked anti-feminist and homoerotic tendencies, evident in anxieties about gender (fear of the 'dangerous woman') and the longing for a male ideal—the lone male, strong, ruggedly handsome, and resisting the confining, emasculating spaces of a domestic life. From a historicist perspective, the frontier influence can also, however, be linked to a yearning not for a human relationship but for a transformation of the existing social order. The form this longing takes can be seen as very closely related to the specific circumstances of 1930s America, to the Depression and Roosevelt-era politics. Carefully placing individual writers in relation to different phases of New Deal liberalism, McCann's *Gumshoe America* interprets the detective story as register-ing the threat to a liberal society. Hard-boiled fiction turns that threat into a manageable tale, a political myth containing the contradictions

---

[5] Plain 2001: 57–9 argues that Chandler's hard-boiled conceits produce so 'intricately wrought' an excess that the depiction of masculinity, in exceeding 'the parameters of patriarchal prescription', actually destabilizes the norms that hard-boiled fiction apparently 'works so ostentatiously to enforce'.

and ironies that bedeviled the efforts to adjust liberal ideals to the demands of an industrialized, urbanized nation.[6]

The tradition's lingering romanticism, most closely associated with Chandler's work, must be set alongside much darker, more cynical generic strains. In contrast to the classic detective, the American private eye does more than simply search for clarification. His manner of intervening in events, which goes beyond the administration of the occasional sound beating with a hunting crop, often carries him some distance outside the bounds of the law. Chandler's Marlowe has numerous fictional descendants who function as very positive figures, committed to values that distinguish them from people 'on the wrong side of the fence' (*The Big Sleep*, [1939] 1993: 105). But there are many other forms of masculine competence, expedient rather than moral, a 'kit of tools' designed for survival in a thoroughly corrupt and insecure world, and it is not really tenable to argue that the private eye's isolation invariably entails a sense of innate rectitude or moral certainty. Hammett, for example, is often credited with inaugurating a hard-boiled lineage much closer to the world of *film noir*, centring on morally dubious protagonists who pursue their questionable ends by deception and manipulation, and he is far from being the only writer to create such protagonists. Many hard-boiled detective figures, such as Hammett's Ned Beaumont, are implicated in the world of corruption they investigate, damaged men who struggle to exert even minimal control over the chaos of contemporary experience. Entering into a scene of disorder, they acknowledge their own anarchic tendencies and their capacity for violence. Deeply flawed and decidedly unknightly, these 'compromised' investigators are near relations of the crook-as-investigator protagonists who emerge in other thrillers of the early thirties.[7] They are key figures in

[6] McCann 2000: 6–7, 36–7. Hard-boiled fiction, McCann argues, 'was uniquely positioned to bring out the contradictions and ironies that dogged the period's reconstruction of liberalism [i.e. New Deal liberalism]. Dashiell Hammett cast himself as the literary correlative to the era's democratic realists, but his fiction tended less to celebrate the victories of intelligence over myth than to portray the delusions that undermined the pretense to intellectual leadership. Raymond Chandler imagined a redemptive public taste inspired by popular vitality. But his fiction constantly depicted the exploitation and erasure of that popular spirit. More tellingly, it revealed the way that the "corporate" vision of democratic life which he shared with [John] Grierson and [John] Dewey might easily culminate in an invocation of an imperilled racial republic.'

[7] For example, amongst writers of the early 1930s, such corrupt investigative figures were created by Paul Cain (*Fast One*) and Raoul Whitfield (*Green Ice*).

the evolution of literary noir, which, as it develops in the late 1920s and the 1930s, uses the hard-boiled idiom to create a much more disturbing kind of crime fiction. In the latter part of this chapter and in Chapter 3, we will explore the mutation of tough guy writing into transgressor-centred narratives (for example, Ed McBain's *Candyland*, Jim Thompson's *The Killer Inside Me*)—tracing a process of diversification so rapid as to render suspect any generalizations about the 'inherent conservatism' of hard-boiled fiction.

The *Black Mask* boys

Dashiell Hammett, *The Glass Key* (1931); Raymond Chandler, *Farewell, My Lovely* (1940)

No publication was more instrumental in encouraging and marketing the hard-boiled crime story than *Black Mask* magazine, founded in 1920 by H. L. Mencken and George Jean Nathan. Sold a year and a half later, it was increasingly given over to crime, adventure, and Western stories, particularly to those containing tough, realistic action. Dashiell Hammett started writing for the magazine in the early 1920s, and most of his stories were published first in *Black Mask*, as were those of Raymond Chandler a decade later. The identity of the magazine became more sharply defined when the editorship was taken over in 1926 by Captain Joseph T. Shaw, who encouraged a high standard of colloquial, racy writing, favouring 'economy of expression' and 'authenticity in character and action'.[8] As the circulation of *Black Mask* grew, other pulp magazines (for example, *Dime Detective, Detective Fiction Weekly, Black Aces*) entered the market, but it is in *Black Mask* that the hard-boiled private detective fired his first shot. Carroll John Daly's December 1922 story, 'The False Burton Combs', is often taken to be the first of *Black Mask*'s hard-boiled stories, and his best-known series character, Race Williams, has been cast as 'the true progenitor of the American private eye'. At first, Daly was more popular than his co-contributor Hammett. The boastful exploits that he penned for his protagonist projected a rugged individualism that

---

[8] Joseph T. Shaw, quoted by Pronzini and Adrian 1995: 9.

gave him the appeal of the traditional adventure hero: Race Williams was an unmistakable heir to the frontiersman and the gunfighter.[9] But of the early *Black Mask* writers it is, of course, Hammett whose reputation has survived. He created his fat, middle-aged, unnamed protagonist, the Continental Op, in a story called 'Arson Plus', published in 1923. His most famous detective, Sam Spade, made his appearance in 1929, in the serialized parts of *The Maltese Falcon*. Ned Beaumont, who fulfils the function of the detective although he is in actuality the associate of racketeers and corrupt politicians, was introduced in the 1930 stories which were published in book form as *The Glass Key* (Hammett's own favourite amongst his novels). Spade, of course, is the figure with whom Hammett is most closely identified, and Humphrey Bogart's defining performances, first as Spade and then as Chandler's Marlowe, did more than anything to establish the popular image of the private eye. Indeed, hard-boiled fiction is difficult to detach from these compelling figures, whose joint preeminence is also responsible for a misleading tendency to elide the very marked differences between Hammett and Chandler.

The two writers are, however, substantially different. The Hammett tradition of hard-boiled writing is an altogether darker, more violent and morally ambivalent tradition than that initiated by Chandler. Hammett's lasting influence owes much to his creation of a distinctive voice, a true 'hard-boiled' style. He wrote spare, unembellished prose that was appropriate to his down-to-earth protagonists and that was an implicit rejection of bourgeois hypocrisy and conventional values. There is considerable critical agreement with Chandler's assertion, in 'Simple Art', that realism is one of Hammett's leading traits. He paid far more attention to verisimilitude than a writer like Daly, creating flawed protagonists whose cynical perceptions of contemporary life gave his novels a capacity to lay bare the 'heart, soul, skin and guts' of a corrupt town (Hammett [1929] 1982: 12). He brought to pulp publishing a modernist sense of irony and ambiguity. His fragmented, subjective narratives undermine binary oppositions between good and evil, order and disorder, imbuing his writing with a thoroughgoing scepticism.

Hammett sought to make crime fiction something of 'avowedly literary' worth, addressing a readership that might be expected to

---

[9] Geherin 1985: 8–16. See also Reilly 1985: 234–7 and Durham 1968: 67–8.

understand the ways in which he was transforming the genre. As Chandler observed, however, he also spoke to readers who were indifferent to the literary merits of his style. This non-élite audience would have been more impressed with Hammett's tough guy credentials: as an ex-Pinkerton operative, he possessed an experience that allowed him to speak with first-hand knowledge of the life of the streets (McCann 2000: 91–3; Raczkowski 2003: 629–59). Hammett's ideological appeal was to readers who had felt the effects of the greed and exploitation consequent on unrestrained capitalism. As McCann notes, 'When Hammett wrote for *Black Mask* and later for Knopf during the twenties, the pulps were a reviled form of publication and the urban, working-class audience to which they were targeted appeared outside the mainstream of American life' (McCann 2000: 147). In narratives that offer little by way of consolatory resolution, Hammett creates an atmosphere of deceitfulness so ubiquitous that moral chaos and betrayal seem the norm rather than the exception. Anarchic human appetites, particularly the lust for wealth or power, disorder all relationships, from the most personal to the political and economic. Playing all factions against one another in *Red Harvest*, the Continental Op realizes that his own character has been infected with the 'poison' of violence; in *Maltese Falcon*, the quest to obtain the fetishized falcon, worthless in itself, is emblematic of the universal scramble for riches; in *The Glass Key*, actual betrayals and corruption offer a grim reminder of how improbable it is that neo-progressive blueprints for progress could be put into effect.

The Glass Key, though it was founded on a realist diagnosis of the ills of contemporary society, questioned the viability of the 'realist cure', given that 'The public world of politics, like the private sphere of love, ran not on consent and reason, but on cruelty and dominance' (McCann 2000: 137–8). As in other Hammett novels, bonds of trust disintegrate, with deceit undermining the possibility of sustaining social relationships. Senator Henry betrays his daughter by using her attractions to secure the support of Paul Madvig, and, having killed his own son, shows himself willing to kill Madvig so that he will carry the blame for the earlier crime. Though this killing is averted, the end of the novel leaves Ned Beaumont staring 'fixedly' through an open door, and we are left pondering the question of whether Madvig stands any chance of 'cleaning house' and ultimately managing to 'get the city back' (Hammett [1931] 1982: 783).

The henchman of a racketeer, Ned Beaumont is a long way from the stereotypical image of the man possessed of honourable, sound individualistic values. An investigative protagonist who lacks even the partial legitimation of the private eye, he is a gambler whose conduct is frequently unscrupulous. He plants evidence and acts on the basis of dubious values and cloudy motives, telling harsh truths about some things and lying about others. The milieu in which he moves is only a small remove from that of the gangster protagonists of the 1930s (*Little Caesar, Scarface*). Indeed, *Black Mask*'s editor, Joseph T. Shaw, found it necessary to defend the inclusion of as criminally-orientated a story as *The Glass Key*, arguing that its serialized parts were the magazine's only story in which 'the gangster' was in any sense 'the hero'. Shaw further justified the decision to publish *The Glass Key* by pointing to the serious danger to the body politic caused by alliances between corrupt politicians, public officials, and organized crime. In such a context, Hammett's story was a demonstration of 'one of the most serious illnesses, to put it mildly, that our body politic has ever suffered from'.[10] With or without this kind of justification, however, the use of criminal or semi-criminal protagonists became increasingly common, in *Black Mask* and elsewhere, during the course of the 1930s. Ranging from the morally dubious to the criminally culpable, they are members of a tradition that has continued to flourish ever since, populating the stories of such late twentieth-century authors as James Ellroy, a writer who explicitly situates himself in the Hammett tradition.

The Glass Key can also be read as a deconstruction of what would generally be seen as conventional hard-boiled assumptions about masculine assurance and control. Our pleasure in reading hard-boiled detective fiction is often taken to reside in its demonstration of male mastery—in the protagonist's assertion of a powerful masculine self. Greg Forter, however, sees in *The Glass Key* a particularly striking example of the pull of hard-boiled writing towards the pleasure of traumatic violation (2000: 17). As in the analysis of classic detective fiction, our view changes if we shift our attention from the end (which, even in the case of hard-boiled fiction, can involve at least partial resolution of conflicts) to the events of the narrative, the vicissitudes

[10] Joseph T. Shaw, 'A Letter to the Editor of *Writer's Digest*' (Sept. 1930), in Metress 1994: 111–12.

of the protagonist's struggle. Looking at the text in this way, we may recognize that the sources of our enjoyment in reading the novel are equally, or indeed more, related to the 'masochistic erotics' of the struggle itself. A psychoanalytic reading of traditional detective fiction says that the detective, in investigating a scene of violence, returns to the trauma of the primal scene, allowing the reader to triumph over the passivity of that moment, with the solution to the mystery bringing mastery of traumatic events (Forter 2000: 12–13, 17, 29–30). In *The Glass Key* there is little actual mastery. The reader is encouraged to identify with a protagonist who seems to have a masochistic urge to invite pain and physical trauma. Particularly in the central part of the novel, Ned can be seen as 'erotically transfixed by the prospect of his own destruction'. His brief periods of masterful activity alternate with passive endurance of the series of savage beatings he receives, suggesting an identification with rather than a repudiation of the corpse (Forter 2000: 25, 30–1). Jeff Gardner, who beats him senseless at O'Rory's, comments wryly on Ned's tendency towards masochistic surrender: ' "I never seen a guy that liked being hit so much or that I liked hitting so much" ' (Hammett [1931] 1982: 662). His masculinity can be associated with the glass key of the title, appearing within the text in a dream in which the key shatters as he attempts to unlock the door to the mystery, an effort to reach a solution that engenders a nightmare image of phallic chaos (hundreds of snakes). Whether or not we accept this kind of psychoanalytic reading in its entirety, it is clear that Ned Beaumont's role in the novel runs very much counter to the active hero conventions associated with fellow *Black Mask* writers like Daly—the heroic model of male mastery often taken to be the essence of hard-boiled fiction. Indeed, according to Forter's reading, this psychological profile suggests that Ned is more closely related to the 'effete' protagonists of classic detective fiction than to the 'hypermasculine heroes' who stereotypically belong to hard-boiled fiction. But it would be truer to say that he in fact embodies the two distinctly noir traditions that evolve out of early hard-boiled fiction. He is linked to transgressor-centred narratives by his membership in a murky world of semi-gangsterism. But equally, his mind-set resembles that of the victim-protagonists created by writers like Horace McCoy and David Goodis, figures whose impaired, traumatized masculinity produces a state of near-immobilization.

Hammett's most famous successor, Raymond Chandler, started writing for *Black Mask* in December 1933 (shortly after Hammett published his final novel, *The Thin Man*) and went on to create the body of work that more than any other fiction has been taken to define the hard-boiled detective story. Chandler was a more repetitive writer than Hammett: whereas Hammett attempted something new in each novel, Chandler recurrently involved the same narrator in plots that do not much differ from one another, and this in itself partly explains the critical tendency to use Chandler (like the even more repetitive Christie) as the exemplar of an entire sub-genre. He was, however, a writer who brought to crime writing a very different sensibility to that of Hammett, and indeed, to that of most other hard-boiled writers. Compared to Hammett's prose, Chandler's has a consistent lightness of tone, combining witty detachment with an underlying sentimentality, qualities heightened in the most famous Chandler film adaptation, Howard Hawks's *The Big Sleep* (1946). Although Chandler and Hammett are routinely linked as creators of the private eye, their novels diverge not only in style but also in themes, narrative patterns, and attitudes to action. They are distinctively different in their representations of male desire and identification, and in their relationship to the politics of the time (McCann 2000: 140–5; Forter 2000: 32). As Frank Miller says, though he 'deliberately clouds it with cynicism', Marlowe is 'a compulsive do-gooder [. . .] a poet [. . .] a knight in dirty armor, whereas the darkness in Hammett is much deeper.'[11] Unlike such figures as Ned Beaumont and the Continental Op, Chandler's Marlowe resists the incursions of the outside world, not simply the physical onslaughts to which the hard-boiled investigator is subject, but any personal relationship made repellent by the threat of bodily violation (as in encounters with forceful, sexually attractive women). Chandler's judgements are more clearly gendered than those of many other hard-boiled writers, and he is one of the few writers of this period to make substantial use of the figure of the *femme fatale*. In fact, he habitually places the dangerous woman at the centre of his plots, in what many have interpreted as a neurotic response to the sexy manipulative

---

[11] Frank Miller, interview with Christopher Brayshaw, Dec. 1998, in *Frank Miller: The Interviews, 1981–2003*. Seattle: Fantagraphics Books, 2003: 83.

woman,[12] associated with 'the nastiness' of which Marlowe fears he has become a part. Resistant to the depraved society around him, Marlowe assumes a role often compared to that of the questing knight, undergoing tests that involve skill in arms, fearlessness, and integrity. Marlowe's knightly qualities are hinted at by the history of his naming: the 'Mallory' of an early *Black Mask* story, 'Blackmailers Don't Shoot', eventually became 'Marlowe', a 'coded version' of the medieval romance-writer's surname. Chandler further drew attention to the image of the knight-at-arms in his description of the man 'good enough for any world', who must go down 'these mean streets' ([1944] 1988: 18). In creating such a protagonist, Chandler can be seen as promoting the positive side of what Auden calls the 'Great Wrong Place' myth: against this pessimistic vision, he sets the American dream of the 'last just man' whose alienation guarantees his honour.[13]

This idealized version of the private eye has not escaped the attention of psychoanalytic critics wishing to reveal the obsessions and neuroses driving both Marlowe and his creator. Whereas analyses of 'apolitical' golden age fiction often attempt to reveal its underlying socio-political meanings, strong readings of the hard-boiled tradition—of Chandler's writing even more than Hammett's—tend to centre on the personal traumas lurking under its socially conscious surface. The knightly protagonist can be read as an ideal of mastery generated by a misogynistic author. This tortured self perceives women as threatening his identity and fears losing control. Such anxieties are projected, for example, in the fascinated disgust Marlowe expresses for effeminate men like Marriott in *Farewell, My Lovely*, Lavery in *The Lady in the Lake*, and Geiger in *The Big Sleep*. Chandler objected to the representation of sexuality in pulp fiction (the writing of James M. Cain, he thought, smelled like a billy goat), and his own novels contain nothing that is sexually explicit. Under the surface of his stories, however, many critics have detected undercurrents of

---

[12] This can plausibly be linked to the repeated motif of Marlowe sinking into unconsciousness and to his many losses of control and erectness, the feeling he has of 'fragmenting'.

[13] Auden [1948] 1987: 151 writes: 'I think Mr. Chandler is interested in writing, not detective stories, but serious studies of a criminal milieu, the Great Wrong Place, and his powerful but extremely depressing books should be read and judged, not as escape literature, but as works of art.'

unfulfilled homoerotic longing.[14] As Gill Plain says, 'In his search for the lost ideal man, Marlowe pursues a desire that cannot be articulated in an attempt to compensate for a loss that can never be grieved.' In *Farewell, My Lovely*, we see Marlowe on a punning quest for Mrs Grayle, but his stronger commitment is arguably to Moose Malloy—a 'magnificent masculine icon' who enters the narrative as 'a semiotic irruption, a substantial return of the repressed, that wreaks havoc on the order around him' (Plain 2001: 63–6). The narrative opens with Marlowe literally and metaphorically in the grip of Moose, whose claim on 'little Velma' Marlowe seems not to question. Towards the end of the novel, his search for Moose's hiding place brings him into contact with Red Norgaard, 'the giant with the red hair and the violet eyes, who was probably the nicest man I had ever met' (Chandler [1940] 1993: 353). This oversized embodiment of a less flawed male ideal helps Marlowe on his perilous journey to Laird Brunette's boat. His idolization of Red seems acceptable because Red is such 'an edifice of the masculine': 'his butchness is highly significant, as it is only in its distance from the feminine that the homosocial's descent into the homoerotic is legitimized' (Plain 2001: 72–6). Politically, this vision of masculine fellowship can be seen as providing a place to stand in opposition to the corrupting powers of monopoly capitalism. There are suggestions of 'a decentralist Utopia of male camaraderie' reminiscent of frontier values. It functions as a contextualizing ideal for Chandler's critique of a Los Angeles in which institutional corruption flourishes and any positive vision of community seems impossible (McCann 2000: 140–5).

Separated from the conditions that would make this sort of sustaining fellowship possible, Marlowe has developed self-protective defences, above all his distinctive variant of the hard-boiled style. Witty, ironic, and aloof, he is a narrator whose verbal dexterity both evaluates and works to contain the moral disorder of the society he investigates. Hammett's protagonists are also capable of speaking with a satirist's mocking insight, but Marlowe's perceptions are expressed

---

[14] This is not, in fact, out of keeping with Chandler's Arthurian legend motif, given that these stories, particularly the *Morte D'Arthur* and *Sir Gawain and the Green Knight*, are seemingly structured around the (normally chaste) retrieval of a feminine object of desire (the grail-cup, Guinevere, someone else's wife), but are emotionally and thematically centred upon a core group of male–male relationships and the vexed homosocial bonding of hero and villain.

in ways very unlike the savage ironies of the Continental Op. *Farewell, My Lovely* amply illustrates this habitual form of self-defence, teasing, elegantly phrased, and ironically guarded. So, for example, explaining to Anne Riordan what Bay City is really like, Marlowe provides a playful but telling image of its total corruption and at the same time directs our attention to his own discernment and fastidiousness: ' "Sure, it's a nice town. It's probably no crookeder than Los Angeles. But you can only buy a piece of a big city. You can buy a town this size all complete, with the original box and tissue paper. That's the difference. And that makes me want out" ' (p. 295). The use of a fanciful image, the satirical diminishment, the arch manner, and the detached voice are all characteristic features of Marlowe's method of simultaneously judging the world and holding himself apart from it. His humour distances him from the brutal scenes that we as readers witness, and even under extreme duress Marlowe's self-ironizing manner never falters. Confronting Dr Sonderborg after having been knocked on the head, 'shot full of dope and locked in a barred room', he has barely recovered from his ordeal but can still be buoyantly self-mocking: ' "Don't make me get tough," I whined. "Don't make me lose my beautiful manners and my flawless English" ' (p. 289). Marlowe's superiority to his environment is never simply a matter of physical toughness, and it is his wry, carefully modulated voice that most clearly defines his character. His wit is as important as the gun he holds, and his use of violence is never excessive: in contrast to Hammett's Op, Marlowe would never 'go blood-simple'.

Brought up in England, Chandler was fascinated by ordinary American speech. Unlike Hammett, he never completely belonged to the American scene, much less to the mean streets that he made his subject as a writer. But in creating his own distinctive version of the American voice, rich in similes and colloquial-sounding metaphors (some of which, like 'the big sleep', he invented), he imbued his writing with a humour resembling that of the frontier tradition, a style that placed him somewhere between romanticism and cynicism. For critics like McCann, who see sentimental populism at the core of Chandler's work, his use of language reflects his nostalgia for lost frontier virtues—a preoccupation with 'the effort to hold onto an ever-fading democratic legitimacy' (McCann 2000: 148–9). As in Marlowe's terse summing-up of the deceptiveness of decent appearances in Bay City, social commentary in Chandler's novels tends to emerge from his meticulously crafted and highly idiosyncratic version of tough guy speech.

The seriousness of Chandler's socio-political critique has often been questioned. It can be argued that, in comparison to Hammett, Chandler focuses far less on the disorder and corruption of the American city, concentrating instead on more individual and familial sources of disturbance. What his novels do accomplish, however, is a subtle and quite complex intertwining of public and personal crimes. He places the private transgressions that Marlowe investigates within the context of larger-scale financial and political misdeeds: the crimes of power-hungry politicians, government officials in league with gangsters, shady businessmen, and crooked cops. These forms of corruption give a public dimension to Chandler's narratives, a dimension which usually turns out to be involved in the disordered individual lives of families like the Sternwoods in *The Big Sleep* or the Grayles in *Farewell, My Lovely*. As Marlowe says in *The Big Sleep*, 'it all ties together' (Chandler [1939] 1993: 158–9). It might be said that Chandler's objective is to demonstrate the way in which personal crimes are inescapably bound up with wider socio-political dishonesty and wrongdoing. At the same time, however, critics have plausibly argued that the intrusive forces of urban criminality function mainly as background in his novels. As Docherty points out, the 'big bosses', the corrupt businessmen and political manipulators, are often perceived by Marlowe as 'presentable and decent', and Chandler is perhaps more inclined to exculpate gangsters than to imply that all businessmen are really gangsters. It might also be said that Marlowe himself, though he is the main source of satiric observations on the state of contemporary society, acts to muffle Chandler's critique because he is so reassuring a figure. Although he is significantly less in control than, say, Holmes or Poirot, his presence as the series narrator is a protective one. Essentially good and honourable, he provides the reader with a stable, trustworthy perspective, his detachment placing him much closer to the masculine competence and 'rightness' of traditional detective fiction.

Chandler often emphasizes Marlowe's marginality: it is part of the detective's claim to integrity that, for no more than 'twenty-five dollars a day and expenses', he is willing to risk getting himself 'in Dutch with half the law enforcement of this country' (*Big Sleep*, [1939] 1993: 81). But however at odds he is with 'law-abiding society',

Marlowe does not occupy any position outside the law other than that of lowly independence. Indeed, as I have suggested, of all the early private eyes, it is Marlowe who most clearly serves as a touch-stone of the integrity and moral fibre of the hard-boiled investigator. He is the possessor *par excellence* of a common decency that (like Holmes's uncommon rationality) has served as a model for sub-sequent writers. Chandler created, as Knight suggests, what is perhaps the most 'clear and imitable' model for hard-boiled fiction (2004: 116). Hammett's very different model has also made a strong impact. But in many later detective series the honourable ghost of Marlowe is near at hand, encouraging the nobler possibilities within the hard-boiled tradition, bringing to the fore the moral integrity, the compassion, and the tough-sentimental view of life that infuse the investigative narra-tive with a redemptive potential. On the other hand, of course, for those aiming to transform hard-boiled writing, Marlowe's morally confident masculine ethos makes him an obvious point of departure, the very embodiment of an assumption of moral superiority on the part of a white male private eye.

The mid-century paperback revolution

Mickey Spillane, *One Lonely Night* (1951); Ross Macdonald, *The Doomsters* (1958)

In the decades following the end of the Second World War, 'the pulps'—*Black Mask, Dime Detective,* and their numerous competi-tors—were replaced by the paperbacks. This was a publishing revolu-tion that transformed popular reading habits, and by 1946 there were over 350 softcover titles in print, three times as many as in 1945. Pocket Books, Avon, Popular Library, Dell, and Bantam were all publishing in the paperback format and many of the best post-war crime novel-ists (for example, David Goodis, Jim Thompson, John D. MacDonald, Ross Macdonald, and Mickey Spillane) were about to begin writing paperback originals.[15] Spillane is often seen as the key figure in this

---

[15] O'Brien [1981] 1997: 22–5. The paperback revolution is discussed in detail by Server 1994: 21–55 and McCann 2000: 198–250.

tale of sudden and spectacular transformation. Living in a tent and trying to build his own house, he needed a thousand dollars for the materials, and so wrote *I, the Jury*. Published first in hardback in 1947, it sold only about 7,000 copies, but, when re-released as a Signet paperback, sold over 2 million copies in two years, an achievement that 'electrified and inspired the softcover book industry'.[16] Gold Medal astutely seized on the possibility of publishing paperback originals, and they were soon providing an entirely new kind of market for crime writers, whose work could now for the first time go directly into cheap softcover editions. And so began the 'gloriously subversive era' of American paperback publishing. The heyday of the paperback originals, with their lurid cover art and sensational cover copy, was over by the early 1960s.[17] But some of the most notable paperback writing careers spanned the period, extending from the immediate post-war years through the 1960s and beyond (Ross Macdonald's final Lew Archer novel was published in 1976; John D. MacDonald wrote his last Travis McGee novel in the mid-1980s).

The early years of the paperback revolution were, of course, a time of American prosperity, of expanding military and economic power, and a degree of affluence that made the Depression seem a historical aberration. Increased wealth also bred materialism and conformity, contributing as well to a Cold War mood of self-righteous aggressiveness. Those on the right feared Communism abroad and dissent at home, leading to the McCarthyite persecution of anyone regarded as seditious or subversive. It was a period in which American society hunted out difference and suppressed and marginalized dissent, and liberal critics identified a post-war malaise characterized by caution, repression, and intellectual retreat (Bradbury and Temperley [1981] 1998: 262, 256–8). The paperback writers emerging during this period reconfigured the conventions of the earlier pulps, responding to the anxieties of post-Second World War audiences. Playing self-consciously with the conventions established in the pulps, they carried hard-boiled fiction in a variety of new directions. Some writers, like

---

[16] Mickey Spillane, the *Guardian* interview, National Film Theatre, 29/7/1999; Collins and Traylor 1984: 5–7; Server 1994: 21–42; O'Brien [1981] 1997: 19–34. Although their great mass market impact was as paperbacks, most of Spillane's novels were first published in hardcover by Dutton.

[17] Server 1994: jacket copy. Bill Pronzini ('Forgotten Writers: Gil Brewer', in Server *et al.* 1998: 193) says that 'The last piece of true pulp-as-art was published circa 1965.'

Jim Thompson and David Goodis (discussed in the following chapters), abandoned the investigative form altogether, whilst others, like Mickey Spillane and Ross Macdonald, retained the private eye model but transformed both the character and the ideological orientation of the sub-genre.

Chandler himself had, by the 1950s, decided that hard-boiled writing had lost its momentum. He announced the demise of the tradition that he himself had helped to define. *Raymond Chandler Speaking*, published in 1962, made public a selection of Chandler's private correspondence, put together just a few years after his death in 1959. The book included a 1949 letter to the critic James Sandhoe, criticizing Ross Macdonald's first novel, *The Moving Target* (1949), for being pretentious in its phrasing and choice of words, and asserting that the tradition of detective fiction was now exhausted. He speculated that it might survive in the form of suspense fiction but not in the established form of hard-boiled detective fiction. As we will see in Chapter 3, this was in some ways prescient, since one of the strongest traditions to emerge from early hard-boiled was the transgressor-centred fiction of Jim Thompson and others, and, although he was wrong in his prediction of the demise of hard-boiled investigative fiction, Chandler was clearly right in foreseeing generic fragmentation. Looking back on the period, we might say that, in the event, the foundational resistance of hard-boiled fiction to the formulaic and its prioritizing of content over form gave it a kind of vitality and variety, saving it from the descent into self-caricature that Chandler foresaw.

The private eye fiction of the 1950s, however, does to some extent bear out Chandler's analysis. In the work of Mickey Spillane and Ross Macdonald (whose real name was Kenneth Millar), we see two very different kinds of generic transformation, each of which exercised considerable influence over subsequent generations of writers. This is a significant bifurcation of the tradition. Spillane moved towards the creation of the super-macho punisher-hero, prototype for countless later protagonists who are 'out for vengeance'. Macdonald, on the other hand, favoured a version of the erring, guilt-ridden protagonist, investigating crimes that take place amongst genteel characters suffering from middle-class neuroses. Following Chandler's line of argument, one can unquestionably see both writers as succumbing to the pressures of their age. Their contrasting lines of development produced a rupture in the union that Chandler himself had sought to achieve between the popular and the 'literary', Spillane opting for what Chandler saw as a lowbrow 'mixture of violence and outright pornography' and Macdonald abandoning popular expression for literary affectation.[18] Each can be seen as having simplified the genre, circumventing the challenge of combining the diverse, often conflicting elements that had vitalized it in earlier decades. Hammett's and Chandler's 'ambivalent meditations on artistic authority, popular legitimacy, and mass entertainment' make way for detective fiction that in effect narrates 'a pair of complementary tales of cultural victory', one telling of 'triumph from below', the other of 'condescension from above' (McCann 2000: 201). Both types of tale achieved huge sales: these were representations of post-war life that appealed to substantial audiences, addressing anxieties that many felt as America moved into the Cold War era.

In Spillane's Mike Hammer novels, the tough ethos of Hammett's protagonists is presented with little of the earlier writer's irony. The Hammer novels spoke most directly to those for whom the virility and vitality of aggressive individualism offered a way of combating Cold War insecurities at a time when the national mood was one of self-righteousness and hostility to all who could be construed as undermining 'the American way'. The form of reassurance offered by Macdonald, on the other hand, was based on a middle-class valorization of the inner life. Both writers saw 'dangers within'. Spillane was preoccupied with vigilante-style crusades against those who were undermining American moral fibre from within. He attacked those responsible for urban vice (narcotics, prostitution, blackmail), the corrupt post-war bureaucracy, and the treacherous political subversives. Macdonald instead looked within the human mind, finding internal enemies to psychic well-being and the good life. Lew Archer was given the task of exorcizing the demons of the troubled soul.

Of the two, Spillane is plainly the more 'hard-boiled': as Bill Ruehlman puts it, 'His stuff is so hard-boiled you could break bricks with it.'[19] The first mass-market novelist to define himself principally

---

[18] Chandler, *The Selected Letters of Raymond Chandler*, ed. Frank MacShane. New York: Columbia University Press, 1981: 311, quoted by McCann 2000: 199.

[19] Ruehlman, 'Spillane, McBain Heroes Fight Foes Above and Below', *Virginian Pilot*, 28/12/2003, online at www.highbeam.com. There are many accounts of the Spillane publishing phenomenon: e.g. Maxim Jakubowski, 'The Tough Guy Vanishes', in the *Daily Telegraph*, 2/5/1998; O'Brien [1981] 1997: 104, who quotes the 1953 New American

as a paperback writer, unashamedly commercial in his insistence that he should be seen as a 'writer' rather than an 'author', he always readily admitted that he was interested only in writing what he was sure would sell.[20] His six early Hammer novels, written between 1947 and 1952, were a publishing phenomenon, with over 15 million copies sold by 1953, and his success was unquestionably related to the uncompromising extremity of his macho ethos. Spillane exploits the possibilities of the style in ways that sweep aside the self-mocking, self-doubting, ambivalent qualities of Hammett and Chandler. The witty, civilized, somewhat effete Marlowe has little share in Mike Hammer's line of descent, which goes directly back to the 'harder-boiled' heroes of the pulps—Race Williams, for example, the dispenser of rough justice (' "Call it murder if you like—a disregard for human life. I don't care. I'll run my business—you run yours." '[21]). Though not a criminal, Hammer is a brutally aggressive revenge-seeker, allied to such later vigilante figures as Dirty Harry and Paul Kersey (*Death Wish*). Having originated as a comic-book character, he is established through a first-person narrative that is entirely consistent with the image established on Harry Sahle's cover for the unpublished 'Mike Danger' comic, which was the basis for *I, the Jury*: 'A vibrant personality [. . .] as ROUGH as he looks!' (Collins and Traylor 1984: 4–6).

Unlike many earlier hard-boiled writers, Spillane was led by his sense of life's viciousness towards right- rather than left-wing views. His novels can be seen as narrating the enfranchisement of the enlisted man: Hammer is the 'apotheosis of the ordinary Joe' (McCann 2000: 202–4), an American male eager to bring down retribution on his country's enemies. This is the populist rhetoric of Cold War militarism, and Hammer acts out McCarthyite paranoia. His self-righteous anger is directed not at capitalism itself but at hidden, conspiratorial organizations subverting American life, chief amongst them the Communist Party. Other thriller writers of the time expressed

Library boast that 'over 15,000,000 copies of [Spillane's] books have been published in Signet editions'; and Server 1994: 22, estimating that there have been '150 million or so' copies of Spillane's books sold to date (i.e. by the mid-1990s). Spillane took up the series again in 1962, with *The Girl Hunters*.

[20] Spillane NFT interview 1999 (n. 16 above).

[21] Daly, *The Third Murderer*. New York: Farrar and Rinehart, 1931, quoted by Geherin 1985: 12.

anxieties generated *by* McCarthyism, creating outsider protagonists who are endangered by repressive forces at work in 'normal society'. Their enemies personify McCarthyite persecution, its enforcement of absolute loyalty and its willingness to sacrifice the interests of the individual in the name of the collective good. Spillane, however, was articulating the anxieties that *motivated* the McCarthyite witch-hunts. Hammer's savage one-man crusade is that of the disgruntled moral majoritarian, the scourge of a variety of demonized others suspected of subverting American life. What results is a macho conservatism that has brought down on Spillane years of criticism.[22]

The violent, often sadistic action and masculinist values of Spillane's novels are accentuated by his vigorous, no-holds-barred way of writing. His style is hyperbolic, even surreal and hallucinatory in its evocation of the sensual or grotesque: the physical detail of his novels creates, in Leslie Fiedler's phrase, 'brutal semi-pornography' (Fiedler [1960] 1998: 477). His novels habitually move towards a point at which extreme physical punishment is meted out to the villain, as when he strangles 'the greatest Commie louse of them all' on the last page of *One Lonely Night*: 'I laughed while his tongue swelled up and bulged out with his eyes and his face turned black. I held him until he was . . . dead as he was ever going to be'. There is irony here, but only in the twist Hammer gives to his vengeance, laughing again as he prises the dead man's fingers apart to put evidence in them that will make people think 'their favourite hero has been knocked off by the reds', thus spurring them to embark on a witch-hunt 'that won't stop until the issue is decided' (Spillane [1951] 1987: 158–9). Presented in this manner, the superhuman endurance of the protagonist shades into grotesque brutality. Capable of surviving whatever tests he is subjected to, Hammer's ferocious assaults on others and the relish with which he recounts them seem to place him outside normal civilized humanity. His insistence (at the beginning of *My Gun is Quick*) that he in no way resembles his armchair-bound reader is more than just a boast of unillusioned knowledge. It is an assertion that the truly hard-boiled protagonist retains no vestiges of the tame and the domestic. The implication, as in contemporary vigilante

---

[22] Anthony Boucher, for example, suggests that *I, the Jury* resembles 'required reading in a Gestapo training school'. See also Jakubowski, 'The Tough Guy Vanishes'; and Ruehlmann 1974: 3–11, which sets out the lines of attack against Spillane.

films, is that it is the man furthest beyond the bounds of common decency and civilized restraint who is actually free to defend the liberties of the common man. As Hammer explains, 'the people' and the justice they desire are distinct from the corrupt society represented by the legal system.

One Lonely Night, the most politically right-wing of Spillane's early novels, is also the one in which Hammer is most emphatically an outcast and most unequivocally the champion of the ordinary man's democratic ideals. The novel opens with Hammer alone on a bridge in cold, fog-like rain, suicidally depressed, brooding on the way he has been denounced by a 'little judge' who, though reluctantly acquitting him, leaves him feeling branded as 'a guy who had no earthly reason for existing in a decent, normal society'. Going home, he dreams that his gun has become 'part of me and stuck fast' (pp. 5–13). This image of violence that has inextricably merged with the protagonist's identity is central to a novel in which Hammer feels both marginalized and a pillar of the American way, his aggression and paranoia linked to the collective hatreds and fears of the American right. By choosing a 'Commie bastard', Deamer, as his villain, Spillane taps into the anxieties of a very wide 1950s audience. He is as 'lonely' at the end of the novel as at the beginning, but his individualism is placed in the service of group hatreds. His antagonist is a transgressor whose crimes are exacerbated by the fact that he pretends to be a champion of the American people he is routinely betraying. The twin brother motif makes Deamer the very embodiment of the Cold War nightmare of the indistinguishable enemy in our midst, whose treacherousness is taken to justify the abandonment of the whole liberal machinery of law, restraint, and civil rights.

In the novels of Ross Macdonald, too, there is heightened emphasis on the crime writer's standard theme of concealment. The hidden threats in this case are family secrets, traumatic memories, and repressed emotions. The inner states he writes about are like subversive ideologies in that they can be seen as having more than individual significance, being symptomatic of the wider society's ingrained delusions and psychic distortions. Macdonald's repeated reworkings of these themes earned him praise as more than just a detective story writer—most famously in Eudora Welty's review of *Underground Man* (1971), which celebrated him as a more serious and complex writer than either Hammett or Chandler. Like Spillane, but with a different audience, Macdonald enjoyed enormous popular success. His reputation grew throughout the 1960s, until by the end of the decade he was the country's best-selling crime writer and also the one regarded as bringing the genre into its closest proximity with 'serious literature'. In addition to Welty's review, there were other evaluations to consolidate his respectability, such as that of Anthony Boucher, who praised Macdonald for having mastered the strengths of 'the authentic Hammett–Chandler tradition' and for being, moreover, 'a considerable, serious novelist—possibly the best current depicter in fiction of the people and manners of Southern California'.[23]

Spillane's contribution to crime fiction has arguably been under-valued because of the extremity of his style and vision: as Ed Gorman, for example, writes, Spillane was 'the great American primitive whose real talents got lost in all the clamour over the violence of his hero. He brought energy and a street-fighter's rage to a form grown moribund with cuteness and imitation Chandler prose.'[24] Ross Macdonald, on the other hand, has conceivably been over-praised because of his very different conception of the hard-boiled aesthetic. Macdonald moved the genre towards liberalism and non-violence, his detective, Lew Archer, being more given to talking than fighting. As O'Brien notes, even Macdonald's villains are more cultivated than the norm. He wrote from within and for the liberal élite, a college-educated mid-dle-class audience; he created a fictional world more familiar to the officer class and the 'G.I. Bill intellectual' than to the ordinary enlisted man. In his very bourgeois fictional world, the respectable institutions include psychotherapy and higher education, and the detective himself is closer than at any previous time to the role of the analyst. Rather than exploring the murky underside of the urban world, he examines the disturbing depths of the human mind. Archer finds that he has to turn head-shrinker himself in *The Doomsters*, for example, so that he can counter the oversimplifying psychiatric framework applied by the self-interested forces responsible for incarcerating his young client Carl. As a detective-analyst, Archer is

---

[23] Boucher quoted in Michael D. Sharp, 'Plotting Chandler's Demise: Ross Macdonald and the Neo-Aristotelian Detective Novel', *Studies in the Novel*, 22/9/2003, online at www.highbeam.com.

[24] Ed Gorman, quoted by Jakubowski, 'The Tough Guy Vanishes'.

paired with a psychiatric social worker called Miss Parish, who, while she has her own problems, is given a reasonably straight run at diagnosing the Freudian tangles of the family: '[Carl] felt as though his efforts to cut the umbilical cord had actually killed her. From there it was only a step to thinking that he was a murderer . . . it's right out of the textbook' (Macdonald [1958] 1990: 120–1).

Although Lew Archer replies, ' "I haven't read the textbook" ' (p. 121), Macdonald himself clearly had: he was well versed both in pop psychological analysis and literary history. When he was invited in the early 1970s to the Popular Culture Association's conference in Chicago to receive the Association's Award of Merit (an occasion on which scholarly work on Macdonald was presented), he gave a speech in which he constructed an elaborate literary genealogy for himself.[25] As Chandler had done in 'The Simple Art', Macdonald defined his contribution against the limitations of earlier writers. Charging his predecessors with frivolity, Chandler had dismissed classic detective fiction as moribund and formulaic; given his turn, Macdonald characterized the hard-boiled tradition as primitive and unrefined. Recent critics have been less inclined to accept Macdonald's high estimation of his own contribution to this tradition. His novels have declined in popularity in comparison, for example, to the work of a writer like Jim Thompson, whose current cult status is partly due to his having been so far beyond the world of polite literature at the time he was writing. Macdonald's influence on many later writers, however, has been undeniable, not simply because of his embourgeoisement of the genre and his promotion of its literary status, but because of the way he shifted its emphasis. Structure, themes, and protagonists were all affected, and the influence of Macdonald's updating of the hard-boiled detective (making him sympathetic, humane, and compassionate) can still be seen in the work of many writers: amongst others, Robert B. Parker, Bill Crider, Michael Collins, Bill Pronzini, Sue Grafton, Joseph Hansen.

There was an early tendency to see California-based Lew Archer as heir to Chandler's Marlowe, with his civilized sensibilities, smart repartee, and avoidance of brutality, and this has persisted, with many readers categorizing his achievement as 'Chandleresque'. Macdonald himself acknowledged the importance of Chandler's influence. From

---

[25] Sharp, 'Plotting Chandler's Demise'.

the late 1950s on, however, after Chandler had written his hostile assessment, classing Macdonald amongst the literary eunuchs, he began to dissociate himself from his assumed mentor. As his career progressed, Macdonald increasingly distanced himself from Chandler, and indeed from the traditions of 'genre fiction'. He aimed to build instead on what he saw as the detective story's kinship with classical tragedy and its indebtedness to Aristotle's *Poetics*.[26] A partiality for design is what sets Macdonald apart from Chandler, whose plots have not generally been counted amongst his chief strengths. In 'Simple Art', scene and style are given precedence as the carriers of 'reality', with Chandler disparaging the mechanical contrivances and end-orientated artifice of classic detective fiction. In moving back towards a plot-centred aesthetic, Macdonald makes the case for structure as metaphor. The mystery itself is symbolic of all that is repressed: it manifests the hidden psychological damage inflicted on whole families. In explaining the importance of this facet of his writing, Macdonald said that (in contrast to Chandler, for whom 'any old plot will do') he tried to make his plots carry meaning, 'and this meaning [. . .] determines and controls the movement of the story [. . .] I have a tendency to subordinate individual scenes to the overall intention, to make the book the unit of effect' (T. Nolan 1999: 133).

The Doomsters, which can be seen as a pivotal novel, is the one in which Macdonald began moving away from 'the Chandler tradition', towards narratives focused on human interiority rather than on action and externalities. Bringing to the fore the complexities of human psychology, as opposed to the dangers of the mean streets, *The Doomsters* presents 'the shadowy wreck of family history'. It shares common ground with stock Chandler plots, concentrating as it does on the family of a father figure who is a man of some power and who has connections with a corrupt local power structure. But whereas Chandler uses the outside community and the urban space it controls as pervasive presences, Macdonald gives the communal power structure only a weak presence (in the person of the local sheriff), putting the tangled Freudian guilt of the Hallman family at

---

[26] 'Maybe we can find a better label than hard-boiled, better sponsors than Hammett and Chandler. They're my masters, sure, but in ways that count to me and a lot of good readers I'd like to sell books to, I'm beginning to trace concentric rings around those fine old primitives' (T. Nolan 1999: 182–3).

the heart of the mystery. Archer's client, Carl, is imprisoned by his past: even after he escapes from the State Hospital, he carries with him a 'queer air of being confined, almost as though he were trapped in the past, or in himself' (p. 14).

In contrast to the early hard-boiled writers, Macdonald gives us Freudian cultural determinism rather than economic determinism, creating characters who are not primarily driven by the remorseless pressure of socio-economic circumstance. Although *The Doomsters* includes greed in the motivational structure of the plot, the wrongs exposed are not principally those of inequity or social injustice. First and foremost, his characters fail to understand themselves. To Archer, the populist rhetoric of earlier decades seems sentimental and out-moded. The emphasis on class divisions does not merely reflect the assumptions of an earlier era: it implies a fundamental misconception about the important human values. It places 'political man' above 'salvation of the individual soul' and the inner life (McCann 2000: 205–7). *The Doomsters* takes its title from a Hardy poem ('To an Unborn Pauper Child') about a child doomed by socio-economic circumstance, an allusion linked within the novel to the threat that a young woman's child, if born, will live its life in poverty. At a deeper level, however, the title attaches not to the spectre of economic deprivation but to devouring maternal possessiveness and a circuit of collective guilt, an inescapable cycle of familial suffering: 'Fear of the treacherous darkness around us and inside of us, fear of the blind destruction that had wiped out most of a family and threatened the rest' (p. 125).

From Lew Archer's opening dream about a hairless ape who lives in a cage (p. 5), kept in a state of 'nervous tension' by people trying to get in, Macdonald directs his attention to the inner traumas of a small cast of characters. Like classic detective fiction, *The Doomsters* con-fines its crime drama within a guilt-ridden family circle, exposing a degree of familial '[g]reed and hate and snobbery' (p. 35) that would be familiar to any reader of Christie novels. In contrast to the world of classic detective fiction, however, these are not conflicts that can be resolved by the expulsion of a single culprit. Macdonald's psycho-analytic narratives suggest not only that guilt seems to 'run in the family' (p. 63) but that blame can be extended outward. Order cannot be restored by the expulsion of a single destructive element, since the whole of the social set-up is characterized by shared guilt and indeed by a degree of insanity. Archer himself, like the protagonists of Hammett and Chandler, has no real solutions to the criminal confusions he investigates. Worse still, his investigations seem to lead him back to his own culpability. Though isolated in the traditional way (divorced, standing outside the family), he feels himself implicated in the insanity. When taking on Carl as a client, he says, ' "I must be crazy? Go ahead and say it. I'm not proud. I've got a friend in psychiatry who says they should build mental hospitals with hinged corners. Every now and then they should turn them inside out, so the people on the outside are in, and the people on the inside are out. I think he's got something" ' (p. 10).

Macdonald's meticulous plotting uses the intertwined causes of family traumas to sustain suspense, but, in obvious contrast to the British tradition, he uses this complex structure to undermine the detachment of the detective, banishing illusions of mastery and immunity. The broad outlines of the plot would be familiar to any reader of classic detective fiction: the detective tenaciously staying on a case in order to demonstrate the innocence of a man wrongly accused; an investigation impeded by uncertainty over timing, with confusion caused by the temperature of the corpse; an earlier crime that took place in a locked room; a murder disguised as a suicide; and an elaborately deceitful criminal (in the case of the doctor who committed the first murder in the chain). The mystery is even unravelled in the traditional detective–villain confrontation, during which the killer gives a detailed explanation of the circumstances of the murders. This classic scene of resolution, however, is followed by a coda in which the back story is expanded to include the detective's own past actions, making him part of the plot in a very full sense: his own earlier indifference and failure are in part what has allowed the mystery he has been investigating to unfold in the way it has. The detective is bound to the story at the very origin of the series of killings, and, far more than, say, Marlowe at the end of *The Big Sleep*, he is now part of the corruption.

Six years before the publication of *The Doomsters*, a Pocket Books editor had criticized Macdonald's books for failing to provide a 'sharp contrast between good and evil', and at some points *The Doomsters* reads like a direct response to such a complaint. Lew, at the end, knows that he does not 'want to be stuck for the rest of my life with the old black-and-white picture', and, extending his compassion to the murderess he has exposed, he reflects, 'Mildred was as guilty as a girl could be, but she wasn't the only one. An alternating current of guilt ran between her and all of us involved with her. The current of guilt flowed in a closed circuit if you traced it far enough' (pp. 181–2).

Contemporary investigations

Charles Willeford, *The Way We Die Now* (1988); Ed McBain, *Candyland* (2001); James Sallis, *The Long-Legged Fly* (1992)

The last half-century of crime writing has demonstrated that Chandler was wrong to predict the demise of the hard-boiled detective novel. It has also, however, confirmed his sense that the tradition was in the process of fragmenting: looking back, we see a huge diversity of efforts to dissociate the hard-boiled detective from a clichéd image of macho individualism and to undermine the sense that what detective novels are offering readers is a confirmation of the status quo. Black and female crime writers, in particular, have contributed to this trend, and I will discuss them in the last two chapters of this study. The revitalizing of the tradition can also, however, be attributed to revisions of the formula accomplished by white male writers, many of whom have taken class, gender, or race as central themes (themes that are in this section treated, respectively, in the novels of Willeford, Hunter/McBain, and Sallis). They have also created as their protagonists investigative figures far removed from the stereotypical hard-boiled private eye—figures so lost, floundering, marginalized, guilt-ridden, alcoholic, or just generally defective that no one could mistake them for masculine role models.

Unlike non-investigative crime fiction, the detective novel and its near-relation, the police procedural, tend to use series characters as their protagonists. There are considerable commercial pressures at work here: as James Sallis notes, 'There is a strong pull among publishers for writers, especially in the mystery field, to write a series.'[27]

---

[27] James Sallis 9/2/2004. Sallis was answering questions as guest author on the rara-avis site (www.miskatonic.org/rara-avis) in Feb. 2004.

In the work of all three writers discussed in this section we will see the tensions this can generate between the darker themes of the contemporary crime novel and the demand for a commercially viable series featuring a likeable investigative figure who is sufficiently resilient to keep going novel after novel. Sallis, in his Lew Griffin series, bends the conventions of the private eye novel virtually to the breaking point. After many years of writing noir crime novels (the transgressor/victim-centred fiction that we will examine in the following chapter), Charles Willeford ultimately only made an audience-pleasing move into a detective series when he started to write his Hoke Mosley books in the mid-1980s. Salvatore A. Lombino, writing both as Evan Hunter and as Ed McBain, has written non-series as well as series novels, with the 'series' part of his persona securing far and away the greatest popular success.

The writers treated here represent only a small sampling of the huge amount of hard-boiled detective fiction published since the mid-twentieth century. During the 1970s and, even more, the 1980s, we can see the inception of a large number of new investigative series, with a variety of strong regional identities.[28] *Fadeout* (1970) introduced Joseph Hansen's gay series detective, Dave Brandstetter, solving crimes in and around Los Angeles; also in the seventies, Lawrence Block began a series of novels featuring an ex-cop, New York investigator Matt Scudder, and James Crumley started writing about his hard-drinking, tough-talking Montana investigators, Milodragovitch and Sughrue. In the eighties, Loren Estleman began his Detroit-based Amos Walker series; in the nineties, Sam Reaves introduced his cab-driving Vietnam veteran Cooper MacLeish, who first appears as a Chicago investigator in 1991; Louisiana crime has been investigated not just by Sallis's Lew Griffin but by Dave Robicheaux, the Cajun detective who features in James Lee Burke's novels; another Cajun investigator, Rene Shade, has been created by Daniel Woodrell. The hard-boiled style has also been developed in an identifiably British way during the eighties and nineties by writers like Ian Rankin (dubbed by Ellroy 'the King of Tartan Noir'), David Peace (in his dark and disturbing 'Red Riding Quartet', set around the time of the

---

[28] The settings of literary noir and *film noir* are discussed, respectively, by Willett 1996 and Nicholas Christopher, *Somewhere in the Night: Film Noir and the American City*. New York: Free Press, 1997.

Yorkshire Ripper investigations), Julian Barnes (writing as Dan Kavanagh, in a four-novel series relating the seedy but generally humorous and upbeat adventures of a bisexual private eye called Duffy), Mark Timlin (in his long-running Nick Sharman series), and Robin Cook (Derek Raymond, whose Factory novels are amongst the darker investigative series).

In the American context, the upsurge of interest in investigative crime fiction can plausibly be related, as Woody Haut suggests, to the proliferation of official investigations during the 1970s. Events such as the Watergate investigation and the Pike and Church Congressional Committees, investigating the CIA and the FBI, helped to generate an atmosphere of secrecy, duplicity, and paranoia, ideal circumstances for a renewal of interest in the fictional private eye: 'With state crimes so glaringly apparent, the problem facing private-eye writers in the early 1980s would be one of locating new boundaries, redefining the relationship between the private-eye and the state, and investigating the role of the investigator' (Haut 1999: 72–3). The Reagan era brought other anxieties, with deregulation, the renewal of the Cold War, and the emphasis on aggressive individualism, rising unemployment, and disparities of wealth—a decade, Haut argues, in which 'the freelancer emerged as a cultural phenomenon' (1999: 77). This was also, however, a period during which the alienated, individualistic private eye was increasingly joined by his more regularly employed counterpart in the police department. In the work of Ed McBain we see one of the best-known examples of the increasingly popular form of the police procedural, in which the individual investigator becomes part of or indeed is replaced by an official team of investigators, and emphasis is on the collective rather than the individual effort. With corporate structures supplanting the independent gumshoe, there tends to be more focus on the established routines of solving cases and the techniques of a police investigation (ballistics, forensic technologies, electronic databases, surveillance). This generic shift has arguably been encouraged by a recognition that the private eye is a fantasy figure, irrelevant to real criminal investigations: James Ellroy quotes Evan Hunter as saying that 'the last time a private eye investigated a homicide was never.'[29]

---

[29] Ellroy quoted in Cathi Unsworth, 'Crime and Punishment', *Melody Maker*, 25/2/1995: 32.

In a sense, elements of the police procedural can be glimpsed much earlier. In the 1920s, for example, Hammett's Continental Op, though he is in essence as much of a lone wolf as Sam Spade, is part of the Continental Detective Agency and must ultimately report to 'the Old Man', who gives him 'merry hell'—something an unconventional police detective is always likely to be given by his superior officers. The move towards the true police procedural, using a team of police officers as protagonists, was slow to come in a genre most often associated (in both its classic detective and hard-boiled forms) with the portrayal of policemen as corrupt and/or stupid. The individualistic bias of detective fiction means that novels involving an institutional investigative force are often pulled back in the direction of the loner cop who bucks the system (as Willeford's Hoke Mosley does). But from the 1940s on, film and television began to present various incarnations of the team-centred police detective. The *Dragnet* series, for example, first on radio (from 1947) and then on television (1952–9), used the files of the Los Angeles police department for its storylines, reflecting 'the professionalisation of real-life law enforcement and of national security concerns incited by the Cold War'.[30] And increasingly in recent decades the police procedural has come to the fore as one of the major forms of crime fiction.

There has been much recent critical debate about the ideological implications of replacing the single protagonist of detective fiction with the official investigative team of the police procedural. Knight (2004: 154–7) links the development to a wartime need to develop disciplined, co-operative methods of controlling disorder. Other critics have described this move towards crime-solving within a bureaucratic context as a validation of the invasive, controlling state apparatus. Some even see it as implying an acceptance of Panopticon-like institutional control, implemented by an investigator who is an instrument of the hegemonic order.[31] But although the police procedural does place the detective more firmly within the context of bureaucratic state control, these two types of investigative novel overlap in many respects. The individual investigator often retains considerable autonomy in the police procedural, particularly in

---

[30] Phillipa Gates, 'A Brief History of the Detective Film', online at www. crimeculture.com.

[31] Ibid.; Messent 1997: 12.

narratives that move towards an exposure of the injustices and failures of the official machinery of law and order.

Much contemporary detective fiction, both private eye and police procedural, does underwrite the values of 'the controlling agencies of modern society' (Messent 1997: 9–12). But there are many writers who use these forms to explore the contradictions of contemporary experience, creating what Andrew Pepper calls a 'discontinuous' tradition that in a variety of ways has challenged normative thinking (existing social and racial hierarchies, the assumed power structure, establishment values). Such writers have led readers to question the assumptions they make about this form of genre fiction, forcing them 'into an active, interpretative role, since meanings are not secured or legitimized within texts themselves' (Pepper 2000: 32). The texts discussed here all modify the form and meaning traditionally associated with hard-boiled investigative fiction: they mix the investigative format with other elements, shift the balance between criminal and detective, aim for less conventional representations of colour and gender, and focus the reader's attention through an investigative figure who is the antithesis of the confidently 'right' male authority.

Charles Willeford's most experimental reworkings of conventional formulas are to be found in the non-investigative literary noir that he wrote from the 1950s through the 1970s. This period produced, for example, *Pick-Up* (1955), with its challenge to racial stereotyping, and *The Burnt-Orange Heresy* (1971), which satirizes pseudo-intellectual theories of modern art. Wider recognition, however, came only with *Miami Blues* (1984), the first of his Hoke Mosley novels (the last of which, *Shark-Infested Custard*, was published in 1993). Following the success *of Miami Blues* Willeford was pressed to write more Hoke Mosley novels. His first response was to produce a novel called *Grimhaven*, in which Hoke kills his daughters and conceals their corpses in the shower stall of his run-down hotel room. His publisher thought this a less than commercial sequel. It remains unpublished, and Willeford's impulse to write it suggests the strength of his inclination to produce noir rather than investigative fiction. It is not surprising that in the sequels he did publish Hoke's control over his own life is ever diminishing. Although Hoke is a Miami homicide detective, and the series novels are near police procedurals, Willeford's emphasis is much more on Hoke's eccentric personal life and his individual investigative role. Like his literary noir, in fact, Willeford's detective fiction works to establish the outsider's perspective on contemporary society. He uses both his transgressors and his investigator (particularly when he goes undercover) as commentators on the injustices of class and on a system that seems preoccupied with owning and controlling human life.

In *The Way We Die Now* (1988), Hoke comes to be detached completely from his ordinary identity, going undercover to investigate rumoured atrocities in a migrant labour camp. Introduced with a quote from Burroughs—'No one owns life. But anyone with a frying pan owns death'—the novel weaves together various sub-plots involving the 'owning', controlling, and destruction of human life. Hoke's method of moving outside of respectable society requires more than the sort of Holmesian disguise that can be readily discarded. He has to transform himself in essential respects, descending to the level of a tramp, symbolically toothless, exposed to humiliation of every sort ('I didn't have my badge, weapon or even my teeth' (Willeford [1988] 1996: 220)). He is on his own in the dangerous Florida outback, surrounded by all of the marginal people that America tries to conceal, the hidden underside of commercial society. As the different strands of the plot are resolved, we see that the novel's middle-class murders are not fundamentally different from the crime of dumping Haitian workers in the swamps: money alone matters. Americans 'hate anyone who is more successful than they are' (p. 80) and can with impunity dispose of anyone sufficiently less successful to have become invisible. Moving downwards, away from any toehold on American affluence, Hoke increasingly receives treatment that reflects his appearance. His own standards of law-abidingness change: 'he wasn't Sergeant Mosley. He was Adam Jinks, itinerant fruit tramp. Fuck Brownley, and fuck the law' (p. 130). When he decides to 'take out' the pair who have been murdering the Haitians, his action is sufficiently beyond the law for him to conceal it, though he in the end finds that nothing has been concealed and that he has both fulfilled official expectations and given his superiors a hold over him. As Hoke reflects on his new assignment, the 'rotten job' of 'looking for dirty cops', *The Way We Die Now* comes to its close. As police procedurals often do, the novel ends with an uneasy and not readily resolved dialogue between individual and official moral frameworks.

Much more centrally associated with the development of the police procedural, Ed McBain has, from the mid-1950s on, been one of the key figures in popularizing the form. He is credited with being the first to use 'the ensemble story', which has since been widely imitated, often plot lines and all, in television crime dramas like *Hill Street Blues* and *NYPD Blue*. McBain combines a prolific talent for producing formulaic best-sellers (over fifty 87th Precinct novels) with a commitment to the more experimental crime fiction he writes under his other main pseudonym, Evan Hunter. McBain has said in interview that, over the years, his police procedurals have darkened in tone and approached his non-investigative fiction in theme. In addition, he stresses, there were connections between the two strands of his writing from the outset, in particular a common core of urban realism and a determination not to shy away from issues of gender, class, and race. As Evan Hunter, he wrote *Blackboard Jungle* in 1954, and the first of the McBain 87th Precinct novels, *Cop Hater*, followed two years later. Both novels dealt with what he describes as 'the ethnic breakdown in the school system and also in the police force', and during the last few decades the 87th Precinct novels 'have become even closer to *Blackboard Jungle* than the early ones' (Silet 1994: 394). As the series continued, justice did not always necessarily triumph and social commentary was brought increasingly to the fore, though always, McBain suggests, kept in check by his recognition that what the reader wants is a mystery—'Hey, hey, hey, get back to what we're supposed to be doing here. We're supposed to be solving a murder.' McBain's grasp of 'what readers want' is in no doubt, bringing him worldwide sales of over 100 million. By his own account, however, he keeps going by setting himself 'new challenges', varying the popular formula as much as possible, trying to ensure that institutional law enforcement is represented as an imperfect instrument, with ' "bad guys" within the squadroom as well as outside'—'stupid cops', 'bad cops', 'bigoted cops, you know, the whole bag' (Silet 1994: 398, 395).

The boundaries became still more blurred in a 2001 novel which brought his Evan Hunter and McBain personas together in what many critics have seen as his most ambitious book. Further developing one of the chief characteristics of the police procedural, the use of multiple perspectives, *Candyland* contains two separate parts. The first, Evan Hunter-authored, section tells the story of Ben Thorpe, a middle-aged architect visiting New York, following him through a single evening of sexual obsession. The second half is a typical McBain police procedural, except that it is not set in 'the 87th Precinct' (in the symbolic city Isola, which McBain created by turning New York 90° clockwise). Instead, it follows a group of New York cops pursuing the killer of a masseuse/prostitute who worked at the establishment that had ejected Thorpe the previous night. The 87th Precinct novels are not noted for their attention to gender issues, but *Candyland* tackles such issues very directly: its central events are rape and murder. Hunter/McBain shows himself willing to venture into controversial territory, splitting the narrative in a way that allows him to explore two radically different perspectives on sex crime. Readers first experience a night with a man we come to suspect is capable of rape and murder, then shift to the perspective of Emma, a young policewoman. Like many other writers in the era of police procedurals, McBain uses his policewoman to explore issues of female integration into law enforcement agencies—ingrained sexism, the assumptions about gender underlying institutional politics, the essential maleness of police departments (Walton and Jones 1999: 13–15). He also, however, explores her perspective in ways more closely related to the act of rape itself. Although the crimes of rape and murder at the centre of the narrative have nothing to do with either Ben or Emma, each in his or her own way acts as a reflection of the situation. A close third-person narrative follows Ben, a potential transgressor, through a night when he hovers on the brink of sexual violence; and Emma is not only a police officer assigned to the case but someone whose personal circumstances give her a heightened affinity with the woman whose murder she is investigating.

The intimate, present-tense narrative of the Ben section functions (not dissimilarly to the first-person narrative of, say, Jim Thompson's *Hell of a Woman*) to expose a male mind characterized by an obsessive and self-deceiving misogyny. Ben is a man who categorizes and sexually evaluates every woman he encounters. Since McBain's psychological portrait is not as savagely satirical as Thompson's dissection of the male gaze, or as Bret Easton Ellis's exposure of Patrick Bateman in *American Psycho*, we are more easily drawn into a degree of sympathy with Ben. Our identification is made possible by hints that he has undergone an unspecified childhood trauma, and our judgement is muted because he does not, as it turns out, actually kill anyone. Unquestionably, though, the 'Ben' section of the novel brings the reader unnervingly close to a mind like that of the actual killer. We are made still more uncomfortable by the realization that the analysis of Ben's disturbed psyche doubles as an exposure of the self-aggrandizing, self-deceiving commercial world that he is part of. From the first page, we see the impersonal nature of the world he inhabits, the technology and space of a grandiose male self-image, and the detachment from others that goes with Ben's predilection for phone sex. Ben habitually thinks of himself in terms of his place in the male hierarchy: 'He is Benjamin Thorpe, Esquire, famous architect whose multilevel concept echoes the very precepts of the law, exalted justice on high, abject supplicants below' (McBain and Hunter 2001: 10).

Structurally, Hunter/McBain uses the fact that the inverted murder story is a known pattern (from Austin Freeman to Columbo), so that it is not inconceivable that what we have witnessed in the first half may well be the prelude to the murder that is being investigated. As more and more evidence is found to link him to the massage parlour on the night in question, and it is established that he has the psychological profile of someone who would commit this sort of crime, Ben does indeed become the main suspect. Although he is not the actual murderer, he indulges in the same kind of obsessive behaviour, rationalizations, and self-deceptions: ' "Thing you have to remember is these guys all lead double lives," [Jimmy Morgan, the actual killer says]. "I know these guys, believe me [. . .] These guys are obsessed, you know. They try to stop themselves, but they can't." ' (p. 210).

Jimmy is in fact the cop who is investigating the case with Emma, and the doubling of Ben with Jimmy is paralleled by the doubling of Emma with Heidi, the female victim. As a police officer Emma inhabits a male space, but she is there on sufferance. As a vulnerable and (in her domestic life) victimized heroine, she functions to efface the victim/hero dichotomy, acting as a solving 'hero' but worrying that she identifies to an unusual extent with the victim. Her relationship with her serial adulterer husband makes her a kind of double for both Ben's wife and the actual victim: in the process of obtaining a divorce, she regards her husband's sexual relations with her, from the time he began his infidelities, as a form of rape. This means that, in the police procedural part of the novel, the crime is in effect being investigated by the (actual) killer and the (doubled) victim. It is a device that very much shapes the way we read that traditional mystery story ingredient, the conversation between the investigator and the transgressor in which the latter is gradually forced to admit what he has done. The parallel between Ben and Jimmy is heavily underscored. An inner assertion of his official position, public identity, and place in the male hierarchy all come into the killer's mind as ways of trying to dissociate himself from the crime. The self that kills Heidi emerges, as it were, as a younger self, not the official male grown-up self but the inner child who has been traumatized, trying as an adult to make up rules to keep himself in line—a parody of the 'law of the father'.

In the same year as *Candyland*, the sixth novel in James Sallis's Lew Griffin series was published. *Ghost of a Flea* begins with the paragraph:

After a while I got up and walked to the window. I felt that if I didn't say anything, if I didn't think about what had happened, didn't acknowledge it, somehow it might still be all right again. I listened to the sound of my feet on the floor, the sounds of cars and delivery vans outside, my own breath. Whatever feelings I had, had been squeezed from me. I was empty as a shoe. Empty as the body on the bed behind me.

Sallis's suffering, erring private eye, contemplating his inner emptiness with a dead body near at hand, has a dark, existential complexity. He has understandably found favour with a somewhat smaller audience than that for McBain's 87th Precinct novels. When Paul Duncan, interviewing Sallis, admits that he cannot remember the plots of any of the Lew Griffin novels he has read, Sallis replies, 'That's because there aren't any! [. . .] When I first tried to describe the first book to people, I said—Well, he's a detective that keeps going on missing persons cases, and he never finds anyone.' In spite of pressure from his publisher ('he wants pumped-up plots so that he can sell 50,000 copies'), he finds plot 'very uninteresting'.[32] His experimentation, his allusiveness, and his determined disruption of generic expectations make Lew Griffin one of the most interesting of contemporary incarnations of the world-weary, marginalized, hard-boiled detective.

The first of the Lew Griffin novels, *The Long-Legged Fly* (1992), is more of a riff on the nature of the crime novel than a crime novel itself. As Woody Haut says, 'These are detective novels that question

[32] Paul Duncan interview with James Sallis, 'Professional Liar', in Duncan 1997, online at www.grasslimb.com.

the very purpose and meaning of detective novels.'[33] Sallis himself, in the Duncan interview, muses on the fact that many of his readers seem nevertheless to read the novels as though they were straight detective stories: 'They have no idea what the ending is all about [. . .] What book had they read?'[34] *The Long-Legged Fly* is the first in a sextet of novels in which the traditions of hard-boiled crime fiction are only one strand in the narrative Sallis builds up, gradually filling in the life story of his protagonist, which spans the 1960s through the 1990s—*Moth* (1993), *Black Hornet* (1994), *Eye of the Cricket* (1997), *Bluebottle* (1999), and, in 2001, *Ghost of a Flea*. The four sections of *The Long-Legged Fly* (1964, 1970, 1984, and 1990) offer what Sallis calls 'a kind of introductory overview of the entire narrative trajectory of the Lew Griffin novels [. . .] an arc, beginning as fairly standard pulp fiction and circling ever more inward towards a kind of auto-biography for Lew.'[35] As the Lew Griffin novels build into a series, the narrative circles back to the different decades of Lew's life (he has at various times been a skip tracer, a bodyguard, a teacher, and a crime novelist whose novels possibly constitute his own story). In the sub-sequent novels, Sallis fills in gaps during and after the period covered in *The Long-Legged Fly*. It is a series that is far from being a 'series' in any conventional sense, repeatedly reminding readers of the slipperi-ness of all narrative, the unstable relationship between narrative and identity, and the unreliability of memory, with snatches of narrative that resemble Lew's own patchy recall of his life during his periods of descent into alcoholism—'A few bright frames, all the rest lost' (p. 183).

Other notable writers have played in a 'literary' way with the conventions of crime fiction (for example, Paul Auster, Martin Amis, Bret Easton Ellis). Unlike these contemporaries, though, Sallis is writing from within the genre, pulling in not just literary references,[36]

---

[33] Woody Haut, 'James Sallis: An Overview', *Crime Time*, 22, 2001, online at www.crimetime.co.uk.

[34] Sallis, rara-avis discussion, 25 Feb. 2004: Sallis also says, 'Do I think of the Lew Griffin novels as crime novels? Well, yes . . . and no. The whole idea of those books was to create a new kind of novel, something that combined the delights of crime fiction, what I love about it, with the delights of "literary" fiction. I'd estimate that about half my readers see them as simply novels, the other half as mysteries or crime novels. Then there are those who find them unsettling and too in-between, neither fish nor fowl.'

[35] Ibid.

[36] Sallis's sources of inspiration include e.g. Joyce, Borges, Queneau, Pynchon, Moorcock, Cortázar, DeLillo.

but a whole series of allusions to the conventions of crime and detective fiction. His critical books, *Difficult Lives* (on Goodis, Thompson, and Himes, published in 1993) and his highly acclaimed biography, *Chester Himes: A Life* (2001), show him to be a writer bound strongly to the earlier traditions of hard-boiled writing and literary noir, though at the same time committed to stretching generic boundaries and to breaking down the distinctions between genre fiction and 'serious literature'. It is in the structure of his novels that Sallis departs most radically from the private eye tradition: his plotting is circular and inconclusive, refusing satisfying resolutions and answering questions not asked rather than clarifying the initial problems posed. He says that, when reading the crime fiction of other writers, he most responds to atmosphere and, above all, voice. In searching for a satisfying combination of ' "literature"—for lack of a better word' and detective fiction, what he most wanted to take from the latter was 'the edgy atmosphere and crisp dialogue', whilst focusing more fully on the ways in which character and milieu interact. His intention, he says, was not to 'subvert' the genre, but to bring to the fore possibilities within it that could be exploited in more adventurous ways.[37] Although he brings a postmodern sensibility to bear, it is an approach that has its roots in the agenda Chandler set for hard-boiled fiction, with its central emphasis on the prioritizing of language, mood, and scene over plot.

Sallis's play with the traditions of the genre takes in both detective narratives and transgressor-centred narratives. Thus the opening scene of *The Long-Legged Fly* presents Lew's revenge killing of a man who, without compunction or compassion, has been responsible for the death of a young girl: wielding a leatherworker's knife, Lew tells the man a story and then opens him up. Sallis has said that he wanted to start in this way and then to secure the reader's sympathy for the man who kills, a man who can be, as another character says, 'crazy as shit' (Sallis [1992] 1996: 72), having killed a man he didn't even know. The narrative then segues into something closer to the standard plot structure of a traditional hard-boiled detective story, with Lew looking into mysterious disappearances (a 'locked plane' disappearance, followed by a 'girl in the big city' disappearance). But neither yields the satisfactions of a conventional investigation. We never learn what

[37] Duncan interview, *Crime Time.*

has motivated the events of the first investigation; Lew cannot prevent the death of the second girl he pursues, and the man responsible for her death is himself a tragic figure, whose filming of his own suicide bears comparison with Lew's own self-destructive hopelessness. In the traditional detective story, the movement towards at least partial resolution can be taken to confirm the possibility of some kind of competent agency.[38] The pattern of Sallis's novels, on the other hand, is a reflection of his view that things may change but not improve: ' "Things'll get better, Lew." "Now you're bullshitting me. Things never get better, Don. At the very best, they only get different" '(p. 98).

The voice Sallis creates for Lew Griffin is unmistakably that of the world-weary hard-boiled private eye, but he is given more to struggle against than corrupt cops and vicious gangsters. Lew himself is one of the lost ('I felt as though I'd lost something, lost it forever, and I didn't even know what it was, had no name for it' (p. 78)). When he wakes up with the light slamming into his eyes like fists in the Truro Infirmary, it is a Chandler moment. The damage, however, has been inflicted by Lew's own self-destructive instincts rather than by the novel's bad guys. Sallis uses both his protagonist and his missing persons, then, to chart the many paths to the gutter—to show how easy it is to let go, suffer the loss of community and the loss of agency.

Lew is further marginalized by his colour. Race emerged as a central issue for Sallis in the early stages of creating the series. *The Long-Legged Fly*, he recalls, developed out of a long short story, initially just the first scene and the murder Lew commits, but then: 'I wondered where all his rage came from. Twenty pages in, I realized this man was black. That was the only thing that could explain all this rage and anger boiling out of him, usually at inappropriate times. So I went back and started writing it again, and found out more about who Lew Griffin was.'[39] Sallis himself is white, but has often been

---

[38] The positive resolution of such narratives is mocked in the film Lew watches towards the end: 'It was a forties-style detective movie, all stark blacks and whites, full of women flaunting cigarettes, silly hats and wisecracks. The hero was a one-time idealist turned mercenary and gone more recently to seed and gin. Ninety minutes later he'd become a solid citizen and, left behind there in movieland when the curtain closed, was probably scouting out real estate just north of town and a few new suits. It was wonderful' (p. 182).

[39] Duncan interview, *Crime Time*.

mistaken for a black writer and has been seen by many readers, both black and white, as accomplishing a generic transformation comparable to that achieved by such black crime writers as Chester Himes and Walter Mosley. A black journalist, Gene Seymour, writes, 'I was three and a half books into James Sallis' extraordinary sextet [. . .] before I found out that Sallis wasn't—as I'd assumed all along—Black Like Me. Apparently I wasn't alone in this misapprehension.' After much online debate about Sallis's racial background, speculation was finally put to rest, Seymour recalls, when Sallis

disclosed in interviews that he was white—or, if one prefers, 'nonblack' [. . .] Some could use this disclosure to scold Sallis for indulging in literary minstrelsy. You won't hear any gripes from me. I wouldn't have misperceived Sallis' racial background in the first place if I hadn't found Lew Griffin such a persuasive rendering of an intellectually supple, physically tough and emotionally wounded black man struggling to negotiate security and self-respect for himself in late 20th century New Orleans.[40]

In creating early twentieth-century hard-boiled fiction, Hammett and Chandler 'thought of themselves as engaged in a complex and unlikely effort to mediate the popular and the literate' (McCann 2000: 199–200). They aimed to establish a form in which vernacular speech, tough action, and oppositional politics had a force and subtlety that went beyond the ephemeral appeal of a 'popular genre'. The political agenda has been updated, and the balance between the popular and the literate is ever-changing, but this broad objective is still visible in contemporary transformations of the hard-boiled tradition.

[40] Gene Seymour, 'Review of *Ghost of a Flea* by James Sallis', *Newsday*, 24/3/2002, reproduced by *No Exit Press*, online at www.noexit.co.uk.

3

Transgression
and Pathology

THE murder that Lew Griffin commits in the first chapter of *Long-Legged Fly* has a visceral, firsthand intensity that impresses itself indelibly on the reader's mind. The protagonist in this scene becomes *like* the criminal in a very disturbing way: 'Nigger's gonna carve you up *like you did her* [. . .] I let him see the knife in my hand then, a leatherworker's knife [. . .] Then I bent down and opened his wasted belly with the knife' (Sallis [1992] 1996: 4–5, my italics). Sallis's intention of turning the murderer of this dark vignette into the protagonist of his series is accomplished by his authorial act of opening Lew to our view, often as brutally and degradingly as Lew has opened the terrified addict. Late twentieth-century crime fiction has increasingly shown its readers the physical opening of bodies, the psychological exposure of damaged minds, and the inscription of personal traumas on the bodies of victims. The main objective of this chapter is to look at the development of some of the forms of crime fiction in which the mind and actions of a killer dominate the narrative, a focus often accompanied in recent decades by the delineation, in grotesque detail, of the ways in which crimes are written upon bodies. The killing of the tramp in Sallis's novel is only a brief section in a narrative otherwise centred on Lew's activities as a private eye and his inconclusive enquiries into the nature of loss. Other writers, however, have specialized in creating crime fiction in which investigation recedes or disappears entirely, and we, as readers, are drawn into a much closer relationship with transgressors and their pathologies.

It can be argued that detective-centred fiction is itself a kind of aberration in a longer tradition of crime fiction. All the texts discussed in this chapter have strong affinities with gothic fiction and with other 'parent traditions' like Defoe's criminal-centred narratives and the Newgate novels of the nineteenth century. Gothic materials recurrently surface in the literature of crime, and it is clearly not just contemporary readers who interest themselves in the romantic figure of the outlaw, the psychological make-up of the criminal, the criminal's own experience of violence, pursuit, and betrayal, and the 'sensational' stories of particularly brutal murders. Even during the heyday of detective fiction, novels and stories written from the perspective of the criminal continued to be written. Although early hard-boiled fiction tends to be stereotypically associated with the figure of the private eye going down mean streets, much of the most powerful crime writing of this period was non-investigative. During the Depression years, fascination with the figures of the gangster and the outlaw is apparent in both film and fiction. Protagonists of these narratives struggle to achieve some measure of success, driven by myths of limitless opportunity in a society characterized by economic injustice and failure on a massive scale: for example, the gangster sagas of W. R. Burnett's *Little Caesar* (1929) and Armitage Trail's (Maurice Coons's) *Scarface* (1930), and the outlaws on the run in Edward Anderson's *Thieves Like Us* (1937). This was the same period during which James M. Cain wrote his hugely influential stories of love-triangle murders, *The Postman Always Rings Twice* (1934) and *Double Indemnity* (1936), in which characters follow their crooked paths in pursuit of the American dream and, in the process, secure their own defeat and entrapment.

At the time of the paperback revolution, transgressive voices of this kind came to the fore in some of the most interesting and original work to come out of mid-century crime writing: Jim Thompson, Charles Willeford, Charles Williams, Harry Whittington, Gil Brewer, John D. MacDonald, Peter Rabe, Patricia Highsmith, Margaret Millar, and many others were producing literary noir that explored the psychopathology of killer protagonists, revenge-seekers, and those murderously determined on achieving upward mobility.[1] When Chandler said that the future of the crime novel lay in the novel of suspense, he did not have this new generation of paperback writers specifically in mind, but their work in a way is a fulfilment of his

---

[1] Crime fiction focusing on the upwardly mobile serial killer is discussed in some detail in Horsley 2001: 112–19.

prophecy. As we have already seen in looking at the transformations of hard-boiled detective fiction, there has been a pull towards transgressor-centred narratives throughout the second half of the twentieth century. It is apparent not just in novels that abandon the investigative structure altogether but also, especially in the 1980s and 1990s, in investigative forms like the police procedural. In the hands of the writers discussed here (James Ellroy, Thomas Harris, Patricia Cornwell), this form is stretched almost to the breaking point by the inclusion of criminal pathologies, vividly imagined competing centres of consciousness, creating what Martin Priestman calls 'split-level' narratives. In these investigative texts, the body is not neatly arranged in a locked room, and murderers are not necessarily apprehended: we are far from the libraries and drawing-rooms of classic detective fiction. Decomposing corpses (in the novels of Patricia Cornwell, for example) become central characters; serial killers like Harris's Hannibal Lecter seem destined to roam at large forever.

The novels discussed in the first two sections of this chapter abandon an investigative structure altogether, falling into the category of 'crime' as opposed to 'detective' fiction. That is, although detection (often notably unsuccessful detection) is still taking place, our interest as readers is invested almost entirely in the transgressors. There have been many attempts to clarify the differences between crime and detective fiction, and to label the sub-generic variants in ways that adequately take account of the structural differences. One of the better known models is that of Julian Symons, whose influential *Bloody Murder: From the Detective Story to the Crime Novel* (1972) gave impetus to a shift of genre criticism, away from a concentration on detective formulas and towards the broader analysis of the many variants of crime fiction. In distinguishing 'the crime novel' from the detective story, Symons constructs a useful table of differences, bringing out the implications of some of the most obvious changes. So, for example, since the crime novel need not have a detective, it does not require clues or forensic details; it builds a narrative around characters and their psychological make-up rather than the investigative process; it often radically questions 'some aspect of law, justice or the way society is run' (Symons [1972] 1992: 201–3).

Another way of identifying these texts is to say that they are thrillers. The Todorov model that we have already introduced defines thrillers simply by saying that they are narratives that suppress the 'first story' of classic detection and vitalize the second story, so that the narrative coincides with the action and interest is thrown forward rather than backward (the narrative is prospective rather than retrospective). Todorov distinguishes the thriller from the suspense story (which retains the element of mystery), but more recent criticism— for example, Martin Rubin's *Thrillers* (1999)—tends to see both forms as having a common core of identifying features. These traits include excess, especially excessive violence; emphasis on feeling and sensation, as opposed to the rationality implicit in the structure of the classic detective story; suspense, arising from the involvement of the protagonist in menacing events (in contrast to the detachment of the traditional detective); the evocation of fear and anxiety; the creation of contrasts due to threatening eruptions in the normal; ambivalence; vulnerability; and a sense of being carried away, control-vulnerability being 'a central dialectic of the thriller, closely related to sadism-masochism' (Rubin 1999: 5–7, 17–32).[2] David Glover, stressing the extent to which the label 'thriller' conveys the importance to this sub-generic variant of intense literary *effect*, quotes the *New York Times Book Review*'s description of Harris's *Red Dragon* as 'an engine designed for one purpose—to make the pulse pound, the heart palpitate, the fear glands secrete'.[3]

A third category useful in understanding these texts, more explicitly defining their mood, is literary noir or 'the noir thriller', which can be seen as accentuating fear and anxiety, ambivalence and vulnerability (for example, by the destabilizing of roles). Literary like cinematic noir is characterized by its stress on the subjective point of view, by the shifting roles of the protagonist, and by the ill-fated relationship between the protagonist and society, generating the themes of alienation and entrapment. The noir thriller overlaps to a significant extent with hard-boiled fiction, but they are not coterminous. That is,

---

[2] As Rubin observes, the label 'thriller' has been contentious, and in formulating his own definition he rightly jettisons, for example, the widely applied definition offered by Jerry Palmer in *Thrillers: Genesis and Structure of a Popular Genre* (London: Edward Arnold, 1978), viz., that a thriller requires just two ingredients, a hero and a conspiracy. This is, as Rubin argues, both too wide (including, for example, the classic detective story) and too narrow (excluding many texts and films that would generally be counted as 'classic thrillers', such as Greene's *Confidential Agent*, Highsmith's Ripley novels, and Hitchcock's *Psycho*).

[3] Cover copy of Dell edition of *Red Dragon*, quoted by Glover 2003: 135.

hard-boiled novels with an upbeat resolution are probably not 'noir', and many noir thrillers (for example, those of Patricia Highsmith) do not have the distinctive attributes of the hard-boiled style. The protagonists of literary noir can be victims, transgressors, or investigators. They cannot, however, be the confident, all-solving investigators we have encountered in classic detective fiction. The hard-boiled investigator is more likely to be the central figure in a noir narrative: we have already encountered investigators whose positions are problematized, whose masculinity is traumatized. Hammett's Ned Beaumont and Sallis's Lew Griffin, particularly the latter, are quintessentially noir protagonists. The noir narrative is frequently focused through the mind of a single character who is bemused or disingenuous; it ironizes his evasions and disguises; it calls into question his judgements; it foregrounds the difficulties of interpreting a mendacious society. Noir plots turn on falsehoods, contradictions, and misinterpretations, and the extent to which all discourse is flawed and duplicitous is a dominant theme. 'Like high art,' James Sallis writes, 'these stories [. . .] unfold the lies society tells us and the lies we tell ourselves' (1993: 5). The unsettling effect of the manipulation of point of view is heightened by the unstable position of the protagonist. The iconic figures of noir are more complex and ambiguous than the traditional detective, the cowboy, or the action hero. We are brought close to the mind of a protagonist whose position *vis-à-vis* other characters is not fixed. Treacherous confusions of his role and the movement of the protagonist from one role to another constitute key structural elements in noir narrative. The victim might, for example, become the aggressor; the hunter might turn into the hunted or vice versa; the investigator might double as either the victim or the perpetrator. Even within the traditional mystery story, we have seen writers destabilizing what readers assume to be a 'reliable' triangle of detective, victim, and murderer, but literary noir carries this process of destabilization much further.

Noir is 'the voice of violation', acting to expose the inadequacy of conventional cultural, political, and also narrative models.[4] The fact that *film noir* was created in the post-war United States is often attributed to an atmosphere in which American society 'came into a more critical focus' (Telotte 1989: 4–5). More generally, the noir sensibility

---

[4] For a fuller discussion, see Horsley 2001: 1–13.

may come to the fore at any time of discontent and anxiety, of disillusionment with institutional structures and loss of confidence in the possibility of effective agency. The kind of social, political, and cultural circumstances to which noir thrillers have historically responded are, for example: the unprecedented disruptions brought by two world wars; economic crises; the rise of aggressive ideologies; racial conflicts; McCarthyism and Cold War paranoia; the emergence of the consumer society and the Thatcher–Reagan years. Concentration on the psychological states of those who stand outside (but might pretend conformity to) mainstream society provides a means of exploring social and psychological malaise. The damaged self of the psychopath can act as a metaphor for society's aberrations, or the perspective of the criminal outsider can serve to critique the sociopolitical world that he stands against—what, in *The Killer Inside Me*, Jim Thompson's Lou Ford calls the 'screwed up, bitched up world' ([1952] 1991: 118).

Increasingly, the violated body of the victim has also come to act as a symbolic focus for the crime narrative. Trends in crime fiction are, of course, only one indication of a pervasive fascination with the spectacle of the traumatized body. The idea of the late twentieth century as a 'wound culture' has gained wide currency. In the 1990s in particular, physical wounding and psychological trauma were amongst our cultural preoccupations and the 'cult of abjection' was a defining feature of the decade's artistic and literary theory.[5] There was, Hal Foster argues in *The Return of the Real*, a sense of 'a symbolic order in crisis' and a tendency to see the truth of contemporary culture as residing in the traumatic or abject subject. Anxieties about invasive disease and death, particularly the AIDS crisis, recession, systemic poverty, and rapid technological advance alongside violent crime all played a part.

Such anxieties clearly intersect with the central elements of crime fiction, given that most crime novels are likely to involve violation of boundaries, threats to established structures of meaning, and the centrality of the corpse—the corpse given over to objecthood being amongst the main images of abjection (Foster 1996: 149).[6] The

---

[5] See e.g. Creed 1993: 10–15; Seltzer 1998: 109–10; and Foster 1996: 166.

[6] Other 'abject materials' that the taboo-violating artist can incorporate include, e.g. dirt, dead animals, rotting food, and such bodily wastes as blood, vomit, and excrement.

killer-protagonist narratives we are examining build their plots around the breaching of boundaries. Bringing the killer's victims to the centre of the stage can have even more disruptive effects. The extreme conditions present in scenes of dead bodies or damaged body parts are, of course, the *sine qua non* of the murder story, but in the classic detective fiction we have examined the corpse is, for the most part, sanitized, 'sacrificial', possessing a reassuring corporeal integrity that is 'a talisman against death's fragmentation and dissolution'. The work of many late twentieth-century crime writers, however, is more likely to be strewn with 'semiotic' bodies, fragmented, grotesque, gruesome.[7] The body is represented as the 'uncontainable excess' of the abject, turned inside out, 'the subject literally abjected, thrown out'. Physical violation becomes a metaphor for the fragility of all our boundaries: this breaking down of borders (of the body, the law, social orderings) is part of the very structure of the transgressive crime novel. As death infects life, we experience both repulsion and fascination, an unnerving dissolution of meaning but at the same time a sense that trauma guarantees the subject and gives it a kind of absolute authority. In crime fiction as in trauma discourse more generally, 'the subject is evacuated and elevated at once' (Foster 1996: 148–9, 168).

The sub-genre of crime fiction that has most obviously reflected late twentieth-century 'trauma culture' is the serial killer novel,[8] which opens to our gaze the wounded psyche of the killer whose aberrations are expressed in the wounds he inflicts on others. In its most common form, this is a narrative in which the reader's attention is fixed on the horrifyingly exposed mind of a killer. This dark artist 'redistributes' his own pain by refashioning the bodies of his victims in the image of his own psychic wounds. In narrative terms, he makes the body of his victim speak the language of his own psychosis: for example, the dark parodies of family life constructed by the homicidal couple in Ellroy's *LA Confidential*, who act out their obsessions

---

[7] Plain 2001, in her chapter on Agatha Christie, discusses in some detail the contrast between 'sacrificial' and 'semiotic' bodies: see esp. pp. 33–4 and 53–4.

[8] Novels in the serial killer sub-genre have proliferated since the late 1970s or early 1980s. The best discussion of the fascination with serial killers in relation to American culture is Seltzer's *Wound Culture* (1998), in which he argues that the public fascination with the wound extends to torn and opened psyches as well as bodies.

by 'killing and building hybrid children' ([1990] 1994: 466–7). A still more compelling example is that of Francis Dolarhyde in *Red Dragon*, who furthers 'the majesty of [his] Becoming' by filming his murder scenes, certain that his idol Hannibal Lecter will also understand 'the unreality of the people who die to help you in these things' (Harris [1981] 1993: 96). Some of the most effectively disturbing serial killer novels stay within the mind of the killer: Bret Easton Ellis's *American Psycho* (1991), for example, Joyce Carol Oates's *Zombie* (1995), or Poppy Z. Brite's *Exquisite Corpse* (1996). More common, and more likely to be shelved by bookshops with crime fiction, are the serial killer novels that are either wholly investigative in structure or are set up as a dual or split-level narratives. In the latter, there is, on the one hand, the script of the serial killer himself, with its larger-than-life elements of gothic romance; and, on the other, the script of the profiler. Explicatory 'fact' is set against the killer's own fantasies, often a fairly reductive script in which childhood abuse and neglect are almost the sole explanations of the adult killer. In the final section of this chapter we will look at three police procedurals that have achieved huge popularity with this combination of elements— Thomas Harris's *Hannibal*, James Ellroy's *Black Dahlia*, and Patricia Cornwell's *The Last Precinct*.

The Prohibition-era gangsters

W. R. Burnett, *Little Caesar* (1929); Armitage Trail, *Scarface* (1930)

The rebellious figure of the American gangster became a popular protagonist in both fiction and film in the 1930s, functioning as the dark double of a 'respectable' capitalist society, issuing a doomed but romantic challenge to its claims of legitimacy and parodying the American success ethic. The gangster had a double appeal, allowing readers and filmgoers to experience a sense of vicarious participation in gangster violence but also giving them the retributive pleasure of seeing violence turned against the gangster himself. They could thus identify with criminal rebellion against a corrupt, hypocritical society, but at the same time could indulge in fantasies of revenge against criminals who, particularly in Hollywood films, were conventionally placed in a retributive frame,[9] identified as the 'public enemy' responsible for the decline of all standards of decency and order. A moralizing frame is also sometimes evident in the crime novels of the time, but fictional portrayals tend to type the gangster as representative rather than aberrant, the implication being that the high-profile gangster resembles any man trying to live out a public identity. The analogy hints at the omnipresence of corruption in public life and the criminality of supposedly honest society, as well as posing the question of what drives such a man to succeed and what qualities ultimately undermine his power. Tough and energetic, the gangster can be admired for defying an unjust system: he is a skewed representation of society's legitimate structures, but he also pits himself against the established powers. The fiction of the 1930s created a wide range of gangster or outlaw protagonists, from the urban ethnic gangster to the poor farm boy who has drifted into crime, all of them engaged in a version of American struggle for success. The floundering, unsuccessful fictional gangster, of whom there were many in the 1930s, can be seen as parallel to the countless small men put under pressure by the big businessmen-gangsters, the political bosses, or the two in league together. This is a pattern evident, for example, in Burnett's novels about ageing gangsters, such as *Nobody Lives Forever* (1943). The figure of the outlaw on the run, as in Anderson's *Thieves Like Us*, fulfils a similar function. The rise and fall of the big-time gangster is an enactment of the dark side of the American dream, his pathology just a 'larger than life' version of a drive to succeed. In contrast to the psychopathology of, say, the contemporary fictional serial killer, the gangster's motivations and modes of thought are entirely comprehensible, familiar even to the most respectable of a capitalist society's law-abiding citizens.

During the Depression years the traumatic socio-economic changes taking place undermined American cultural myths, calling into question, for example, belief in 'the middle-class homilies about the virtue of deferred gratification and assurance that hard work and perseverance would bring success' (Sklar 1975: 195–6). In such a context, the gangster became a symbol of rebellion impossible for ordinary

---

[9] Powers 1983: 19–25 analyses the anti-crime mythology of vigilante and G-Men films. The best recent discussion of the representation of the gangster in Hollywood films is in Munby 1999.

law-abiding citizens to enact, and exerted an appeal that was cross-class and cross-ethnic (Munby 1999: 4–5). He expressed with heightened intensity the *desire* for things that are ultimately unobtainable: as Jack Shadoian says, '[t]he gangster is a creature who wants, and though he shares this trait with characters in other genres, the degree of compulsion is probably unique' (Shadoian 1977: 13–14). The heroic rebel image was reinforced by the classic Hollywood gangster films of the 1930s (*Little Caesar, Public Enemy, Scarface*), versions of the myth that were fixed in the public mind by performances of great verve and energy. The famous movie gangsters—Edward G. Robinson, James Cagney, Paul Muni—were heroes 'of dynamic gesture', strutting, snarling, and posturing, possessing a blatant, anarchic appeal. Standing outside the law in a period when Depression America was cynical about all sources of moral authority, they were awe-inspiring, 'grand, even in death' (Powers 1983: 90–1; Shadoian 1977: 59–60). The inevitable fall of the gangster creates a sense of entrapment in an economically determined reality. He is a victim of his own obsession with an illusory goal and of a society in which everyone is corrupt: they are all 'thieves like us'. Burnett wrote, 'if you have this type of society, it will produce such men'.[10]

As Knight argues, these were texts aiming for realism and unusually committed to representing 'the world and the responses of the criminal' (2004: 126). They ask to be read within a very specific historical context. At the same time, however, readers are supplied with a universalizing interpretative frame, perhaps most clearly of all in Burnett's *Little Caesar*, the earliest and one of the best-known examples of the gangster novel. It has been said that, if Burnett's novels were to be judged on the basis of their influence, he 'would undeniably be numbered amongst the most important writers of his time'.[11] His major innovation, as he saw it, was to re-imagine crime from the perspective of the criminal himself. *Little Caesar* was, he said, 'the world seen through the eyes of the gangster. It's commonplace now, but it had never been done before then. You had crime stories but always seen through the eyes of society. The criminal was just some son-of-a-bitch who'd killed somebody and then you go get

---

[10] Burnett, in Pat McGilligan, *Backstory*. Berkeley: University of California Press, 1986: 57, quoted by Munby 1999: 46.

[11] George Grella, in Reilly [1980] 1985: 129.

'em. I treated them as human beings.' As Burnett's title and his own phrase, 'gutter Macbeths', suggests, his decision to write from the viewpoint of the criminal is in another sense not an unprecedented departure but a return to older precedents. One of the ways in which he confers dignity on 'Little Caesar' is by representing him as the modern equivalent of a tragic hero, 'a composite figure that would indicate how men could rise to prominence or money under the most hazardous of conditions, but not more hazardous than the Renaissance'.[12] The perspective of 'the other' is thus shaped in Burnett's novel both by contemporary experience (soaring capitalist ambitions leading to the downfall of the Depression) and by a classic narrative form that confers mythic status on the defeated protagonist.

Like the private eye, the gangster is a figure of immense iconic power whose original complexity tends to be diluted in the countless imitations he inspires. After being filmed in 1930, *Little Caesar* was copied in dozens of early thirties novels and films (Powers 1983: 13), amongst them *Scarface*, which was filmed in 1932 (its author, Armitage Trail, wanted Edward G. Robinson, star of *Little Caesar*, to play the role of Scarface in the film adaptation). Like Tony Guarino in the Trail novel, Burnett's Rico ('Little Caesar') is obsessed with scaling the heights of power, and Burnett makes sure, as Trail does, that readers will understand the qualities that enable his hero to rise. Burnett, however, also places considerable stress on the flaws, the sense of inferiority, and the insecurities in his protagonist's character that spur his overweening ambition, making him akin to the heroes of tragedy and ultimately bringing about his downfall. Indeed, in delineating the characters of the other gangsters as well, Burnett sketches in, from the opening pages on, the psychological flaws in each that lead to their downfall. Lacking the glamour and dynamism of the movie gangster, these are unromanticized characters: Tony Passa is overexcitable, 'unable to control his imagination' (Burnett [1929] 1989: 38); Sam Vettori, lethargic and indolent, worries about Rico 'getting too big for us' (p. 8). Rico himself, as the title suggests, is an ironized 'great man', perceived by another character, Ramón Otero, as a legendary figure to be spoken of in the same breath as the rebel general of the Mexican Revolution, Pancho Villa. Small, pale, and quiet, Rico is above all marked out by his heroic energy and

---

[12] Burnett, in McGilligan, *Backstory*, 57–8, quoted by Munby 1999: 45–6.

single-mindedness (pp. 16–17). All his attention is focused on his image and his dream of upward mobility. He is 'a simple man' who loves only three things—'himself, his hair and his gun' (p. 22). Like the clichéd hard-boiled investigator, he is an isolated figure, unhampered by domestic ties and affections, indifferent to women, fiercely determined, not given to remorse. In contrast to the private eye, however, his dissociation from the past leads not to the condition of living in the present but to an obsessive preoccupation with future goals. Also, unlike the private eye, he is awed by those who are socially above him, and motivated not by the urge to set things right but by the spirit of emulation. There is considerable pathos in Rico's dreams: as he sits, for example, in a reverie reading the story of a rich society girl, he is 'fascinated by a stratum of existence which seemed so remote and unreal to him', inhabited by people who are 'insolent, inaccessible' (pp. 44–5).

Although the 1930s gangster saga is conventionally distinguished from the *film noir* of the 1940s–1950s, the figure of the gangster is in many respects comparable to the noir protagonist, with his extreme vulnerability and his traumatized masculinity. Rico has the illusion that he cannot be stopped, but under his confident exterior there is always a sense of isolation and despair. He is in many ways very unlike the bemused, damaged protagonist of literary noir, but Burnett's analysis alerts us from fairly early on to his 'dangerous' lapses of drive and energy, which would 'suddenly disappear', leaving him vulnerable—a danger he associates with women and their 'ability to relax a man, to make him soft and slack' (pp. 70–1, 81–5). As he struggles to consolidate his power (for example, in his conflict with Little Arnie), Rico begins to weaken physically, and the effect is to expose the self-doubt that has always been a part of his psychological make-up: 'By an effort of the will, he rid himself of an attitude of mind which had been growing on him since his interviews with Montana and the Big Boy. He was nobody, nobody. Worse than nobody' (p. 132). At the core of Burnett's creation of Rico there is the recurrent crime fiction theme of identity, though here (in comparison, for example, to either detective fiction or later serial killer narratives) the problem is reversed. That is, Rico's concern is not with concealing his actual murderous impulses under a falsely respectable exterior but of adequately sustaining a flamboyantly criminal persona that has, under the surface, an essential hollowness. Compelled to go into exile, he cannot bear his insignificance. A look from him now means nothing, since no one knows his true identity. He is completely unable to assert himself and is constantly conscious of his position as 'a lonely Youngstown yegg in a hostile city without friends or influence' (pp. 141–5).

Perhaps suggesting one of the reasons for the gangster story's hold over the popular imagination, Rico's one consolation when his fortunes have declined is the rehearsal of the near-legendary tales of his triumphant ascent. The 'episodes leading to his rise and fall' (p. 150) are fascinating to him even when he is in a position in which 'the very virtues' that accounted for his success are liabilities, now that he has no outlet for his energies, no object for his tenacity of purpose. Like *Scarface*, *Little Caesar* moves towards an end in which irony derives from the contradictions within the protagonist's identity. Rico must hide all knowledge of his past in order to survive, but it is this past that he longs to reassert and, in the end, he is psychologically unable to resist resuming his old identity. His urge to have people know his 'real' (recognizable) identity is his undoing, and the novel ends with him seeing the death of the public self he has so carefully created: ' "is this the end of Rico?" ' (p. 158).

Although Burnett thinks constantly in terms of universalizing the figure of Rico and his tragic flaw of rash ambition overreaching itself, the historical model for this big-time gangster was in part, of course, Al Capone. By the end of the 1920s Capone was the most widely recognized incarnation of American gangsterism. He was seen as 'a force in American life that government was powerless to control', his phenomenal rise to power in Chicago's underworld having made him feared and hugely wealthy. He was also a substantial political influence and an example of how a gangster could make a business asset of his reputation (Powers 1983: 4–6). The most famous fictionalization of Capone's career (including the Valentine's Day massacre) was unquestionably *Scarface*. Written by a detective-story and Hollywood scriptwriter, Maurice Coons, under the pseudonym Armitage Trail, the novel *Scarface* was the basis for the most notorious of the 1930s gangster films. Trail went to some lengths in pursuit of verisimilitude, seeking out Sicilian gangsters and immersing himself in Chicago's gangland in order to gather material for the book. As with Burnett's novel, however, there was also an impulse towards universalization, leading to the creation of a figure symbolic both of capitalist drives and of the conflict between private and public identity.

One of the key issues in the representation of so flamboyantly transgressive a figure is whether the gangster is to be contained within a moralizing frame that functions in the manner of the traditional detective narrative—that is, to judge, disempower, and punish the criminal. When Howard Hawks directed the film of *Scarface*, he came under intense pressure from the film's producers to establish a moral context for the story that would point the finger of blame at the gangster. The film could not be released until scenes were cut and added, allowing spokesmen for official morality to deliver a diatribe about the gangster as an evil force in society.[13] In Trail's novel, however, the frame is rather different, moralizing the career of the gangster but also quite explicitly exploring socio-political causes of gangsterism. Tony Guarino, the Capone figure, is both protagonist and scapegoat, and Trail's method of commenting on the narrative is to interpolate numerous passages that function to establish a normative moral perspective. He insists that, as an exemplary figure, the gangster supplies a cautionary tale rather than a glamorous role model,[14] but he also, from his opening descriptions to the moralizing end of the novel, presents the celebrated career of Scarface as a rebuke to the society that produced him—a lesson that will help in the restoration of decent government. Trail even gives to Scarface himself the role of articulating the causes of his own corrupt ascendancy. Moved by 'the social impulse', Tony Guarino writes before his death a 'damning indictment', setting out his 'great vision' of his own role in creating the 'monster' of his gang and of the corrupt system that has facilitated his rise (Trail [1930] 1997: 170). Perhaps further risking a loss of credibility, Trail also ends the novel by having the publication of this indictment produce 'a complete reorganization of the government and police administration' (pp. 177–8). Tony's vision is not entirely

---

[13] As Munby points out (1999: 58–9), this diatribe was delivered in distinctly Anglo tones, rendering the ideological interference 'visible and audible as such'.

[14] This was in some ways an approach more in keeping than Burnett's with the tendency of Hollywood studios of the time (under pressure to acquiesce in censorship) to add 'crime doesn't pay' riders to gangster films, in an effort to counter charges that their aim was 'to glorify the gangster'. See Munby, 1999: 51 and *passim*. The censors altered *Scarface* by demanding the addition of scenes intended 'to police the meaning of the film', the cutting of a violent scene (the St Valentine's Day Massacre), and a change of title, to 'Scarface, the Shame of a Nation'.

out of character, since it is his insight into the nature of power that has enabled him to attain dominance in the first place and to hone his skills as a political manipulator.

Again like Little Caesar, the character of Scarface can be seen as having certain affinities with the private eye. He is, like the archetypal hard-boiled investigator, separated from his past and his family, and street-smart beyond his years: he is 'shockingly old for his age [. . .] with his wise eyes, cynical mouth and well-developed beard', possessing 'more actual knowledge of mankind and its vagaries than most men acquire in a lifetime' (p. 4). He has a vitality and masculine competence that set him apart from others, as well as a sense of chivalry and pride in keeping his word. But, like Rico, he is separated from most other crime and detective fiction protagonists (whether heroes or anti-heroes) by his drive for power, sustained by a combination of efficient business and efficient violence. It is this that most obviously makes his story not simply an allegory of gangsterdom but of the whole of the capitalist system. A dapper, efficient, post-war gangster, Scarface goes in for 'regular business administration in crime' and ultimately feels 'like many another millionaire' that success is easily achieved if you are not too squeamish (pp. 74–5, 147–8).

The socio-political dimension of Trail's novel is strengthened by the careful placing of the story in an explanatory historical context, starting with a series of developments that are already in motion prior to the First World War. Tony is capable of killing before he goes to war (his first killing is just before the war, at a time before violence was a natural recourse in gangland), but his experience of the war forges his character, demonstrating that he really does possess 'that indefinable "it" of the born leader' and perfecting him 'in every branch of the fine art of murder'. As Trail says with heavy irony, the government then turned him loose with an honourable discharge, and seemingly expected him 'to forget it all immediately and thereafter be a peaceable, law-abiding citizen' (pp. 42–4). Although violence is only one of the means he deploys in order to attain his political ends, warfare is a dominant image in *Scarface*, and the scar itself takes on symbolic importance, constituting his new identity (since 'Tony Guarino' is reported as killed in action). It is his curse as well as his destiny, and, together with his gun, it signifies the inescapability of violence. He is 'a marked man', and the scar leaves him unrecognizable to the family he was close to in earlier life, so guaranteeing his separation from the past and from warm humanity.

The protagonist's identity crisis dominates the end of the novel as it does in *Little Caesar*, except that here it is his human rather than his public identity that is fatal to him. Scarface is forced to confront his own brother, a policeman, and the question is whether his past or his present identity will prevail. He dies at the moment when his past (his human identity) resurfaces in his mind and stops him from using the gun that has constituted his male authority as a gangster. The end is brought about by his knowing more than 'respectable society' knows. Decent folk like his brother cannot see him for who he is, whereas he 'knows' them and conceals the truth from them. He has previously hidden from his mother, for example, knowledge of events that would kill her and of the real nature of the society that has re-created her son as Scarface: 'What a blessing it was that most people actually knew so little' (p. 155).

The killers inside us

Jim Thompson, *The Killer Inside Me* (1952); Patricia Highsmith, *The Talented Mr Ripley* (1955)

The dress, gesture, language, and public persona of the gangster mark him out clearly as a transgressor. His very name ('Little Caesar', 'Scarface') declares his distinct, high-profile identity. The serial killer, on the other hand, has to be singled out and characterized by a 'profiler'. He moves amongst ordinary people unrecognized, 'abnormally normal' (Seltzer 1998: 9–15) in his appearance and behaviour. His next-door-neighbour banality has become part of the profile. Jim Thompson and Patricia Highsmith wrote their first novels about multiple murderers two decades before the term 'serial killer' entered the vocabulary, and, unlike many later novelists, they are not creating their fictional characters on the pattern of some infamous 'real-life killer'. The underlying moral insight—that a murderous potential can lurk in 'everyman'—did not have to wait for the studies of forensic psychologists to be recognized. Both Thompson and Highsmith, in the late 1940s and early 1950s, began to create out of this perception some of the most compelling and disturbing of all the transgressor-centred crime novels: Thompson's *Nothing More than Murder* (1949), *The Killer Inside Me* (1952), *Savage Night* (1953), *A Hell of a Woman* (1954), *The Nothing Man* (1954), *A Swell-Looking Babe* (1954), and *Pop. 1280* (1964); and Highsmith's Ripley novels, starting in 1955 with *The Talented Mr Ripley*, to be followed by *Ripley under Ground* (1970), *Ripley's Game* (1974), and *The Boy who Followed Ripley* (1980).

There was, of course, no shortage of multiple murderers in earlier crime fiction. Such figures were not excluded from classic detective fiction as long as their murders were 'rational and scientific',[15] and in hard-boiled fiction there are numerous tough guys who amass a high body count, both amongst villains and detectives (the Continental Op, for example, when he goes 'blood simple' in *Red Harvest*). As a distinct phenomenon, however, the multiple murderer really comes into his own only in the mid-century years of American crime writing. He is not yet a professionally diagnosed and categorized type, but is created in ways that have lent themselves to the retrospective analysis of those interested in the profiling of serial killers (for example, Mark Seltzer's extended analysis of Thompson's Lou Ford in *Serial Killers: Death and Life in America's Wound Culture* (1998)). Though writing considerably in advance of the refinements of forensic psychology, Highsmith and, even more, Thompson invite (and, in Thompson's case, provide the vocabulary for) psychoanalytic interpretations of the actions of their killers. At the same time, however, both writers raise the issue of whether a psychoanalytic explanation of the mind of the killer is simply a means of deflecting blame from the society on which he preys. They are centrally concerned with providing insights into the ordinary society that their killers mimic.

The killer, like the detective, can be seen as a protagonist working towards revelations. However, whereas the choice of a detective as protagonist, traditionally at least, suggests a narrative moving towards a restoration of some form of order, the protagonist killer is a figure whose objectives are more radical, more disruptive of conventional assumptions. Such a character may act to change a given set of circumstances through retribution, 'cleansing' society, or righting a wrong, though perhaps only a wrong done to himself, as in the case of

---

[15] Van Dine's twelfth rule specifies that only one murderer is allowed 'no matter how many murders are committed'; his fourteenth rule that both the method of murder and the means of detecting it 'must be rational and scientific'.

Tom Ripley, who kills in the first instance to rectify the social and economic injustices inflicted on him by the circumstances of his birth. If he is more radically alienated from 'normality', the killer may satirize the whole crooked, conformist social order, as does Thompson's sadistic, folksy, murderous sheriff, Lou Ford, in *The Killer Inside Me*. Acting as a 'threat to idyllic American domestic existence posed by the vengeful return of the repressed', Lou commits murders that reveal the corruptions of the symbolic order. His insights are those of 'a man that's crazy enough to tell he truth' (Simpson 2000: 91; Plain 2001: 230–1).

Thompson and Highsmith are in many respects very different writers. Highsmith would, for a start, never be grouped with the hard-boiled school, whereas Thompson is clearly a descendant of the early masters of pulp fiction, achieving his effects in part by his twisted use of the laconic style and deadpan wit that are so central a part of the tough guy tradition of Hammett and Chandler. But both Thompson and Highsmith make subversive, darkly humorous use of the conventions of crime writing, manipulating them to construct a critique of contemporary society, its injustices and stupidities, its deadening conformity, and its lack of imagination. Both create protagonists characterized by the contrast between their inner and outer lives. Their killers' minds are split between conformity and violation, their murderous impulses hidden behind affable, innocuous personas. Thomson said that all his novels were about the fact that 'things aren't what they seem' (Polito 1995: 351). This is, of course, true in almost any crime novel, but what is distinctive about the work of Highsmith and Thompson, and what is most compelling, is the insidious way in which they make us, as readers, party to all that is concealed. They make us complicit, forcing us to attend to their protagonists' cynically detached commentaries on the societies through which they move, and perhaps bringing us to see our own suppressed violence reflected in their states of mind.

The most remarkable and ambitious of Thompson's dramas of psychopathology are the first novel he wrote for Lion, *The Killer Inside Me*, and a companion piece written a dozen years later, also for Lion, *Pop. 1280*. Both novels make seductive use of a first-person narrative voice, addressing the reader directly, teasing and unreliable, but appealing for our understanding of the narrative we are being told. The effect is that we look down on this small-town society from the alienated position of a psychopath who is also a scathing observer, stripping off illusory surfaces and denouncing what he sees. In his day-to-day contact with his fellow townsfolk, however, Lou Ford's method of attack is apparently congenial and wholly ironic: his weapons are clichés, multiplied and exaggerated, delivered in so sincere and straight-faced a way that his conversations cumulatively create a savage critique of the small town as a form of living death. This satiric diversion is, for Lou, a substitute for actual killing: 'Striking at people that way is almost as good as the other, the real way' (Thompson [1952] 1991: 5). Much of the surreal, blackly comic force of the novel comes from the juxtaposition of Lou's clichés and his crime wave. When Lou moves on to killing in 'the real way', he tells us that he is just taking to a logical conclusion his critiques of small-town American society, putting into practice the secret wishes that others would act on if only they dared. He is 'typical' not just in the sense of having the chameleon-like ability to impersonate 'normality' but also in that he does 'what other people merely think'.[16] Lou is both (as the town sheriff) an investigator and the killer hunted, and Thompson uses this dual role to undermine the whole idea of a reassuring restoration of order. Conforming scrupulously to the conventional social forms that, as a lawman, he is officially meant to uphold, Lou reveals the essential hollowness of these forms and the 'pretendsy' (p. 187) nature of most people's apparent adherence to them. Lou Ford's role as denouncer of a corrupt and morally bankrupt society is most to the fore in his speech to Johnnie Pappas. Just before he kills Johnny, Lou offers him a fatherly explanation of the moral chaos of the world around them: ' "We're living in a funny world, kid, a peculiar civilization. The police are playing crooks in it, and the crooks are doing police duty [. . .] it's a screwed up, bitched up world, and I'm afraid it's going to stay that way [. . .] Because no one, almost no one, sees anything wrong with it" ' (p. 118).

The speech to Johnny Pappas is both a critique of an unjust society and an invitation to psychoanalyse the critic. ' "I guess I kind of got a foot on both fences . . . All I can do is wait until I split" ' (p. 119), Lou tells Johnny. Thompson uses Lou's schizophrenic personality as an image of the psychosis of an entire society. The faith Thompson had

[16] Frederic Wertham, *Dark Legend: A Study in Murder*. London: Victor Gollancz, 1947, quoted in Seltzer 1998: 161.

once had in populist democracy, evident in an earlier novel like *Heed the Thunder* (1946), had faded by the 1950s, and in *The Killer Inside Me* there remains no possibility of populist collectivism, of a sustaining folk culture, a common voice, or a coherent democratic community.[17] The tension between the two sides of his personality is represented by Lou himself as an internalization of the breakdown and the dishonesty of American society. This is something that, during the course of the novel, he traces back to the deceits inherent in the system of patriarchal authority that formed his character: ' "I was thinking the other day," ' Lou says in one of his triumphant exercises in truism, ' "and all of a sudden I had the doggonedest thought. It came to me out of a clear sky—the boy is father to the man. Just like that" ' (p. 4). The division of Lou's personality has been encouraged by his father, who made him 'typical' to hide his abnormality (p. 28). As Lou draws on pop psychoanalysis to delve into the events of this period in his life, we begin to see the *actual* typicality of this particular benevolent doctor and the upstanding lawman who is his son. Lou himself is just, in more extreme form, the embodiment of everyone's (and especially of his own father's) hypocritical respectability. He discovers, in a Bible concordance, a fragment of his father's past, a photograph, contemplated 'like something coming out of hiding', that reveals his father to have been a sexual sadist willing to go to any lengths to avoid scandal. Outside of his family, patriarchal figures (Conway, for example) are similarly corrupt and culpable. Although classified as abnormal, Lou is not being distanced as 'other' but is presented as a grotesque version of 'normal' society. He is part of a 'fine ol' family' and is the carrier of a badge (pp. 13–15). In short, he is the inheritor and embodiment of both familial and official position. Here and all through the novel, then, we see Thompson's use of the trope of schizophrenia as a means of exposing the moral vacuum at the centre of American society.

As a suspense narrative, *The Killer Inside Me* is sustained by Lou's perspective. 'I want to tell you, and I will,' he says, as he reorders the narrative, withholds information until the time is right and leaves us suspended with ellipses that we have to fill in for ourselves. Suspense is partly created by the unreliability of Lou's narrative, his imperfect knowledge, and his capacity for self-deception, producing a situation

---

[17] This shift in Thompson's thinking is analysed in detail by McCann 2000: 212–25.

in which many of the ironies are generated by his failure to recognize the full reality of the investigation into his own crimes and the ultimate hopelessness of trying to hold retribution at bay. As he pursues the question of the corruption of the patriarchy that has given him his role and his badge, the investigation of Lou himself (until the end glimpsed only in fragments) closes in. The end of the novel is an apocalyptic reversal of the traditional resolution of investigative crime narratives. It offers a bleakly ironic final image of a harmony impossible in the human society symbolized by this small town in Texas. Lou, exploding, 'yelling and laughing' in the final shoot-out, imagines his own death assimilated to a surreal, messianic vision of a celestial reunion of '[a]ll of us that started the game with a crooked cue, that wanted so much and got so little, that meant so good and did so bad' (p. 244).

Having read to the end of *The Killer Inside Me*, we must imagine the Lou Ford who narrates the story as already dead. Although he does, in fact, pop up again in a later Thompson novel, *Wild Town* (1957),[18] he cannot really be counted as a series protagonist, particularly given that *Wild Town* reverses most of what readers 'knew' about Lou from the earlier book. Patricia Highsmith, on the other hand, creates in Tom Ripley a multiple murderer who comes to seem as natural a series protagonist as Chandler's Marlowe and who presides over nearly as many novels. The Ripley saga, which began in the mid-1950s with *The Talented Mr Ripley*, is a fantasy of impunity sustained by lack of narrative closure. Highsmith reworks the conventions of crime writing in a way that is both comic and serious. She saw the serious function of crime fiction as the exploration of our moral confusions and the indeterminacy of guilt: 'I suppose the reason I write about crime is simply that it is very good for illustrating moral points of life. I am really interested in the behaviour of people surrounding someone who has done something wrong, and also whether the person who has done it feels guilty about it, or just, "so what".' Her methods are a blackly comic manipulation of the basic ingredients of the genre—the conventions of sustaining suspense, of hidden identities, paranoid fears, and plodding detection. In *The Talented Mr Ripley*, when the hard-boiled American private eye

[18] Polito 1995: 411 discusses *Wild Town* as a kind of 'parallel universe' in which Lou plays a quite different role to that he occupies in *The Killer Inside Me*.

finally arrives on the scene, Tom frightens himself by imagining an astute investigation of his crimes, conducted with all of the fictional detective's powers of perception, but the actual questions posed by the detective are an anticlimax. The masculine ethos of more traditional detective narratives is consistently undercut in the world of Tom Ripley, a feminized world, well-suited to the myth of Italy as a 'romantic' contrast to rational, 'progressive' northern European cultures. The intellectual endeavour and rational investigative structure of detection have little success in comparison to flair, intuition, dressing well, and shopping discerningly, all of which are satisfyingly rewarded. Ripley, wearing Dickie's jewellery and smile ('dangerously welcoming to a stranger' (Highsmith [1955] 1992: 97)), ultimately eludes with ease all efforts at detection. The Ripley novels are guaranteed *not* to move towards moral closure, and the suspense of the novels is built on tension between the exposure he risks and his success in evading detection, with Tom vacillating between confidence in his luck and fear of nemesis. Asked by a German interviewer whether Ripley would ever lose out, Highsmith declared, 'Nein, nein! Nicht bevor ich sterbe.'[19]

Ripley has often been seen as Highsmith's *alter ego*, speaking in a timbre and tone of voice 'remarkably similar to Highsmith's own': her most recent biographer, Andrew Wilson, records Charles Latimer as saying that 'After Pat's death, John Mortimer wrote a tribute, saying he thought she was in love with Mr Ripley [. . .] but actually she *was* Ripley, or, I should say, she would have liked to have been him.' Indeed, she on occasion signed herself 'Pat H., alias Ripley.'[20] Ripley was, Wilson says, an embodiment of her own creative imagination at work, and perhaps also 'a representation of her unconscious and a shadowy symbol of her repressed, forbidden, and occasionally quite violent, desires' (Wilson 2003: 194–5).

Ripley's irrepressible instinct for survival is also a manifestation of what we might think of as his pioneering spirit. As he sets out on his mission, supposedly aimed at persuading Dickie Greenleaf to return from Europe, it is possible to read his journey as an inversion of

[19] 'Patricia Highsmith im Gespräch mit Holly-Jane Rahlens', in Franz Cavagelli and Fritz Senn, eds., *Über Patricia Highsmith*, quoted by Hilfer 1990: 129.

[20] Interview with Charles Latimer, 2/11/1998, and Patricia Highsmith, Letter to Barbara Ker-Seymer, 24/5/1969, quoted by Wilson 2003: 194.

America as the new frontier. Released from the pressures of conformity and from the snare of poverty, Tom acquires on board ship a 'versatile', magical cap, capable of transforming his character and personality, and his transformation is a parodic (or comic) version of the American adaptability, other-directedness, and upward mobility. He aspires to achieve imaginative rebirth, and his Italian experience enables him to articulate everything in American life that he finds unsatisfactory and narrow. Highsmith explicitly echoes Henry James's *The Ambassadors*, representing Ripley as determined to comprehend European space, conceived of as a vast frontier requiring reading and translation. Tom wants to 'read' Italy in every sense, to acquire the means of knowing it at his leisure, to learn the language, to fully assimilate the experience. More than that, he desires to be assimilated by his new milieu and in the process to be purged of all traces of his former American self. In the Jamesian representation of America and Europe as geographical and moral poles, the traveller encounters a European frontier that 'speaks of an otherness imagined as the perfect alterity'.[21] Constructed as an object of knowledge and discovery, this strange, seductive new world seemingly promises that the most unlikely things—anything you imagine—can be accomplished. Whilst on the boat that carries him away from America, Ripley spends much of his time thinking about what he *hopes* or *imagines* will happen, feeling 'as he imagined immigrants felt when they left everything behind them in some foreign country [. . .] He was versatile, and the world was wide! [. . .] Upward and onward!' (pp. 31–2).

The 'bulky volumes of morbid psychology' that Lou Ford turns to for self-diagnosis (p. 27) would not necessarily be our first choice of texts if we were seeking to understand Tom Ripley. Highsmith leaves open the possibility of interpreting his behaviour as schizophrenic: for example, he is able, once he has returned to his identity as Tom Ripley, to free himself from guilt for a murder committed whilst impersonating Dickie. The emphasis, however, is strongly on his typicality, his American versatility and blankness of character. Viewed in this light, his ability to reinvent himself as the occasion demands and to feel as 'free of guilt as his old suitcase' (p. 154) is symptomatic of

---

[21] Roxana Pana-Oltean, ' "The Extravagant Curve of the Globe": Refractions of Europe in Henry James's "An International Episode" and *The Ambassadors*', *Henry James Review* 22/2, 2001: 188.

the widespread tendency to evade feelings of guilt and responsibility. He has the optimistic American belief in fresh starts, and resorts to murder only when it presents itself as a reasonable means of securing his goal or preserving his freedom. His murders are, as Tony Hilfer suggests, 'not the triumph of the id but the evasion of the superego' (1990: 128–9).

Highsmith adroitly secures our complicity, establishing Ripley's appeal not only by his blithe evasion of guilt but by associating him with a higher good, embodied in the cultural richness of Europe. His participation in these sensual and cultural riches is one of the things that most draws readers into the guilty pleasure of sympathizing with him. We do not want to see him trapped by the facts of his crimes. Rather, we find ourselves wanting him to continue enjoying the 'conceptions of the mind' opened to him by his reverse pilgrimage. Highsmith's biographers attest to her obsession with Europe and her conviction that it was here that the true reality and the possibility of imaginative release were to be found. What Europeans had, she believed, was not just a reverence of the intellect and culture but, above all, freedom. 'Expatriates', she wrote in 1953, 'are accused of escaping. They seek, on the contrary.'[22] Like the gangster of the 1930s, the figure of the killer is used in Highsmith's novels to signify 'wants' with which any reader can sympathize, partly the desire for material things but also a reaching out for something more—power in the case of the gangster, a less tangible intellectual and spiritual liberation in the case of Ripley.

Part of what Tom is escaping is the constricting, deadening effect of democratic ordinariness. In this sense, the Ripley series originates as another manifestation of the 1950s obsession with individuality submerged by mass cultural conformity. Richard H. Brodhead, writing of America's Gilded Age, explores the persistent American tendency to locate class markers in the superior culture associated with Italy, and one can clearly see such a conception operating in the way Highsmith constructs her protagonist. Tom above all desires the means and leisure to cultivate aesthetic consciousness. He is placed in his ascendant position by the facility with which he acquires cultural capital—to some extent the objectified state of cultural capital (books

---

[22] Patricia Highsmith, Cahier 16, 11/20/47 and 22, 10/27/53, Swiss Literary Archives, Berne, quoted by Wilson 2003: 154.

especially) but principally embodied capital (personal growth, competency, learning). He is a character who invests a huge amount of time and effort in the learning necessary to cultural ease and confidence. In order to pursue this objective, Tom commits murders that are perhaps most of all to be seen as a means of securing the inherited wealth he lacks (ultimately making himself Dickie's heir). This is a not entirely effortless enterprise, but it is certainly an excellent method of obtaining sufficient wealth without any of the crude pressures of a day job, thus making it possible to take full advantage of the liberating potential of the European frontier and to leave behind him the dismal life that consisted of 'creeping around New York. In and out of subways, standing in some dingy bar on Third Avenue for their entertainment [. . .] how dull it all was compared to the worst little trattoria in Venice' (p. 185).

Julia Kristeva's assertion that all artistic activity depends on some kind of exile and on the existence of a distance from the mundane and the everyday is relevant to the themes of *The Talented Mr Ripley*. Highsmith invests her serial killer protagonist with a powerful creative imagination. The presentation of the criminal as an artist figure is of course a recurrent element in detective fiction (which frequently gives us the criminal genius who contrives intricate crimes in classic detective fiction, committing murders that are a kind of highly wrought poetic conceit[23]). There is more going on here, though, than the mischievous reworking of literary convention. There is generic play, of course, with the (unapprehendable) killer pursued by investigators who might have fared better in earlier traditions of detective fiction, but who are here comically inefficient. In wider terms, however, Tom Ripley, by his association with all that European culture represents, is made capable of carrying more positive meanings. He acts metaphorically as an embodiment of cultural freedom and as a celebration of the transgressive imagination. Tom is clearly endowed with a writer's inventive skills. His narrative art, nourished by his travels in Europe, produces manifold versions of his life, an open-ended process of self-creation, with each event, or imagined event, prompting further elaborations. His imaginative capacity is hinted at from the outset, but whereas in New York it had found outlet only in

[23] David Lehman, *The Perfect Murder*. New York: Free Press, 1989: p. xvii, quoted by Simpson 2000: 73–4.

petty fraud, in Europe it finds a space adequate to its potential. Here Tom has the freedom to invent and to create himself afresh. His stories and the intensity of his imagination are such that he can virtually hear the conversations in his invented pasts and possible futures, whether they are glorious or doomed.

In this context, murder becomes a punishment visited on those who lack imagination. As soon as Dickie is dead, Tom amuses himself by holding imaginary conversations in both English and Italian, as he sets about the 'real annihilation of his past and of himself, Tom Ripley, who was made up of the past and his rebirth as a completely new person' (pp. 92–4). In inhabiting his dead friend's persona, Tom becomes a very much more discerning and interesting version of Dickie than Dickie could ever have become himself. In spite of acquiring some fluency in Italian, Dickie is not (we are led to believe) a character who could have built on this minimal fluency to become a finely discriminating denizen of his adopted country. Dickie's failure to master the subjunctive signifies more fundamental deficiencies, in particular the want of subtlety that is one of Dickie's most recur- rently stressed traits. A central contrast in *The Talented Mr Ripley* is that between the unsubtle and the nuanced understanding of a for- eign space, associated, respectively, with an impoverished and a lively imagination. In spite of his enjoyment of the place, Dickie's 'eye' and 'ear' for Italy remain relatively crude, as exemplified by his paintings of Mongibello: 'They were all wild and hasty and monotonously similar. The combination of terra cotta and electric blue was in nearly every one, terra cotta roofs and mountains and bright electric-blue seas' (p. 49). Indeed, it is in part by convincing us of the vulgar limitations of Dickie's artistic representations of Italy and of his gen- eral lack of any aesthetic standards (note also, for example, the 'dull yards' of his prose (p. 138)) that Highsmith brings us to collude with Tom's decision to eliminate him. Marge, whose 'dull imagination' (p. 200) is even more obviously found wanting by Tom, is character- ized from the first as limited in her command of her own language, let alone of Italian: 'her speech, Tom thought, was abominable, both her choice of words and her pronunciation' (p. 57). Both Dickie and Marge are aspiring artists, painting and writing assiduously, but neither could be said to possess any form of artistic or imaginative powers. Tom spares Marge's life, and her dull imagination indeed turns out to be unexpectedly helpful to him in his relations with the police. But his other victim in *The Talented Mr Ripley* is even less capable than poor Marge of appreciating European culture. Freddy Miles's responses to a foreign environment are missing all of the finer shades, and he appropriately ends by being taken on a grand tour of Rome that he 'could not appreciate at all' (p. 114). Freddie is, of course, dead at the time. We feel certain, however, that he would not, even if alive, have properly appreciated the tour, and his crude philistinism is one of the qualities of character that make him a victim whose loss we do not for a moment mourn. With his carrot-red hair and 'loud sports shirt, an American' (p. 52), he is a character who seems to live in the garish colours in which Dickie paints— unquestionably one of 'the rude' whom the most famous literary serial killer of the last two decades, Thomas Harris's Hannibal Lecter, specially favours with his attentions.

Serial killers, pathologists, and police procedurals

Thomas Harris, *Hannibal* (1999); James Ellroy, *The Black Dahlia* (1987); Patricia Cornwell, *The Last Precinct* (2000)

The term 'serial killer' was coined in the mid-1970s by Robert K. Ressler, who co-founded the FBI's Behavioral Science Unit. Ressler and his colleague John Douglas have in recent years both written books that have helped to popularize their methods of investigating crime scenes and probing the minds of actual serial killers: Ressler's *Whoever Fights Monsters* (1992) and *I Have Lived in the Monster* (1997) and Douglas's *Mindhunter* (1995). The links between both Ressler and Douglas and one of the best-known of all contemporary crime novelists, Thomas Harris, are confirmed by much cross-referencing: in *Silence of the Lambs* the FBI chief, Jack Crawford, is said to be based on Ressler and Douglas; the frontispiece of *Whoever Fights Monsters* reproduces Blake's Red Dragon with an inscription that reads, 'For Bob Ressler with best wishes, Francis Dolarhyde [the serial killer in Harris's *Red Dragon*] and Thomas Harris' (Seltzer 1998: 16). In his own book, *Mindhunter*, Douglas also thinks in terms of the interconnectedness of life and literature:

We began methodically developing the work of the FBI's Behavioral Science Unit, and what later came to be the Investigative Support Unit, in the late 1970s and early 1980s. And though most of the books that dramatize and glorify what we do, such as Tom Harris's memorable *The Silence of the Lambs*, are somewhat fanciful and prone to dramatic license, our antecedents actually do go back to crime fiction more than crime fact. C. August Dupin, the amateur detective hero of Edgar Allan Poe's 1841 classic 'The Murders in the Rue Morgue' [. . .] (Douglas and Olshaker 1995: 19–20)

Whilst working on a murder case in Missouri, Douglas was, he says, referred to by a local paper as the 'FBI's Modern Sherlock Holmes' (1995: 20). Contemporary writers, he goes on to point out, have sometimes created fictions in which Holmes is put on the case of the serial killer who was committing the Whitechapel murders at the time that Doyle was writing the Holmes stories: Jack the Ripper, whose 'case' has also recently been marked as 'closed' by one of the best-selling crime novelists of the 1990s, Patricia Cornwell.

This skein of references back and forth between fiction and reality has become increasingly commonplace in a period when, Mark Seltzer argues, we have seen a kind of 'switchback or looping effect'. Fictional representations interact with professional analysis, and popularized knowledge about the phenomenon shapes the self-conceptions of actual killers, eroding the distinctions between fact and fiction (Seltzer 1998: 15–16). As the older investigative tradition comes together with the post-1970s currency of the idea of the serial killer, we see the emergence of a narrative structure in which Holmesian methods are combined with serial killer fascination, often within narratives that move towards the kind of closure associated with classic detective fiction (Douglas and Olshaker 1995: 20–2). We also, however, see marked signs of tension, pulling the narrative away from a reassuring traditional resolution. Within the now-established police procedural form, the split-level narrative has been much in evidence. In this form of crime novel, part of the narrative is given over to enough minutely detailed investigative technique to have impressed Sherlock Holmes; the other part offers us a disturbingly intimate view of the psychopathology of the serial killer. At their most symbolic, such texts elaborate the myth of the solving rational intellect pitted against the myth of the inhuman monster. As the titles of Ressler's books suggest, even 'factual' discussions of forensic psychology tend to invoke the idea of 'monstrosity', with its gothic intimations of a darkness beyond our comprehension. This tendency is, of course, even more apparent in those contemporary novels that establish their narratives in the borderland between true crime and fictional crime (Haut 1999: 195). Particularly in the hands of Thomas Harris, the serial killer novel develops into a strange hybrid, in which the veri-similar world of the police procedural coexists with an ever more gothic narrative, centring on a mythic figure who bears less and less resemblance to the psychological profiles of known real-life serial killers.

Profilers of actual serial killers, like Ressler and Thomas Shachtman, argue that the 'typical' motivational structure of the serial killer is founded on two basic themes, 'the dominance of a fantasy life and a history of personal abuse' (Simpson 2000: 128; Ressler and Shachtman 1997: 4). Within the serial killer novel, this received wisdom corres-ponds to the gothic tendency to obscure the boundary between 'fact' and 'fiction'. The implied duality stands behind a concept of the figure of the killer as part damaged human being, part descendant of the supernatural and vampiric characters of gothic fiction, some-times, like Francis Dolarhyde, constructing a self-image around a romantic linkage of criminal acts with art and divinity.[24] This pattern is particularly prominent in Harris's most famous creation, Hannibal Lecter, humanized by innumerable small details and by the account in *Hannibal* of his childhood traumas, but at the same time defiantly resistant to the commonplaces of the profiler. Lecter adds to the professional discourse about the typical patterns of the serial killer, but is himself adamantly 'untypical' and unquantifiable. An increas-ingly mythic figure, he is an artist whose Grand Guignol crimes com-bine with an aesthetics of murder so darkly humorous that we find it hard to resist the force of the images produced by Hannibal's satiric art: the elaborate, precisely crafted tableau of the hunter and deer; the scholarly re-creation of Pazzi's death in imitation of his ancestor's demise, supported by a learned discourse on the linkage in art 'since antiquity' of avarice and hanging (Harris [1999] 2000: 356–7, 229–33).

Lecter's gallery of victims is a high art form of one of the defining traits (profilers and crime writers agree) of serial killers, the objecti-fication of the victim. As Dolarhyde reflects, he can bear the screams of

---

[24] This is well discussed in Simpson's chapter (2000: 13–25), 'The Serial Killer Sub-genre and its Conventions'.

his victims 'as a sculptor bears dust from the beaten stone' (Harris [1981] 1993: 96). Like 'John Doe' in David Fincher's *Se7en*, Lecter differs from the run of serial killers in his close attention to the appropriateness of particular fates to individual victims. The more usual pattern, in texts and films as in life, would seem to involve a killer for whom the victim has no independent individual existence. As Joyce Carol Oates's Quentin P. says of his ill-fated efforts to refashion his victims, 'A true ZOMBIE would be mine forever [. . .] His eyes would be open & clear but there would be nothing inside them *seeing* & nothing behind them *thinking*.'[25] Seltzer notes that the 'normal' image would be of the killer's compulsive expulsion of his own interior state in the act of violence he inflicts on the victim—an 'emptying' of himself on to the mutilated body which entails a perception of all victims as essentially the same. The victim is given a 'symbolic value' that requires 'anonymity and abstractness' (Seltzer 1998: 186). For readers of the crime novel, our sense of narrative resolution depends on our gaining knowledge of this compulsive mind: 'Implicating the viewer into the criminal mind-set occupies an ascendant position in the serial killer narrative' (Simpson 2000: 74).

In contrast to the 'normal' killer, the near-mythic serial killer has a destabilizing effect within the genre. Whereas the 'artistic' dimension of the killer can be connected with the murderers of classic detective fiction, the mythic (vampiric, monstrous) dimension moves the genre so far towards its gothic side that the other (rational, ordering) aspects of the genre are undermined. There is, Simpson argues, a shift in 'the true narratological agenda' away from the interpretative enterprise, the puzzle-solving activity of the detective (2000: 76–7), towards the agenda set by the killer, the production of his own narrative inscribed as a text on the body of the victim. The killer's text is one that works to implicate the detective who decodes it (and thereby the reader and the literary critic) in his own crimes and cultural attitudes. Whilst it would be misleading to suggest that earlier representations of the transgressor do not work in this way (Highsmith, in particular, aims for something akin to this effect), the more excessive and the more gothic the narrative, the more unsettling it is to our facile moral assumptions.

The increased component of body horror in contemporary crime

---

[25] Joyce Carol Oates, *Zombie*. New York: Plume Books, 1995: 169.

fiction has brought the genre yet closer into contact with its gothic roots. With the emergence of crime fiction as a separate genre in the late nineteenth–early twentieth century, gothic excess tended to recede in the interests of realism. So, in Thompson's novels, for example, there is an admixture of the surreal and the grotesque, but these tend to be elements belonging to climactic scenes of violent confrontation or self-destruction (the dismemberment that takes place in the final pages of *Savage Night*, or the castration that ends *A Hell of a Woman*). In 1990s crime fiction, on the other hand, one more often encounters a wholly gothic form of serial killer novel, in which body horror is the substance of much of the narrative rather than just the culmination of an action that is spiralling out of control—for example, in Poppy Z. Brite's AIDS-infested horror story *Exquisite Corpse* (1996). Within more mainstream serial killer fiction, the goth-icizing of the crime narrative is generally handled a little more cau-tiously. The novels of Thomas Harris, James Ellroy, and Patricia Cornwell, particularly in the more recent Scarpetta novels, all have marked gothic tendencies, held in check in ways that stop the novels sliding over into horror fiction, but nevertheless sharply differentiat-ing them from more conventional examples of the police procedural.

The pull in the direction of the gothic is especially evident in Harris's *Hannibal*, the latter part of which is actually taken over by the eponymous serial killer and cannibal. The narratives of *Red Dragon* and *Silence of the Lambs* are ultimately contained within the structure of the police procedural, with the FBI enjoying reasonable success in its exercise of institutional investigative power and fulfil-ling its task as guardian of the existing socio-political order. In *Hannibal*, on the other hand, Starling's actual departure from Quan-tico is signalled as a final break, an irrevocable change: 'She would never see Quantico again' (Harris [1999] 2000: 406). From this point on the narrative is dominated by a figure who would seem to repre-sent all that is repressed in a civilized society, symbolizing what Kristeva calls society's underlying causality, 'the social contradictions a given society can provisionally subdue in order to constitute itself as such'.[26] Hannibal embodies the drives and desires that shape but cannot be admitted to consciousness, not only bringing them to the

---

[26] Julia Kristeva, *Revolution in Poetic Language*. New York: Columbia University Press, [1974] 1986: 153, quoted by Plain 2001: 227; and see Simpson 2000: 73.

surface but encouraging others to do so as well: the doubling of profiler and killer, pushed much further in *Hannibal*, becomes an alliance that radically undermines the rationalist assumptions of the police procedural's investigative narrative.

As the Lecter trilogy develops, then, the structure of the police procedural recedes and the standard moral polarities of a conventional detective story are displaced. In the later stages of *Hannibal*, investigative techniques are in fact increasingly identified with the henchmen of a victim who emerges as the novel's true monster, Mason Verger, a literally faceless exploiter, ruling over his 'meat kingdom' (p. 465) and its abattoirs. Mason's 'team' of scientifically equipped underlings hunts at his bidding, armed with a professional array of tools ('Neatly stored behind the seats were a small chain saw, long-handled metal shears, a surgical saw, sharp plastic zip-lock bags, a Black & Decker Work Buddy to hold the doctor's arms still [. . .]' (pp. 218–19)). The chief investigator, using sophisticated methods to track Hannibal across the face of the earth, is now a butcher.

Mason's hunt is a difficult one, given that his prey (though he is in *Hannibal* supplied with an exculpatory human back story) is drawn on so mythic a scale, and endowed not only with intellectual but cultural superiority. It is partly by way of association with European high culture that Hannibal secures his ascendancy. His aristocratic lineage, part Italian and part Lithuanian (his father a Lithuanian count, his mother a 'high-born Italian' (p. 314)), links him with the Mediterranean and the Baltic, with just a hint of the Carpathians in between. He is a timeless, vampiric figure, committing crimes suggestive of comparisons with ancient evil, but also of Renaissance civilization. His ability to seduce others into his way of life is more potent and subtle than that of Dracula. Preferring the civilized amenities of a settled existence (associated, Harris notes, with the territorial vampire as opposed to the wide-ranging cannibal as identified by behavioural science (p. 336)), his most dearly loved habitat is Florence, itself a city that has contained the extremes of civilization and barbarism. Indeed, a recurrent motif is the figuring of Hannibal as homologous with Florence, and our approach, as readers, to him is implicitly compared to the voyeuristic interest of eager if slightly apprehensive tourists.

As Gill Plain observes, Lecter has a contradictory relationship to the symbolic, dedicated to 'civilized values' but at the same time acting to undermine the symbolic order: 'Lecter's whole being is contradictory. He is an outlaw and criminal dedicated to the preservation of the values of "civilized" society' (2001: 239). Harris strongly emphasizes the contradictions, the paradoxical combination of the highest degree of civilization with the most extreme imaginable forms of violence, and in developing this theme stresses the analogies with Florentine history. It is in keeping with the city's violent past that Lecter creates the opening for a new curator (himself) by killing his predecessor, though this is a low-key crime by the standards either of Florentine history or of Lecter's own personal history. Far worse things are contained in 'the rank black oubliettes beneath his memory palace' (pp. 219–21). Lecter's memory palace itself is imagined in terms of the kind of architectural contrasts that our tour guide has pointed out to us in Florence, whilst reminding us that we, too, have dual natures: 'But this we share with the doctor. In the vaults of our hearts and brains, danger waits. All the chambers are not lovely, light and high. There are holes in the floor of the mind, like those in a medieval dungeon floor' (p. 297), and these are spaces, Harris suggests, within which rational investigation is of little use.

Harris's trope of the killer as aesthete seems aimed at generating a series of challenges to our taken-for-granted assumptions about the nature of civilized behaviour, at compelling us towards a double vision. Hannibal's crimes and his accomplishments alike are perceived within the same high-ceilinged, dark-dungeoned cultural space, and the sheer scale of this space is allied with imaginative freedom and with a thematically central contrast between this world and the narrow and repressive world of a man like Krendler. The commodiousness of Italian architecture (rooms of a size that permit full humanity to flourish) has a bearing as well on Lecter's determination to release Clarice Starling from the limitations of her background. He aims to free her from her employment and her role in an oppressively patriarchal society, and from a past in which her life has, metaphorically speaking, been lived in a soul-destroyingly constricted space: 'was Krendler, and every other authority and taboo, empowered to box Starling into what was, in Dr Lecter's view, her little low-ceiling life?' (p. 529). The climactic dinner scene is imaged in terms of spacious mental and physical architecture, with Hannibal promising her that whilst the tastes and smells of dinner 'are housed in parts of the mind that precede pity', its ceremonies and sights are, at the same time, 'playing in the dome of the cortex like miracles illumined on the ceiling of a church' (p. 541).

The idea of an inherently contradictory, violent, but also freedom-conferring cultural space hovers behind all of Hannibal's murders except for the merely expedient (which are presented in passing, like the pragmatic dispatching of the previous curator), most of all behind this climactic cannibal feast. The significance of the scene is underscored by the strong implicit contrast with the feast hungrily anticipated by Mason Verger as his revenge on Lecter—a scene of raw consumption and torture, in which specially bred wild swine, with savage faces and 'great curved tusks' (p. 489), would, if all went to plan, devour their victim in the most horrifically prolonged manner that Mason can arrange. The methods of consumption contrived by Mason and Hannibal are suggestive of the Lévi-Strauss distinction between the raw (crude, imperfect, savage) and the cooked (synonymous with the refined, tasteful, and beneficial). This potently metaphoric binary can be seen in Lecter's own selection of victims for his symbolic murders—generally speaking, men capable of savagery but not of refinement. Lecter's transgressive behaviour is aimed at accomplishing transformations. When he encounters those who have *within them* the capacity for 'refinement', he finds ways of making them aware of their potential (letting, one might say, the inside out); those whom he judges to be beyond redemption, he transforms in other ways, whether into artful tableaux (the deer hunter; the *Commendatore*) or into exquisite meals, both of which bring the (admittedly unwilling) converts *inside*, assimilating them into civilization as Lecter understands it. Barney, the male nurse who developed a wary but devoted attachment to Lecter when he was incarcerated, explains to Clarice his conviction that the doctor would not pursue him: ' "He told me once that, whenever it was 'feasible', he preferred to eat the rude. 'Free-range rude,' he called them." Barney laughed' (p. 102). Rude carries the sense not just of ill manners but of being completely uncultivated and uncultivatable, and Barney's immunity lies in the fact that he is, though 'unlettered', totally committed to his quest to understand and appreciate the 'fresh experience' of high culture. ' "[H]e shared his mind with me," ' Barney says, and Barney's reward is to be there at the end of the novel, engaged in his quest to see every Vermeer in the world (pp. 102, 559).

In the novel's much-discussed resolution, Dr Lecter draws Clarice into his own personal cultured space, giving us, as Gill Plain comments, Cinderella when we had been expecting Bluebeard (2001: 242). Part of the critical resistance to this part of the novel is presumably due to unease about being seduced ourselves by the vividly conjured cultural spaces associated with what is a traditionally dualistic but also, in this form, a profoundly unsettling conception of civilization. The reader, who has come along as a touristic voyeur, may end the novel shocked at having been so insidiously drawn into the visceral delights and horrors of Hannibal's world, and Harris would appear to be very conscious of the fact that his readers will feel uneasy not just about their own acquiescence in this ending but about the fate of Clarice Starling. Has she escaped one repressive patriarchal system only to be taken firmly in hand by yet another very dubious father figure? In a coda that takes Clarice and Hannibal to South America (another place of creative exile), Harris succinctly acknowledges the question his readers will ask. As the tone becomes more affirmative, he includes a slyly punning reminder that we have moved from a detective story to a sexual consummation: 'The relationship has a great deal to do with the penetration of Clarice Starling, which she avidly welcomes and encourages' (p. 561). As our understanding of 'penetration' shifts from the 'penetrating' mind of Clarice-as-detective to the penetrated body of the villain-hero's beloved, we are prompted to weigh the evidence for these two different readings of the end. As we finish reading *Hannibal*, the question that remains is whether Clarice's 'penetration' is a match for Lecter's—whether she will use her new-found capabilities to assert *herself* or whether she is hopelessly ensnared by Lecter's insidious discourse.[27]

Whereas Harris pointedly abandons the framework of the police procedural about two-thirds of the way through *Hannibal*, James Ellroy and Patricia Cornwell stay (geographically and formally) within the investigative structures of the LAPD and, in Cornwell's case, the office of Virginia's Chief Medical Examiner, working with or against

---

[27] An interesting point in Plain 2001: 230 is that when Lecter takes over Clarice, she is not succumbing to 'the phallic power of the symbolic order' but is coming under the sway of a 'superheroic other': in contrast to the sexism and obtuseness of the men of the FBI—the FBI being her 'adopted father' (who thwart and misperceive her) is 'a fascinating symbol of gratified desire', and a mother as well as a surrogate father, 'a force of truth—sometimes kind, sometimes painful—who will facilitate her rebirth after her sacrifice by the FBI.'

the Richmond Police and the FBI. The novels of Ellroy's ambitious LA Quartet, published between 1987 and 1992, are firmly rooted in the history of post-war Los Angeles. He places himself in the traditions of hard-boiled writing and literary noir and thinks of the 1980s and 1990s as an ideal time for his type of fiction because 'Noir (of the '40s and '50s) was a popular form that expressed futility in a time of great boosterism.'[28] Quick to distinguish himself from certain types of crime writing, especially that which is morally centred on a hero of lonely integrity, he sees Chandler as overrated and identifies himself instead with the work of Dashiell Hammett, whose bleak endings, compromised heroes, and sceptical view of American life have strong affinities with Ellroy's own appropriation of noir conventions: 'I think I picked up the Hammett world view [. . .] Increasingly, I have focused on the bad men of history, on the leg-breakers, and that in essence is what the Continental Op was all about [. . .] It's a dark view.'[29] Ellroy moves the deeply flawed character of the protagonist closer to the psychotic, and focuses more closely on the mind of the killer and the body of the victim, both of which bear the marks of a disturbed and violent society and its hidden horrors. Ellroy is contemptuous of crime novels which allow the reader to emerge 'intact and uncompromised' and which reaffirm 'that on some level decency and kindness prevail': 'In my books the ramifications of bad acts are still continuing as the action closes. I want to leave people with a sense of the real horror of life.'[30]

Seeing his novels as encompassing the broad sweep of American history, Ellroy produces books that seem designed to reflect the sheer scale of American experience—an America seen to contain, in Gore Vidal's words, so much of 'the superstition, the bigotry and the madness' that it is 'richer—richer in horrible detail.'[31] His most characteristic method of representing the hidden guilt at the core of the American dream is his elaboration of the psychopathology of criminal acts. Ellroy is preoccupied with psychological breakdown and

---

[28] *San Diego Tribune*, 29/6/1990.

[29] Charles L. P. Silet, 'Mad Dog and Glory: A Conversation with James Ellroy', *Armchair Detective* 28, summer 1995: 240.

[30] Neil Trotter, 'Moonshine, Bullshit, Beebop and Jive.' *Big Issue*, 1–14/4/1994: 30; Simon Westcott, 'The Lowdown on L. A. Law', *Books in the Media*, 14/9/1990: 12.

[31] Ellroy, unpublished interview with Lee Horsley, London, 7/10/1995; Vidal, quoted by Ginny Dougary in the *Times Magazine*, 7/10/1995: 25.

perverse, excessive sexuality, using pop Freudianism to create a vision of social disorder. He chooses as protagonists men who are bound in complex ways to the crimes they investigate. In the first of the novels comprising the LA Quartet, *The Black Dahlia*, which has at its centre the savage murder of a young prostitute (the 'Black Dahlia' of the title) who had ambitions to be a movie star, the protagonist, Bucky Bleichert, is drawn into a tortured relationship with the victim of the crime, and at the same time experiences the total breakdown of all normative relationships. A man who would seem to be an embodiment of tough masculinity (a heavyweight boxer before he became a cop), Bleichert begins the novel as a 'story book hero' who is part of a 'fairy tale family', but one that turns out to have brutality and silence at the heart of its relationships (Ellroy [1987] 1993: 70–9). As the ugly secrets emerge, he sees himself reduced to 'Stooge. Bumfuck detective too blind to clear the case he was a homicide accessory to', 'a whore with a badge' (pp. 277, 313–14). He moves into a motel room with the Dahlia investigation, no longer able to separate his own life from that of a prostitute 'dumbstruck with cheap dreams, vivisected in a weedy vacant lot', knowing that he 'couldn't go any lower' (pp. 310–14).

Traumatized masculinity is not, however, confined to Bucky in his sordid motel room but is almost the defining trait of post-war Los Angeles. In *The Black Dahlia*, as in the other 'disintegrative narratives' (Cohen 1997: 170) that make up the LA Quartet, as mysteries are resolved, suppressed relationships and unrecognized blood ties are revealed, the family structure is clarified, and we locate the deeper sources of depravity in the patriarchal power structure. The denouement of *The Black Dahlia* is connected to the revelation of the full extent of the responsibility borne by a powerful father figure—a figure equivalent to the gothic villain in his duplicity and in the extent of the damage he inflicts. There are instances, too, of female depravity, but the women themselves tend to emerge as the victims of a corrupt patriarchy. Madeleine Sprague takes on the role of the *femme fatale* and her mother, Ramona, the role of 'torturer murderess', but both have been irrevocably shaped by their relationship with Emmett Sprague. The 'brass girl', his 'ersatz daughter', has been nurtured by the semi-incestuous attentions of her 'robber baron Daddy' (p. 210); her mother has been psychologically destroyed by the humiliations of an intolerable marriage to the ruthless, domineering real estate tycoon (p. 367). As throughout the Quartet, the most disturbing criminal impulses are those generated within a regime of masculine political and economic power, with the course of events determined by powerful figures of male authority whose sins are appallingly visited on their children. The fate of the heirs of the 'strong men' of the Quartet (Emmett Sprague, Reynolds Loftis, Raymond Dieterling, J. C. Kafesjian, and Phillip Herrick) illuminates the failures of the whole legitimizing framework of masculine authority. In deviant families, we repeatedly see the impairment of masculine identity, and potent, controlled masculinity sustained only by repression and deceit.[32]

In *The Black Dahlia*, as elsewhere in the Quartet, the male romance is not just the source of extreme physical violence but also inflicts the kind of psychological harm that ensures a continuity of shameful responsibility and destructiveness, with damaged children wreaking revenge, seeking atonement. Whilst retaining an investigative structure, Ellroy modifies it in ways that give considerable space to the counter-narratives of the transgressors. In contemplating twentieth-century history, Ellroy says, he has always had 'a persistent sense of individual stories trying to get out',[33] and the motif of counter-narratives is important to all four novels of the LA Quartet. The dominance of Hollywood story-telling spurs the disaffected to narrative acts of their own—for example, Ramona Sprague's 'little pageants', in which, using the neighbour's children as extras, she re-enacts and films 'episodes out of Mr. Sprague's past that he would rather forget', speaking 'obliquely of his greed and cowardice' (pp. 163 and 368). But we also see the psychopath 'writing in blood' the story of his inner torments. As in the novels of Patricia Cornwell, we see the assault on the male ethos of the thriller world through the violation of bodily boundaries, through forms of violence and mutilation that are (as a psychopath in one of the other Quartet novels says) 'like symbolism' (Ellroy [1992] 1993: 328). The LA Quartet presents a succession of such symbolic disfigurements and mutilations. What one critic calls Ellroy's tendency to 'hack cartoonery, horror comic stuff' is there for its obvious shock value, but this 'symbolic destruction' also functions as the excessive language of those dispossessed by the

---

[32] The most culpable figures in Ellroy's novels are all in some sense 'city fathers'— the constructors of cities, businessmen, Hollywood icons, and institutionalized myth-makers who have created the actual and the metaphoric landscape of post-war Los Angeles.

[33] Ellroy, interview with Horsley.

masculine power structure—as stories of earlier traumas (Williams [1991] 1993: 89; Ellroy [1992] 1993: 228). The masculine values conventionally associated with dominance can be seen as a kind of 'defensive solidification': strength is associated with firmly defined boundaries, both bodily and social. Opposition to this confidently constituted façade can be signified by fragmentation, the violation of boundaries and the assault on bodily integrity. The horror of Ellroy's narratives repeatedly embodies (in a rather literal sense) the protest of those silenced by the dominant order. In *The Black Dahlia* this is given a literary gloss by a Victor Hugo novel found at the scene of the crime—*The Man Who Laughs*, in which a group of fifteenth- and sixteenth-century Spaniards kidnap and torture children, mutilating them and then selling them to the aristocracy to be used as court jesters (p. 363). For the murderer, as in fact for the many others in the city who come forward to confess to the crime, the macabre death of the Black Dahlia is a declaration of personal suffering: 'The longer I listened the more they talked about themselves, interweaving their sad tales with the story of the Black Dahlia' (p. 147). The body of the Black Dahlia is at the symbolic centre of the novel and the atrocities inflicted on it are inscriptions of the rage generated by the cruelties and humiliations inflicted within a family characterized by 'gothic hyper-dysfunctionality'. A 'text' created by the novel's main counter-narrative, the Dahlia's dismembered corpse resists all tidy and reassuring interpretations: it is a body that 'palpably underscores the resistance of postwar urban history's counter-images to narrative resolution' (Cohen 1997: 184–5).

The traumatized body communicating what has been inflicted on it is even more central and more disturbing in Patricia Cornwell's long-running, hugely popular Kay Scarpetta series (1990–), the best-known of the forensic pathology narratives that have flourished during the last decade.[34] In contrast to the kind of police procedural novel that gives centre-stage to the psyche of the serial killer, the

---

[34] There is a growing number of other novels that confront readers with the 'reality' of the dead body. In some cases (e.g. Kathy Reichs and Priscilla Masters) writers use, as Cornwell does, the figure of the forensic pathologist; in other instances, such as Nicci French's *The Red Room* (2001) and Jan Burke's *Bones* (1999), the female protagonist's reading of the crime is determined by alternative forms of firsthand access to the 'underworld' of the grave or autopsy room, such as that of the crime journalist or criminal psychologist.

forensic pathology novel aims instead to evoke the 'appalling human messiness' of actual crime (Cornwell [2000] 2001: 60–2) through a perspective nearer to that of the victim. By providing readers not only with a body of experts but with an expert on the body, the novelist allows them to listen to the voices of the dead. Scarpetta, as Chief Medical Examiner, sharply distinguishes herself from the conventional homicide investigator. She claims that what her role gives her is privileged access to 'the real' as it is embodied in the torn and open body: ' "You don't put your hands inside their ruined bodies and touch and measure their wounds", I said. ' "You don't hear them speak after they're dead . . . You spend more time with the killers than with those they ripped from life." ' (Cornwell [1998] 2000: 14). Although she admits a degree of unfairness in this tirade against Benton Wesley, there is some force (felt throughout the Scarpetta series) behind her assertion that, whereas she immerses herself in the horrifying reality of the victim's death, an investigator like Wesley need only look at 'clean case files and glossy photos and cold crime scenes' (Cornwell [1998] 2000: 14). By using a forensic pathologist as her protagonist, Cornwell makes possible a more 'corporeally sophisticated' reading of the corpse-as-text, using the body as the evidentiary basis for readings of the crime (Plain 2001: 31–2). But more than that, she creates a central intelligence which is empowered to speak directly about the body as witness to truth. Scarpetta's unmediated access to the traumatized corpse endows her with the almost unchallengeable authority that comes with intimate knowledge of the unbearable and unthinkable; she gives voice to what would otherwise remain simply 'unspeakable'.[35]

This form of investigative empowerment, however, can also be a source of danger to the investigator's own sense of self. It becomes apparent as the Scarpetta series develops how readily texts cross generic boundaries—and again, this is a move from investigative crime fiction into the more ambiguous territory of the gothic. Cornwell is often praised for her 'nail-biting realism', the 'accuracy and expertise' that she herself attributes to working for the Virginia Chief Medical Examiner's Office. The dark flavour of her novels emerges from the fact that these descriptive powers are used to catalogue so unremittingly the details of the autopsy room, producing the text's sense of

[35] See Foster 1996: 166–8: 'for one cannot challenge the trauma of another'.

obsessive and intimate contact with the unspeakable 'real'. While the gruesome *objets d'art* left behind by each killer cannot talk, they are inherently denotative in ways that no living human is. The dead body inspires in the living protagonist nightmares of self-division, of gothic doubling and boundaries violated.

The role of autopsy historically explains something of why this is so. As Jonathan Sawday suggests, the role of those involved in dissection and anatomization has always been a complex and contradictory one:

Matrices of discomfort, pain, death, and social prohibition separate us, in the twentieth century, from our bodily interiors. A paradox becomes apparent. Modern surgical techniques, the skilled technology of penetrative surgery allied to the apparatus of reproduction on film and photographic plate, have made it possible for us to gain an unparalleled access to scenes of our own interiority. But in similar measure, the taboo still exists and we violate it at some risk. (Sawday 1996: 15)

The intimate contact the forensic pathologist has with the corpse means that her 'othering' can even be more extreme that that of the detective/profiler, carrying her beyond the bounds of normal society towards the taboo-violation and voyeuristic display that have, historically, brought infamy to the transgressive probing of the human interior. Within crime fiction, this is a crossing over into shadowy territory, a land of the dead that has the potential for undermining both identity and resolution. The sheer violence of autoptic procedures link them with the criminal act—the dismemberment a further, brutal reduction of the body into constituent parts. In the recent novels of Patricia Cornwell—*Unnatural Exposure* (1997), *Point of Origin* (1998), *Black Notice* (1999), and *The Last Precinct* (2000)—the effort to construct identity from bodily fragments has occupied an increasing amount of narrative space, and the relationship between the pathologist and the corpse sometimes comes to be amongst the most intimate, even maternal, of encounters. By applying medical science to the description of the body, the forensic pathologist in a sense produces the body, both as a specific human being and as an embodiment of larger cultural anxieties. Engaged in reconstructing the victim's suffering and identity, the pathologist must (for the narrative to move towards closure) bring the abject back within the symbolic order. The resolution of the crime novel most often makes instrumental and admonitory use of its grim material, evoking disgust with the crime committed, registering breakdowns of order which might be remediable—that require action, if only condemnation. To this end, the forensic pathologist has in effect to reconstitute a narrative by reassembling the fragmented body parts. The task involves recontaining the horror, reconstructing the abject body, negotiating amongst different possible scriptings of the victim's fate, reincorporating the body within a narrative structure that will rescue it from abjection. The work of the forensic pathologist (like that of the anatomist historically) can be presented as 'a reinscription of order', a stay against the chaos and misrule that brought the body to the autopsy table. The pathologist is constantly having to negotiate the border between the unspeakable corpse and that which is articulable. The confrontation with decomposition must be followed by an act of composition: the pathologist is charged with bringing the narrative back from the horror of non-being and non-meaning to stability and reasonable form.[36]

In a novel like *The Last Precinct*, this restorative movement, the pathologist's reinscription of order, is fraught with difficulty. Cornwell darkens the macabre atmosphere of the autopsy room, and builds more on the taboo nature of anatomical investigation, sliding towards nightmarish images of violating the deeply rooted prohibition against looking into our own bodies. She focuses increasingly on Scarpetta's visions of self-dissection, the repeated intrusions into her 'inner space', the extremity of her knowledge, and the constant sense that her work makes her a transgressor, a violator of nature. Critical discussion of the role of Scarpetta conventionally notes the balance in the Cornwell novels between the prototypically male activity of gathering information and the more 'feminine' recognition of the limitations of objective, unemotional knowledge. What is more apparent here, however, is the extent to which the pull in the direction of gothic excess destabilizes Scarpetta's role. With female subjectivity there goes a heightening of visual and auditory senses, touch, and smell, intensifying the experience of immersion in a realm of fragmentation and dissolution. Scarpetta's very sensitivity threatens to disable her in her role as a restorer of lost wholeness and as a defender of an ostensibly liberal, enlightened agenda.

[36] See Sawday 1996: 82–3; and Plain 2001: 34, 42–3. The restorative, therapeutic function of the pathologist requires, by the end of the narrative, the transformation of the corpse into a 'grievable' body, the rescue of the corpse from the site of abjection.

As has been apparent so far in crime fiction generally, generic mutations (and our categorization of texts) depend very much on the ways in which characters shift between the roles of victim, murderer, and investigator—the traditional and fixed character triangle of classic detective fiction. Cornwell's protagonist, an investigator who is perceived by others, and often perceives herself, in the roles of intended victim and actual or potential malefactor, suffers from uncertainties that interfere with the main element in her role, her ability to read bodies. Her difficulties do not simply arise because *public* conflict leads to the (standard) fears of the loss of an official position but because private immersion in trauma and Scarpetta's encounters with unreadable interiors (including her own) ultimately destabilize her own identity. In *The Last Precinct* Scarpetta's own sense of self and motivation are being broken down during the course of the narrative. Her friend Anna, furthering the dissection of Scarpetta by probing her psychoanalytically, asks, ' "What about homicide? [. . .] Wrong? Immoral? Is it always wrong to kill? You have killed [. . .] You killed Carrie's partner and then she killed yours. A connection, perhaps?" ' Scarpetta's response—' "Because I killed him, he will forever be part of me" ' (pp. 114–15)—is one of the central themes of *The Last Precinct*, a dissolution of the boundaries between investigators, killers, and victims that is again and again picked up in the metaphoric structure of the novel. Scarpetta herself, as the narrative progresses, is 'othered' by the community, and her response to this ostracism is repeatedly conveyed in images of internal invasion. Even Marino's dark jokes—' "It's just a damn good thing people are dead when you do shit like this to them" ' (p. 311)— reinforce the confusion of boundaries that has its most disturbing image in the autopsy room itself.

The further stage of this dissolution of identities is to be seen in the way that Scarpetta herself is metaphorically put on the autopsy table. This is much more than the conventional move of casting the protagonist as the next possible victim. The familiar narrative pattern which has a female investigator doubling as retributive agent and eroticized victim of male violence (Plain 2001: 224–5) here becomes an intense inner struggle, with a more radical permeability of roles. For all of Scarpetta's efforts to stay within the confines of her 'clinical, fact-only' lawyer's and physician's mind, she increasingly gives way to a tendency to see herself in the place of the victim, her interior self exposed and open to inspection by hostile eyes. This tendency is greatly exacerbated by the physical and psychic wounds that Scarpetta acquires. In one of Cornwell's earlier novels, *The Body Farm* (1994), Cornwell represents Scarpetta as attending to her own wounds in looking at the victim: Scarpetta's business of interpreting wounds can readily be seen to be part of a 'feminine' dimension that includes a kind of co-victimization (Vanacker 1997: 76). Cornwell also, however, uses Scarpetta's role as a forensic pathologist to develop this theme considerably beyond its use in conventional crime fiction. Increasingly in the later books of the series she elaborates the theme in relation to one of the most deep-seated taboos to be found in anatomical investigation, the prohibition against looking into our *own* bodies (Sawday 1996: 7–8). This impossible self-inspection emerges as a central metaphor in the later Scarpetta novels, both in nightmarish imaginings of herself on an autopsy table and in the actual events of plots that subject her to the trauma of looking into the deaths of the men she loved, Mark James and Benton Wesley. These appalling deaths, which involve the reduction of both men to the extreme of abjection—Mark in a bomb blast, Benton by means of horrific torture and fire—leave Scarpetta with two corpses that she can neither inspect nor interpret, either literally (in autopsy) or psychologically, by confronting the full knowledge of their deaths.

The more terrible truth, however, is that these are, for Scarpetta, bodies that are unreadable and that cannot be given meaning. They remain repressed because she cannot bring them within the compass of her interpretative skills. She must short-circuit her process of knowing Benton's death, which will remain illegible to her because she has to stop her own ability to imagine what his body will be like in an autopsy room with which she is all too familiar. The personal loss of Benton for Scarpetta means that she is perceived as on the run from pain, in hiding from herself. In *The Last Precinct* Anna asks Scarpetta how she would have felt if she had been able to watch on film the murder of Bray—or of Benton: if she used her imagination as she has done before professionally, she could ' "reconstruct in detail the last minutes of Diane Bray's life [. . .] if you went through that looking glass [. . .] where might it end? [. . .] Ah. Maybe it would not end, and you would be forced to watch the footage of Benton's murder" ' (78–9).

The Last Precinct is a novel that begins by unravelling the ending of the previous Scarpetta book, *Black Notice*, and the sense of not knowing 'where things will end' is strong in both of these novels. As Scarpetta's personal and professional life come increasingly under scrutiny, the narrative turns progressively more inward, towards her own interior, imaged both in her house and her body. Berger, with 'the sharp edge of a prosecutor', drives home the comparisons: ' "I'm sure your patients wouldn't enjoy being naked on your table and under your knife, to have their pockets and orifices explored, if they knew [. . .] you aren't going to like my probing" ' (p. 259). One of the novel's most persistent images is of Scarpetta's own body inspected and violated. At the very beginning, she presents her inability to subject herself to 'anatomically correct images of [her] own mauled dead body' (p. 2), and she is preoccupied with thoughts of resistance to the image that Chandonne tried to ' "project onto me" '. Even had he succeeded in killing her, she reflects, ' "I would just be dead. Not changed [. . .] Just dead" ' (p. 31). But the state of her potential 'deadness' and its possible meaning resurfaces throughout the narrative. Her life, Anna tells her, ' "reads like one of your more complicated death certificates" ' (p. 44); she feels ' "as dehumanized as [her] dead patients" ' (p. 76). Thinking back to Bray's murder, Scarpetta reflects that to see someone dead is to see them 'completely degraded' (p. 157), and Scarpetta cannot shake the sense that she herself is inescapably trapped by this kind of degradation, 'the dismantling, the humiliation of me for all the world to see' (p. 262).

This, then, is a novel in which both the conventional investigative structure and the protagonist's own sense of identity and agency are eroded by the gothicizing of the narrative, most importantly by the 'matrices of discomfort, pain, death, and social prohibition' that accompany the violation of 'our bodily interiors' (Sawday 1996: 15). The figure of the forensic pathologist is empowered by her access to torn, opened bodies and the realities they reveal, but this access only comes at a price. Towards the end of *The Last Precinct*, Scarpetta has what she describes as ' "an out-of-body experience, looking down on myself after something terrible and final has happened . . . I am dead like other people whose brown paper bags end up in that evidence room" ' (pp. 436–7). The sense of a protagonist who has not quite returned from the realm of the dead remains overwhelmingly dark, in a novel whose very title suggests death: 'The Last Precinct was death.' The novel does, of course, have a solving conclusion, but by no means all questions are reassuringly answered: the 'Y' of the forensic pathologist's incision is no longer followed by the kind of conventional closure in which the 'uncontainable excess' of bodily interiors can simply be recontained at the end of the autoptic investigation.

4

Crime Fiction as Socio-political Critique

EVAN HUNTER argues that crime fiction is a genre 'wide enough not to be subverted if you want to make social comments'; it is, James Ellroy maintains, 'the perfect vehicle' for social and political criticism.[1] The remainder of this study will focus on writers who, like Ellroy and Hunter, see detective and crime fiction as effective instruments of socio-political critique, using the genre to address issues of class, race and gender, to expose corruption, and to explore the nature of prejudice. There are always elements of 'subversion' involved in using crime fiction to put forward an oppositional socio-political agenda. Several of the writers included in this study (particularly those discussed in Chapters 5 and 6) have seen themselves as adapting the genre in subversive ways, defining the tradition that preceded them as antithetical to their own ideological position—as conservative, say, or patriarchal or racist, or as fundamentally unconcerned with the state of contemporary society. Hunter's point, however, is a legitimate one. The genre itself is neither inherently conservative nor radical: rather, it is a form that can be co-opted for a variety of purposes. There has always been within it a capacity for socio-political comment, and using it in this way is facilitated by the very nature of crime fiction. Although particular forms of protest are likely to entail the overturning of some earlier form of detective or crime fiction, the

---

[1] Ellroy, interviewed by Charles L. P. Silet, 'Mad Dog and Glory: A Conversation with James Ellroy', *Armchair Detective* 28, summer 1995: 243.

genre itself contains characteristics that lend themselves to political and oppositional purposes.

To put this in another way, crime and detective fiction can readily be combined with the transformative mode of satire. For a start, both obviously deal with *crimes*, with the 'evils' of contemporary society— the transgressions of the 'other' who threatens established values, perhaps, but also the corruption and misconduct of establishment figures themselves and the injustices of the system they serve. A number of the texts discussed in the preceding chapters could equally well have been included here, particularly those that belong to the traditions of hard-boiled detection and literary noir. Amongst those with a strong emphasis on contemporary social and political realities are Jim Thompson's excoriating satire of small-town America, Ellroy's sweeping indictments of unchecked ambition and the abuses of power in mid-twentieth-century urban and national life, Charles Willeford's exposure of the brutal treatment and exploitation of marginalized groups of people, Ed McBain's/Evan Hunter's representation of the assumptions about gender embedded in institutional politics, and James Sallis's exploration of the sources of his black protagonist's anger and his struggle to attain self-respect. In the present chapter, the aim is to look more formally at this aspect of crime fiction, analysing a range of texts with a well-defined critical and satiric purpose, grouping together texts with common themes to clarify some of the ways in which crime writing as a genre lends itself to a strong socio-political agenda. Since Chapters 5 and 6 focus on issues of race and gender, the intention in this section is to bring to the fore other issues that have been prominent in crime writing from the late 1920s on: class prejudice and exploitation, commercial greed and the plundering of the environment, consumerism and the politics of economic self-interest.

Satirists write to lash the crimes and vices of their own age, and just as their agendas alter with the times so do those of the socially or politically alert crime writers. The nature of the crimes, the forces impinging on the protagonist and the injustices and prejudices underlying the narrative all change markedly from decade to decade. Having come to maturity during the years of the Depression, American tough guy writing had from the outset a marked preoccupation with political corruption and economic exploitation. As we have seen, the lives of hard-boiled characters are shaped by a succession of socio-political determinants, and corrupt alliances between politicians and big business are seen as dominating urban life. These are themes that run through early twentieth-century crime writing, but in some novels they emerge with unusual force. The examples included here are Dashiell Hammett's *Red Harvest* (1929), Horace McCoy's *They Shoot Horses, Don't They?* (1935), and David Goodis's *The Blonde on the Street Corner* (1954), all three of which are texts bent so emphatically to their purpose that the generic structure is quite radically reshaped.

The post-war years were, of course, a time of prosperity, bringing an expanding economy and the augmentation of American military and economic power. Unprecedented affluence was beginning to make it seem that the Depression had been a historical aberration (Bradbury and Temperley [1981] 1998: 262). In crime writing, what surfaces most often in this period is a preoccupation with the inability or refusal to conform to conventional expectations. The characteristic scenes of crime fiction are as often the claustrophobic small town as the big city—the small town, like the city, acting as a microcosm of American society, within which, at the mid-century, we see crystallized the pressures to impose conformity and to sweep aside impediments to the creation of a buoyantly commercial American system. Liberal critics of the time often focused on the ways in which American society hunted out and marginalized dissent. There was a proliferation of plots centring on the suppression of difference. Sometimes these were directly linked to the fears generated by McCarthyism, but they also treated many other forms of stereotyping, moral platitudes, social and racial prejudice, and hostility to deviance. Jim Thompson's novels are particularly associated with the satiric dissection of the closed community, but numerous other writers of the time, amongst whom John D. MacDonald is probably the best known, directed their attention to similar themes. We will look in this chapter at the way in which MacDonald, at the beginning of the 1960s, merged the critique of conformity with an extended diatribe against the ecological destruction being inflicted on Florida by the developers. This is a line of attack picked up again in the 1990s crime novels of Carl Hiaasen, who sees MacDonald as one of his own inspirations. Recruited to write an appreciation of MacDonald for the reissue of the Travis McGee novels, Hiaasen told the publisher that it was in reading MacDonald's work that he realized the possibility of using crime fiction to write about serious subjects.

Neither economic injustice nor social exclusion and victimization have disappeared from view in contemporary crime writing, but a preoccupation with consumerism and commercialization has come increasingly to the fore, particularly in crime novels that take issue with the public and private morality of Reaganite America and Thatcherite Britain. The protagonists of contemporary crime novels, rather than being lured into a dangerous demi-monde, find themselves endangered by a seductive commodity culture and a society of spectacle, in which complicity and assimilation are major sources of anxiety. These shifts are particularly evident in literary noir, which is one of the most inherently critical forms of crime writing and is also one of the variants most likely to slip its generic moorings, crossing over into mainstream fiction.

Whatever the shifts in the nature of the critique, one can see writers adapting the basic elements of detective and crime fiction in ways that invest them with wider meaning. This is a process that several writers and critics have tried to illuminate by considering the relationship between the various sub-genres of crime fiction and the traditional literary genres. The generic affinities of detective fiction in particular have been much debated, with classifications depending on which aspects of the sub-genre were emphasized—whether crime and punishment, the quest for truth, or the exposure of the sordid realities underlying social pretence. The diversity of detective fiction itself accounts for much of the disagreement. Ross Macdonald, for example, stressed its connections with tragedy;[2] W. H. Auden (in 'The Guilty Vicarage'), drawing on comments that Edmund Wilson made, also classified the structure of the detective novel as tragic, its effect as cathartic. G. K. Chesterton, in his 'Defence of Detective Stories', suggested that it was essentially romance. George Grella, on the other hand, argued that in the case of classic detective fiction the most important links were to be seen with comedy, particularly with comedy of manners; but that with the shift to hard-boiled, what we essentially see is a generic relationship to romance, with the emphasis on

---

[2] Michael D. Sharp, 'Plotting Chandler's Demise: Ross Macdonald and the Neo-Aristotelian Detective Novel', *Studies in the Novel*, 22/9/2003, online at www.highbeam.com.

the male quest.[3] Alternatively, and of more relevance here, detective fiction can be analysed in relation to the structure and the techniques of satire. One can argue that some of the stock elements of satire are visible in detective fiction from the outset just in the conventional triangle of characters—the investigator whose task it is to reveal corruption; the transgressor who embodies highly recognizable social and moral flaws; the victim whose unsuspecting innocence, like that of the satiric naïf, functions to reveal the treachery of those around them. In response to Grella's analysis, Rick Eden questions whether there is in fact such a marked switch to be observed as we move from classic detective fiction to hard-boiled: 'What engages us is the satiric action of the detective exposing the real, sordid nature of the meretricious society in which the murder occurred' (Eden 1983: 279). Eden's aim is to bring out the continuities between classic detective fiction and hard-boiled, and as our analysis so far has suggested it is right to question the conventional compartmentalization. Drawing on Northrop Frye's *Anatomy of Criticism* (1957), Eden stresses the difficulty of distinguishing between an ironic comedy and a comic satire. Comedy might be said to begin where satire ends, with a sudden plot twist bringing a shift in tone, and enhancing rather than diminishing our view of the 'redeemed' society represented. Comic satire, on the other hand, humorously reveals the deceptions and usurpations of impostors, but this state of affairs is not transformed. The flawed society remains basically the same. In the latter, the satiric 'hero' is either himself ironized or is less effective than his comic counterpart, accounting, as Frye suggests, for the fact that in satire we see the disappearance of the heroic. Further extending the ideas contained in Frye's analysis, Eden posits that the difference between classic detective fiction and hard-boiled detective fiction is actually that between Horatian and Juvenalian satire. Hard-boiled fiction has moved towards Juvenalian satire, becoming more violent, naturalistic, and urban, but there is nevertheless a considerable amount of overlap between the two forms, and the associated binaries (rural/urban, English/American, upper class/lower class, intellectual/physical) should not be overemphasized. There are, however, some key differ-

---

[3] George Grella, 'Murder and Manners: The Formal Detective Novel', *Novel*, 4, 1970: 30–48; Eden 1983: 279–81. See also Hanna Charney, *The Detective Novel of Manners*. London: Associated University Press, 1981.

ences, most importantly that what Frye calls the 'alazonic society' (the society of impostors) is larger and more threatening in hard-boiled fiction, and the satire is correspondingly darker, the tone less amicable, the irony more strongly marked (Eden 1983: 291–2).

In Chapters 5 and 6 we will examine in detail the contemporary politicization of detective fiction, the oppositional and satiric potential of which has been most strikingly exploited by the growing number of black and female writers who have made polemical use of the form. In this chapter, however, the texts discussed belong to the sub-genre of crime rather than detective fiction: although Hammett's *Red Harvest* has the Continental Op as its detective-protagonist, it can in fact be read (see McCann 2000: 78) as a dismantling of the detective story, since the original murder case is solved less than half-way through the novel, before the bloodbath in which the Op himself goes on a killing spree. In the other texts discussed, though some contain characters analogous to the detective, such figures are implicated in the crimes they investigate and lack agency, and the narratives created are most closely allied to the transgressor-centred world of crime fiction. Within the less predictably structured, more open-ended form of the crime novel, any partisan agenda is likely to tend towards excoriation, disruption, and provocation rather than towards resolution and the articulation of positive norms.

In looking at critiques of this kind, one of the more useful frameworks is Alvin Kernan's mid-century analysis of the dynamic of satiric exposure, *The Cankered Muse* (1959), which pays particular attention to the scene of satire. As was apparent in our discussion of hard-boiled fiction, the emphasis on milieu was crucial in defining the American departure from classic detective fiction. The 'world gone wrong' through which the private eye moves has obvious affinities with the most characteristic scenes of satire, and when the protective presence of the private eye is withdrawn the discordances of the scene itself dominate the text. The satiric scene, in Kernan's analysis, tends to be sordid, disorderly, grotesque, and crowded, with characters represented, indeed often caricatured, as depraved, malicious, villainous, and greedy. The 'sheer dirty weight' of their possessions can be overwhelming: 'in the satirist's vision of the world decency is forever in a precarious position near the edge of extinction', and the satirist underscores the destructive power of vice (Kernan [1959] 1971: 254). Even at the more 'realistic' end of the satiric spectrum,

there is a strong pull towards the symbolic mode. All of these characteristics can be observed as well in the more satiric forms of crime
fiction. These give readers a solid sense of a specific scene represented
in a harshly realistic way, but also use the selection of detail to establish the metaphoric significance of the scene, shifting the narrative
towards the fantastic and the symbolic. The symbolic force of a crime
novel can be generated, for example, by incorporating the details of a
particular milieu into surreal descriptions of threatening and oppressive forms of entrapment, or by building out of them what is cumulatively a hellish landscape in which brutality, destruction, and
violence prevail. This is a process that is very evident, as we will see, in
such novels as Hammett's *Red Harvest*, Hiaasen's *Stormy Weather*,
and Ellis's *American Psycho*. As David Madden argues in *Tough Guy
Writers of the Thirties*, the coupling of abrasive realism and satiric
intensification is a hallmark of tough guy writing, creating 'the
nightmare version of the American Dream' (Madden 1968: pp. xxv–
xxvi), and this combination, carried into crime writing outside the
hard-boiled tradition, continues to be a powerful resource in the
contemporary crime writing of both Britain and America.

In contrast to the 'over-plottedness' and the neat conclusions of
classic detective fiction, crime fiction can often be said to 'go
nowhere', and here again Kernan's description of the pattern of
action in satire can be applied to the dark world of crime fiction—in
particular to the literary noir examined in this chapter:

If we take plot to mean, as it ordinarily does, 'what happens,' or to put it in a
more useful way, a series of events which constitute a change, then the most
striking quality of satire is the absence of plot. We seem at the conclusion of
satire to be always at very nearly the same point where we began. The scenery
and the faces may have changed outwardly, but fundamentally we are looking
at the same world. [. . .] Whatever movement there is, is not plot in the true
sense of change but mere intensification of the unpleasant situation with
which satire opens. (Kernan [1959] 1971: 271–2)

The movement within the plot of the noir crime novel often has
the circular effect of patterns repeated over and over. Looking at
novels that focus on America during the Depression in the section
that follows, we will see the image of movement without progress:
the piling up of dead bodies in *Red Harvest*; the ceaselessly moving
marathon dancers in *They Shoot Horses Don't They?* These are people
caught up in the capitalist dream, endlessly, desperately going

through the motions of trying to attain an end that always proves illusory. The existence of a strong expected pattern also, of course, makes possible satiric reversal: in *The Blonde on the Street Corner*, Goodis exploits the reader's anticipation of violent action by presenting a scene emptied of active people. Our expectation of some dramatic event lingers on until an ending in which we finally realize that the 'closure' Goodis provides lies simply in the fact that these are lives that have been brought to a complete halt.

Despairing of the Depression

Dashiell Hammett, *Red Harvest* (1929); Horace McCoy, *They Shoot Horses, Don't They?* (1935); David Goodis, *The Blonde on the Street Corner* (1954)

Hammett, McCoy, and Goodis all provide descriptions of scene and circumstance calculated to persuade readers that they are encountering a brutally realistic picture of contemporary society. Though each creates, with nightmarish intensity, symbolic patterns of action that take on the generalizing force of a satiric vision, this vision, in the work of all three writers, is firmly rooted in American political and economic life of the inter-war years. The stock market crash of 1929 and the Great Depression were, Madden argues, the forcing house of the hard-boiled hero: 'An unusually tough era turns out the hard-boiled hero. A traumatic wrench like the Depression, its evils and despair touching all facets of human society, causes a violent reaction in these men as they find that they lay down in the great American dream-bed in the Twenties only to wake up screaming in the nightmare of the Thirties.' The hard-boiled hero reacts 'in kind' to the violent world he finds himself in, responding 'objectively to a world that treats him like an object. "Not reason," says Leslie Fiedler in *Love and Death in the American Novel* (1960), "but only counter-violence can defeat decadence and corruption" [. . .] In his actions more crucially than in his attitudes, he takes revenge on the forces that shaped him; however, they usually defeat him' (Madden 1968: pp. xvii–xviii). We have seen these qualities in hard-boiled fiction generally, much of which acts as socio-political critique. In some novels, however, we see the critique pushed further, as in the three essentially left-wing crime novels discussed in this section, in all of which the image of the tough protagonist is invoked but undercut. In Hammett's *Red Harvest*, the Continental Op could be said to embody hard-boiled agency in an exaggerated form. The elements that Madden emphasizes are central: the appropriation of violent means, the reaction against being treated like an object, and the taking of revenge on a corrupt society. But the Op's actions are so extreme and so ultimately fruitless that the reader must question this form of resistance. In the novels of McCoy and Goodis, these purposeful hard-boiled energies have disappeared almost entirely, but there are repeated reminders of a form that would conventionally bring such qualities to the fore, and we are therefore aware throughout of their absence.

Dashiell Hammett's *Red Harvest*, first called *The Cleansing of Poisonville*, was serialized in *Black Mask* between November 1927 and February 1928. Published in the following year by Alfred A. Knopf, it became his first hard-boiled novel—indeed, *the* first hard-boiled novel, and one of the most radically unsettling the genre has produced. Along with *The Glass Key* (1931) it is the most directly political of Hammett's novels, but its methods are far more extreme and, with its grotesque, spiralling violence, it is more obviously akin to the surreal and symbolic world of satire, in which vice is opposed but never eradicated: as the Op wearily concedes at the end, the fundamental problems will not have gone away. His frantic cleansing of Poisonville has been a short-term remedy, but the effect is ultimately to call into doubt the viability of the radical individualism of the hard-boiled ethos.[4] Hammett was involved in leftist politics in the mid-thirties (a few years after he published his last novel), and because of this there has been a marked critical tendency to read back into his novels—*Red Harvest* especially—a Marxist political agenda.[5] But although its representation of the greed and exploitation of unrestrained capitalism in many respects constitutes a left-wing critique, any proposals for reform would stand small chance of success in the society that

---

[4] In an elaboration of this, McCann 2000: 78, for example, reads the novel as a critique of the Ku Klux Klan vision of moral reform and orderly community.

[5] See e.g. William F. Nolan, *Hammett: A Life at the Edge*. New York: Congdon and Weed, 1983: 77–8, excerpted in Metress 1994: 5.

Hammett depicts. The world he created is characterized not by remediable political-economic ills but by deep-seated moral disorder.

The Montana mining town in which the novel is set has an element of historical specificity, but Hammett from the outset emphasizes its wider meaning. It is a town known by two names, both metaphoric. As 'Personville' it suggests a representative population and, in terms of the power structure, one man's presumption in taking over the whole town, making it in every respect his personal property ('Elihu Willsson was Personville'). The name 'Personville', then, embodies the American ethos of opportunistic individualism. The insidious nature of the corruption Willsson presides over gives rise to the town's other name, 'Poisonville', suggestive of crookedness and violence spreading like a toxin through the body politic, not just in one small town but (given the representative nature of the name) through the whole of American society.

Hammett was distinguished from his *Black Mask* contemporaries by his development of sophisticated ironies, his ambiguity and complexity, his disruption of reliable narrative and of binary oppositions between good and evil, order and disorder. His protagonists are never immune. Indeed, we remember them for their imperfections, their human weaknesses and self-distrust. The Continental Op (an operative of the San Francisco office of the Continental Detective Agency, and the nameless narrator of *Red Harvest, The Dain Curse,* and other stories) is fat and middle-aged, and is frequently up against things that undermine his strength and competence and make him feel that he has lost his moral bearings. In *Red Harvest,* his own character is, he says, 'infected' with the poison of violence. He plays all factions against one another and abandons himself to the violent atmosphere in full awareness of the corruption of his own character and motives: 'It makes you sick, or you get to like it.' The Op's investigation leads him into a 'red harvest' of violence. He tells the book's bad–good woman, Dinah Brand, that after sixteen murders in less than a week he fears he himself is going 'blood-simple'. In the following chapter, 'The Seventeenth Murder', the Op wakes from a surreal dream to find that his right hand is holding an ice pick, the six-inch blade of which is buried in Dinah Brand's breast. The nightmarish final chapters, though they bring some of the answers, also bring more carnage. After the Op's frenzy of cleansing and retribution, he has merely given the town back into the same hands as before. Personville is 'all nice and clean and ready to go to the dogs again', and the Op is under no illusions that he has achieved something of lasting value.

As a satiric fable, *Red Harvest* can be read in different ways. One of the things that makes it so unsettling a novel is that readers find it difficult to agree about the direction of Hammett's critique. The destabilizing effects are akin to those encountered in Swift's satires, as when we look through Gulliver's disillusioned eyes at the state of civilization but also consider whether the responses of Gulliver himself are entirely balanced. *Red Harvest* can be read as a reaffirmation of the powers of the individual at time of major crisis in American individualism and in the political philosophy of modern capitalism: Dennis Porter sees in it the myth of heroic frontier individualism and 'average American-ness' standing against big business, government, labour, and the criminal corruption of institutions (Pepper 2000: 21; Porter 1981: 173–8). Alternatively, as McCann argues, it is a critique of programmes of individualistic reform. In this reading, *Red Harvest* begins from the principles of popular reformism, as the Op sets out on a campaign that shares a vocabulary with the vigilante activities of the Ku Klux Klan: 'The Cleansing of Poisonville' (the title of the first *Black Mask* instalment) shares something with the Klan's vision of an 'organized crusade' to 'reform and cleanse' political institutions. The novel at first seems to promise a story in which corruption is routed, and democracy and social health are restored. As Hammett abandons a more conventionally 'restorative' detective narrative, however, the narrative lurches towards an ending in which the Op has only achieved the dubious peace of a state of martial law. This resolution arguably embodies the degeneration of a reformist agenda into the pursuit of righteous violence, giving encouragement to the indiscriminate murder of power brokers and small-time henchmen alike. Even betraying 'the working-class men he might claim to represent', the Op has carried out a crusade that ultimately becomes 'a pathological search for personal gratification' (McCann 2000: 78–80). The ambiguities in the Op's role are similarly emphasized by Andrew Pepper, who sees them as being produced by the contradictory functions the protagonist fulfils: he has been 'contracted by a capitalist megalomaniac in order to reinscribe that person's authority' (Pepper 2000: 21). This is, then, another reading of the protagonist as ironized. The implication is that the novel builds to a sweeping satiric vision of a society in which effective autonomous action seems all but impossible. It is a critique from which neither the industrial-capitalist state nor popular reformism are exempt.

With the economic disasters of the 1930s, many other crime writers conveyed an even stronger sense of hopelessness than Hammett does in retailing the Op's activities in Poisonville. It is a period during which we often encounter protagonists worn down by harsh circumstance: for example, the destitute young outlaws of Edward Anderson's *Thieves Like Us* (1937) and the ageing gangsters in the early 1940s novels of W. R. Burnett, *High Sierra* (1940) and *Nobody Lives Forever* (1943), which, like Hemingway's *To Have and Have Not*, are studies of exhaustion and defeat, of unremitting struggle and poverty. Some of the most strongly critical of later crime novels acknowledge this sense of ultimate defeat not simply by a weary admission at the novel's end but by shaping the whole of the narrative to reflect the hopelessness of the task. In these we do not see the would-be purposeful violence of Hammett's Op. Instead, our view is confined to the pointless movement of characters in McCoy's *They Shoot Horses, Don't They?* or the total stasis of paralysing despair, in David Goodis's *Blonde on the Street Corner*. The latter was written in 1954 but offered a take on the whole relationship between the crime novel and a time of national demoralization. The implication is that the action-orientated nature of the hard-boiled novel implies the possibility, at least, of satisfying retribution, whereas for those trapped within the Depression years the reality was that there was no cathartic release, only an unending cycle of apathetic resignation. Economic collapse and the corruption and indifference of those in power not only deprives people of control over their lives but brings them to accept their objectification and to lose all will to resist.

In contrast to Hammett's Op, who has affinities with the figure of the excoriating satirist, the protagonists of McCoy and Goodis suggest comparison with the satiric naïf—a victim whose innocence and suffering acts as a foil to the corruptions of society. Within the generic conventions of crime fiction, a very similar sort of function can be served by the victim-protagonist of literary noir. Unlike hard-boiled investigators (and for that matter transgressive figures like the career criminal) this type of weak protagonist lacks the kind of masculine competence that would enable him to achieve some degree of mastery in a hostile world. His innocence acts as a foil to corruption, and his helplessness makes him the embodiment of pervasive enervation and despair. As in much mid-century literary noir, the protagonists of McCoy and Goodis (in their other novels as well as those discussed here) are born victims, completely lacking in the macho competence of the private eye. They are decent, gullible, ineffectual men who are simply not able to deal with a corrupt world. Their unpreparedness for life's traumas is summed up by one of Horace McCoy's narrators: 'and then I said something to myself I had never said before (but which I now knew had always been in the back of my mind): *I should have stayed home*'.[6]

McCoy was a contemporary of Hammett, and Chandler, and wrote for *Black Mask* from 1927 on. Like James M. Cain, he was a writer admired by European audiences, who saw him as having anticipated the themes of existentialism, and indeed his alienated protagonists struggling in an absurd universe were an influence on the existentialists. McCoy's absurdist themes, however, were strongly tied to American life of the thirties: few other crime writers expressed as starkly as McCoy did the deprivation and despair of Depression years. He imagines an everyday world in which violence and corruption seem matter-of-course, and which have no counter-force to stand against these things. As in much other satiric crime fiction, the protagonists are unable to separate themselves from the crooked world that is bearing down on them. A recurrent McCoy character is the ordinary man too vulnerable, insecure, and inept to avoid disaster. He is humiliatingly aware of being in an inferior position, unable to assert his masculine authority, to control his fate, or to entirely grasp what is happening to him.[7] McCoy pushes the genre to its boundaries in narratives that almost cease to be recognizable as genre fiction, but which in fact work as satires. In part this is because they play against the audience's knowledge of those generic conventions which function to create a framework of expectations: in violating these conventions, his novels remind us of the *absence* of any redemptive possibilities.

McCoy's essentially left-wing critique does not entail the

---

[6] *I Should Have Stayed Home*, New York: Knopf, 1938: 142.

[7] Krutnik 1991: 125–63, in his analysis of male figures in *film noir*, offers many insights into the noir victim, particularly in his chapters on 'the "tough" suspense thriller' and 'the criminal-adventure thriller'; Foster Hirsch, *Film Noir: The Dark Side of the Screen*. San Diego: A. S. Barnes, 1981: 175–90, also provides a useful account, taking in a range of films that illustrate different patterns of victim noir.

development of any overt or programmatic political position: in fact, he actually edited out topical references in *They Shoot Horses* (Sturak 1968: 148). Like Hammett and the proletarian writers of the thirties (such as Edward Anderson), McCoy shows clearly the socio-economic factors producing the world he describes, but he also works to give them 'universal' as well as historically specific meanings. *They Shoot Horses*, the story of a deadening and dehumanizing dance marathon, can be seen as an absurdist parable. The contest enfolding the action is so constricting and de-natured that you are disqualified if you open a door to the outside: it provides McCoy with a powerful satiric image of a society in which people are crowded together, trapped in a wholly pointless and soul-destroying form of competition. This works, of course, on a general level. With its repetitive movement, the marathon signifies that 'There is no new experience in life' (McCoy [1935] 1995: 53). Futile motion is interrupted only by random violence, like the shooting that closes down the marathon, or Gloria's suicidal decision to 'get off this merry-go-round' (p. 120). The novel is also, however, a protest against the casual viciousness of the American economic and social system. It exposes the cruel deceptiveness of the American dream, spurring so many in the thirties to pursue illusory goals, only to end by having their fragile hopes (that they might, for example, be 'discovered' in Hollywood) worn away by weariness and defeat.

McCoy's narrative not only lacks the possibility of vigorous intervention on the part of a tough hard-boiled hero but removes the uncertainty of the suspense novel by framing the novel with a fate that is already irrevocable. The ceaseless movement of the dancers around the floor is paralleled by the oppressively circular structure of the plot. *They Shoot Horses* is framed by the death sentence passed on the protagonist, broken into sections that precede each chapter, with the type becoming larger and larger as his final doom is read out. There is a savagely ironic juxtaposition of the utterly cold, formal, deterministic frame of the sentence with the puzzled, innocent, first-person narrative of how Robert Syverten actually came to shoot Gloria, his 'very best friend', because she asked him to kill her. The containing of the narrative in the judicial death sentence sets up two discourses, and there is a strong implication that the remorseless legal judgment omits all that is humanly important and that the individual is punished for sins that are the responsibility of society. There is no possible *legal* answer to the question of 'why sentence should not now be pronounced', but the human reasons are compelling, and the gap between these two discourses constitutes the condemnation of official morality. Like Goodis later, McCoy uses the genre to censure a whole society: his iconic figures are both victims, neither carrying guilt. The '*femme fatale*', Gloria, is guilty only of despair, a pathos-filled version of the woman-as-temptress, tempting the narrator not to sex but to nihilism and death. The 'killer', Robert, is touchingly bemused ('I try to do somebody a favour and I wind up getting myself killed' (15)). The opening phrase of the legal pronouncement ('The prisoner will stand') starts a run-on sentence that acts throughout as an increasingly insistent reminder of the fate that awaits Robert. At the same time, there is a close-up (everything 'plain as day') of the murder itself, with Gloria smiling for 'the first time' when Robert is forced to agree that the only act of friendship to someone in so alienated and friendless a state must be to shoot them.

The illusion that there might be a better life and a promised land is a still more insistent presence in the Depression novel written in the mid-1950s by David Goodis. In *The Blonde on the Street Corner* the theme is more present because it is more remote than in McCoy's novel, and therefore a constant element in the mental life of the protagonist and his friends as they stand on street corners in the bitterly cold Philadelphia winter. Written nearly two decades after McCoy's novel, *The Blonde on the Street Corner* returns to the immobility of the 1930s, during which economic circumstance weighs so heavily that the characters no longer have the capacity to choose a different life or to take action against the system that is oppressing them. Writing at the height of the mid-century paperback revolution, Goodis adapts the conventions of the noir crime novel to capture a mood of crippling despair. In Goodis's other work there are generally the conventional elements of suspense and action: in *Cassidy's Girl* (1951), for example, violent action achieves at least some kind of partial resolution (the defeat of Haney Kenrick), even though Cassidy still feels a great 'heaviness' of spirit; *Down There* (1956—filmed in 1960 as *Shoot the Piano Player*), though it ultimately moves towards despair, has a strong pursuit-and-resistance plot. In *Blonde on the Street Corner*, however, Goodis sets up an expectation of violent action but, although there are occasional violent acts, they do not come together to constitute a crime narrative. It is a novel that perfectly illustrates how the violation of generic conventions can in itself make a strong statement: the implication is that the rupture brought about by sudden, violent, transgressive events (the stuff of the thriller) embodies a potential for change that is absent in the intolerably drab life of the Depression years. If you look at the original cover—with a provocative blonde posed in an urban scene—it is easy to see how the initial package signalled its conformity to a well-known generic type. In a sense the novel's wrapper misrepresented it to the paperback buyers who would have picked it up at a newsstand in the mid-1950s, only to encounter lives of such quiet and passive desperation that even sex and violence assume only routine and diminished forms. *The Blonde on the Street Corner* poses the question, 'How could a guy just go on and on—not doing a thing?' (Goodis [1954] 1998: 30). Its lament for wasted years—'just standing on the corner and waiting, waiting' (p. 5)—is extended to a critique of the kind of society that could leave 'Millions of guys on the corners in the big cities. Standing around' (pp. 36–7). A character called Dippy has the refrain-like line, 'What is this?'—an unexplained phrase, directed at no one in particular. Over the course of the novel it comes to express a profound bafflement, a failure to move forward in any sense, or to acquire any knowledge: it was 'the "sum total of all that he had learned through all the days of his existence" '.

The jobs intermittently available are 'slow death' (p. 31), and the effect of Goodis's novel is to persuade its readers that this process of attrition is in its way worse than the eruption of random violence. There are only a few violent episodes in the novel, all characterized by the pointlessness of the Depression years. In one, the protagonist comes to the aid of a man goaded by one of the 'bastards from upstairs', and we see his potential for violence, the wildness in his eyes, recalled by his friends as a trait with him since childhood. But the only consequence (other than being fired) is that Ralph is left wondering 'what the hell he should do' (pp. 115–26). The climactic violence is sexual: he is cornered by the blonde, Lenore, and seduced into losing control. In the low-key closing chapters, however, the significance of this event is shown to lie in the fact that it is Lenore who impresses on Ralph the gap between dreams and realities. Nothing, then, occurs that can in any significant way change the conditions of life for those who spend their days having to 'walk up and down' in the cold, grey streets of Philadelphia. It is a locale impossibly far from the imagined warmth of Florida, which is used through-out—rather as the South and Africa are in the Harlem novels of Chester Himes—as a misconceived idyll of unobtainable release from suffering and entrapment. Florida is, like the possibility of trans-formative action, conspicuous by its absence—a remote, imagined place where 'everybody's happy . . . It's warm, it's nice'—'I got a good mind to pick me up and shoot down there this week. Why not tomorrow?' (pp. 5, 15).

Despoiling Florida

John D. MacDonald, *A Flash of Green* (1962); Carl Hiaasen, *Stormy Weather* (1995)

'Trees with oranges. Big oranges. He reached up to grab one': Ralph's dream near the beginning of Goodis's *The Blonde on the Street Corner* captures the allure of Florida for anyone who actually looked out to see '[g]rey winter . . . freezing itself onto the alley' (p. 7). The Florida that beckoned to Depression-era Philadelphians trapped in their freezing northern city was, like California, a terminus of the American dream, and in its turn it became an important locus for crime fiction. In the 1930s crime novels of writers like James M. Cain and Horace McCoy, California was, to use Nathaniel West's phrase, the 'dream dump': there wasn't, West wrote in *The Day of the Locust* (1939), 'a dream afloat somewhere which wouldn't sooner or later turn up on it' (West [1939] 1991: 99). It was a fabled place of opportunity trans-formed into a site of disappointment and failure, of disastrous end-ings for rootless characters arriving at a dead-end of hopelessness. Florida, similarly, comes to be associated with the betrayal of people's dreams of a better life. As Bruce Stephenson writes in his book about St Petersburg, *Visions of Eden*, 'Florida epitomizes the potential of modern life. The forces of genius have transformed this once uninhabitable wilderness into an air-conditioned version of the American Dream.'[8] As the Florida idyll disappeared under the onrush

---

[8] Bruce Stephenson, *Visions of Eden: Environmentalism, Urban Planning and City Building in St. Petersburg, Florida, 1900–1995*. Columbus: Ohio State University Press, 1997: 10.

of successive migrations of cold Northerners, reinforced by ever-greater numbers of holidaymakers, all catered for by armies of developers, the despoiling of the state became a prominent theme in the Florida-centred crime fiction of the second half of the twentieth century—most notably in the work of John D. MacDonald (in the 1960s and 1970s) and (from the mid-1980s on) Carl Hiaasen.

The study of environmental literature—'environmental literary criticism' or 'ecocriticism'—is credited with adding place to the categories of race, class, and gender used to analyse literature.[9] As ecocriticism has developed within the last couple of decades, both MacDonald and Hiaasen have come to be seen as important contributors to the literary campaign against the destruction of the physical world, using the satiric potential of crime fiction to raise serious moral questions about human interactions with nature. Florida, as Hiaasen says, is a natural habitat for the tacky developers, constructing their ever-more invasive versions of the Dream, and therefore also a natural habitat for satirists. Those moving in to exploit the state—the amoral, greedy builders of 'wall-to-wall condos and wall-to-wall malls', the shady lawyers, the unscrupulous real-estate agents, the Disney Corporation—are 'so bizarre and so extreme, so dependably and incompetently corrupt' that it is a satirist's paradise.[10] What Hiaasen sees as making Florida 'a little bit unique' is its colossal growth rate: 'There's a sort of Klondike mentality that not only brings new settlers from all parts of the hemisphere, north and south, but also the opportunists, the scammers, the con men, the outlaws. They're not flooding into South Carolina because the opportunities aren't there,' whereas Florida still has 'a breathtaking amount of unspoiled area to be exploited if you're so inclined'. It is 'a place in which there's no such word as "enough" ', but only the question of 'how many more people can we cram in and how much can we sell them and how much beach can we cut up into little tiny pieces and tell them this is their little piece of paradise'.[11]

John D. MacDonald, an early conservationist and a novelist cited by Hiaasen as one of the most significant influences on his own work,

---

[9] See e.g. K. J. Winkler, 'Inventing A New Field: The Study of Literature about the Environment', *Chronicle of Higher Education*, 9/8/1996.

[10] Dan Cryer interview with Carl Hiaasen, 'Florida Follies', *Newsday*, 21/1/2002.

[11] Ibid.; and Thomas Sutcliffe, 'The Thursday Interview: Carl Hiaasen', *Independent*, 3/7/2002.

was a writer who took the function of literature very seriously, as a protection against fanaticism and self-delusion: the non-reader, he argued, is 'defeated by histories that illuminate the past', but 'the man who reads is using the fabulous memory storage and relationship analysis of the brain his ancestors developed eons ago. He is facilitating his survival in the contemporary world.'[12] MacDonald has often been discussed as an heir to a Puritan–Calvinist tradition. Underpinning his writing, there is a belief in 'evil' in a radical sense, and, although he is not overtly religious, he projects a foreboding of retribution following on man's transgressions against the natural world. One can indeed see a strong apocalyptic strain in MacDonald's writing, with his excoriating voice (whether a third-person narrator or the first-person voice of an increasingly disillusioned and cynical Travis McGee) predicting not just the irretrievable breakdown of cities but the cataclysmic destruction of the planet (Lott 1997: 182–3). MacDonald's long-serving series protagonist, Travis McGee, is, as Woody Haut says, 'renowned for his thundering moralisms and corrosive observations regarding the shortcomings of others' (Haut 1999: 18), particularly those of capitalist exploiters and of the self-satisfied middle classes. Commercial greed and the plundering of the environment are rampant in many of his novels—for example, both in McGee novels like *Pale Gray for Guilt* (1968) and *The Green Ripper* (1979) and in such non-series novels as *A Flash of Green* and *A Key to the Suite* (both 1962) and *Condominium* (1977), which, like Hiaasen's *Stormy Weather* (1995), centres on the devastating results of a hurricane hitting buildings built under code.

A Flash of Green, which precedes the Travis McGee series, was written before the environmentalist movement was particularly active, but, in a vigorously satiric, occasionally melodramatic way, establishes many of the environment-centred themes that recur in later work. Focused on the efforts of a group of local citizens to block the plans to fill in the 800 acres of 'Grassy Bay', on Florida's Gulf Coast, for an ill-thought-out 'upscale' housing scheme, the novel is a sustained assault on the real estate scammers, on the bulldozing developers, and on the money-grubbing, power-hungry local businessmen and politicians, who are willing to countenance bribery and corruption to achieve their ends. The effectiveness of MacDonald's

---

[12] John D. MacDonald, 'Reading for Survival', online at www.2think.org.

satire is perhaps suggested by the fact that, when Victor Nunez directed a film adaptation of *A Flash of Green* (in 1984), a group of
developers took legal action to stop its release.

The 'flash of green' of the title, explained within the novel as a rare,
evanescent phenomenon—a flash of green sometimes to be seen
bursting across the horizon when the sun sets in the Gulf of Mexico—
is used as a reminder of the transient natural beauty threatened by
the encroaching malls, housing tracts, and high-rise, beach-side
townhouses. It is one of several images, scattered through the novel,
of what will be lost; but by far the strongest of MacDonald's images
are of the densely packed horror of what will replace it, and of the
human appetites that pose the threat. Dedicated to those opposed to
'the uglification of America', *A Flash of Green* is (like *The Blonde on
the Street Corner*) a crime novel that very freely adapts the conventions of crime writing to indict not a particular criminal but the
criminality of all of the social, commercial, and political interests
colluding in the despoliation of the Florida landscape. The fact that *A
Flash of Green* is not really a murder story means that our attention is
turned towards the dozens of other small, corrupt, self-serving,
greedy, or cowardly acts that thwart the efforts of those who are
trying to oppose the destruction of their environment by hugely
lucrative commercial schemes. Like so much other mid-century crime
fiction, this is a novel that has at its centre the small-town imposition
of conformity and the hunting out of the dissident. Those who want
to save Grassy Bay from the attentions of Palmland Development
Company—'All the damn bird watchers and do-gooders and nature
boys' (MacDonald [1962] 1983: 92)—are easily portrayed as an eccentric, marginalized lot whose failure to conform to modern commercial pressures makes them very susceptible to the attacks launched
by a group of extreme right-wing, fundamentalist Christian back-
woodsmen, 'the Army of the Lord'. The conservationists themselves
know that their stance will be interpreted as an anti-American defiance of the imperatives of free enterprise. They are fully aware of how
they are viewed by the larger community: ' "Who are those nuts to
try to take the bread out of our children's mouths? They just don't
want their view spoiled. They're just a bunch of rich, nutty, degenerate
Communists" ' (p. 112).

In common with Hammett's *The Glass Key, A Flash of Green* has as
the protagonist a corruptible man, Jimmy Wing, who is drawn into

the activities of a politically ambitious employer, and whose cynical representation of his own moral dereliction takes us inside the kind of mind that can accede to any form of corruptly expedient action without too much interference from conscience. Like Hammett's investigators, Wing has both a satirist's eye and a full complement of flaws that render him almost indistinguishable from the world on which he cynically reports back. Aware from the outset of his own weaknesses, he charts with some insight his descent into complicity with corruption, knowing exactly the qualities of mind required for such collaboration: 'Were a man able to use his own fictions and realities interchangeably, he could be much more at home in a mud-died world' (p. 19). Wing has been tempted into his role by the argument that we are all powerless to change anything, and one of the fictions that sustains him is the illusion that, as a reporter, he is even more of a detached observer than others, a man free of responsibility: 'Nothing could seriously touch him who watched. No blame could accrue' (pp. 56–7).

Wing's ultimate self-recriminations are the satirist's assault on the average reader's complacency. We are all complicit, and some of the most nightmarish passages in the novel present the invasion of Jimmy Wing's inner life by the morally chaotic world from which he has held himself apart. As he is sucked into the universe of the symbolically named Bliss, he pictures his own mind as a kind of surreal cave in which leech-like distortions, betrayals, and corruptions cling, making themselves increasingly at home—'a cave pink and membranous, where the things too easy to believe were like flat leech-creatures which inched up from the dark floor to affix themselves to the soft walls [. . .] They made a comfortable muffling, a padded toughened wall, as opposed to a Calvinist rawness' (p. 119). When Wing ultimately reverses roles, repudiating the smear campaign of which he has been a part, he feels driven to take revenge on the man who suborned him. He imagines himself as a Wild West gunslinger, but he evens the score not in the manner of the traditional hard-boiled protagonist, with guns blazing, but instead by becoming the very type of the outcast satirist, a transformation that is accompanied by a sense that logic is being replaced by images. His mind is taken over by irresistible images of corruption and retribution, by 'some pictures, and some darkness', and by the urge to make-up parables and fables that caricature the relationship he has had to corrupt power (pp. 296, 301–2). Having publicly told the truth about the methods and the monstrosity of the man of power, he experiences the satirist's compulsion to court harm by speaking out, suffering threats and beatings in order to continue inventing rhymes that mock and parody the commercial exploiters, 'little verses people have learned by heart [. . .] I make them very simple, very easy to remember' (p. 333). By ultimately having nothing, and therefore nothing to lose, he becomes what other people cannot be, a resisting voice that does actually curb the corrupt power of Bliss.

A Flash of Green echoes one of the most famous earlier fictionalizations of Southern corruption, Robert Penn Warren's *All the King's Men* (1946), in which (as in MacDonald) a journalist employed to get the goods on someone is caught up in the rise and fall of a charismatic populist politician (in Warren's novel, Willie Stark, a character modelled on Louisiana's Huey Long). The monstrous quality of Bliss and of the construction company is conveyed in images of conspicuous consumption. Describing his political ambitions to be Governor of the Sunshine State, Bliss says, ' "God knows where we'll be by then. Boy. Depends on the size bite I can take . . . To get it all, and keep it coming, I have to take the right-size bite at the right time . . . I want the meat in my mouth and room to taste the juice. There's getting to be so many people crowding the earth, it makes it easier" ' (pp. 53–5).

The hunger of Bliss is fed by the hordes of people who, responding to their own hunger, crowd into the state he wants to run. Florida is indeed the antithesis of Philadelphia: it is the classic satiric scene of swirling activity, the crowded rush towards commercial progress. Elmo sees himself as the kind of man who comes to the top when the crowds—the mass of democratic mediocrity—create a demand for someone who has star quality. The motif of consumption associated with Bliss is part and parcel of the basic human hunger that brings people in their thousands to Florida in the first place, hunger for food, land, success, material comforts, bringing 'oceans of squirming people, from sea to sea [. . .] Mankind is on the march, heading toward that golden day when there's nothing to eat but each other' (p. 73). The land suffering under this onslaught is seen in a visionary moment by Wing as a dying, tortured creature, like 'some great fallen animal' with 'a noisome, festering wound, maggoty and moving, draining blood and serum into the silent Gulf' (pp. 192–3). Wing, even before he takes on the role of the satirist, conveys to the reader an unillusioned view of this scene of despoliation, the overlaying of the natural scene with an excrescence of indistinguishable tourists gathering momentum until they coalesce into just one endlessly repeated elderly couple. The pressure to profit from this ceaseless activity fills the local business community with the fear of what would happen if it were to stop, leaving them with a ludicrously useless agglomeration of tourist trash, 'the picture postcards and sun glasses and straw slippers and cement pelicans'. Driven by this anxiety, hundreds of operators converge on the 'sun coast', filling the swamps, clearing palmetto scrub lands, and 'constructing the suburban slums of the future' (p. 24).

Carl Hiaasen, a journalist himself, has been exposing corruption as a feature-writer for the *Miami Herald* since 1976. His breakthrough as a novelist came with *Tourist Season*, published in the mid-1980s. More self-conscious and outspoken than MacDonald about his use of crime fiction as a vehicle for satiric attack, Hiaasen has repeatedly taken as his theme 'the ravaging of Florida' by the 'thousand fortune-seekers [who] took up residence in the state every day' (Hiaasen 1995: 120). He uses his novels to take a series of grotesque, comic revenges on those he holds responsible for the plundering of Florida, devising gruesome and appropriate ways of killing them off. Hiaasen himself has the satirist's sense of purgation and, as in MacDonald, there is a kind of Old Testament fervour and sense of mission. Within the novels, the voice of the satirist is invested in Skink, one-time governor of the state, now an eccentric recluse who lives on road kill, judged to be a 'mentally unstable' wild man (pp. 118–19). Turning up in several Hiaasen novels, Skink is the outsider who punishes and admonishes, inflicting symbolic humiliations on those who violate the state. In a slightly different sense to Jimmy Wing, he is a character who has been inside the system, but then has left it in disgust; he is a more mythic, apocalyptic figure, but similarly functions as an *alter ego* for the satirist.[13] In *Stormy Weather*, Skink's wrath has a powerful ally in a devastating hurricane, another form of purgation which, like the storm in

---

[13] The back story of Clinton Tyree's time as governor of Florida establishes his credentials as the voice of the satirist: 'No previous governor had dared to disrupt the business of paving Florida. For seventy glorious years, the state had shriveled safely in the grip of those most efficient at looting its resources. Suddenly this reckless young upstart was inciting folks like a damn communist. Save the rivers. Save the coasts. Save the Big Cypress. Where would it end?' (Hiaasen 1995: 118–19).

MacDonald's *Condominium*, sweeps away the excrescence of shoddy developments, ripping off the flimsy pretence that all is well in the Florida paradise. The lies (like the hurricane-proof roofs) are blown away, leaving the bizarre remnants of consumer society, with some of the residents clinging on precariously to the fragments that are left. In the pieces of 1980s–1990s journalism collected in the section 'Stormy Weather' (in *Kick Ass*), Hiaasen includes a column addressed to God in the wake of Hurricane Andrew. He tells the Almighty that he now has the attention of Florida's residents, who, ignoring warnings, had crammed 4 million people along the coast, ill-provided for and unprotected, in their substandard housing, against the fury of God's storm (Hiaasen [1999] 2001: 273–4). When the fictional hurricane arrives in *Stormy Weather*, Skink worships the 'gorgeous fury inside that storm,' though he hoped for something more 'biblical' (pp. 147, 35). A Swift-like satiric device, the hurricane washes together con men, victims, and avengers, whose paths cross in blackly comic ways; it takes roofs off, depositing people with unlikely companions and so stirring up the human mixture of tourists, thieves, 'low-life hustlers, slick-talking scammers and cold-blooded opportunists, not to mention pure gangsters and thugs' (pp. 198–9). It energizes Skink's mission of retribution and cleansing by bringing to the surface the grotesque, chaotic corruptions of the Florida scene, as out-of-state opportunists swarm to Florida 'in orgiastic wonderment at the employment opportunity that God had wrought' (p. 339).

As in MacDonald's novel, only with much more comic energy, Hiaasen achieves his satiric effects by the creation of packed scenes: 'the streets were clogged with out-of-towners who treated the hurricane zone as a tourist attraction' (p. 79). What they see is a landscape of destruction that itself functions as a satiric image of rampant materialism, stripped of the thin veneer of civilization, not by communist incursions but by the greed and carelessness of capitalism itself:

Edie had never seen such destruction; it looked like Castro had nuked the place. Houses without roofs, walls, windows. Trailers and cars crumpled like foil. Trees in the swimming pools. People weeping. Sweet Jesus, and everywhere the plonking of hammers and the growling of chain saws [. . .] Bonnie was stunned by the devastation; Max himself was aglow. He held the Handycam on his lap as he steered. Every two or three blocks, he slowed to videotape spectacular rubble. A flattened hardware store. The remains of a Sizzler steak house. A school bus impaled by a forty-foot pine. (p. 14)

Hiaasen's detailed creation of his symbolic scene is central to the novel, and much of its action takes place amidst the remnants of domestic life incongruously strewn about by the storm, the detritus and trivia of sleazy commercialism, assault rifles, and brass chandeliers, tea sets and a cheap laminated 'Salesman of the Year' award hanging on a rain-soaked wall. Even murder seems a natural part of so surreal a post-storm landscape—indeed, a healthy reversal when 'the world's upside down' (p. 25). The actual murderers—the salesmen and inspectors who guaranteed the trailers and houses—roam free or try to make their getaway, while a few desperate residents whose lives have been blown away try to hunt them down and take their revenge.

Hiaasen also peoples his scene with more reprehensible predators, like the grotesquely caricatured Snapper, whose disfigurement runs through the novel as an image of twisted ambition and violent greed—his face, like his name, emblematic of his moral nature. But, although he is an actual criminal, he is not inherently worse than the others who pursue the same sorts of ends by underhanded methods: ' "They're turning it into a sump hole. Some with guns, some with briefcases—it's all the same goddamn crime" ' (p. 327). In fact, as the northern tough guy, Ira Jackson, reflects, the 'shitty construction' and other commercial crimes going on in Florida are 'exactly the kind of thing that [gives] corruption a bad name' (pp. 122–3). In a satiric scene crowded with so many varieties of corruption, very little progress towards a resolution is possible. There is partial justice meted out (some characters punished, others saved), but the main hope seems to reside in those who withdraw from society—the reclusive dropouts, those who join Skink on the margins, finding a place from which they can articulate anti-commercial values and report back satirically on the society they have escaped from. And this is in a way, of course, just a slightly more extreme version of the private eye's lonely integrity, the battered shamus in his dusty urban office replaced by 'the guy at the lake' who lives in a cabin that 'looks like a glorified outhouse' (Skink, in *Double Whammy* (1988)).

The politics of self-enrichment

Bret Easton Ellis, *American Psycho* (1991); Iain Banks, *Complicity* (1993); Jason Starr, *Cold Caller* (1997)

All three of the texts considered here use murder in a symbolic way, as an analogue for the crimes of the society represented: in *Complicity* each murder acts as a symbolic punishment for the crimes of those who have abused their power; in *American Psycho*, Patrick Bateman's cannibalism is just another form of excessive consumption, accompanied by a failure to recognize the humanity of others; and in *Cold Caller*, murdering your way to upward mobility captures the whole competitive structure of a society. This is a very small sampling of an increasing tendency, during and after the Thatcher–Reagan years, for crime writers in both America and Britain to use the genre for satirizing the economic and political crimes of those in power, the atmosphere of blithe self-interest, the whole-hearted commitment to self-enrichment, and the addiction to the pleasures and games of a consumer society. In America, the years of Reagan's presidency were, of course, associated by their critics with the encouragement of a commodity culture, with the promotion of selfishness, greed, a get-rich-quick mentality, and the rise of the yuppie; in Britain, the Thatcherite 1980s, during which personal wealth rose 'by 80 per cent in real terms', were similarly a time of rapidly expanding affluence and consumption.[14] Anthony Sampson's recent *Who Runs This Place?* quotes Hugo Young as saying that the Establishment, 'whether in politics, in business or in intellectual life, is all of one colour. There is little point in being anything else', and that colour, Sampson adds, 'is the colour of money. The new elite is held together by a desire for personal enrichment, its acceptance of capitalism and the need for the profit motive, while the resistance to money values is much weaker and former anti-capitalists have been the people least inclined to criticize them once in power.' With the end of the Cold War bringing a huge expansion of the global marketplace, rich investors have benefited on a previously undreamt-of scale, and '[a]bove all,

---

[14] Martin 1997: 52–3; Hutton 1995: pp. xi–xii and 54; York and Jennings 1995: 42.

the rich feel much less need than their predecessors to account for their wealth, whether to society, to governments or to God'.[15] Although 'all the totems of an advanced consumerist society' had been present in the seventies, it was really only in the eighties that the consumer paradise arrived. As Peter York says, in a comment that applies equally to Britain and the US:

the eighties effect took quite a lot of things coming together; the right time, right place, right people, right feelings, right fistfuls of cash. This wasn't *just* a consumer boom. Yes, we did go out and buy more—more TVs, more VCRs, state-of-the-art hi-fis, etc.—but it was really a new generation of consumerism with changes in advertising, retailing, financing, attitudes and expectations. And it's *still with us*: it set the pattern for the next ten or fifteen years. (York and Jennings 1995: 40)

The sheer proliferation of goods to accumulate and the excesses of individual self-enrichment have fed a growing body of crime literature satirizing contemporary society and elaborating the relationship between crime, commercialism, and consumption. Writers on both sides of the Atlantic have focused on characters' resistance to the power of the consumer society to 'consume' people or on characters whose psychopathic and satirically presented excesses embody the all-devouring nature of consumerism. Aside from Hiaasen's exuberantly satiric Florida novels, there have been, for example, the novels of Charles Willeford and Elmore Leonard, also partially Florida-based and using rampant consumerism as the context of their fictions, a satirically heightened scene that functions to establish the moral perspective within which we judge their gallery of criminals, with consumer greed acting as a metaphor for moral bankruptcy. In Leonard's *Stick* (1983), for example, Chucky is a caricature of acquisitive energy, wheeling and dealing in a crude imitation of Barry, whose taste in colour-coordinated cars and chauffeur's uniforms epitomizes his concept of the American Dream; or, in *Split Images* (1981), Robbie, the psychopathic millionaire who puts on his dark cashmere and a light canvas shooting coat, assembles his most impressive consumer durables (a $4,000 video camera and an elaborately decorated, 'compact little submachine gun'), and sets out in his silver Rolls Royce to film the death of a rich acquaintance whose main offence is that he never remembers Robbie's name. For American crime writers of the

---

[15] *The Observer*, 28/3/2004, extracts from Sampson 2004.

1990s, consumerism and self-enrichment have continued to be strong themes, as we will see in looking at the savagely comic literary noir of Jason Starr and at the unsettling use of the materials of crime fiction in Bret Easton Ellis's *American Psycho*.

In Britain, some of the most interesting contemporary crime writers have also satirized a society in which everything is subordinated to consumption. The New Wave British crime novelists have been very much influenced by American noir fiction—by Jim Thompson, Chester Himes, and Charles Willeford, as well as by more recent writers like Elmore Leonard and Carl Hiaasen.[16] Amongst the best-known recent British crime writers are Jeremy Cameron, Nicholas Blincoe, Ken Bruen, Iain Banks, Christopher Brookmyre, and Irvine Welsh, all of whom include a large admixture of surreal and comic elements, building up sharply satiric pictures of British socio-economic and political life from the time of the 'Thatcher revolution', drawing in characters whose personal consumption is most conspicuous—Thatcherite yuppies, for example, in pursuit of the 'fistfuls of cash' that will buy them state-of-the-art commodities. Both Christopher Brookmyre and Iain Banks chronicle the dirtiness of British society from north of the border. In a continuing series that starts with *Quite Ugly One Morning* (1996) and *Country of the Blind* (1997)—the most recently published addition is *Be My Enemy* (2004)—Jack Parblane, Brookmyre's hard-boiled journalist, investigates conspiracies and dirty deals in 1990s Scotland, where the entrepreneurial activities and shoddy morality of the Thatcherite 1980s continue to flourish.

Iain Banks, whose *Complicity* (1993) is one of the more 'mainstream' post-Thatcher era thrillers, has been described as 'an old-fashioned socialist, forced by distaste for the former Conservative administration into nationalism'. 'After Thatcher came to power,' he says, 'I felt alienated and a lot more Scottish.'[17] Banks's themes are very forcefully articulated. As Scott McCracken observes, *Complicity* is a novel that will sustain a psychoanalytic interpretation, bringing out its representation of transgressive desires lurking under the performance of 'normal' masculinity. This is, however (as McCracken

---

[16] These are amongst the influences mentioned by Nicholas Blincoe, 'The Same Mean Streets Seen from a Fresh Angle', in 'Murder, They Write', *The Times*, 18/4/1998:17.

[17] Iain Banks, interview with Robin Eggar, *The Times*, 14/11/1997.

himself points out), a very narrow reading of a text that so clearly invites us to consider personal traumas within a very firmly established historical context. In such a reading, the repressed mutual attraction between Cameron (the investigative protagonist) and Andy (the novel's serial killer) primarily serves to reinforce the doubling of investigator and murderer, underscoring the (manifestly political) implications of the title: we are all complicit in the crimes of our society. The novel provides its readers with much more overtly moral and political argumentation than most genre fiction attempts: ' "We have chosen to put profits before people, money before morality, dividends before decency, fanaticism before fairness, and our own trivial comforts before the unspeakable agonies of others" ' (Banks [1993] 1995: 301). Such straightforward statements of theme are recurrent, signposting instances of cynicism and moral bankruptcy, commercial selfishness and corruption, and relating these crimes to the wider framework of law, democracy, and political allegiance. Connections become more explicit as increasing numbers of the prominently corrupt are appropriately dispatched: *Complicity* is a text that, like the gothicized police procedurals discussed in Chapter 3, imagines the psychopath as writing his grievances on the bodies of his victims, except that in Banks's novel these grievances are public rather than private—a diatribe against those in power conducted by means of gruesome physical violations. The piling up of grotesquely murdered bodies acts, as does the crowded scene of satire, to provide an overwhelming reminder of the difficulty of acting in any logical sequential way, either to bring investigative closure or to set things right in any wider sense. Rather in the way that Jim Thompson does in his first-person killer novels, Banks uses the psychopath both as a metaphor for and a critic of a sick society: as Andy himself argues, in a 'climate of culpability' with such widespread 'perversion of moral values', nothing that he has done has been out of place. He knows that he is complicit himself. He is a product of the system, 'a businessman' (pp. 299–301), settling accounts for the exploited, tipping the balance against those who can afford to live in houses with views over golf courses, can own Range Rovers and foxhounds, and enjoy richly carpeted floors, black leather furniture, chrome-and-glass tables, and all the hi-tech luxuries that money can buy (pp. 34, 56–7, 85–6).

Complicity is saved from becoming simply a diatribe by the complexity of Banks's narrative methods, which both destabilize point of view and help to implicate us in the scenes we witness. Using the second person for the graphic descriptions of each murder creates suspense by making us unsure who is speaking (it could be Cameron), but it also involves us in the killer's choices: 'You couldn't decide when you were planning this whether to infect him with HIV-positive blood or not; you couldn't make-up your mind whether he really deserved it' (p. 38). The question of whether the victims deserve the retribution inflicted on them is central, as is the question of whether one can remain detached (as Cameron attempts to do), or whether one in fact is *always* choosing and must come to terms with the moral implications of one's choices (almost the last words Andy says to Cameron are ' "Your choice" ' (p. 304)). The friendship between Cameron and Andy raises the issue of complicity in compli-cated ways, creating a narrative space within which Banks's characters are able to debate the issues raised by Andy's murders. Cameron's own complicity is repeatedly highlighted by Andy when he quotes back at Cameron the words that lie behind (or have been literalized by) Andy's actions. As Andy explains, his performance has been based on ideas that Cameron, as a journalist, has put into print but does not himself choose to act on: ' "Don't you see? I'm agreeing with you; I listened to all your arguments over the years, and you're right: the twentieth century *is* our greatest work of art and we *are* what we've done [. . .] and *look at it*" ' (p. 301).

The detached, cynical voice of the writer is itself one of Banks's themes. He is using the convention of the cynical outsider observing from the margins the goings-on in a totally immoral society, but he is also turning his own critical armoury on the presumption of the observer. Cameron would like to occupy the role of the detached investigator ('If I was some fucking private eye [. . .]' (p. 169)) and imagines himself as 'some tough cookie' (p. 183) but, arrested on suspicion of the murders, feels a disintegration of this detached self rapidly setting in. The metaphor of the computer game 'Despot' is used throughout the novel to establish Cameron's view of the strug-gle between civilization and barbarism as nothing more than a game. Andy's murders, however, force his involvement in fundamental ways. As a journalist and as a game-player, Cameron has in fact imagined himself to be secure within a genre that is rather more familiar and reassuring, only to find that he is not a competent, uninvolved investigator but party to the horrors he reports on.

McCracken actually categorizes *Complicity* as a gothic horror rather than crime fiction, but it is perhaps more true to say that, like other crime fiction that moves towards the gothic, it is structured in a way that undermines the too-easy sense of rational control afforded by the traditional investigative narrative. The gothic extremity of Banks's conception is crucial to his satiric effect, enabling him to create monstrosities (the symbolic murders) that draw us in, challenge us to feel both guilt and revulsion, and confront us in a very visceral way with one man's vision of the horrors of modern society.

Brett Easton Ellis's *American Psycho* (1991), the most satirically extreme of the novels we are discussing, draws substantially on the conventions of both the gothic and crime writing. Closely linked to the techniques and materials of contemporary literary noir, *American Psycho* makes devastating use of the figure of the serial killer to launch an attack on 1990s consumer culture. It is a book that clearly claims its status as a 'mainstream' novel, though of so radical and disturbing a kind that it has divided critics ever since its publication. The huge furore over *American Psycho* has in fact been plausibly attributed to this mainstream status, to its publication by Alfred A. Knopf as one of its Vintage Contemporary paperbacks rather than in a familiar genre niche, as horror or crime fiction (Skal 1993: 375–6). Many other immoderately violent novels had been published in the 1980s, both noir thrillers (there are grisly killings aplenty in Ellroy's LA Quartet novels) and horror novels, such as the best-selling 'splatterpunk' novels of Clive Barker. From their radically different perspectives, both Ellis and Stephen King depict, as Robert Skal points out, 'the monstrous spectacle of the consumer consumed. Ellis's world of blood-soaked designer labels recognizably upgrades the voracious mall zombies in *Dawn of the Dead*: they shop till they drop, eat your brains, then shop some more' (Skal 1993: 376). Skal suggests, in explanation of the outrage over *American Psycho*, that excess of this kind may be accepted in popular film and genre fiction but not within the mainstream: if the 'hideous progeny' of the genre writers is allowed to 'start tracking blood up the staircase of the Manhattan castle', it is quite another matter.

There is a Swiftian extremity in Ellis's novel, and a corresponding technique, disorienting to many readers, of providing what looks like enormously detailed surface realism but including it for its satiric effect on the reader. Part of Ellis's satiric point is that the cumulative exposure to anything desensitizes our minds, makes us inured to things that should be profoundly shocking. The whole method of *American Psycho* is to crowd the novel with such an accumulation of consumer goods, consumers, and sensory details that it all ceases to register. The novel's opening details establish a world of commercial oversaturation in which the most common reaction is one of 'total and sheer acceptance' (Ellis 1991: 5–6), a numbed response to the omnipresence of commodification and objectification. An extraordinarily dense texture of product descriptions, saleable surfaces, and beautification rituals create the context within which we read Patrick Bateman's later, and ever more disturbing lists, building from such early sequences as 'a Soprani jacket, two white Brooks Brothers shirts and a tie from Agnes B. still covered with flecks of someone's blood' (p. 81) to the full-blown horrors of passages gruesomely detailing the killing and consumption of women, in the same flat, affectless style as used for Ralph Lauren shirts, Toshiba portable compact disc players, and Mitsubishi rechargeable electric shavers.

The crowded scenes of *American Psycho*, then, are packed with commodities and people reduced to commodities, but the chief horror here resides in the way in which this mass of objects is assimilated by the novel's centre of consciousness. The use of a heavily ironized narrator, who embodies the failures of his world but also (if unreliably) reports back on them, is an important part both of satiric tradition (most famously Swift's use of ironic masks) and of literary noir—particularly of mid-century transgressor-centred novels like those of Jim Thompson (the folksy psychopaths of *The Killer Inside Me* and *Pop. 1280*; Dolly Dillon in *A Hell of a Woman*); Charles Williams (*Hell Hath No Fury, A Touch of Death*); Gil Brewer (*Nude on Thin Ice*); and Harry Whittington (*Web of Murder*). The tensions within Ellis's ultimate consumer are the most extreme imaginable, and his narrative is so thoroughly destabilized that we are hard put to know whether the external world constitutes the whole of his interior world or his perception of the external world is merely a projection of his own disordered mind. If we accept his narrative as an account of real events, then one of the main things it records is Patrick Bateman's struggle to maintain his own surface, the insipid ordinariness of a façade that progressively disintegrates: 'I'm having a difficult time containing my disordered self' (p. 301). In the 'bone season', his 'mask of sanity' is 'a victim of impending slippage' (p. 279). The nature of the society that surrounds him is all too apparent in its persistent failure to see Bateman as he really is: ' "You're not really comprehending any of this [. . .] *I* chopped Owen's fucking head off. *I* tortured dozens of girls." [. . .] "Excuse me," he says, trying to ignore my outburst. "I really *must* be going" ' (p. 388). The killing can be seen as an expression of Bateman's inability to cope, but more fundamentally it is an expression of the dehumanization of the society to which he wants to belong (and into which his sickness and inhumanity do actually 'fit'). The depersonalization of this world is 'so intense' that 'There wasn't a clear, identifiable emotion within me, except for greed and, possibly, total disgust' (p. 282).

One of the reasons *American Psycho* is so disorientating to the reader is that inner and outer landscapes come to seem indistinguishable, to such an extent that readers disagree about whether Bateman's crimes belong to the real world or are simply part of his disordered imagination. Recording his growing sense of the meaninglessness of all higher ideals and emotions, Bateman reflects on an inner world that consists entirely of meaningless external 'geography', a 'desert landscape [. . .] devoid of reason and light and spirit [. . .] Surface, surface, surface was all that anyone found meaning in' (pp. 374–5). This is a society in which the ideas of both decency and indecency are defined in terms of tastes. Stash cannot be '*perfectly* decent and nice' if he asks for '*chocolate chip sorbet*'; 'evil' is just a casually used endearment; 'insane' is a description of someone wearing tasselled loafers; you're 'crazy' if you fail to join a tanning salon (pp. 20, 24, 31, 48). The satiric world created by Ellis stands at the opposite extreme from David Goodis's *Blonde on the Street Corner*, and our relationship to class is reversed: instead of locating ourselves within the mental universe of characters immobilized by poverty, we are instead swept along with a current of essentially mindless, affectless activity amongst a cast of rich characters for whom the impoverished class is virtually non-existent. The omnipresent bums and beggars, viewed with brutally comic callousness by Price, Bateman, and their like, define the lowest social boundaries of the society, and are used by Ellis as a heavily stressed reminder throughout the novel of the nobodies in a world where '*Everybody's* rich [. . .] *Everybody's* good-looking' (p. 23). By the end the lists are a Swiftian compendium of the disorder and meaninglessness of the contemporary history that has made its way into Bateman's consciousness, the violent acts that he is able to invest with no meaning: 'blood pouring from automated tellers, women giving birth through their assholes, embryos frozen or scrambled (which is it?), nuclear warheads, billions of dollars, the total destruction of the world' (p. 343).

American Psycho has the kind of satiric plot described by Ronald Paulson in *Fictions of Satire* as an 'unholy parody' of an orderly world, creating an 'absurd universe' in which the assumptions of the worst of mankind have come true: 'The crowd, which was formerly only one element, has become the main one, and the impotent villain is now its king'—or, in these democratic times, is now its most fully representative citizen, taking within himself (he is, after all, a cannibal) all of the materials and qualities of this fallen world. As in Pope's *Dunciad*, this is a 'society upside down, overrun by fools, with a human ideal or two hiding to remind us that fools are not the ideal' (Paulson [1967] 1983: 125–6). In *American Psycho*, the most important reminders are Patrick Bateman's own moments of terror or despair at his passing recognition of the nature of his inner and outer reality: 'Individuality no longer an issue [. . .] Justice is dead. Fear, recrimination, innocence, sympathy, guilt, waste, failure, grief, were things, emotions, that no one really felt anymore' (p. 375). Emptied of every human value, the ultimate urban hell is also inescapable. There is no prospect of a release from the horrors recorded. The closure of the novel's end is present in its first sentence, which reports that ' "ABANDON ALL HOPE YE WHO ENTER HERE" ' is scrawled in blood red lettering on the side of the Chemical Bank. The frame is completed at the end by another sign, again in red, 'THIS IS NOT AN EXIT' (pp. 3, 399). The end of the novel is both closed and open. The entrapment is total, the prediction of the book's beginning wholly fulfilled. At the same time, however, the traditional end of the murderer eludes Bateman, although he seeks it by confessing to his murders. His confessions are not credited or even comprehended; his carnage is routinely and unquestioningly cleaned up by others. We finish the novel not knowing whether anyone will ever believe that he is not 'the boy next door' but 'a fucking evil psychopath' (p. 20).

If both Banks and Ellis—the latter in particular, of course—seem to be standing so far outside the constraints of genre fiction that their novels are not 'really' crime novels, it is perhaps finally worth emphasizing that the satiric messages writ large in these hybrid texts are also strongly and effectively present in numerous contemporary novels that have incontestably been conceived and marketed as genre fiction. My example here is the work of one of the best of the younger generation of American crime writers, Jason Starr, who has been praised by Bret Easton Ellis as 'the first writer of his generation to convincingly update the modern crime novel'.[18] Like Ellis, he writes about the corruption of the American success ethic and has a satiric agenda that invites comparisons with the more canonical American plays and novels that have exposed the 'straight for the jugular' implications of the American way—the savagery of the vigorous commitment to frontier capitalism expounded, for example, by Teach in David Mamet's *American Buffalo*: 'the freedom [. . .] Of the Individual [. . .] To Embark on Any Fucking Course that he sees fit'.[19] But unlike Ellis, Starr can unproblematically be placed within the traditions of crime writing. His first novel, *Cold Caller*, was published in 1997; his sixth, *Twisted City*, in 2004. Critics have compared his work to that of Jim Thompson, Patricia Highsmith, and Charles Willeford; and technical and thematic comparisons can also be extended to include other writers of literary noir who used the form for satiric ends, particularly those (for example, Charles Williams, Gil Brewer, and Harry Whittington) who chose deeply flawed protagonists. Starr makes similarly insidious use of a taut, edgy first-person narration to take readers inside a mind on the verge of disintegration: 'I could forget about my dreams of finding another job in advertising, of starting a family and moving to the suburbs. I was going to be a loser again,' Bill Moss, protagonist of *Cold Caller*, reflects. 'Then I stopped thinking. I tackled him from behind and went right for his throat' (Starr 1997: 120).

The most important of Starr's satiric techniques is his mastery of voice, tempting us to listen sympathetically to telemarketer Bill Moss's self-justifications and evasions, whilst at the same time leading us to see ever more clearly his slide towards insanity—towards the stage at which the 'beautiful thing' he fantasizes about changes from a dream of his gloriously rapid progress up the ladder of success to an almost equally satisfying vision of wrapping his hands around the neck of whoever is standing on the rung above him. Moss, at the beginning of his narrative, is precariously employed in a part-time

---

[18] Jason Starr's website, online at http://members.aol.com/Jasonstarr.
[19] David Mamet, *American Buffalo*. London: Methuen, [1975] 1996: 71.

job that involves phoning people to try to sell them on the idea of meeting a salesman who will try to sell them long-distance phone services—a form of remote and roundabout salesmanship that in itself suggests a deferral of any actual 'communication'. The sales-man, a kind of legitimized conman and liminal trickster figure, has traditionally, of course, held a strong fascination for American writers. As a specialist in phony realities, he depends for his success on his skills as a performer, tailoring his performance to whatever audience he is trying to con. In Starr's novel, as elsewhere, the sales-man's strengths (his adaptability and his powers of invention) are perverted in the service of a criminally irresponsible capitalist ethos. His adaptability erodes all firm sense of self, and his slick (and often not so slick) deceptions displace all other forms of communication. The brash self-assurance of the 'cold caller', able to establish a tran-sient connection with any stranger via the telephone, eventually hardens into the coldness of complete emotional detachment.

The indifferent urban 'crowd of strangers' in Starr's novel is fur-ther removed from individualized humanity by being reduced to voices and functions. Relationships with others are perceived entirely in terms of power and powerlessness, and *Cold Caller* is particularly effective in the way it charts the protagonist's dehumanization, his alternating self-abasement and brutality. Turns of fortune carry him from shame and fear of failure to euphoric interludes when he redis-covers the joys of callously exercising power. The firm Bill works for ensures that ritual humiliations in front of multitudes of co-workers are part of the daily routine. The first traumatic event of his narrative is the ordeal of apologizing to the entire office: ' "No deals," Ed said. "You either apologize to everyone or you walk out that door" [. . .] I don't know if I've ever felt more humiliated' (pp. 32–3). Learning to dissociate himself from the others who surround him, Bill commits himself to moving upwards in the hierarchy, reflecting that his des-peration to hold on to his job is such that 'I was prepared to do anything not to let this opportunity slip away. If it meant literally getting down on my hands and knees, stripping off Mr. Simmons' pants, and kissing his butt cheeks, I was ready to do it' (p. 85).

In comparison to this method of career advancement, the act of murder seems like a new-found form of forcefulness and self-assertion. And indeed, the office murder he commits at first appears to be a shrewd career move: 'The way I saw things, it was the difference between the end of my career and a new beginning. Killing Ed was definitely the right thing to do—it was the only thing to do under the circumstances' (p. 125). It looks as though everything is going to turn out as he had hoped it would before he committed the murder, 'except that things were going to happen ahead of schedule' (p. 146). He is already tasting the pleasures of wielding control over those eager to kiss his own butt cheeks: 'The next couple of days my dream life continued. The telemarketers treated me with fear and respect, making it incredibly satisfying to come into work every day' (p. 167).

As in *Complicity* and *American Psycho*, the competent male agency of the protagonist is constantly at issue. Starr uses the shifts in Bill's voice and self-perceptions to make him the embodiment of the traumas attendant on an unswerving commitment to the success ethic and to an American dream conceived (in Mamet's phrase) as 'basically raping and pillage'. In Mamet's *Glengarry Glen Ross*, failures to achieve that dream are emasculating. In *Cold Caller*, the spectre of losing his job renders Bill Moss impotent, except in a brief encounter with a prostitute. His sexual potency, however, returns when he thinks he is on his way to prosperity, and after he 'makes a killing', his rediscovered capacity for inspiring respect means that he again feels vigorous and manly enough to qualify as the protagonist of the stereotypical American success story. Regaining his ability to 'perform' is, of course, just a side-effect of his workaholic character reasserting itself, rather than a manifestation of warm human interconnectedness. From his earliest years, Bill Moss has cultivated his work ethic, and Starr underlines the irony of his childhood conviction that if he dedicates himself to earning money he can protect himself from 'my aloneness in the world' (p. 13). It is a goal that proves as illusory as paying back his $10,000 in student loans. The truth of the matter is that his pursuit of upward mobility leads only to his utter isolation and to dissociation not just from others but from himself. We witness the reduction of his whole sense of himself as a functioning human being: 'When I looked in the mirror I didn't recognize the man staring back at me [. . .] it was his eyes that frightened me most. They were two dark, dull circles that didn't seem to be alive' (p. 71). There is no longer a man to whom others can relate. Ultimately his whole existence seems to him 'to be someone else's life that I could view like scenes in a movie. I could rewind it and repeat certain events and none of it was real' (p. 211).

The end of *Cold Caller* is characterized by the pointless circularity of the satiric narrative. The lies that come naturally to the lips of a salesman become increasingly frantic and increasingly necessary to his survival. He begins to realize that his invention of false narratives has been a little less skilful than he has imagined, and the struggle to hold his elaborate fictional constructions together grows desperate. From the outset, murder has presented itself as an essential prop for his habitual untruths: it is to cover up a lie about his past that he kills his boss; it is to preserve the lie of his innocence that he kills a prostitute. As his stories begin to unravel, his foolhardy measures become a grotesque caricature of the American dream of upward mobility, his 'progress' reduced to a surreal journey towards Harlem on the subway, carrying a severed head in a trash bag.

5

Black Appropriations

CHESTER HIMES said of the creation of his Harlem-centred crime novels, 'The detective story originally in the plain narrative form—straightforward violence—is an American product. I just made the faces black.'[1] Himes touches here on one of the main issues addressed in this chapter, that is, the relevance of this form of genre fiction to the black experience of American life. He also, in his self-deprecating description of his own contribution, skirts round a crucial question: what are the ramifications, in so white-dominated a form, of 'making the faces black'? The Harlem cycle is an obvious starting point for a discussion of black appropriations of the crime novel. There were earlier black writers of crime fiction, most notably two Harlem Renaissance writers, George S. Schuyler, whose detective-spy novella, *The Ethiopian Murder Mystery*, was first serialized in the 1930s, and Rudolph Fisher, whose Harlem-set version of a classic detective novel, *The Conjure-Man Dies*, was published in 1932. Himes's achievements in the genre, however, have had a far more lasting impact. Although they were for a long period neglected and often harshly criticized, the ten Harlem novels that he wrote between 1957 and 1969 remade the genre in a powerful and distinctive way. As the reassessment of Himes's whole body of work continues, his crime novels have significantly contributed to the case for recognizing his importance, helping to make him, in the eyes of some, 'America's central black writer' (Sallis 2000: p. xii).

The years during which Himes wrote his Harlem novels were amongst the most turbulent and momentous of the African-American fight for civil rights. The Harlem cycle draws into its fictional world the violence of this struggle, escalating until, by *Plan B* (the last book

---

[1] Himes in interview with John A. Williams, 1970, 'My Man Himes: An Interview with Chester Himes', in Fabre and Skinner 1995: 48.

in the series), it had reached what Himes saw as the 'beginnings of an apocalypse', a spectacle so appalling that he found he could not move forward to the novel's completion: 'I've tried to imagine what would happen, and write it as a documentary. But I've had to stop. The violence shocks even me.'[2] In Himes's use of genre fiction to represent the conflict between black and white America, we encounter the difficult questions begged by his throw-away line about substituting black characters for white, a phrase that makes light of the generic changes that will inevitably accompany such a substitution if the writer actually confronts the implications. During the last decade in particular critics have begun to explore the complexities of this apparently simple change in the colour of the crime novel, and the work of Himes himself, like that of the other novelists discussed in this chapter, shows very clearly the radical revisioning attendant on such a reversal of the racial binary, a reversal that produces significant transformations in the language, structure, and meaning of the genre.

In identifying the hard-boiled novel itself with 'straightforward violence', Himes focuses our attention on a controversial aspect of generic definition: does the tradition of hard-boiled fiction that he takes as his starting point bear the indelible impress of mainstream, conservative American ideology? Himes (using a definition broad enough to encompass 'crime' as well as 'detective' fiction) argues that American violence, which 'is public life', finds its literary correlative in the form of the detective story.[3] What this implies is that the genre's codes and conventions are an *expression* (rather than a *containment*) of all that is disruptive and explosive in American society. The genre as Himes conceives of it, then, is a hybrid form quite distant from the classic detective story, one that is not primarily about the process of detection, and that does not centre on the reassuring restitution of order. It is, rather, an unsettling embodiment of the competing forces in American public life—of the violent official imposition of the will of the dominant culture, to be sure, but also of the many other kinds of violence that seem to him to be the very fabric of American life. As we move on to our discussion of the

---

[2] Himes quoted in H. Bruce Franklin, *Prison Literature in America*. New York: Oxford University Press, 1989: 227, in Sallis 2000: 223; Himes in interview with Philip Oakes in 1969, 'The Man Who Goes Too Fast', in Fabre and Skinner 1995: 22.

[3] Himes quoted by McCann 2000: 251.

last half-century of black crime writing, it is important, I think, to bear in mind Himes's description of the genre as, first and foremost, a fictional embodiment of America's violently competing interests, its disturbed and disturbing cultural-political spaces. We have looked, in the earlier part of this study, at some of the ways in which, from the late 1920s on, American hard-boiled detective and crime fiction accommodated the perspective of the morally dubious investigator, the outlaw and the victim, breaking down neat binaries and undermining stable identities. White writers as well as black have seen the genre's potential for challenging racial stereotypes: amongst Himes's contemporaries, such writers as Charles Willeford, Dorothy B. Hughes, and William McGivern used black protagonists to tackle the issue of race from a white liberal perspective.[4] The inherent transgressiveness of this form of popular fiction is one of the reasons it has held such an appeal for those who are themselves on the margins of conventional society and who are aiming to further extend generic boundaries by altering the crime novel's handling of, for example, gender, race, and ethnicity.

Somewhat paradoxically, another important reason for the genre's appeal to the transgressive writer is the clichéd image of hard-boiled fiction as narrow, deeply conservative, and therefore ripe for inversion. The investigative narrative (whether private eye or police procedural) is the most popularly recognizable form of the genre. It is easily reducible to formulaic elements, with white male detectives tackling violators of the status quo and presiding over narratives that proceed in a fairly linear fashion towards the re-establishment of order. As Maureen T. Reddy argues, in *Traces, Codes, and Clues*, 'it is therefore basically reassuring and conservative, because it suggests, first, that it is not only desirable but actually possible to banish or destroy disruptive social elements, and, second, that the greatly-to-be-desired continuation of bourgeois, white, masculinist society depends on general acceptance of a masculine authority figure who alone is capable of explaining the world satisfactorily' (2003a: 54–5). There is much investigative fiction that conforms to this description, but it is a reductive construction, narrowing the huge variety of crime narra-

---

[4] The novels referred to here are: Willeford, *Pick Up* (1954), Hughes, *The Expendable Man* (1963), and McGivern, *Odds against Tomorrow* (1957). For a fuller discussion see Horsley 2001: 168–73.

tives to the sub-genre of detective fiction. A further delimitation of the sub-genre results from taking Chandler and Hammett as its progenitors and, having elided the differences between their novels, identifying them as the primary exemplars of the 'hard-boiled ideology' (Reddy 2003a: 7–8). Understandably enough, black novelists themselves sometimes construct their own achievements with reference to this oversimplified model of the tradition of white-authored crime fiction, using it as a foil for their own handling of the genre. Mike Phillips, in discussing his development as a novelist, says that he came to see crime fiction as 'a genre whose conventions were part of a racist polemic about society', and thus as a form that could only be employed by a black writer who revised it radically, not just 'changing the colour of the protagonist' but challenging 'the order of the convention' in a very thoroughgoing way.[5] Both critics and writers have constructed the 'parent' genre in a way that allows it to stand in for the larger society that is being challenged. It is obviously not without basis to argue that race and ethnic otherness have been for detective fiction amongst the main traditional signifiers of criminality. The reality, however, is both more complicated and more interesting. In what follows we will examine strategies of resistance that draw in a great variety of ways on the actual diversity of earlier, white-dominated crime writing. In a closely allied process, these approaches also respond to other black literature, to more mainstream writing as well as to genre fiction.

Particularly in the 1990s, there has been a proliferation of black crime writers, both in the USA and in Britain, both male and female. The selection in this chapter takes in a range of writers, from Himes in the 1950s and 1960s to contemporary novelists such as Walter Mosley, John Ridley, Mike Phillips, BarbaraNeely, and Charlotte Carter. We will draw in some of the key issues debated by recent critics, centring on the question of how a challenge to generic whiteness becomes transformational. The growth of interest in black crime writing since 1990 in itself prompts the question of whether what we are seeing here is another example of the widespread commodification of the black image, with clichéd representations devaluing the work being produced. Chester Himes went to France in part because he hoped to encounter there less racial prejudice in the publishing

---

[5] Phillips quoted by Wells 1999: 210.

industry ('America only allows one black man at a time to become successful from writing'[6]). In contrast, contemporary black writers, and white writers who choose to write about black protagonists, can be accused of producing their novels simply to cash in at a time when 'race sells': Paul Cobley suggests that 'in the realm of production and consumption there have been numerous arguments to the effect that "black popular culture" in the twentieth century is the creation of white business' (2000: 135).

As a question about the texts themselves, what this most obviously relates to is the issue of whether the racial dimension is just a super-ficial exploitation of racial themes, or whether the text genuinely interrogates white ideology. By creating black characters, and by look-ing through their eyes at white characters and at a society in which wealth and power are in white hands, novelists can provoke resistance to ingrained habits of thought. They can disrupt the reader's ten-dency to take whiteness for granted, thus countering the effects of the kind of white-authored crime fiction that comments only on the race of non-white characters. This reversal of the racial binary in itself, however, may be charged with leaving binary habits of thought and racial categories intact. A strategy that involves the creation of posi-tive images of blackness can be as reductive as negative stereotyping, simply reinscribing the black–white binary in a different form. Issues such as these are at the heart of most discussions of black crime fiction. Do black writers bear a 'burden of representation', requiring them to represent all the diverse effects of racial marginalization? How best are they to avoid oversimplifying constructions of racial identities? Is there such a thing as an 'authentic' form of blackness, as suggested by the Black Arts and Black Power movements of the 1960s–1970s?

One centrally important element in the response to such questions has been the concept of diasporic culture, which suggests the limita-tions of a commitment to 'positive' images of blackness. It also gives support to the argument that well-meaning positive but reductionist constructions of racial identity might be regarded as hardly less racist than hostile stereotyping. Cornell West, for example, proposes a 'cul-tural politics of difference', a rejection of a 'homogenizing impulse'

---

[6] Himes in interview with Jean Miotte, 1977, 'Conversation with Chester Himes', in Fabre and Skinner 1995: 121.

(West 1993: 17) that offers sameness rather than acknowledging the heterogeneity of black subject positions and multicultural diversity. Amongst British cultural theorists, it is perhaps Stuart Hall who states the case against oppositional modes of thought most persuasively. Drawing on the Bakhtinian idea of a dialogic way of thinking, he sees the interpretation of culture as requiring a recognition of the dialogues taking place amongst a variety of marginalized voices: 'The emergence of new subjects, new genders, new ethnicities, new regions, new communities, hitherto excluded from the major forms of cultural representation, unable to locate themselves except as decentered or subaltern, have acquired through struggle, sometimes in very marginalized ways, the means to speak for themselves for the first time.'[7] In what follows, it will become apparent how significant 'subaltern' postcolonial voices are to a reading of black British crime fiction of the 1990s. All the novels we will be looking at, however, can to some extent be seen as trying to avoid 'either–or' conceptions of racial identity, and to be addressing the problem of representing a diversity of 'decentred' discourses.

One of the better-known analyses of the creation of a distinctive voice in black crime fiction is that of Stephen Soitos in *The Blues Detective* (1996). Soitos uses the metaphor of the blues to signify the African-American ability to recreate European or American art forms to their own ends (Soitos 1996: 9). He identifies four key 'tropes' or 'figures of thought': the detective persona, double consciousness, black vernaculars, and hoodoo. The analysis draws on vernacular criticism, and in particular on the argument of Henry Louis Gates in *The Signifying Monkey* (1989) that black texts employing 'the conventions of literary form that comprise the western tradition' do so in ways that significantly alter these traditions. Gates sees black difference as manifesting itself 'in specific *language* use', particularly in the ironic reworking of what is appropriated, what Gates calls 'repetition with a signal difference' (Gates 1989: 52). The liberatory mimicry of reverse discourse invests its negative categories with positive meaning. The creation of black rhetorical styles functions to 'turn' a discourse

---

[7] Hall, 'The Local and the Global: Globalisation and Ethnicity', in *Culture, Globalisation and the World System*, ed. Anthony D. King. London: Macmillan, 1991: 34, quoted by Wells 1999: 209.

like hard-boiled fiction, offering a way of 'claiming the I'.[8] Within the
tradition of hard-boiled crime fiction, the argument runs, this is an
important form of resistance, because voice is so crucial an element
in most white-authored examples of the genre.[9] The tough masculine
persona of the hard-boiled protagonist has almost invariably been
white, and a transformation of voice is seen as crucial in detaching a
novel's centre of consciousness from the ideology and racial identity
conventionally associated with the genre. As we will see, there is a
wide variety of such alternative voices, ranging from the Jamaican
patois of the coke-snorting gang boss in Victor Headley's *Yardie* to
the tartly satiric inner voice of BarbaraNeely's outwardly deferential
black maid, Blanche White. Whether or not one agrees that the
tripled subject position of white-male-hetero is 'sacred, unchallengeable' in hard-boiled fiction, it is clearly the case, as Maureen T. Reddy
notes, that many contemporary black writers have seen their detective
series 'as motivated at least in part by their desire to create an
"authentic" or "true" voice in that genre for a person of their own
race/ethnicity, asserting that the genre has been missing such a voice'
(Reddy 2003a: 48).

The detective or crime story is an ideal form for the exploration of
suppressed realities. The investigative structure provides a ready-
made instrument for unearthing the previously invisible crimes
against a people—the events preserved in oral history that Gary
Phillips calls the 'hidden history' of a city like Los Angeles. The act of
looking at what has been hidden is in itself fraught with meaning.
The development of an 'authentic voice' is inextricably linked to the
establishment of an angle of vision that allows readers to see the site
of crime in a different way—to escape the limitations of the (white)
observing eye that has constituted otherness and marginality whilst

[8] Campbell and Kean 1997: 82; as Gruesser 1999: 237–8 points out, the strength of
this counter-discursive strategy lies in the fact that it is 'distinctively black' without
claiming to reflect a 'black essence', and without simply repudiating assertions of black
inferiority.

[9] Reddy 2003a: 8–9 quotes Bethany Ogdon, 'Hard-Boiled Ideology' (*Critical
Quarterly*, 34/1, 1999: 74): 'I think [the centrality of voice] is the element that most
attracts writers interested in challenging hard-boiled racial and sexual codes—because
the voice is everything. To change the voice, to let the Other speak, is to transform the
genre by replacing the traditional central consciousness with another that does not
share the ideology or the racial (or sexual or gender) identity around which the genre
formed.'

not recognizing its own act of looking.[10] The Du Boisian theme of double consciousness is strongly present in the work of the writers we are examining here. Each novel in its way represents the difficulties of 'always looking at the world through the eyes of others, of measuring one's soul by the tape of a world that looks on in amused contempt and pity'.[11] In revisioning the relationship of race, class, and crime, the eye of the protagonist also catches whiteness in the act of perception. Rather than being taken for granted, racial construction now operates in the opposite direction, and the 'implicitness' of whiteness is undermined. Just as feminist crime novels self-consciously reverse the male gaze in the process of appropriating the 'I' of the private eye novel, black writers use the centrality of vision in the crime novel to turn the tables, and, because the genre is so centred on perception, the result is 'a degree of reflective interrogation as to the mechanisms of scrutiny' (Walton and Jones 1999: 158–9, 198).

Structurally, the reversal of the gaze goes with a shift in agency. Unless the protagonist is ultimately unable to act, this reversal goes with a redistribution of power and with a refocusing of investigative objectives. Assuming that the disruption of the black/white binary is more than a superficial change, this reversal must be accompanied by a re-examination of the full implications. Race and its encodings will function as a mainspring of the narrative, not merely as an issue that is discussed in passing. In the analyses that follow, we will be considering some of the ways in which race *is* placed at the centre of the plot, influencing the attribution of guilt and the shaping of narrative patterns (for example, Walter Mosley's narratives of 'passing' in contrast to the gangster-centred 'Yardie' novels of Headley or Neely's take on the classic detective novel). The novels discussed also make the scene of the crime a carrier of meaning, exploring the racialized spaces of different urban locations, which are also psychological locations (Reddy 2003a: 82). There are significant changes in the handling of urban space over the last few decades, evident if we contrast, for example, the claustrophobic enclosure of Himes's Harlem cycle with more recent novels representing the movement across the racial

---

[10] This is analogous to the all-encompassing 'English eye' that Stuart Hall describes as seeing everything but failing to recognize 'that it is itself actually looking at something' (Wells 1999: 212).

[11] W. E. B. Du Bois, *The Souls of Black Folk. Essays and Sketches*. Chicago: A. C. McClurg, 1903: 215; and see Campbell and Kean 1997: 80.

boundaries of a sprawling Los Angeles. Like much of the mid-century American writing that transformed the earlier investigative structures of detective and crime fiction, then, the most interesting black crime fiction moves towards distinctive reworkings of the plot structures, the crimes and threats at the heart of the narrative. It re-imagines the characteristic urban spaces and resolutions of the genre, compelling readers to re-examine their assumptions and stereotypes.

As this suggests, the role of the reader is also at issue here. The aim of the writer who sets out to revise a popular genre is presumably to provoke a degree of unease in the reader, to unsettle preconceptions. This negotiation with readers, however, is by no means a simple matter to gauge, if we are justified in assuming that readers themselves play a very active role in this process, constructing their own meanings, transgressive or otherwise, through their interaction with the text. Discussions of the novels included here often address the question of the racial identity of the readers themselves: that is, of whether particular groups of readers will simply content themselves with the most superficially obvious meaning. When a publisher like X Press turns out novels about Jamaican drug dealers, will the black audience at which they are aimed see them as a glorification of violence? Will white readers of such novels come away with no more than a sense of stereotypes confirmed? Does a writer like Walter Mosley, who has a very substantial white audience, bring his readers to identify with his black protagonist in such a way that they need to negotiate differing subjectivities? Or does Mosley's huge popularity amongst white liberal readers who occupy an 'always already determined' position suggest that he is insufficiently disturbing, distancing the struggles of Easy Rawlins to such an extent that we are able without discomfiture to identify with a man who is the victim of white prejudice? Such questions are related to the wider debate of whether we are really only capable of the passive consumption of popular culture or whether we can resist our 'interpellation within the racial status quo' (Reddy 2003a: 188–9). One function of criticism is to encourage readers to apply more rigorous standards in their own interpretative acts—to make white liberal readers, for example, examine the easy assumptions they are inclined to make about what constitutes a progressive treatment of racial issues. As Reddy suggests, we might want to ask whether the novels examined do in fact 'force the white reader into the position of the Other's Other' or whether they permit the white reader to escape the positioning of whiteness in the novel and to stand instead with the black protagonist, identifying with his or her rebel status (2003*a*: 79).

'A Harlem of my mind'[12]

Chester Himes, *Blind Man with a Pistol* (1969)

No black crime writer has provoked more debate about how we should read him than has Chester Himes. Himes's writing career spans over four decades, from the early 1930s, when he began writing short stories whilst imprisoned in Ohio State Penitentiary for armed robbery, to the 1970s, when he published his two-volume auto-biography. In his early writing, he was determined to play a part in the black struggle against oppression. The mid-1940s, when he published his first novels (*If He Hollers Let Him Go* in 1945 and *Lonely Crusade* in 1947), was a time that saw an increasingly interventionist federal attitude, with the Truman administration, for example, appointing a Presidential Committee on Civil Rights in 1946, heralding twenty years of effort, in the face of Southern intransigence, to secure legislation that would achieve desegregation. Himes, however, left the United States, moving to France in 1953, and it was there that he was commissioned by Marcel Duhamel of Gallimard's Série Noire to write his Harlem cycle. The move came just a year before what is generally seen as the key judicial breakthrough in the civil rights movement, the day seen by much of the South as 'Black Monday'—17 May 1954—when Chief Justice Earl Warren gave the judgment of the Supreme Court in the case of *Brown* v. *Board of Education of Topeka, Kansas*, that 'in the field of public education the doctrine of "separate but equal" has no place. Separate educational facilities are inherently unequal.'[13] This was a decision followed by some of the most dramatic events of the mid-century battle for civil rights: the sending of

---

[12] Himes in interview with Michael Mok, 1972, 'Chester Himes', in Fabre and Skinner 1995: 105–7.

[13] Bradbury and Temperley [1981] 1998: 167. The landmark Supreme Court case of *Brown* v. *Board of Education* (1954) settled the question of whether or not blacks and whites can receive an education integrated with or separate from each other. Linda

federal troops to Little Rock, Arkansas;[14] the spread of Klan-like groups resisting change by resorting to mob violence and murder, burnings, and bombings; the broadening of the battle against segregation in, for example, the Montgomery Bus Boycott. Himes's departure from the United States removed him from the possibility of active involvement in the civil rights movement, and the fact that he was living in France and writing at the behest of a French publisher has led some critics to question whether the body of fiction that he wrote while living there can in fact be classed as 'black American crime writing' (Cobley 2000: 36–7).

There is no question that the mid-1950s was a watershed for Himes, but it cannot be conceptualized in terms of simple uprooting and separation from the African-American struggle. His emigration to France marked not just his movement away from his earlier novels of social protest, but also a shift in his view of whether American racial conflicts were susceptible to solution. Sean McCann, in *Gumshoe America*, argues persuasively that it is important to understand the ramifications (in literature as well as in terms of social justice) of the fact that the *Brown* v. *Topeka* decision represented a change in emphasis from economic factors to social and psychological factors, and that this was of considerable significance in separating Himes from the new generation of black writers who came to prominence in the 1950s, most notably Ralph Ellison and James Baldwin.[15] The

Brown was an 8-year-old black child who had to cross Topeka to attend grade school, instead of going to a school a few blocks away, because the Topeka School system was segregated (under the 'separate but equal' doctrine, this arrangement was acceptable and legal). Linda's parents sued on the basis that separate facilities for blacks were inherently unequal.

[14] In September 1957, three years after the Supreme Court's *Brown* v. *Topeka* decision, a federal court ordered Little Rock, Arkansas, to comply by ending their public-school segregation. Governor Orval Faubus defied the court, and eventually President Eisenhower dispatched 101st Airborne Division paratroopers, putting the Arkansas National Guard under federal command. The nine African-American students (the 'Little Rock Nine') finished out the school year under federal protection.

[15] Bradbury and Temperley [1981] 1998: 168–9, characterizing both writers as liberal, argue that Ellison sees 'the alienated plight of blacks [as matching] that of all modern sufferers of disorientation and persecution, and urges the need for the individual to accept a private and public responsibility for reality'; and that Baldwin, in spite of strictures on liberals, is to be seen as liberal in the sense that he has a 'belief in the integrity and reality of the individual, his model of a society of socially responsive individuals, his stance as moral teacher, his devotion to the human being, his freedom and fulfilment'.

Supreme Court decision, McCann suggests, is an important element in the transition between New Deal liberalism and 1950s liberalism. In the 1930s and 1940s, thinking about race was influenced by the Depression-fostered, New Deal prioritizing of economic issues and a preoccupation with class consciousness: black leaders had tended to think, in the phrase of W. E. B. Du Bois, of the Negro standing amongst 'the throngs of disinherited and underfed men'.[16] From the mid-1950s through the late 1960s, however, liberals and civil rights leaders were much less inclined to see the black cause as inextricably linked to economic disenfranchisement and a wider class struggle. Those like Himes and Richard Wright, who had invested their hopes in this ideal of 'interracial populist brotherhood', saw the earlier sense of promise recede with the decline of the leftist politics of the Roosevelt years. Himes continued, but more pessimistically, to think in predominantly economic terms of creating in his crime novels a Harlem deformed by economic disenfranchisement, a brutal environment, and white exploitation. He saw it cruelly deceived by those who pretended to offer redemption of a different kind, whether religious salvation or a return to 'roots'.

From Himes's own perspective, this shift of the mid-1950s was crucial in bringing him to realize that the kind of protest novel he had written in the 1940s would not accomplish the transformations he had looked towards. He did, however, see fundamental continuities between his earlier work and the Harlem cycle. In interview in 1970, he said of his crime novels:

[M]ore and more readers have realized that the essence of these stories lies in the fact that there really are people who live like this, and because they do, this is the way they will act when living under racist oppression. Recently, people have begun to think that these stories represent a bolder kind of racial protest than the explicit protest novels I wrote years ago.[17]

Asked in another interview to class himself in terms of the mid-century protest movements, he said that he did not consider himself 'an activist', but that he had 'written the most militant prose ever printed to condemn American racism', and that he did believe that ultimately

---

[16] Du Bois, 'My Evolving Program for Negro Freedom', in *What the Negro Wants*, ed. Rayford W. Logan, 65, quoted by McCann 2000: 258–9.

[17] Himes in interview with Willi Hochkeppel, 1970, 'Conversation with Chester Himes', in Fabre and Skinner 1995: 26–8.

'organized revolution with violence' was probably 'the only way for the blacks to instill enough fear into the whites to make them back down'.[18]

These and other interviews that Himes gave in the 1970s constitute an implicit response to the charge that the move to France detached him from his role as a black American writer. He stressed how deeply his perspective was embedded in the history of mid-century American racial conflict. He had fully experienced the hurt and anger of the 'inescapable fact' of racism in his own working life: 'it seemed to stick to me. It contaminated everything,' he said of his years in LA.[19] After his departure to France, he followed closely the achievements of the black activists of the 1960s, and came increasingly to see his novels of that period as his own form of protest. Though he emphasized that the Harlem of what he called his 'domestic novels' was his own imaginative construct, 'a Harlem of my mind', he also talked frequently about his sense of himself as always writing out of his own experience of being black in America. One can argue, then, that Himes's crime novels are in part such compelling reading because of the brutal directness with which they confront the racial conflicts of mid-century America, reshaping the genre to confront the pain and violence of this period. Interviewed by Philip Oakes in 1969, Himes said that he felt the novels of the Harlem cycle had become parables of the plight of African Americans.[20]

Himes's frequent reference in interview to the question of his responsibilities as a black writer is not surprising, given that the continuing controversy over the Harlem cycle almost invariably centres on some aspect of the burden of representation. As Henry Louis Gates has observed, even if a black writer has devoted his writing career to demonstrating that the burden of representation is an illusion, he realizes that 'it follows you everywhere like your own shadow'.[21] Himes's critics from the 1950s on have demonstrated the

---

[18] Himes in interview with David Jenkins, 1971, 'Profile of Chester Himes', ibid. 102.

[19] Himes in interview with Francois Bott, 1964, 'Chester Himes: An Interview', ibid. 14.

[20] Himes in interview with Mok, in Himes 1995: 105–7; Himes in interview with Oakes, ibid. 21–2.

[21] Michiko Kakutani, 'Coping with the Idea of Representing One's Race', *New York Times*, 28/1/1997, online at www.pulitzer.org/year/1998, quoting from Henry Louis Gates, *Thirteen Ways of Looking at a Black Man*. New York: Random House, 1997.

truth of this, coming back repeatedly to his refusal to provide 'positive images', to his statement that his 'parables' offer 'no solution', and to his vision of what appears to be unending and unredeemed violence. Claire Wells, for example, writing in Klein's *Diversity and Detective Fiction*, argues that Himes's black detectives, Coffin Ed and Grave Digger Jones, are 'brutal characters driven by a deep rage to beat and kill other blacks—a sort of psychotic reaction to systematized racial self-hatred'. She charges that in the Harlem cycle white readers are introduced to a 'moral underworld' that would have been seen as an accurate reflection of black life, creating stereotypical characters 'seemingly without much sense of authorial irony', thus confirming the racist preconceptions of the time: 'Himes seemed engaged in publicly taking revenge on his blackness, reworking an internal conflict about himself into an urban fantasy' (Wells 1999: 211–12). The black British crime writer Mike Phillips says (in interview with Wells, 1999: 212) that when he began writing he 'took Chester Himes as a dreadful object lesson'.

Many other recent critics, however, have found in Himes's fiction 'lessons' of a much more radical and transformative kind, and have looked for ways of constructing meanings in his fiction that would give support to his own judgement that, although they offer no solution, 'they go some way towards explaining the violence of the current situation'.[22] Amongst the most persuasive lines of analysis are those clarifying the fact that, although he may have been living in France, Himes's satiric responses to the times he was living through were very firmly grounded in the socio-historical context of an America from which he never really detached himself. Perhaps the most obvious question to be addressed is that of tone. Whereas Wells, for example, bases her judgement of Himes in part on what she sees as an absence of authorial irony, others have argued for the presence of considerably more sophisticated rhetorical strategies. The 'moral underground' of Harlem is presented in ways that render it grotesque and surreal (a strategy closely akin to that of the other satiric crime fiction discussed in Chapter 4). This heightened, absurdist vision,

---

[22] Himes in interview with Oakes, in Fabre and Skinner 1995: 21–2. Himes added, 'In fact, I've come to believe that the only way the American Negro will ever be able to participate in the American way of life is by a series of acts of violence. It's tragic, but it's true.'

crowded with carnivalesque details and ludic inversions,[23] can be seen as allied with the ironizing impulse of reverse discourse. The first question here is perhaps, if the Harlem cycle is read in this way, what are the objects of Himes's satire? In a period in which race relations were seen as undermining America's Cold War image as the defender of democracy, the Harlem cycle is an assault on the optimistic liberal consensus. It calls into question the belief that integration is just around the corner.

In the mid-1960s, the integrationist ideal of an easily assimilated black citizenry could perhaps be seen as exemplified by Sidney Poitier playing Virgil Tibbs, 'a white man with a black skin' (Cochran 2000: 96), in the film adaptation of John Ball's novel *In the Heat of the Night* (1965; film version 1967). In the year following the publication of Ball's novel, Himes's addition to the Harlem cycle was *The Heat's On*, a novel which centres on an alternative image of a black man approximating to whiteness. Pinkie, the giant albino, is a bizarre, fatherless, displaced version of the white black man. Instead of the Virgil Tibbs nose, 'almost like a white man's', and his 'straight and disciplined' lips, Himes gives his readers a 'milk-white albino with pink eyes, battered lips, cauliflowered ears and thick, kinky, cream-colored hair', wearing 'a white T-shirt, greasy black pants held up with a length of hemp rope, and blue canvas rubber-soled sneakers'.[24] Harlem itself, like Pinkie, cannot be conveniently packaged for the reassurance of white liberals, but threatens at every point to erupt with catastrophic consequences: ' "The Valley", that flat lowland of Harlem east of Seventh Avenue, was like the frying pan of hell. Heat was coming out of the pavement, bubbling from the asphalt; and the atmospheric pressure was pushing it back to earth like the lid on a pan' (Himes [1966] 1996: 343).

The extremity of these images, characteristic of the whole of the Harlem cycle, gives Himes a way of breaking up conventional pieties and false assurances that the conflicts can be resolved. The naturalism of Himes's early novels is still in evidence, particularly in his insistence on the warping effects of environment. In the Harlem cycle, however, naturalism combines with absurdism to produce an inversion of

---

[23] This aspect of Himes's work is well covered by McCann 2000: 251–308 *passim*.

[24] Ball, *In the Heat of the Night*. New York: Harper and Row, 1965: 13; Himes, *The Heat's On* (1966), in *The Harlem Cycle*, ii Edinburgh: Payback Press, 1996: 325.

all redemptive possibilities, whether these involve signs of harmonious co-operation with white society or the hope for a discovery of roots and of connections with a nourishing ancestral heritage.[25] Himes provides a powerful picture of the material conditions of Harlem, the poverty and deprivation, but, pushing his prose more towards the symbolic than the realistic, he shifts our attention from causes to consequences. He structures his narratives around the activities of assorted con men who all, in one way or another, exploit the desperate hopes of the people of Harlem for escape or salvation (fool's gold and empty political promises, tickets to heaven or tickets back to Africa). But the con men who swarm through Harlem are ultimately less guilty than the attitudes towards race, the capitalistic greed and exploitation of American society as a whole. Himes's pessimism about the possibility of an imminent resolution to this distress and conflict is apparent in the progression of the Harlem cycle as a whole, in which a growing preoccupation with consequences is to be seen in the increasingly unresolved nature of the narratives. If the novels of the cycle are categorized simply as 'detective stories' (with their structural commitment to the discovery of causes), then the last completed novel of the cycle, *Blind Man with a Pistol*, can be seen as the ultimate breakdown of the form under pressure of violence that has no single identifiable cause. More accurately, however, we might say that the initial combination of crime and detective story in the series undergoes a gradual shift towards crimes and their consequences (the structural pattern of the crime novel, which moves from cause to effect). That is, if we ask what the form itself signifies, we see the irresolvable effects that white racism has produced. The real 'villain', the construct of a white society, is 'skin'—a form of villainy routinely punished by white institutional law and order (Walton and Jones 1999: 146–7). Himes's pessimistic vision of race relations in mid-century America is imaged in increasing structural fragmentation and in plots that seem less and less susceptible to resolution. By the time of *Blind Man* (published in 1969), narrational breakdown is extreme, with temporal confusion, the non-solution of crimes, the refusal to subordinate any of the proliferating plots to a

[25] See Cochran 2000: 281, on how Himes systematically inverts the ideals of Baldwin in particular.

master plot, the 'leakage' between plots, and the tendency of characters to metamorphose into one another, with consequent disturbances of identity. For Himes, one can argue, this fragmenting and confusion embody the state of the society he's representing, a 'literary ruin' that mirrors the 'dilapidation' of the Harlem Himes depicts (Forter 2000: 174–80).

There is a strong contemporary political resonance. Published in the year after the assassination of Martin Luther King, *Blind Man* represents a preacher urging non-violence as the first one to be shot by the blind man; his next shot kills a white cop who saw himself as protecting 'the whole white race' from the gun-wielding black man. The eruption of the blind man's violence was based on an actual incident, Himes said, that sounded to him 'like today's news, riots in the ghettos, war in Vietnam'.[26] The shootings he depicts are in one sense random and pointless, but also fortuitously appropriate. Most obviously, perhaps, the blind man can be seen as acting out the repressed rage of Harlem's deluded and downtrodden inhabitants. He is unwilling to admit that he cannot see or that he does not know what he is doing, but feels compelled to take some action against those who are tormenting him. The incident can be read, as can the whole of the Harlem cycle, as an expression of Himes's own inner rage and hurt. Whilst this could, of course, be, as Wells alleges, the projection of his own 'internal conflict about himself' into an 'urban fantasy' (1999: 212), it can clearly also be argued that, drawing on his own deep-seated anger, Himes understands but also despairs of acts of violence in response to the actual and psychological damage inflicted on African Americans. If minoritization is in effect a form of emasculation, then the blind man, however irrational his act, has seized a means of masculine empowerment. Though he brings destruction on himself, he has briefly overcome his impotence in the face of racist oppression.

A psychoanalytic reading of the Harlem cycle can be pushed further, towards seeing it as an exploration of the pathological effects of racism. One of the more sophisticated of such readings is that of Greg Forter, whose *Murdering Masculinities* (2000) argues that Himes's crime novels use white conceptions of blackness, incorporating them

---

[26] Himes's Prefatory note to *Blind Man With a Pistol*, [1969] 1997: 193.

in a 'waste' in which white readers are unconsciously implicated. In this reading, Himes's Harlem is the repository of the psychic waste of white society: stereotypes exploded from within are thrown back at white readers as '*psychic* waste', and Himes asks his readers to 'assimilate the inassimilable'. Extending this argument, Forter analyses the way that Himes uses excremental imagery to produce an 'interpretive meltdown', with white readers in effect being asked to incorporate the refuse of white identity, the 'externalized blackness' that results when they 'find in the image of a human "other" a darkness they cannot own in themselves' (Forter 2000: 173–4, 186–7, 191–2). This confrontation with the 'waste' of Harlem, then, is being seen as the enforced reinternalization of racial stereotypes. Such an interpretation obviously goes considerably beyond the performative resignification of reverse discourse. It presents white readers as compelled to encounter the degraded images through which they habitually 'see' blackness—to encounter the 'excremental blackness' created by a white community that is not just socially destructive but psychotic in its insistence on 'an impossible racial purity' (Forter 2000: 201–3). Read in this way, *Blind Man*'s eponymous gunman fulfils a more complex function than a simple expression of suppressed rage. Most importantly, he can be read as a subversive echo of the visual power associated with Himes's detectives, who are repeatedly figured in the novels as moving invisibly through the darkness of Harlem but empowered because they can 'see in the dark', thus participating in 'a symbolic and scopic register from which African American masculinity is habitually excluded'. The binary in question (white looking and power as opposed to black objectification and powerlessness) is challenged in a different way by the blind man. Like Coffin Ed and Grave Digger, he wields a pistol and is thus identified with the symbol of phallic power, and he believes that he possesses the power of vision. But since he is actually blind, his refusal to acknowledge his visual impairment is a form of insanity, analogous (Forter suggests) to the self-delusion of black cops who identify with the white masculine power structures that confer authority on them (Forter 195–6).

Although their work does not, on the whole, sustain such complex readings, there were, amongst Himes's contemporaries and successors, a number of other black writers who have attracted the same sorts of criticism for their work as has Himes. Wells, interviewing the black British crime writer Mike Phillips, observes that it is 'perhaps indicative of a certain consensus about what has traditionally been commercially viable in black crime writing that more recently several writers have followed Himes's descent into the moral underground' (1999: 212). This is obviously in a sense true, and in spite of the movement within black cultural studies beyond 'positive images', many critics are still reluctant to extend their approval to such raw (many would argue unredeemed) images of black crime and violence. A number of earlier 'black underground' writers added to the tradition of harsh, grim urban crime (as opposed to crime plus detective) novels. Perhaps the best-known of the novels encompassed in this sort of generalization are the tough, brutal narratives of writers like Robert Beck (Iceberg Slim) and Donald Goines, both of whom had even more experience than did Himes of street life and criminality— of pimping, hustling, drug-dealing, and violence. Iceberg Slim, who worked in the Chicago area for over twenty years as a pimp, was imprisoned several times, including a stretch in Leavenworth; Goines, a pimp, thief, bootlegger, numbers runner, and heroin addict, spent over six years in prison, and was shot to death in 1974, at the age of 39, according to some versions as a result of a failed drugs deal. Both were published by Holloway House, who bill themselves as the 'World's Largest Publisher of Black Experience Paperbacks' and aim to produce an 'alternative' black literature in paperback. Like Himes, both made powerful use of the noir sense of otherness and marginality as an equivalent for racial exclusion. Writing mainly during the 1970s, both admired the radicalism of the Black Panthers more unequivocally than Himes did. Goines, writing under the pseudonym Al C. Clark, wrote a series of four novels, the protagonist of which, Kenyatta, is the leader of a militant group dedicated to expunging drugs and prostitution from the ghettos. Iceberg Slim's first autobiographical novel, *Pimp: The Story of my Life*, was published in 1969, at a time when he could be marketed along with such black militants as Eldridge Cleaver and Malcolm X.

Though neither Goines nor Beck has received the kind of critical re-evaluation that has been given to the work of Himes, both used their unpolished crime stories to express black anger and to present unflinchingly the evils of ghetto life and a hatred of white values and hypocrisy. One might suggest that this shift in itself has contributed to their neglect. Those novelists who retain at least strong elements of a detective structure leave open the possibility of inserting some more positive scenes within their hard-boiled fiction—'scenes of instruction' or 'a more progressive handling of race' (Reddy 2003a: 66–7, 188–9). The choice of a straightforward crime structure, on the other hand, means that Goines and Beck do not technically qualify for inclusion in studies of black detective fiction. But their exclusion is also in keeping with the attitudes of such studies to the 'pulpier' end of pulp fiction and the extremity of content that this entails. So, for example, all mention of Beck and Goines is omitted from Soitos's *The Blues Detective*, from Paula Wood's excellent anthology, *Spooks, Spies and Private Eyes*, and from Maureen T. Reddy's ground-breaking study of race and detective fiction, *Traces, Codes, and Clues*. By drawing boundaries, though not always consistently,[27] around detective as opposed to crime fiction, such analyses exclude work which is focused through the perspectives of transgressors—that is, work considered as not just too far beyond the pale, perhaps, but too far inside the ghetto. In such fiction, the genre is brought uncompromisingly into contact with 'the life' in so unmediated and so 'unliterary' a way that (in spite of their own sense of writing against white oppression) Beck and Goines are not seen as employing genre fiction to serious and responsible ends. They are, as Paul Cobley says of Goines, marginalized because they 'do not fit nicely with current critical predilections'.[28] Obviously the present study does little to remedy this neglect, but as we move on to the great explosion of black crime writing in the 1990s, it is important, at least, to bear in mind that such writers are another important generic voice, and one against which many subsequent black crime writers have defined themselves, as they do against the ideology and conventions of white-authored crime fiction.

[27] So Reddy, for example, includes discussion of novels, like Charles Willeford's *Pick-Up*, which are not detective stories; and Soitos's discussion of Himes pays close attention to the mixed nature of his narratives.

[28] Cobley 2000: 137. Cobley has substantially contributed to redressing the balance in the case of Goines, whose work he analyses in a chapter called 'Sambos or Superspades?' (pp. 123–45).

Writing the other Los Angeles

Walter Mosley, *Devil in a Blue Dress* (1990); John Ridley, *Love is a Racket* (1998)

The 1990s saw a phenomenal increase in the number and variety of black crime novels, and, as Denise Hamilton (interviewing Paula Woods) suggests, 'Today's black writers are also expanding away from the gritty urban canon of authors such as Donald Goines and Iceberg Slim.'[29] Since the late 1980s, there have been twenty-five to thirty new black crime writers, some of whom have published half-a-dozen or more books. The success of such hugely popular black authors as Terry McMillan, Toni Morrison, and Alice Walker is often cited as one of the factors encouraging this phenomenon, as are the novels of Walter Mosley: 'Mosley's popularity', Paula Woods says, 'has paved the way on the part of publishers to say, "We'd like to have one like that, or two or three." '[30] Mosley is the best known member of an extremely vigorous Los Angeles crime-writing scene, and his work amply illustrates some of the ways in which the crime novel can be used, in the words of James Sallis, 'to say something about American society today', and specifically about race, the 'one big "story" there is to write about'.[31] Los Angeles (LA) has come to be seen as a kind of microcosm of American race relations in the 1990s, with its rapidly growing multi-ethnic population (making it the most multi-ethnic city in America). The riots that set the city ablaze in 1992, together with the rapidly rising numbers of hate crimes and of racially motivated violence, brought to national attention the fact that life in the poorest areas of the city had become intolerable. There is, then, a vast amount of contemporary material for the crime novel to assimilate, and several of the city's black crime writers of the 1990s have very deliberately set about creating novels that revise mainstream historical accounts of inner-city turmoil, providing counter-histories both

[29] Denise Hamilton, 'Black Women Writers Put their Brand on the Suspense Genre', *Los Angeles Times*, 20/1/1999, online at www.woodsontheweb.com.
[30] Woods, quoted by Hamilton, *Los Angeles Times*.
[31] Sallis quoted by Lawrence Donegan, 'Skin Deep in Crime', *The Observer*, 4/8/2002, online at: http://observer.guardian.co.uk/review/story.

of specifically African-American and of multi-ethnic experiences. Gary Phillips, for example, has been particularly explicit about his agenda in this respect. Coming out of a background of community activism, Phillips says he aims to write a suppressed 'people's history', and he draws into his Ivan Monk novels (from *Perdition USA* in 1996 to *Only the Wicked* in 2000) a very detailed knowledge of class and ethnic conflict in a turbulent Los Angeles.[32] Gar Anthony Haywood, like Phillips, sets his work in contemporary LA and similarly conceives of it as a highly politicized city. In his Aaron Gunner novels (for example, *Not Long for this World*, published in 1990, and *When Last Seen Alive*, published in 1997), he constructs plots which reflect this urban politicization: 'If I have an agenda,' he says, 'it's to make people more aware of what it's like to be an African American in contemporary Los Angeles [. . .] the built-in paranoia. I want them to see a viewpoint they may not have seen before.'[33] In creating his protagonist Aaron Gunner he tries, he says, 'to attach some issues near and dear to my heart, like the re-emergence of black militancy, gangs in the inner-city and [problems between] the African American community and the LAPD'.[34]

Although his writing of the Easy Rawlins novels has been influenced by contemporary events (such as the beating of Rodney King in 1992), Walter Mosley reaches further back into LA history, to the mid-1940s, for the start of his series, reclaiming what he sees as forgotten dimensions of the city's history. Reading him alongside Himes, one is struck by the fact that Mosley's first-person narratives are markedly more distanced and contained than the feverish novels of the Harlem cycle. This is partly, of course, a matter of tone: the phrase 'a Harlem of my mind' suggests, rightly, a place re-imagined in all the intense anger and frustration that beset Himes himself as he contemplated the black experience of America. But this distancing is also a consequence of the historical nature of Mosley's project in the Easy Rawlins novels, of his controlled progression from the immediately post-war period up to the present. Mosley sets about reconstituting the racial landscape of the city over a period of half a century

---

[32] 'Gary Phillips Interview', by Joyce Park, online at www.mysteryguide.com.
[33] Scott Timberg, 'A Darker Shade of Noir', 27/5/1999, online at www.woodsontheweb.com.
[34] Haywood, quoted by Hamilton, *Los Angeles Times*.

or more (ultimately aiming, he says, to take an ageing Easy up to 2000), tracing the power relationships involved in creating the 'other' LA that developed in the wake of the Second World War. This is a process of re-mapping urban spaces that has both positive and nega-tive dimensions. In part, Mosley is reaching back to a sustaining memory of communal closeness. There is a nostalgic sense of what preceded the 'criminalized ghettos' of the contemporary imagination. The Easy Rawlins series begins in *Devil in a Blue Dress* by returning to LA itself as one of the dreams of salvation, the sort of thing that characters in Himes's Harlem long for, a paradisal California: 'People told stories of how you could eat fruit right off the trees and get enough work to retire one day. The stories were true for the most part but the truth wasn't like the dream. Life was still hard in L.A. and if you worked every day you still found yourself on the bottom' (Mosley [1990] 1992: 34). Having arrived in California, Easy Rawlins is still in many respects a migrant. His spatialized conception of the American Dream as property ownership constitutes a kind of fixed point in the narrative, but mobility within the wider city is a constant necessity, whether as part of the liberatory process of 'making it', or as trans-gression into alien parts of the city, as mobility across the colour line. These are narratives of 'passing' in various senses, with white restric-tions on black movement evident at every turn. The complex dis-criminations this introduces into the novels militates against any simple conception of a racial binary, as does the multicultural and physical character of Los Angeles itself: the idea of the 'split city' familiar from the Harlem cycle (the 'normal' world opposed to the urban 'underworld') is replaced by the fragmentation of the LA sprawl (Voss 1998: 159).

Whereas Himes's Harlem novels respond as the series continues to the turmoil of the times, ultimately spinning out of control by the last novels, Mosley's Easy Rawlins series is contained and ordered in numerous ways, thus conveying a much stronger sense of historical progression. Andrew Pepper uses the term 'circumspect' to describe Mosley's exploration of this difficult terrain (2000: 122), and one might add that it is restrained, both emotionally and formally. This is not the interiority implied by 'a Harlem of my mind'. The use of a detective rather than a detective-cum-crime structure imposes a sense of resolvability that is ultimately impossible in the Harlem cycle. The act of reaching back into the past implies a series of events to which there is a known outcome. The internal dimension of Mosley's history is primarily to do with the ways in which his central character struggles to interpret the experience of crossing into unfamiliar, white-dominated parts of the city. He is forced to confront rifts in his own identity, emerging as he tries to negotiate the hostile, treacherous power structures of the city, alternately resisting and compromising in his efforts to achieve some kind of control over his own life.

The complexity of Mosley's picture is there from the first novel of the series, *Devil in a Blue Dress*, which is centrally about the shifting categorizations of colour that Easy encounters as he moves through this racially divided landscape. The novel opens with a challenge to the racializing white perspective and a reminder of how embedded this perspective is in the LA crime fiction of earlier days. *Farewell, My Lovely*, perhaps the most widely known representation in genre fiction of LA in the mid-1940s, is strongly echoed, with Mosley reversing the binary. Where Chandler treats whiteness as invisible and inserts a caricatured black presence, Mosley interrogates whiteness, using Easy's black perspective to draw attention to whiteness as such, removing its taken-for-grantedness. As the novel develops, however, in keeping with the shift within black cultural politics away from understanding race in binary terms, it broadens out considerably beyond this. In doing so it builds on the moral confusions of earlier traditions of literary noir, whilst revising the tradition by bonding these confusions to issues of racial identity and empowerment.

Devil in a Blue Dress brings about generic transformation in part simply by focusing our attention on the voices in which the protagonist speaks, the inner divisions wrought by his black and American 'twoness'. It also makes the difficulties involved in encoding race central to Easy's Chandleresque quest for a missing woman. Easy's own sense of self-division is evident throughout, for example, in his self-confessed tendency to speak in different voices. He has, as Joppy says, tried to better himself, but the consequence is that educated and vernacular speech in themselves divide him. His voice is further fractured by his divided strategies for dealing with rage and frustration, and for trying to take control. In the presence of white characters whose interpellating gaze threatens to deprive him of his own identity, he reverts to a boyhood habit of self-preservation: 'Sometimes, when a white man of authority would catch me off guard, I'd empty my head of everything so I was unable to say anything' (pp. 176, 21). This silencing of Easy's voice is set against a 'hard' inner voice that comes to his aid at 'the worst times', telling him how to survive like a man. When he was under fire during the war, for example, 'The voice told me to "get off yo' butt when the sun comes down an kill that motherfucker. Kill him an rip off his fuckin' face with yo' bayonet, man. You cain't let him do that to you. Even if he lets you live you be scared the rest'a yo' life. Kill that motherfucker" ' (p. 21). The destabilizing of the masculine self is a recurrent element in literary and cinematic noir, in which even investigative figures tend to be flawed and vulnerable. What Mosley is doing, then, is adapting the familiar figure of the traumatized and self-divided protagonist to his racial themes, locating the source of Easy's traumas in the near-intolerable pressures of racial oppression and in confusions over racial identity.

Easy's struggle to overcome the rifts in his sense of self is closely linked to his desire to find, within the fragmented city, a space that is his own, psychologically as well as physically. The apparent attainment of this goal is in itself, however, fraught with dangers and contradictions. The house, figuring placement in American society as well as a secure sense of self, is in actuality more important to Easy than is the *femme fatale* of the title: 'that house meant more to me than any woman I ever knew. I loved her and I was jealous of her and if the bank sent the county marshal to take her from me I might have come at him with a rifle rather than to give her up' (pp. 19–20). The relationship between Easy and his house is heavily ironized. He secures his self-respecting black identity by the possession of his suburban American house, which in turn draws him ever more inexorably into the whole white-dominated system of capitalist exchange: ' "We all owe out something, Easy. When you owe out then you're in debt and when you're in debt then you can't be your own man. That's capitalism" ' (pp. 107–8). It is his mortgage that necessitates the formation of threatening relationships within the white community, subjugating him, making him dependent and, as things get out of hand, leading the white outside world to invade the sanctuary of his house. In short, his property ownership leads him to compromise at every turn his independent black sense of self. Arguably, the house can be seen as analogous to the woman who belongs to the figure of the father in classic *film noir*. It makes the intersection of masculine domination and white racial domination painfully clear, given that his possession of his house, his claim to a position as 'a man of property', can be classified as illegitimate in the eyes of white society.

The plot of *Devil in a Blue Dress* turns on the ambiguity both of Easy's position (the contradictory nature of his empowering/endangering roles as home-owner and detective) and of the object of his quest, Daphne Monet. Like Mrs Grayle in *Farewell, My Lovely*, Daphne is not what she seems. But again, Mosley recasts the character's deceptions and inner contradictions in terms of race, shifting the focus of our attention on to the arbitrariness of the colour line and the mistakenness of essentialist thinking about racial identity. Daphne is a site of uncertainty about racial identity but also of uncertainty about the reliability of Easy's own perceptions. When his confident placing of her as a white woman turns out to be wrong, it alters his understanding of the nature of his quest, and of the relationship in which he has been involved. Although Daphne does not herself emerge as a fully developed character, she is sufficiently complex to mirror in her own way Easy's sense of a divided self. In her case, this entails a sense that she exists both as her mulatto self, Ruby, and as Daphne, the more empowered but still vulnerable self that passes for white. Like the traditional *femme fatale*, Daphne/Ruby embodies aspects of the protagonist himself, desires that he seeks to deny. Here, however, rather than suppressed sexual desires or the transgressive pursuit of money and freedom, what she most clearly signifies is an entirely legitimate longing for a fulfilment of desires. Most importantly, it is the recognition of her colour (rather than the revelation of any guilt on her part) that denies her this fulfilment. Easy, like the traditional noir protagonist, is compelled to recognize his connection with her. Again, though, this is not a connection founded in actual guilt but in the divided natures forced upon each of them by the society that has shaped the nature of their 'twoness'.

Criticisms of Mosley's novel tend to crystallize around the question of whether it disturbs its readers too little. Is it perhaps a more 'comfortable' read for white readers than it ought to be? Does the novel's resolution too readily gloss over contradictions and conflicts? Affirmative answers to these questions are, it is argued, confirmed by the popularity, prizes, and commendations that Mosley has received, ranging from Edgar awards to the approbation of President Clinton. One approach is to place strongly positive emphasis on the effects of crossover: Valerie Wilson Wesley, for example, sees her Tamara

Hayle series as facilitating the kind of crossover between white and black, male and female that assists readers in negotiating differing subjectivities (Walton and Jones 1999: 160–1); Maureen T. Reddy, on the other hand, argues that such a process softens a novel's more uncomfortable and challenging themes (2003a: 95–7). The assumption here is obviously that white readers *should* find it profoundly unsettling to read about a black protagonist struggling against evils inflicted on him by the white world; they *should* feel deeply disturbed by a novel's representation of whiteness. The wide readership of *Devil in a Blue Dress* suggests that readers do not feel this kind of acute discomfiture. The explanation, it is suggested, is to be found both in the 'pastness' of the narrative and in its comforting sense of closure, which means that the novel ends by reinforcing the ideological views it purports to disrupt. Readers indulge themselves in the temporary pleasures of identifying with the outsider, a positioning facilitated by the historical setting. This enables them to participate in Easy's encounter with a temporally distant white culture in which they do not themselves feel implicated.

Carl Franklin's film adaptation (1995) has been accused, even more than the novel, of opting for this reassuring closure. In a narrative that figures the American Dream as property ownership, the nostalgic glow of the closing sequence, with the warmth and satisfaction of Easy's voice-over, can seem like (and arguably for most audiences will be) an ending that conveys a sense of sentimental resolution. This spatialized nostalgia, however, can itself be seen as an essential element of Mosley's/Franklin's re-mapping of black urban experience. It can be read as a counter-image to the stereotypical placing of black masculinity in the criminalized territory of the urban ghetto and a relocating of criminality in white rather than black LA. It is clearly part of Mosley's intention to establish this tenuously secured black migrant community as living and vital, the antithesis of the clichéd images of the 'hood', representing Watts at a time when it embodied black hopes of prosperity, even if the hopes are illusory, rather than a strife-torn ghetto. The 'pastness' of the narrative can, in the same way, be read not as a comforting method of distancing and reassuring white readers but as a construction of the past of Los Angeles that repeatedly brings to the fore historical betrayals. It is an important part of the African-American experience that so many blacks were lured to California by the prospect of jobs in the defence industry and of affordable housing. For an African-American able, like Easy, to own property because of the GI Bill, there is a constant struggle (imaged in both book and film) to retain this toehold on the American Dream, given the reality of discrimination and the consequent difficulty of holding on to a job. The sun-drenched suburban haven has to be perceived within the context of the spatial injustices that were an inescapable part of the black history of California. Franklin's *Devil in a Blue Dress* makes this apparent in the rhythms of the plot: we see the repeated incursions into Easy's treasured suburban space by violent and corrupt representatives of white society, whether Dewitt Albright or the Los Angeles police. The point is reinforced at the end of the film by the juxtaposition of the suburban idyll with a pointed reminder that the post-war black hold on the bottom rung of the ladder of success was threatened by an imminent backlash, heralded by the newspaper headline proclaiming, 'Negroes Angered by New Property Restrictions', a reminder of the restrictive housing regulations that were soon to reconfigure the space of LA for its black inhabitants.

In the novel as well as the film, it can be argued that an attentive reader will observe much that remains to disturb apparently comforting resolutions. Although we see Easy, taking on the role of detective, acquiring some degree of agency and acquiring greater mobility across boundaries within Los Angeles, we can say of the end of the narrative (as of the end of a Chandler or Hammett narrative) that the divisive character of the city remains. In Mosley's novel, this involves not just the layered corruption of an irredeemably hierarchical capitalistic society but the racially determined injustices that compound abuses of power—that produce boundaries, distort identities and constrict possibilities in ways that (whatever Easy's access to new individual assurance) will mean that his mobility within his city is always limited. In fact, part of Mosley's theme throughout the Easy Rawlins series is that every move towards upward mobility brings with it different forms of restriction and moral compromise, the harshly deterministic socio-political world against which Easy's liberal humanist ethos is a fairly flimsy defence. It might be argued that, in reading Mosley, we have to reverse the critical strategies deployed in support of Himes. That is, as readers of Himes we might choose to defend him against the charge of 'dreadful' extremity by emphasizing the pointedness of his critique of American society. In the case of

Mosley, we might feel that a balanced reading requires looking under the surface to find unresolved tensions, discovering what Andrew Pepper calls 'the underlying bleakness of Mosley's vision'.[35] Like many other hard-boiled writers, white as well as black (Himes, of course, but also, say, Hammett, Ellroy, Sallis), Mosley writes novels that cannot be neatly slotted into a political category, presenting us with a marginalized detective figure who is ultimately able to make only the most tenuous advances in an intractable society.

Another Los Angeles crime writer of the 1990s who has earned a place in the 'uneasy', unsettling school of hard-boiled writers is John Ridley, who draws, with darkly comic skill, on a range of literary and cinematic sources. The vision underlying his non-series, non-detective novels is of the nexus of class and race as a brutal determinant. In *Love is a Racket*, the market society and its controlling motivations are reduced almost wholly to appetitive self-interest: 'Truth,' his protagonist says, 'People like me—people at the bottom of the barrel regardless of race, but especially so if you've got any tint to your skin—the only rights we had were to get shoved around, beaten up, slapped to the floor, then shut up and take it and be happy that was all that had happened to us. God bless America' (Ridley [1998] 1999: 219). In contrast, say, to Beck and Goines, Ridley's firsthand knowledge of 'the life' is presumably not all that extensive, given that he was born in suburban Milwaukee, has a degree in East Asian culture and languages from New York University, and worked as a stand-up comedian before moving on to writing scripts for film and TV shows such as 'The Fresh Prince of Bel-Air'. He writes, however, from the street perspective of the small-time crook and grifter. A gifted parodist and comic writer, Ridley adds a layer of ironic awareness to the representation of the criminal protagonist. As in Himes, the satiric and grotesque elements alter the relationship of the reader to the grim content. Ridley's tone is inseparable from his use of a crime rather than a detective structure: there is no link with the order-restoring

---

[35] 2000: 135–6. Pepper develops his argument by saying that 'Himes and Mosley, like [. . .] all the "best" crime writers, cannot be neatly situated somewhere on the political spectrum. Their writing and characters are manifestations of an at times bewildering mixture of attitudes, ideologies, politics and ambitions; moving between hegemonic and counter-hegemonic positions, their detectives consciously subvert the values of an established or dominant culture while simultaneously policing its not so fluid boundaries.'

potential of detective fiction, and no real distinction between legitimate and illegitimate violence. Instead, the narrative moves towards a satiric vision of a society without the capacity for sane and civilized stability, in which violence remains meaningless and dehumanizing, both for those who suffer it and for those who inflict it. Society in consequence seems fundamentally anarchic, and the end of the narrative offers no closure, in the sense of a restoration of 'law and order'.

Ridley represents objectification by means of violence as one of the inescapable realities of the urban underworld his characters inhabit. This reduction of characters to things signifies, as it does in Himes's Harlem cycle, a world in which economic necessity or greed combine with economic power sustained by violence to deprive people of the ability to connect with others, to sustain any kind of fraternal feeling. The opening act of *Love is a Racket* is one of extreme violence unwillingly inflicted by one black man on another: Ty, a brutal but sympathetic heavy, breaks the fingers of Jeffty, the narrator, leaving him feeling that he has been reduced to a worthless object ('I got cozy with the dirt and rubbish' (p. 14)). It is a scene that introduces one of the central relationships of the novel, between two men who have, we find, not only their colour but much else in common. Their potential ability to connect with one another, however, is rendered impossible by economic imperatives: in Ty's case, these draw him to work for a Haitian gang boss, in Jeffty's, to the inveterate pursuit of the get-rich-next-time schemes of the hustler and con man.

The repeatedly thwarted con man is, for Ridley, a sympathetic (if also pathetic) everyman figure. Whereas Himes's novels reserve their worst scorn for the hustlers who take advantage of people's desperation, peddling bogus dreams of escape or redemption, there is in Ridley's city a democracy of delusion, and the figure of the con man deludes himself as much as others. His 'bottom of the heap' status is the main thing that drives the plot, his constant efforts to find a quick fix out of his situation invariably ending in disaster. Jeffty's self-delusions and his self-confessed weaknesses and viciousness are as much in view as they are in the case of a Jim Thompson protagonist, and the rhythms of his life are such that the death of one dream seems to require the immediate emergence of another, equally remote. The final scam he embarks on is a wholly self-serving version of the investigative figure's grail quest—the refashioning of his 'angel', a street girl who looks like Pier Angeli. It is 'a crazy swinger of an idea. An idea that could only be induced by a cocktail of booze and death. In a moment of high intoxication and crystal clarity, I was swept up in the rapture. Religion that had escaped me my entire life now over-flowed from inside me, and with it a vision came and went like a sighting of the Grail: a perfect, shining scam' (p. 175).

The antithesis of the confident masculinity associated with the clichéd image of the detective, Jeffty can be considered in relation to the 1990s cinema trend to depict black masculinity in more complex and humanized ways. He is one of those guys who are 'too small for people to ever step up and take notice of what we do' (p. 204). The highly visible forms of black masculinity that Ridley sends up in his blaxploitation parody, *Undercover Brother* (directed by Malcolm D. Lee, 2002), provide a perspective on the creation of Jeffty, who is so marginal and invisible that his 'nothingness' is in a sense protective. The representation of Jeffty's 'masculinity in crisis' is a theme that runs through the novel, in its events, its language, and its images. He has a gun he cannot bring himself to use, in contrast to the *femme fatale*, who of course uses his own gun to shoot him; he is virtually the antithesis of the blaxploitation action hero, conning 'mom and pop' stores out of small change, ineffectual, completely unsuccessful with women, a clownish figure, utterly uncool. The back story of what led to his falling out with his friend Nellis centres on the way in which Jeffty acted as a whore himself, using his offer of sex and flattery to get money out of his wife. All sense of unified or confident masculinity is undermined not just by a series of humiliations but by his persistent feminization, in incidents that reduce him, in his own estimation, to bitch or little girl.

Mosley, as we have seen, creates a protagonist who routinely experiences a splitting of identity: his self-division that can immobilize him at moments of crisis. In Ridley's comic vision of a much bleaker reality, the protagonist is fragmented both racially and sexually to such an extent that he almost ceases (ultimately does cease) to function altogether. There is no stable sense of a unified black identity. Like other LA crime writers, Ridley is very attuned to the ways in which a multicultural city challenges and erodes the sense of racial identity. The protagonist has a fairly unsympathetic view of 'the other', a miming of the social, sexual, and racial prejudices ascribed to the Hammett–Chandler era variety of hard-boiled hero, and to Shaft, for example, in the blaxploitation films of the 1970s (McCann 2000: 132). Here, however, such views are not a reflection of the protagonist's casual confidence in his own identity but a further element in the breakdown and fragmentation of his sense of self, a manifestation of his paranoid recognition that a multicultural LA can no longer, even in its seediest and most dangerous reaches, be considered as 'his city'.

Diasporic identities in contemporary Britain

Victor Headley, *Yardie* (1992); Mike Phillips, *Point of Darkness* (1994)

It was not until the end of the 1980s (with Mike Phillips's *Blood Rights* in 1989) and the 1990s that black British writers began to exploit the potential of crime fiction for developing a complex discourse of race. Conceiving of blackness in diasporic terms, these are writers who explore racialized identities in ways that not only bring multicultural-ism to the fore but that take the formation of multicultural cities as a central theme. The first wave of large-scale Caribbean immigration to Britain having taken place in the 1950s and 1960s, the crime novelists of the last decade or so tend to belong to a new generation of Caribbean migrants. The very different forms of crime fiction to emerge from this period might in itself be taken to be in accord with the contemporary emphasis on the heterogeneity of black identities. Victor Headley, the first and best-known of the X Press 'Yardie' novel-ists, writes a form of violent, criminal protagonist fiction that very deliberately sets out to provide a take on black experience in Britain that will discomfit the 'Afro-Saxon élite'. Mike Phillips is part of that élite. Phillips co-wrote *Windrush: The Irresistible Rise of Multi-Racial Britain* (1998) to accompany a BBC television series telling the story of the Caribbean migrant workers who settled in post-war Britain. As a novelist, he writes crime fiction that tries to convey something of this broader historical perspective, not just the Caribbean diaspora but the diverse, overlapping histories of black migrants in both London and New York. What Headley and Phillips share, apart from their diasporic conceptions of blackness, is a strong thematic pre-occupation with race and class. Both see the blame attaching to a capitalistic system and stress the way in which this system further fractures black experience by the competition it generates between communities that might otherwise find common ground. Phillips, for example, says in interview:

The result is that readers who identify with our heroes have their universe turned upside down. In our worlds we are the goodies, and the real threat of the mean streets is the paranoia of the white world about our presence. Around us are conditions which, for our families and friends, have often squeezed shut the avenues to economic survival, except for petty crime. (Wells 1999: 213)

In thinking of what separates Phillips from Headley, the phrase 'petty crime' here is perhaps the key thing to focus on. Grant Farred, in 'The Postcolonial Chickens Come Home to Roost', suggests that trying to resist the stereotyping of blacks as always already 'criminals', post-colonial authors have generally preferred to represent petty thieves, as, say, in Sam Selvon's *The Lonely Londoners* (1956), rather than big-time drug dealing and gangland violence: 'the potency of the existing stereotype is given as a reason for avoiding the kind of literary representation to be found in Yardie novels' (Farred 2001: 298–300). The Yardie novelists' representation of the black experience of Britain is from the vantage point of the 'subaltern' postcolonial underclass, the culturally disenfranchised voice of the inner-city, wholly resistant to acculturation, to the imposition of law and order, or the 'regular' economic activities involved in upward mobility. The Yardie is a figure who cannot be comfortably thought of as 'colonized'. What we see in comparing Phillips and Headley is a distinctively British version of the literary rift in black American crime writing between 'underclass' crime writing (Beck, Goines) and more upmarket detective fiction of the kind produced, for example, by Walter Mosley.

The form of postcolonial pulp fiction or 'street literature' centring on the Jamaican Yardies is disliked by the more 'respectable' voices of postcolonial criticism. The black literary élite has been charged with excluding such work from consideration, in the interests of sustaining enlightened, intellectually sophisticated literary standards and values. As a review of Headley's *Yardie* in an American newspaper observes, 'Britain's growing drug and criminal subculture is rarely acknowledged in polite conversation, let alone written about.'[36] In an

---

[36] Martha Ann Overland, 'Black Authors Find their Audience—the Hard Way', *Washington Post*, 13/7/1993, quoted by Farred 2001: 289.

increasingly multicultural Britain, the Yardie remains one of the unassimilable members of the black British population. Young underclass Jamaican men engaged in drug dealing and violent crime are seen as the very embodiment of criminal deviancy and self-interest, committed to nothing other than their own advancement within a brutally amoral capitalist environment. They are 'undesirable aliens', not easy to incorporate within the rhetoric that celebrates a multicultural, cosmopolitan environment and a smoothly functioning plural society. By focusing on a highly recognizable type of criminal protagonist, the Yardie novelists leave themselves open to the charge of reinforcing damaging, reductive images of black masculinity and of the cityscape-as-battlezone that they dominate.

The major influence in the creation of Yardie fiction has been X Press, which, like Holloway House in the USA (the 'black experience' publisher of Goines and Beck), has produced fiction dealing with black street life, marketed to appeal to a youthful, metropolitan black readership. The Jamaican-born Headley, together with two black journalists, Steve Pope and Dotun Adebayo, set up their publishing house in 1992, publishing, along with Headley's novels, books like Donald Gorgon's *Cop Killer* (1994) and Karline Smith's *Moss Side Massive* (1994). It has been an unexpectedly successful venture, credited with 'reshaping the black reading public in Britain'.[37] Headley's *Yardie* and his second novel, *Excess* (1993), sold something like 50,000 copies: in one of his rare interviews, Headley said that '*Yardie* will be remembered in years to come as the book which got black people into book shops in large, large numbers' and started a literary movement that 'touched some kind of nerve' in the black community.[38]

Yardie opens with the arrival at Heathrow of 'D', a Jamaican cocaine courier who double crosses his supplier, escaping with enough cocaine to finance his own drug distribution operation and to establish himself as a gang leader. Whereas Mosley, for example, represents the crossing of boundaries within LA, Headley's narrative of 'passing' involves the crossing of national boundaries, and he interrogates white perceptions of blackness in a somewhat different way. 'D' is short for posse don (we never know the name of the young Jamaican who is about to detach himself from his old identity) and as he enters

[37] Overland, *Washington Post*, quoted by Farred 2001: 295.
[38] Tony Sewell, 'New Boy in Town', BBC Arts Windrush site, at www.bbc.co.uk.

Britain he 'passes' under another's identity, unrecognized because the black arrivals are indistinguishable to the immigration officials. Having crossed a national border as an illegal immigrant, he enters into a new way of life that is 'the biggest ride he had ever taken' (Headley [1992] 1993: 8). This is not the kind of upward mobility into a privileged life that is presented, for example, as an enticing possibility for Daphne in *Devil in a Blue Dress*, but a dangerous, knife-edge existence, an 'escape' into the British inner-city from a Jamaican 'yard' so impoverished and a ghetto life so embattled that it makes Hackney look good by comparison. D's credibility as a gangster and 'bad bwoy' has already been established on the Jamaican streets, where his violence and ruthlessness enabled him to make 'a name for himself in West Kingston' and they now help him to secure his identity 'on this side of the world' (pp. 7–9). The reference back to Jamaica is both a contextualization of D's present actions and a way of validating the novel's sense of black masculinity: 'This dualism of feeling left out of the mainstream of Britain and looking towards Jamaica as an authenticating force for your masculinity, has been a key driving force in black male expression,'[39] exerting an anti-heroic fascination comparable to that of the American gangsters discussed in Chapter 3. It is a comparison perhaps supported by the fact that the recent re-release of Brian De Palma's *Scarface* in the USA was apparently targeted primarily at black audiences, its appeal attributed to its representation of a determination to fight back regardless of the consequences on the part of a protagonist who is 'the apotheosis of raging, self-destructive defiance'.[40]

The serious objectives of the X Press writers, however, are not confined to the representation of a particularly controversial form of black masculinity. The 'nerve' that Headley claimed to have touched is equally to do with the novel's effort to re-map the British inner-city's terrain, focusing attention on black social decay and institutionalized racism, and developing a critique that has something in common with the socio-economic determinism apparent in Himes's novels. Yardie fiction, it can be argued, implicitly demands a reassessment of the postcolonial economic and cultural circumstances that make the Yardie underworld possible. Economic necessity

---

[39] Sewell, review of *Yardie*.
[40] Sean Macaulay, 'Yes, It's the Great American Dream', T2, *The Times*, 18/9/2003: 6–7.

is, for Yardie gang members, of overwhelming importance, leaving them without the dimension of personal and emotional ties. Although this is by no means a moralizing novel, it can certainly be argued that Headley does not minimize the self-destructiveness of this lifestyle and that, far from holding D up as a model, he uses other perspectives (particularly that of the Rasta movement) to frame the choices made by the posse don. Under the romance of the Yardie gangster he makes apparent the social and personal costs. But whatever moral distancing one may detect, Yardie novels, like the gangster films of the 1930s, have been widely read as manuals of criminal conduct. Adebayo, one of the founders of X Press, professed himself bemused by the fact that the police appeared to take *Yardie* as an accurate insider's socio-psychological profile. Even if the editors and authors downplay the politically awkward implications, it has to be acknowledged that there is a substantial group of readers whose construction of such fiction is highly politicized, positioning the press and its novels in a political crossfire that involves Scotland Yard, the media, black activists, and inner-city black youth culture.

Mike Phillips, who started publishing two or three years before the first Yardie novel, represents an antithetical approach to the representation of diasporic identities and black subjectivity. He is preoccupied not with immigrant survival in an inner-city jungle but with the nuanced understanding of the varieties of black experience. The choice of sub-genre—of investigative as opposed to criminal-centred narratives—was obviously, for Phillips, an important part of a strategy that would enable him to disrupt a tradition he sees as embodying pernicious modes of thought, especially the binaries of good–evil, white–black. His fairly narrow construction of existing generic conventions—taking white investigative crime writing to consist mainly of golden age puzzles, arid mysteries constricted by class prejudices and ingrained mental patterns (Wells 1999: 206–7)—allows him to situate himself as an adversarial voice whilst still putting forward an instructive agenda mediated by a perceptive narrator. Phillips locates himself in opposition both to 'white' generic conventions and to black appropriations that he regards as irresponsible and extreme representations of black masculinity. By identifying the nature of the genre as morally tidy and conventional, Phillips is able to claim a kind of 'outlaw' status for his protagonist, Sam Dean. He presents Dean as a character who is 'continually obliged to reconstitute his own moral code within a culture where he is a moral outlaw',[41] though not as the sort of romanticized outlaw that in Phillips's view is one of the more worrying ways in which television and the media construct and exploit black crime for their own purposes. To Phillips the Yardie novels are simply a reinforcement of media constructions of the black immigrant underclass as criminal, and his fourth novel, *An Image to Die For* (1995), has Sam Dean resisting exactly this kind of construction.

One of Phillips's most interesting novels, published in the previous year (1994), is *Point of Darkness*, in which he moves his protagonist, Sam Dean, to New York, where he searches for a close boyhood friend's runaway daughter, in a city in which he feels doubly alien, a black person who confounds white expectations by speaking in an English accent, a charming anomaly which also means that he lacks the New York-born African-American's ability to negotiate the treacherous territory of a violent city. There are self-ironizing gestures on Dean's part towards the earlier detective footsteps in which he follows—for example, his *Maltese Falcon* moment when he ponders what it was that was stolen ('A great golden bird with jewels for eyes flashed through my head and I laughed out loud. Pure fantasy.' (Phillips [1994] 1995: 133)).

New York's greater complexity not only endangers the innocent abroad but confronts him with rapidly accumulating examples of false binary conceptions of racial identity. From the opening, Sam Dean is reflecting on the habits of thought that stereotype the ethnic other, facile generalizations quite at odds with the diversity of African-American, Hispanic, and Caribbean people he encounters as he tries to 'learn' New York: 'The irony was, I thought, that white people's notions about African America were bounded by images of jazz, blues, and rap music; tap dancing; riots, and heavyweight boxing; street violence, guns, and poverty. But then, as all the world knows, black people have different dreams' (p. 6). The influence of Stuart Hall on Phillips has been noted, particularly of Hall's essay 'Minimal Selves', which argues the value of hybridity over binarist models of identity and emphasizes race as a construct, with 'black' as in every sense (culturally, politically, psychologically) an 'unstable

[41] Phillips, quoted by James Procter, 'Mike Phillips', online at www.contemporarywriters.com/authors.

identity', far from being a 'simple—if I can use the metaphor—black or white question', especially 'in the diaspora'.[42]

In *Point of Darkness*, one of the key tensions in the back story is between different conceptions of blackness, particularly between an upwardly mobile black society on the one hand and 'street life' on the other. The plot in fact might be said to turn on the contrasts between the two types of crime novel, with those most closely allied to the detective (those who are in one way or another 'making it') juxta-posed with the lure of street life and semi-glamorized criminality that lead the missing girl into trouble. In contrast to Daphne in *Devil in a Blue Dress*, for example, the girl for whom Sam is searching is trying to escape middle-classness, as embodied by the couple she goes to stay with in New York. The biracial Mary, who grew up feeling that she 'didn't belong anywhere' (pp. 180–1), is in search of her own identity and is acting on a set of 'distorted notions' about being 'a real black person' which, Phillips implies, are actually media-generated: 'Mary would have come here looking for adventure, her only knowledge about the country gleaned from English TV and newspapers [. . .] in Carmen and Rupert [the middle-class couple] she would have seen a pair of snobs living in luxury' (pp. 34–5). For those like Carmen, who worked her way up from poverty, Mary's behaviour opens the doors to the threat of the street life they have fought against in their own drive to succeed—a life in which addiction and murder are everyday occurrences, and young black men seem to be 'in some kind of obstacle race with death and disaster' (p. 68).

The introduction of Claude, the villain of the piece, is in the con-text of a debate about how the Jamaican immigrant achieves upward mobility. The protean Claude is someone who knows very well how to signal the shifting aspects of his persona, and his story has enough common features with other immigrant 'making it' stories to make Sam Dean believe in it (about his upbringing in Jamaica, he says, 'Tough place [. . .] Kids, younger than me, used to get a gun, go out and shoot someone. You know why? For a few dollars.'). He now 'owns some of the buses', having arrived aged 15, skipped college, worked as a car salesman, then 'set up his own business, working on his first million'. Like Headley's Yardies, he dismisses the

---

[42] Hall, 'Minimal Selves', in *The Real Me: Postmodernism and the Question of Identity.* London: Institute of Contemporary Arts, 1987: 136, quoted by Wells 1999: 207–9.

conventional routes to success: 'He said the establishment culture was a trap designed to keep things the same. You couldn't win, and the only way to beat the system was to pretend it wasn't there' (pp. 135–41). Claude, however, who has cynically mastered the various narratives of immigrant experience, is simply availing himself of the confusions caused by diasporic differences, swapping identities as it suits him, with little sense of integrity, constant only to his upwardly mobile self-interest. His story is the dark shadow of the 'making it' ethos, and his inauthenticity is apparent in his mimicry of both narratives and voices: 'When I first saw him he'd been speaking a Jamaican dialect with a Jamaican accent; when he talked about the politics of the city he'd sounded like an African-American, up from the South a generation ago; now French with a Haitian accent. I wondered whether he spoke Spanish too' (p. 141).

The New York setting presents Phillips's protagonist with a great range of immigrant experiences and expectations, and if this diverse milieu facilitates criminal deceptions of a clever chameleon, it also demonstrates the falsity of essentialist thinking. It exposes the misjudgements of the white observer who thinks in stereotypical binary terms, as well as revealing the confusions of the black observer who himself wants to think of others as belonging to familiar categories. The struggle of Sam Dean revolves around the correct reading of race. As in *Devil in a Blue Dress*, the search for a missing woman forces the protagonist to re-examine his own preconceptions in order to 'find' her, in the sense of understanding her identity and the reasons for her disappearance. This is (as for Easy Rawlins) a matter of grasping the fact that categories have been rendered inadequate by the actual complexities of black experience. In the case of Daphne/Ruby, these categories create a woman who is both black and white; in Sam Dean's case, confusions over categorization in terms of a black–white binary are replaced by confusions over the socio-political identities, the kinds of belonging he associates with particular types of black experience. Like Easy, having insisted throughout the novel on a nuanced understanding of black experience, he finds that his own habits of categorization have misled him. There are no simple routes to understanding the complexity of racial identity.

Detectives, mammies, bitches, and whores

BarbaraNeely, *Blanche on the Lam* (1992); Charlotte Carter, *Walking Bones* (2002)

Some of the genre's most subtle explorations of the projection of multiple identities have been in the novels of the black women writers who have emerged in the 1990s, particularly in those of BarbaraNeely and, in a quite different way, those of Charlotte Carter.[43] Both are writers building within genre fiction on the strengths of half a century or so of black female writing, during which time novelists have carried the representation of black women beyond stereotypes, and showed the ways in which the black woman herself could 'project the intensity, complexity, and diversity of the experience of black women from their own point of view' (Christian 1985: 16). Within the crime novel's dynamic of aggression and submission there is a ready-made context for exploring the relationship of dominance and degradation built into slavery itself. The power violently exerted over a victim and the historical shaping of the compliant black female role is of particular interest. As Barbara Christian writes,

Specifically in America, the definition of the enslaved African woman became the basis for the definition of our society's Other. It is now a truism to say that the peculiar history and culture of Afro-American women comes out of the peculiar institution of slavery that left a legacy of racism in its wake [. . .] The woman, as enslaved and black, is not included psychologically or philosophically in the pre-twentieth century American definition of woman. (1985: 160–1)

What Neely and Carter have in common is their exploration of the intersection of gender, class, and black female self-definition. In the creation of their protagonists, they subvert two of the most common stereotypes in white Southern literature, the mammy or Aunt Jemima figure (black, fat, nurturing, kind, strong) and the concubine (Christian 1985: 2–3). They take women who at first sight seem to conform to familiar images, but so thoroughly explore their personalities

---

[43] Other black female voices of the 1990s include Eleanor Taylor Bland, Penny Micklebury, Nikki Baker, Delores Komo, and Valerie Wilson Wesley.

that the cliché is demolished. Both construct narratives around the culturally produced 'invisibility' and passivity of black women. Neely's *Blanche on the Lam* and Carter's *Walking Bones* use women who present themselves in submissive roles but at the same time assert themselves very forcefully, defying their assumed categorization. These are protagonists who are in a sense very unlike the dynamic female sleuths discussed in Chapter 6, but the apparent contradictions in their make-up constitute serious play with taken-for-granted cultural norms.

Neely's choice of form places her in some respects at the very traditional end of the crime fiction spectrum. *Blanche on the Lam*, her first novel, is a near relation of the English country house murder mystery, as are the later novels in the series, such as *Blanche among the Talented Tenth* (1994). The historical setting of the house in Neely's first Blanche novel separates it quite sharply from this tradition, with Southern racism compelling an attention to socio-political issues that is rare in the world of, say, Agatha Christie. The traditional closure of the 'golden age' form, however, poses questions about the implications of Neely's adaptation (particularly, for example, in the conclusion of *Blanche on the Lam*, which arguably reinscribes some of the most familiar Southern stereotypes). Andrew Pepper asks whether the contained world of the classic model acts to distance Neely's narrator and detective—and in fact the reader—from the actual problems she is addressing, imposing limits on Blanche's ratiocinative 'triumphs' by unproblematically restoring the status quo (2000: 87). Is the effect perhaps to suggest that any apparent success achieved by those who are poor and black will always be circumscribed in this way? Does the form itself stand in the way of a broader critique? Or does this sort of reading depend more on the reader's politics than on those of the author?

It is clear that Neely's own agenda involves using the conventional traits of the form (in particular, of course, the way in which it would conventionally marginalize a woman such as her heroine) to get a purchase on a range of issues. In her creation of Blanche, Neely not only takes on the doubly disadvantaged position of black and female but adds a strong dimension of class by making Blanche a woman who works in the kind of servant capacity that would have placed her in the caricatured role of the black mammy or in the walk-on part of the black domestic. But although Blanche occupies the most 'traditional' role of any of the protagonists we have considered, Neely is careful to stress that she has deliberately chosen her identity, at the cost of considerable conflict with a strong mother figure. She enters into the role with no illusions, insisting on not being fooled into seeing the relationship with her employers in anything other than cynically down-to-earth terms. She does not suffer from 'Darkies' Disease': 'What she didn't understand was how you convinced yourself that you were actually loved by people who paid you the lowest possible wages' (p. 48). Constantly thoughtful of the differences between the way in which she undertakes this kind of subservient role and the older generation's form of submission, Blanche reflects on the importance of rejecting the 'turn-the-other-cheek fantasy land' of an older generation (p. 73) and is determined instead to tap into the traditional strength of the black woman:

If Diana [Ross] could move from the welfare and the housing projects of Detroit to the top of the music charts and starring roles in movies, certainly Blanche could get herself out of this mess she was in, just as black women had been getting themselves and their people out of messes in this country since the day the first kidnapped African woman was dragged onto these shores. (pp. 77–8)

By choosing a role so obviously not transgressive, Blanche is in fact asserting and confirming her extremely individual transgressive-ness—what Frankie Y. Bailey sees as her role as a 'resistance fighter' (1991: 192–4). Sustained by the only community (friend, children) that matters to her, she puts herself in a lonely position, as solitary as that of the private eye, in that she must rely entirely on her own resources without any structure of social-legal support. In *Blanche on the Lam*, her isolation is confirmed by her alliance and rapport with the white family's 'idiot cousin', Mumsfield, sharing with him the fact that neither of them is 'taken seriously as a person', that they are both 'invisibles' (p. 83).

The culturally produced invisibility and silence that are the trad-itional attributes of the black domestic are very tellingly exploited by Neely's protagonist, and are central elements both in the creation of Blanche's role as a detective and in the metaphoric structure of the novels themselves. Neely's strategy is one of ironic reversal, as in the doubly ironic naming of her protagonist ('Blanche White'). Using the trickster qualities of masking and signifying, she outwits and manipulates those around her. The motif of hiding runs through *Blanche on the Lam*, the 'on the lam' part of the plot, which places her in actual hiding, interlaced with her detailed account of how she makes space for herself within the white society by hiding her reality, with scene after scene presenting Blanche's double consciousness. In her investigative activities, Blanche's knowledge-conferring invisibility is coupled with her knowledge-withholding silence, and her white employers are in consequence utterly unaware of how much she has observed. As she goes about her *own* business, there is a kind of constant counterpoint to her servant persona that goes on inside Blanche's head—calling her employers Sir and Ma'am to their faces, for example, but by their first names in her mind, and reserving 'Sir' and 'Ma'am' for her cats (p. 27). For us, as readers, Blanche is both highly visible and entertainingly audible, and her performance of her subservient identity is used throughout to make us aware of the absurdity of the white stereotypes she parodies via her complex role-playing. Her inner resources, wit, and intelligence enable her to turn perceived passivity and quiescence into agency, and her perspective on the white perspective gives us from the start a kind of double gaze: Blanche is constantly aware of how white society looks at her. Like Nettie in Carter's *Walking Bones* she is attuned much more than are male protagonists to her 'looked-at-edness', and combines this with sharply critical perceptions of those she looks at herself: for example, 'Blanche chopped down her usually wide stride to match the pace of the woman in front of her. A stone could walk faster, Blanche tsked to herself'; or, 'Blanche smiled and nodded. She ain't got no more idea what's going on in her house than a jackrabbit' (pp. 12, 14). The ready smile and the accommodation of her pace to that of her employer signify Blanche's habit of outward co-operation and, particularly in the case of the shortened stride, a concealment of her natural strengths. Neely explicitly addresses the question of how far a person can carry the business of hiding her true self under a performance of stupidity. The climax of the novel comes when Blanche emerges with effective violence in her confrontation with the caricatured representative of white neurosis, repression, and debilitation. It is an action that produces quite a different sort of smile: 'A slow, satisfied grin spread over Blanche's face', and her final decision at the end releases her from her self-imposed silence. The movement of the narrative is ultimately towards the breaking of this silence, the final decision Blanche must make being that of whether she should conceal or publicize the crimes of her white Southern employers.

Charlotte Carter, too, writes a detective series, featuring Nanette Hayes, a hedonistic, independent, jazz-loving street saxophonist, in novels like *Rhode Island Red* (1997), *Coq au Vin* (1999), and *Drumsticks* (2001). In addition, however, she has written a non-series, non-detective novel, *Walking Bones*, of which she says, 'If nothing else, the *Walking Bones* characters are a messed up lot. Maybe they are my way of asking, "Is this dark enough for you?" ' When she started to get feedback on the novel and saw the word 'noir' a lot, she wanted, she said, 'to say Hooray! Finally I'm noir. I haven't yet reached the mecca of being "transgressive", but at least I'm noir.' Influenced by the more noirish of American hard-boiled writers—Willeford, Hammett, Himes, Thompson, Highsmith, McCoy—she structures the novel in such a way that readers must, at the end, reassess what they have read. Carter is writing against the implications of progression contained in seriality, using as chapter titles the letters of the alphabet, A to Z plus 'The End', which is actually a beginning that forces us to reconceptualize the 'progression' of the earlier chapters. The dual linear narrative of detective novels is replaced by a mockery of the notion of beginnings and endings. Part of Carter's objective, she says in interview, is to explore the whole question of racial guilt without saying 'poor us' or 'shame on them'.[44]

Carter's female protagonist, Nettie, is a reworking of the stereotype of the *femme fatale*. Her subjectivity is at the centre of an often dreamlike narrative that explores her self-construction, and the contradictions of a character that is both potentially powerful and abjectly submissive. Having come to New York to be a fashion model, Nettie has outgrown the conventional dimensions of the role, and is now a 'handsome and powerfully built woman of color standing nearly six feet tall. Irreversibly too big for the runway. Her descent commenced [. . .] She moved into darker and darker neighborhoods' (Carter 2002: 3). Her downward spiral halted (with the help of her black, gay friend Rufe), she reclaims the power to control the gaze, self-confident enough to intimidate others and to be labelled a bitch by other women. Her whole sense of self depends on projecting a

---

[44] Carter, in 'Charlotte Carter's *Walking Bones*', *Online Publishing*, www. serpentstail.com.

figure that is looked at. But although Nettie has reinvented herself more than once, she is bound to her past in ways that become fully apparent only at the end of the novel. The core of the narrative is a dangerously aberrant sado-masochistic relationship between Nettie and a wealthy white middle-aged man called Albert Press—as Carter describes him in interview, 'a quirky, profoundly troubled white man who is a kind of wash on a familiar character in fiction: the innocent Anglo who unwittingly sets all kinds of tragedies in motion'.[45] His deeply ambiguous attraction for Nettie is made explicit: 'But this man was not like any of those other partners. This was a man who had elicited in her murder and degradation and unbelievable tenderness' (p. 96). The initial violent meeting with Press takes place in the small sphere of a New York bar that appears to be unaligned in terms of either race or class. The encounter with Albert, however, transforms it into a racially charged place, and the sequence of events there (a coarse proposition, a glass smashed in Press's face by Nettie) begins both a strange affair and a diagnosis of guilt that is a painful exploration of racialized patterns of dominance and submission. The allocation of blame is a recurrent theme in the novel, as is the appetite for degradation, glimpsed, for example, when Nettie's protective friend Rufe discovers the truth about a black prostitute paid by Albert to humiliate him. Rufe's diagnosis, leading to his murder of Albert, is that he is engaged in a form of enslavement of Nettie: 'Albert Press acted out all his vilest wishes on a surrogate for Nettie—and while he lavished chaste love and bank-breaking gifts on Nettie, she was his surrogate skanky black whore. One was the other' (p. 179). The implication throughout is that it is the pattern of submission and dominance built into slavery itself that is exerting so strong a pull on their relationship. Both seem compelled to think in terms of such patterns (enslavement, revenge, humiliation), rendering impossible the loving relationship that may in some sense be there. The complexity of Nettie's own psychological make-up does not emerge fully until the final chapter, when we glimpse her at the age of 12, involved in an incident with a white salesman in which she rapidly transforms herself from willing temptress to rape victim to self-righteous avenger. Never fully in control of the performance of her alternating identities,

---

[45] Bob Cornwell, 'Sophisticated Lady', interview with Charlotte Carter, *Online Publishing*, www.twbooks.co.uk.

Nettie would seem to carry more guilt than we first imagine. But Carter also puts into the balance the fact of her racial past. When she imagines herself back into slavery we see the institution itself as responsible for her fractured sense of self, her vacillation between abject submission and violent retribution, echoing the relationship of submission and dominance in her relationship with Albert. She dreams at some times of herself, motherless and fatherless, and of a 'fine-looking colored man, who loves her', but who is sold, after which the overseer 'finds her floating face down in the stream'; at other times her dream leads to a revenge fantasy in which she 'gets hold of an ax, starts at the top floor, kills them all, the big house is running blood'; and at others, of 'the master's son [coming] to her at night, a mendicant, and [pouring] out his heart' (pp. 21–2). The more open-ended form of the crime novel, as opposed to the detective novel, enables Carter to place at the heart of her narrative the indeterminacy of guilt and the contradictions of black female identity produced by the institution of slavery. It also helps to make *Walking Bones* a novel that seriously addresses racial issues but that also ranges more widely, breaking free from many of the clichéd ways of writing a 'black' version of a 'white' genre. Carter says in interview:

Funny. I've probably said a hundred thousand times that it's tragic, sick, dumb, grotesque, etc., that black writers in the U.S. can't seem to get published unless they write about race. So, given the chance to publish a small, arty kind of novel, I wrote about race. But not entirely. Also on the platter, the platter being *Walking Bones*, are alcohol, masochism, jealousy, fate, the city of New York, and race in the city of New York.[46]

[46] Serpent's Tail review article.

6

Regendering the Genre

When Mary Wings's highly successful lesbian detective novel, *She Came Too Late*, was published in the mid-1980s, the *Elle* reviewer welcomed it with the line, 'Roll over Raymond Chandler, and tell Philip Marlowe the news: the lady has a pistol in her pocket.'[1] The phallic nature of the lady's pistol is made more obvious by the reader's discovery that the protagonist of Wings's novel neither owns nor uses a pistol. In fact, she deliberately dismisses the possibility of keeping a gun in her house, let alone in her pocket.[2] If she does not have an actual gun, then, what is it that she has picked up from male private eyes? The *Elle* reviewer presumably intends an echo of Marlowe's famous line in *Farewell, My Lovely*—'She gave me a smile I could feel in my hip pocket'—and certainly one implication here is that the 'lady' has been transformed into a female dick/phallic woman, appropriating the potency, the agency, and the provocative style of her male predecessors. Much feminist crime fiction creates its protagonists in just this way, but by no means all. When we come to look at Wings more closely, in fact, we will see that in many respects she deliberately avoids the stereotypical 'chick dick dyke lit' image, creating a protagonist who is neither a hardened investigator nor a tough cookie kicking male butt, but who has both femme and butch

---

[1] Cover blurb on the Women's Press (1995) edition of *She Came Too Late*, quoted from *Elle* review.

[2] Whereas, when she gets broken into, Stacy goes out and learns how to use a gun, Emma confesses her continued gun-lessness: ' "So, what did our mother of conception, Stacy Weldemeer, do after her break-in?" "She went out and bought a gun and enrolled in a course to learn how to use it." "Well isn't that swell. I haven't graduated to the bullet stage of fear yet. I don't want to live with a gun in my house" ' (p. 143).

sides. Since the mid-1970s, there has been a phenomenal increase both in women crime writers and in female investigative protagonists (the number of fictional female investigators soaring from thirteen in the late 1970s to over 360 in the mid-1990s (Walton and Jones 1999: 28–30)). In the present chapter's small sampling of feminist crime fiction, we will be looking at crime as well as detective novels, and will examine some of the most popular incarnations of the case-hardened, gun-toting female private eye. We will also, however, find that feminist protagonists are not invariably feisty ladies who literally carry pistols in their pockets.

In a chapter which analyses some of the ways in which contemporary women writers have 'talked back to the genre' (Walton and Jones 1999: 94–5), we should perhaps also take note of the fact that empowered women and female subjectivity are by no means wholly absent from the detective and crime fiction of earlier decades. In both male- and female-authored texts, the genre itself has offered, through its female characters, alternative perspectives that have stopped it from being monologic. Pierre Bayard is more mischievous than serious in suggesting that the central character in *The Murder of Roger Ackroyd* is actually Caroline Sheppard (in his reading, she is a representative of Christie herself, a double of Miss Marple and the real murderer—'the only dangerous person, the only decisive—one would be tempted to say phallic—person' ([1998] 2000: 129–45)). But his deconstruction of Christie's novel is a useful reminder that the role of women in the crime and detective fiction of earlier decades is often much more central and complex than is assumed. Although we might not want to follow the convoluted path of Bayard in our reading of more traditional detective fiction, there are many exceptions to the clichéd image of crime fiction's unredeemed generic 'masculinity'. One hint we might follow in Bayard's 'revelation' of the true importance of Caroline Sheppard is that his conception of her role involves both investigative and transgressive ascendancy. This double for the detective is doubly (or indeed trebly) potent, a murderer as well as a solver of crimes, and even, as a seemingly omniscient figure, a stand-in for the author herself. The novels most commonly discussed in the context of feminist rewritings of the genre are those featuring female investigative figures. It is important to emphasize, though, that in examining the 'regendering of the genre' we are not talking simply about the substitution of a female for a male detective.

The recovery of female subjectivity is more complex than this: there are other key roles that female characters occupy. The revisionings of the female transgressor—and indeed victim—are as significant as the better-known series which recast the investigative role.

An often-voiced feminist criticism of male-authored crime fiction is that women's roles tend to be confined to clichéd versions of the victim or transgressor—the good but weak woman who is the murder victim; the evil woman who is the *femme fatale*. This not an unfounded generalization, but there are some very notable exceptions to this reductive view, the most interesting of which is the representation of the *femme fatale*. Hollywood was constrained both by the Hays Code and by expectations that the sexual or aggressive woman would be subjugated. For these reasons it tended to contain the *femme fatale* narrative, limiting the 'progressiveness' of the cycle and confirming popular prejudices by reasserting male control over the independent female. Novelists, on the other hand, were free to play much more extensively *against* stereotype, often setting up plots that initially lead us to judge according to stereotype and then reversing our expectations, or complicating our judgements and in the process establishing strong female figures who, though sexual, are admirable and/or indomitable. In novels which focus our perceptions through a single protagonist, some of the most effective mid-century male writers—especially Charles Williams, Charles Willeford, and Jim Thompson—structured entire narratives around the satiric presentation of the male point of view. They implicitly reassessed the role of the tough and triumphant *femme fatale*, subverting male stereotypes and creating a space within which the strong, independent woman could get and even sometimes keep the upper hand.[3] The mid-century also produced women writers of non-investigative crime novels who contributed powerful representations of female subjectivity to the traditions of literary noir. Although she was as capable of misogyny as she was of general misanthropy, Patricia Highsmith's work is important here, and Margaret Millar also wrote several novels in which the female voice was central (ironic pictures of corrupted social and familial relationships, such as *The Iron Gates* (1945) and *Beast in View* (1955)).

[3] For a more detailed discussion of the representation of women in the male-authored thrillers of this period, see Horsley 2001: 125–52.

But it is with respect to detective fiction that there has been a significant feminist critical effort to find exceptions to the maleness of the genre, since it is clearly the case that some of the outstanding writers of detective stories in previous decades (particularly during the first 'golden age') have been women. From the 1980s on, historians and literary critics have been filling out the picture of earlier female detectives: notable studies of the 1980s include Patricia Craig and Mary Cadogan, *The Lady Investigates* (1981), and Kathleen Gregory Klein, *The Woman Detective* (1988). Recent work, like that of Susan Rowland (*From Agatha Christie to Ruth Rendell*, published in 2001) and Gill Plain (*Twentieth-Century Crime Fiction*, also 2001) have reassessed the roles of femininity, sexuality, and female investigators in the fiction of such golden age writers as Christie and Sayers. Of the earlier twentieth-century female detectives, the best-known is unquestionably Christie's Jane Marple, who can herself be placed in a tradition of genteel female investigators featuring in detective fiction from the nineteenth century on, all of whom were to a considerable extent constrained by the conventions and assumptions of Victorian or early twentieth-century England. Uncombative in appearance and approach, Jane Marple and her sleuthing sisters contributed a great deal to the feminizing of the genre, but their creators were not bent on radically challenging or remaking the male tradition. They did not think of themselves as 'regendering' the genre. Although one must not underrate Miss Marple's forcefulness, shrewd intelligence, and 'uncanny' powers of perception, there are many elements in her image (the reserve, the decorous, correct behaviour, the confined sphere of action) that make it hard to visualize her stepping out of the 'cosy' tradition with its largely domestic crimes and taking up arms alongside V. I. Warshawski. Although the earlier 'Queens of Crime' did represent 'tensions over female participation in society' (Rowland 2001: 157–8), they would not have thought of themselves as feminists nor have felt it their responsibility to explore specifically gender-linked issues. Contemporary female crime writers, on the other hand, have been preoccupied with *difference*. Gender differences and the constructedness of gender are explicitly incorporated in narratives that draw readers' attention to the ways in which female-authored texts can be differentiated from male-authored crime and detective fiction. Their investigators are women who set about resisting and challenging the 'inherent maleness' of a genre in which detection would indeed seem (in P. D. James's phrase) 'an unsuitable job for a woman'.

In spite of its many early twentieth-century female practitioners, the 'maleness' of the form itself is often seen as a defining characteristic of crime fiction as a genre. Much has been written on the question of whether so ingrained a trait can actually be resisted by the vigorous new generation of female investigators. However marginal his position, simply by virtue of his maleness the traditional detective is counted as a member of the male power structure.[4] In restoring order within the narrative, he is acting to confirm the rightness and authority of this patriarchal stasis, the male-dominated status quo. The potency (in every sense) of this image has led some feminist critics of detective fiction to see the genre as so *unavoidably* male that the whole project of feminist transformation seems a lost cause. As Paul Cobley suggests, this can be seen as an essentially structuralist line of argument that takes the genre to be 'an omnipotent vessel': regardless of the kind of narrative with which the writer fills it, it will retain its male generic structure (2000: 123).[5] Critics like Kathleen Gregory Klein (*The Woman Detective*, 1988) are sceptical about whether there can be an effective male–female transposition. They stress the difficulties of negotiating with or changing a genre which, particularly in its hard-boiled variant, they perceive as so irrevocably allied to 'oppressive masculinity' that it will simply cancel out any feminist political agenda inserted into it (Walton and Jones 1999: 86–94). In this interpretation, the female character acting as a private investigator must be perceived as a drag performance, and one which reconfirms rather than seriously challenges male power structures. Feminist ideology, Klein maintains, cannot in itself change the nature of the private eye novel, and feminist writers therefore merely end by reproducing the patterns of their male predecessors: 'The predictable formula of detective fiction is based on a world whose sex/gender valuations reinforce male hegemony' (1988: 223). Klein's strategy, in examining the difficulty of reconciling the 'divergent scripts' of 'detective' and 'woman', is to

---

[4] Jane S. Bakerman, 'Living "Openly and with Dignity": Sara Paretsky's New-Boiled Feminist Fiction', *Midamerica: The Yearbook of the Society for the Study of Midwestern Literature*, 12, 1985: 128–9, quoted by Walton and Jones 1999: 191–2.

[5] One of the better-known examples of this critical tendency is Palmer 1978.

narrow her focus in order to isolate a formula so recognizable, and so inherently conservative, that a 'proper woman' could not function as a 'proper detective' (1988: 3–4, 128–9). Another recurrent feminist argument centres on the observation that, historically, this kind of genre fiction, like true crime reporting, has been fascinated with the female victim. This is an argument that can be pushed some way. Klein, for example, neatly sidestepping counter-arguments about the actual content of hard-boiled fiction, invokes Luce Irigaray's argument that 'women constitute the silent ground on which the patriarchal thinker erects his discursive constructs. Or to paraphrase back into pop culture, the Woman is the body in the library on whom the criminal writes his narrative of murder.' Thus gender is said to depend on structural position in the text: the victim, 'despite biology', is always female, just as the detective is structurally always male, 'always in the dominant position in the pairing' (Klein 1995a: 173–4).

This perceived maleness of the genre is of course in itself one of the major incentives to those who rework it. It offers the challenge of a bastion to be conquered, as well as an armoury of weapons to be deployed in the battle, and writers who *do* believe it is possible to seize the bastion are often inclined to hyperbolize the opposing forces. Having constructed the male tradition in bold outline, women writers have skilfully adapted the alienated but 'powerfully contestatory and insightful' position inscribed in hard-boiled codes in particular, in order to confront society's masculinist imperatives (Walton and Jones 1999: 92). Like other projects of reversal and resistance, feminist crime fiction draws strength from having a sharply defined counter-tradition as a point of departure—reverse discourse, as Walton and Jones suggest, depending on 'the reader's recognition of differential textual relationships' (1999: 92). Susan Rowland, in her analysis of the British tradition of female-authored detective fiction, rightly argues that what we see, from the time of Christie on, is sophisticated play with a tradition that women writers have constructed as male, treating the Holmesian tradition 'as if it was a secure construction of masculinity which they can disrupt' (2001: 18). The same sort of process can clearly be discerned in the post-1970s American and British regendering of the genre, with writers constructing their fictions with and against what they posit as the male crime writing traditions of hard-boiled and, to a lesser extent, classic detective fiction. These often playful appropriations are written 'as if' the established genre is indeed a monolithic repository of stereotypical male gestures. These male generic attributes are taken to include assumptions of mastery (whether rational or physical), individualistic modes of thought and action, masculine concepts of justice and traditional hierarchies, 'the voice of authority'. It is precisely these perceived generic traits that make it so effective a site of feminist agency (Walton and Jones 1999: 84–5).

Although classic detective fiction, which can also be read as a demonstration of male ascendancy, has been adapted to feminist ends (by P. D. James, for example, Amanda Cross [Carolyn Heilbrun], and Barbara Wilson), it is unquestionably hard-boiled fiction that has proven to be the most compelling model and, for the purposes of self-definition, the key point of reference for post-1970s women crime writers. The Chandler–Hammett tradition is associated with a cynical, worldly-wise protagonist, inured to corruption and to the harshness of urban squalor. He speaks in a tough, gritty, colloquial way and is in possession of the kind of confident agency, the independence of mind and the self-reliance that recommend themselves to writers interested in female empowerment. As for black writers, it is an advantage that this stereotypical male investigator is *also* an outsider rather than part of an entrenched power structure, and is therefore a figure who might be seen as acting in support of forms of justice that are not simply replications of masculine power relationships. Combined with the generic tendency to use contemporary material, this helps, as we have seen, to make hard-boiled detective fiction a natural site for protest. It supplies a structure for critique that can be significantly changed by the reversal of a basic binary (white to black, male to female), re-situating the protagonist in relation to the existing system.

The preoccupation of women crime writers with strategically altering the defining traits of male-authored crime fiction was much influenced by the experience and the ideals of the liberal feminist activism of the 1960s and 1970s. The real upsurge in female-authored crime writing, however, only got under way after the backlash against feminism had set in during the 1980s, at a time that saw a general turn towards political conservatism, towards a law and order agenda and the resurgence of the 'moral majority'. Sara Paretsky, who joked that V. I. Warshawski should ideally be played by Sylvester Stallone—

Rambo in drag[6]—launched her fictional assaults on institutionalized American corruption in 1982, with *Indemnity Only*. In the same year (the year after the start of Reagan's presidency), Sue Grafton's *'A' is for Alibi* came out; and Marcia Muller, often credited with initiating the trend in hard-boiled female detective fiction (with *Edwin of the Iron Shoes* in 1977), published her second Sharon McCone novel, *Ask the Cards a Question*. As in the 1950s, the great days of male-authored, hard-boiled paperback originals, an atmosphere characterized by conservative retrenchment gave crime novelists a radical edge. There were alarmingly reactionary attitudes and specific abuses of power to be attacked, a context within which individual crimes could readily be perceived as symptomatic of wider socio-political ills. By taking over the male detective's 'professionalized' position (creating heroines who are private investigators rather than just amateur sleuths), the hard-boiled women crime writers gave themselves a more visible and more public place to stand, an independent vantage point from which to comment on the failings of patriarchal institutions. In this kind of gender-bending in detective fiction, the professional female investigator becomes 'a fictional site where the link between gender, capital, and power central to Western economies may be both foregrounded and arbitrated' (Walton and Jones 1999: 31–2).

In appropriating a site of discursive power conventionally seen as masculine, the chick dicks of the 1980s and 1990s (and on into the twenty-first century) are, then, imitating the stereotypical male qualities of the genre. But they are also subverting them, superimposing a different form of marginalization on the marginalized but empowered position of the traditional detective. They imbue the male stereotype (and this is obviously the process in which critics locate contradictions) with qualities intended to differentiate the new, female version from the old-fashioned, culpable male model (*c.* 1930). The qualities retained tend to be instrumental, the means to an end: physical prowess, for example, or qualities of character like tenacity and self-reliance. What change most markedly are the social and moral contexts within which these qualities are brought into play. The 'masculine' quality of agency is important, but the 'female' quality of *community* is equally central. One of the things that

---

[6] Paretsky interviewed by Sarah Jane Evans, 'Sister of the Shock', *The Guardian*, 25/8/1987: 8, quoted by Munt 1994: 41–2.

distinguishes female-authored from other crime fiction is that
community is not just a sustaining presence for the protagonist but
the linchpin both of plot and of the protagonist's own sense of
self-definition. In the former case, damage to the community must
be repaired; in the latter, the importance of community makes us
realize that, to a far greater extent than male private eyes, these are
protagonists defined *by means of comparison.*

The issues we have been considering are most often discussed in
relation to the 'new breed' of female private eyes. But this is only one
variety of feminist crime fiction, and the balance between these competing elements (particularly between agency and community) can
be struck in quite different ways. So, for example, lesbian crime fiction began gaining popularity at about the same time as the series of
Paretsky, Grafton, and Muller: amongst the best-known novels are
M. F. Beal's *Angel Dance* (1977), Barbara Wilson's Pam Nilson novels,
starting with *Murder in the Collective* (1984), and Mary Wings's
Emma Victor series (*She Came Too Late*, discussed in this chapter, was
published in 1986). By refusing heterosexuality, lesbian crime fiction
is arguably better able to avoid the patriarchal binary: 'a lesbian is
outside that binary and by her very presence destabilizes the heterosexual contract and imperative' (Klein 1995a: 174). The effect of
introducing an alternative position—the 'third term' of lesbianism—
has been to shift the genre further from the recognizable contours of
the male detective novel. The commitment to disrupting heterosexual
assumptions is evident, as we will see, in Mary Wings's creation of
Emma Victor. She is an investigative protagonist who is not a detective, who is neither physically nor verbally aggressive, and who sees the
self as performative rather than seeking to emulate the 'unified subjectivity' of the hard-boiled male. Wings's protagonist nevertheless
offers a fantasy of agency, as an independent and active heroine who
presides over a narrative that has female subjectivity at its centre and
who, within the structure of a fairly conventional whodunit, does
undertake a quest. Hence the novel retains the atmosphere of trial
and self-validation through action which constitutes so important a
part of the genre's appeal for feminist writers and readers. Another
claim made for lesbian detective fiction is that, from the point of view
of structure, the destabilizing of the gender binary tends to generate a
plot involving a kind of double unveiling. Not only the truth about
the crime investigated but the truth about the protagonist's sexual

identity is revealed during the course of the narrative. There are intersecting narratives, with the detective's 'coming out' paralleling her investigation of the crime (Klein 1995a: 179). Detecting resembles outing, and the lesbian detective is frequently both discoverer and discovered.

As this suggests, one of the main things at issue here is the question of whether lesbian writers are able to destabilize the genre more effectively than others. Klein suggests that the introduction of the third term of lesbianism means that, if the gender binary can be unsettled, 'so too can the apparently unchanging pairs of criminal/victim and detective/criminal' (1995a: 175). This is true, though it is not really unique to lesbian crime fiction. Rather, it is a new way of occupying a transgressive space that was already there in many other forms of crime fiction, whether investigative or non-investigative, male- or female-authored. As we have seen, these structural binaries (criminal/victim; detective/criminal) had already been radically destabilized in the male crime fiction of the mid-century paperback originals. What we are seeing in post-1970s feminist detective fiction, both straight and lesbian, is that more attention is given to destabilizing gender-determined interactions and pairings. The female detective may find it more difficult to separate herself from the victim and she is more vulnerable than her male predecessors. When violence is inflicted on her, 'voyeurism isn't such an easy option' (Walton and Jones 1999: 175), and if the plot moves towards an unsettling revelation of the detective's own hidden guilt, this is more likely to involve issues of sexual identity. Gender differences between the private eye and the male hierarchy may generate plots even less resolved than those centring on male protagonists, with lack of closure consequent on the powerlessness of a single 'private' woman confronting corporate male corruption.

These 'destabilizing' traits bring to the fore an important point about the development of female-authored crime fiction over the last few decades. Although most criticism of such fiction has focused on detective series, these series themselves, in their destabilizing of the traditional investigator–victim–criminal triangle and in their preference for plots that in some respects remain unresolved, also have affinities with non-investigative forms of crime fiction. Indeed, some of the most interesting developments in female-authored crime fiction have been in non-series, non-investigative novels which bring to the fore the female voice and female subjectivity. Such novels invest female characters with individuality and subjectivity without simply reversing the male–female binary of hard-boiled fiction and without seeing all female transgression in the context of woman's subordination *vis-à-vis* men. They give us narrators and central characters who, at their best, establish a strong, personalized female voice, using a focalized narration to draw readers into the subjective experiences of female protagonists who are positioned in decidedly non-traditional ways with respect to masculine social hierarchies. By writing novels centring on the victim or the transgressor, writers offer kinds of awareness, accounts of society as seen from the margins, that act to expose the perspectives of those at the centre.

The writers of mid-century literary noir (for example, James M. Cain, Horace McCoy, Jim Thompson, Cornell Woolrich, Gil Brewer, Charles Williams, Charles Willeford, and David Goodis) forced a reassessment of the more traditional forms of crime fiction, recurrently representing 'male figures who are both internally divided and alienated from the culturally permissible (or ideal) parameters of masculine identity, desire and achievement' (Krutnik 1991: pp. xii–xiii). In comparison to detective and private eye novels, these texts are not committed to 'proper' hero formation. They are more diverse and less formulaic, and are constantly reworking and deviating from generic expectations. A number of the women writers included in this chapter—Patricia Highsmith, Helen Zahavi, Vicki Hendricks, and Susanna Moore—differ not in being more subversive than the mid-century male writers but in focusing on *female* identity under pressure, substituting engagement with female subjectivity for the concern, in classic *film noir* and the 'tough thriller,' with the 'problematic [. . .] potentialities within masculine identity' (Krutnik 1991: xiii). What distinguishes the noir crime novel from other forms of female crime fiction (particularly female *detective* fiction) is the refusal to offer positive female role models. Instead, women's noir challenges assumptions about female identity. Through the sympathetic representation of 'transgressive' female desire and insecure, fragmented female identities, it subverts the idealized cultural possibilities of stereotypical femininity. We experience the 'both/and' of the character's dialogic consciousness, even if, in the noir world, there is no possibility of a healing resolution.

Mothering feminist crime fiction in the 1970s

P. D. James, *An Unsuitable Job for a Woman* (1972); Patricia Highsmith, *Edith's Diary* (1977)

This chapter has been subdivided decadally—an inexact process of chronologically grouping writers, but one which does at least suggest broad, overlapping lines of development and generational shifts. Patricia Highsmith and the two British 'New Wave' Queens of Crime, P. D. James and Ruth Rendell (who also writes as Barbara Vine), all born between 1920 and 1930, are key members of the 'older generation' of feminist crime writers. Highsmith's first novels appeared in the 1950s, James's and Rendell's in the early 1960s, and the dissatisfactions of mid-century Britain and America can be discerned behind their representations of female characters who either resist or remain trapped within oppressive domestic circumstances. Writing during the period that saw the development of the Women's Liberation Movement, they repeatedly turned to themes that echo the concerns of the liberal feminism of the 1960s and 1970s. All three can be regarded as having a formative influence on the depiction in crime fiction of female subjectivity and on the exploration of female identity in relation to patriarchal oppression, not encountered on Chandler's mean streets but within what Julie Smith calls 'the mean rooms' (Walton and Jones 1999: 214–15). All three might also, however, be seen by more recent generations of feminists as caught between the radical potential of oppositional feminist thinking and the conservative pull of an essentially bourgeois ideology. Sally Munt, for example, argues that the 'contradictory positioning' of liberal feminism can be seen in the female-authored crime writing of the 1970s, in its failures to harmonize surface images of female empowerment with a 'depth text [. . .] which conservatively expunges radicalism, extremism, and even an acknowledgement of difference from the sphere of liberation' (Munt 1994: 204–5). In both of the novels considered in this section, we will look at what they contribute to liberal humanist 'woman-in-control-of-her-own-life' feminism, but also at the tensions and contradictions they contain.

Of the two main texts discussed here, one is investigative (*An Unsuitable Job for a Woman*) and the other (*Edith's Diary*) is an example of literary noir, a non-investigative psychological crime novel. In both, we enter the minds of female protagonists whose sense of deprivation or isolation has been due to their position within families or societies that deny them recognition as equal subjects. This shift in perspective (from male to female) goes with an intensified interest in the impairment of social bonds and the absence of mutuality. Like their successors, these are writers who disrupt masculine authority and expose gender stereotyping, but the focus of writers like Highsmith, James, and Rendell is generally speaking more domestic than that of the female detective novelists of the 1980s (for example, Paretsky, Grafton, Muller). Community is as important (or more important) than agency in both periods, but here it plays a greater structural role: the true site of crisis is the family. These mothers of feminist crime writing in fact often bring to the fore the subjectivity of the mother, a figure most likely to be introduced into male crime fiction only to account for the instability of a male transgressor (Mrs Bates in *Psycho*, for example, or Ma Jarrett in Raoul Walsh's 1949 film, *White Heat*). In both *An Unsuitable Job for a Woman* and *Edith's Diary*, the juxtaposition of parental figures functions to develop a critique of male-dominated society which is in part played out as a conflict between the formative influences of mothers and fathers.

P. D. James's first novel to feature Cordelia Grey, published in 1972, has been placed at the beginning of the feminist counter-revolution, 'the first novel by a woman author featuring a "counter-traditional" professional female private investigator' (Walton and Jones 1999: 16). As the title implies, *An Unsuitable Job for a Woman*, like the American private eye novels of the 1980s, foregrounds the relationship between gender and genre, underscoring the fact that in conventional crime fiction, as in conventional society, the work of the professional investigator is not seen as belonging within the sphere of proper and acceptable female occupations. The eventual second novel to feature Cordelia Grey, *Skull beneath the Skin* (1982), is regarded as having backtracked considerably, moving towards conservatism in a Thatcher-era betrayal of James's feminist credentials. The first Cordelia Grey novel, however, is seen as containing a cluster of social concerns associated with a liberal feminist agenda of the 1970s—

concerns appropriate to a novel that can be neatly slotted between Britain's Equal Pay Act of 1970 and the Sex Discrimination Act of 1975. It is, as Nicola Nixon argues, Cordelia's independence of character and her sense of solidarity with other women that make her 'a touchstone of early seventies feminism' (1995: 30). This single, dedicated, and hard-working protagonist is the prototypical 'new woman', involved in a plot that raises issues of both male guilt and female empowerment.

Like the next decade's female investigators, Cordelia is self-sufficient and resilient, her independence underwritten by her orphan status (a standard qualification for female private eyes). There is, however, a curious doubleness about this orphaning, and one that is telling if we are considering the differences between male- and female-authored detective fiction. Independent, isolated male protagonists, whether of the Sherlock Holmes or Sam Spade variety, may, of course, also have been orphaned at a tender age, but we do not really know—and this is the point. It is hard to imagine our being given this sort of information about the male investigator (who always seems, like Jay Gatsby, to have sprung from his Platonic conception of himself). For a female protagonist like Cordelia, on the other hand, her orphaning is an ever-present psychological reality. Indeed, she defines herself in relation to her dead mother: as for other female investigators, relationships are an essential part of her sense of self. In a narrative in which 'real' mothers are either absent or unable to mother, Cordelia creates an inner replacement for her dead mother. She constructs an ideal mother whose subjectivity is coterminous with that of Cordelia and who sanctions her daughter's divergence from more traditional patterns of 'womanly' behaviour. Her mother having died when she was born, the question of what she would 'approve of' is dealt with by Cordelia's ability to 'evolve' a 'philosophy of compensation' out of childhood deprivation: 'Now, in imagination, she consulted her mother. It was just as she expected: her mother thought it an entirely suitable job for a woman' (James [1972] 2000: 12–13). This mothering of herself is both consoling and liberatory—giving her the strength to resist a patriarchy that is life-denying and destructive.

In the larger pattern of the novel, mothering relationships are more positive and less destructive than fathering relationships. Cordelia, in turn, feels a motherly connection with the young man who is murdered, who has never known (in a somewhat different sense) his actual mother. The connection between Cordelia and Mark is secured by the belt she 'borrows' from him, an object that has female rather than male connotations. More important to Cordelia's survival than the (generally unloaded) gun she sometimes carries, the belt used to hang Mark becomes Cordelia's salvation. An umbilicus-like cord, it is strangely protective and reassuring, 'The strength and heaviness of the leather so close to her skin was even obscurely comforting and reassuring as if the belt were a talisman' (pp. 150–1). When Cordelia is thrown into the womb–tomb of a well, her efforts to escape are explicitly compared to a difficult birth, and emerging alive requires an *active* process of, in effect, giving birth to herself, fighting to avoid the temptation of easeful death, struggling towards the light: 'The temptation to stay in comparative safety and ease was almost irresistible and she had to will herself to start again on the slow tortuous climb. It seemed that she had been climbing for hours, moving in a parody of a difficult labour towards some desperate birth' (pp. 154–5). It is a scene that invites comparison to the Hélène Cixous theme of raising and inventing ourselves, of rebirth, with the self taking on the role of mother.[7]

In comparison to the strength women demonstrated in the novel, its male figures (with the exception of P. D. James's series detective Adam Dalgliesh) are repressive and inadequate, and the male symbol, the gun, is of very questionable potency. Cordelia's biological father has reduced her to a parody of female subservience, a 'wandering life as cook, nurse, messenger and general camp follower to Daddy and the comrades' (pp. 64–5). Her first father-substitute, her partner Bernie, who commits suicide at the beginning of the novel, has constantly suffered from a sense of his own inadequacy and impairment. Rather like Cordelia, he has created his own inner parent. 'The Super', however, is an internalized father figure who, in contrast to Cordelia's strongly supportive inner mother, is a disapproving 'paragon', a male voice so condescending and uncompromising that the effect on Cordelia is to considerably strengthen her distrust of male authority: 'She in turn had devised a private litany of disdain: supercilious,

---

[7] The idea is developed in the Hélène Cixous essay 'Coming to Writing', in *Coming to Writing and Other Essays*. Trans. Sarah Cornell *et al.*, ed. Deborah Jenson. Cambridge, Mass.: Harvard University Press, 1991.

superior, sarcastic Super; what wisdom, she wondered, would he have to comfort Bernie now' (pp. 8–9). Bernie's final message, bequeathing to Cordelia '*all* the equipment' (p. 6), pointedly includes the gun, which he makes it possible for her to keep by not using it for his suicide. The gun itself, however, is a 'boyish' rather than a manly weapon, in keeping with Bernie's relationship with it: 'She had never seen it as a lethal weapon, perhaps because Bernie's boyishly naïve obsession with it had reduced it to the impotence of a child's toy' (pp. 8–9). It has been fired in practice with blanks, a harmless symbol of the manhood Bernie craves, and one that Cordelia drops into her handbag before the police come. Her treatment of the gun whilst at the cottage is equally an emasculation of it, hiding it separately from the ammunition (pp. 58–9). The explanation that Cordelia finally gives of the murdered man's possession of her gun, although a fabrication, captures accurately the relationship—the 'father' in the case is said to have taken the gun from her on the grounds that *he* could be held responsible in case of its use.

It is the irresponsibility of this particular father, however, and his deformation of family life, that is at the heart of the narrative. Mark's father reduces the son in death to a 'false woman', depriving him of his male sexual identity, dressing him, in a sense, as a traitor to his sex, as he is, in his father's eyes. Mark's weak, effeminate refusal to take his inheritance and with it his role in his father's world has threatened not only to undermine the authority and prosperity of his father but to destroy his carefully constructed professional self-image. Characteristically, his threat to Cordelia, to try to prevent her from revealing what she has discovered, is to make her 'unemployable' (p. 173). Pursuing a career that relies on methods not in keeping with the standards of respectable society (' "You can't do our job, partner, and be a gentleman" ' (p. 87)), in possession of an *unlicensed* gun (reflecting her unlicensed position *vis-à-vis* the patriarchy and officialdom), Cordelia has only a precarious hold on her professional position. She is pitting herself against a yet more illegitimate male professional position, and for her to win the contest is by no means the same as for her to secure legitimation: 'It was a pity, she thought drily, that she couldn't get a reference from Miss Leaming. Alibis arranged; inquests attended; murders efficiently concealed; perjury at our own special rates' (p. 207).

The end of the novel leaves Cordelia balanced between one female and one male relationship, with her sense of self and her position under negotiation. She has, on the one hand, an unofficial bond with the female murderer, and—testing this bond—she undergoes her final confrontation with the true father figure of the book, 'the Super', Adam Dalgliesh. Whilst Cordelia allies herself with Miss Leaming, the link is not one of affection or community. Given that they don't even like one another, Cordelia's only reason for making common cause with Miss Leaming is because she is Mark's mother. What there is in their alliance is a joint recognition of their superiority to men: 'Miss Leaming suddenly laughed and said with revealing bitterness: "What is there to be frightened of? We shall be dealing only with men." So they waited quietly together' (p. 182). This ascendancy over the Law of the Father is qualified by the role of Dalgliesh at the end. His 'second solution' in a sense replicates Cordelia's solution, and Dalgliesh treats her almost as an equal, even going along with the 'unsolved' resolution that protects Miss Leaming. But the question of how far this undermines Cordelia's fulfilment of her 'job' remains. It is, as well, this element in *An Unsuitable Job* that opens the way for the much less feminist narrative of *Skull beneath the Skin*, in which the more strongly asserted influence of Dalgliesh is felt to weaken Cordelia's independent new woman status.

As Nicola Nixon argues, *An Unsuitable Job* is something of a one-off for P. D. James (1995: 44). Given the comparative conservatism of *The Skull beneath the Skin*, it is only the earlier novel amongst her detective fiction that challenges British patriarchalism. James has also, however, written non-detective fiction centred on female subjectivity. These are not novels that image female empowerment in the way that investigative novels do, but a novel like *Innocent Blood* (1980), for example, is a complex exploration of the mother–daughter bond in which the subjectivity of each is paramount, and in which all father figures are weak or corrupt. Amongst the female-authored crime novels of the 1970s, it is in fact the case that some of the most interesting treatments of female subjectivity are in novels that, like *Innocent Blood*, are non-investigative. Britain's other 'Queen of Crime', Ruth Rendell, writing as Barbara Vine, has produced, for example, *A Dark-Adapted Eye* (1986), a narrative of maternal obsession, breaking down the nurturing mother–destructive mother duality, centring on a character who, although she commits murder, commands the reader's sympathy because of the intensity with which her subjectivity and her maternal devotion are presented. It is not true to say, as Sally Munt does, that the psychological crime novel is 'the mainstream legacy of the changes wrought by women writers on the genre' (1994: 204), given that writers like Jim Thompson, for example, were of such importance to this kind of fiction from the 1950s on. It is certainly the case, however, that women writers have contributed as interestingly to the non-investigative psychological thriller as they have to detective fiction. We will, in the final section of this chapter, be looking at a handful of 1990s examples of the psychological thriller, the work of Helen Zahavi, Susanna Moore, and Vicki Hendricks. The combination of transgressor- or victim-centred crime narratives and social satire to be found in the 1990s, however, is also a hallmark of the work of Patricia Highsmith from the 1950s on. The most famous of these novels belong, of course, to the series beginning with *The Talented Mr Ripley*, but, from the point of view of feminist criticism, the more interesting text is Highsmith's 1977 novel, *Edith's Diary*, which uses the figure of the mother as a focus for Highsmith's fierce critique of post-war American culture and society.

Edith, who is the centre of consciousness for most of the novel, is an articulate, self-aware character, and the combination of diary entries with close third-person narration ensures that we are in contact throughout with the subjectivity of the mother as she moves from being a woman with a public role (writing articles, active in the community) to being a woman whose voice is only to be heard in diary entries that attest to her total isolation and powerlessness. Superficially summarized, the plot of *Edith's Diary* sounds closely analogous to that of a matrophobic text such as Robert Bloch's/ Alfred Hitchcock's *Psycho*: a mother figure, abandoned by her husband, shares a house with an overly dependent son who is a murderer, and for whose crime the mother might be said to bear a heavy burden of responsibility. What Highsmith does, however, is to use this basic idea for quite different ends, transferring blame from the guilty mother to a guilty society. This is not, to borrow E. Ann Kaplan's phrasing, a novel that could be viewed as a mother-blaming construction serving 'to deflect attention from the economic, political, and cultural ills no one knows how to cure' (Kaplan 1990: 142). Rather, it is a deeply sympathetic construction of motherhood as a parallel to the helplessness of a 'motherly' liberal ethos confronted with incurable socio-political ills. Further, it is an examination of

some of the ways in which post-Second World War American society
shaped and also betrayed an ideal of mothering that might be said to
embody some of the most generous and selfless of liberal values—
compassion, tolerance, gentleness. Edith is only 'one single woman
. . . in a small town in Pennsylvania' (Highsmith [1977] 1980: 285), but
her life, as she drifts towards true 'self-lessness', comes to seem a
reflection of a very widespread sense of loss and bemusement.

It is because we enter so fully into the mental space of Edith that
we understand the ways in which she tries to live up to these values.
And it is our immersion in her subjectivity that gives us a grimly
ironic, unequivocally noir sense of the gap between the world of the
liberal ideal and the criminally deranged world that Edith actually
inhabits and that judges her to be mad. As Edith writes in her diary,
'The difference between dream and reality is the true hell' (p. 265).
The 'dream' for Edith contains the idealized mother and family, an
image of perfection that she only finds possible to preserve in the
realm of domestic fantasy she creates in her diary. Writing her diary is
for Edith a release from the silence required by her habitual tact and
reticence: her not saying things in awkward social situations, whether
they involve adultery or murder; her determination to bear up, not to
make scenes, not to 'fight' because it's 'too sordid' (pp. 100–1, 108).
Edith has tried hard to conform to the role of the idealized wife/
mother and one of the novel's ironic reversals is that her diary contains a secret that is not dark but radiant—a fictional realm in which
Edith imagines that she has fulfilled the ideals of the conventional
good mother and has reaped its rewards (e.g. p. 62). As a 'mother-
author', what her voice increasingly expresses is a sustaining literary
lie, a dream of her son Cliffie's successful movement into marriage
and a career, allowing him to separate himself from his mother but
still to remain close to her, a fantasy only intermittently disrupted by
intimations of her secret fears—by the opposing image of herself as a
'bad' mother whose existence is meaningless and wholly devoid of
intersubjective relationships.

What *Edith's Diary* achieves is an ironic exposure of the male view
of the mother, undermining all positions of male authority that
would conventionally provide closure in a detective novel. It is devoid
of sympathetic male characters, certainly of any who would be capable of performing the restorative functions of the active, solving
male—the traditional detective or the hard-boiled thriller hero. The

men in Edith's life are so ineffectual that they are dependent in the way that the patriarchally constructed female is. Edith's son, Cliffie, who is particularly marked by inertia, is happiest of all when he is 'mummified', 'wrapped up like a mummy so that he couldn't even move a hand or arm' (p. 45). He is in one sense just 'a minor human failure' insignificant in the larger scheme of things, but in another sense, his failures are the embodiment of national apathy, loss of will, aimlessness, and paranoia (pp. 61, 114). The other main men in the narrative are also passive: Uncle George, a bedridden, immovable object; Edith's husband, Brett, unable or unwilling to act to have George institutionalized. The only occasion on which Brett seems moved to act is when he (despicably, we feel) tries to take on the role of detective, wanting to prove that Cliffie murdered George and 'trying to stir up a case of murder' (pp. 211–12, 247). Highsmith ensures that we share Edith's aversion both to the 'smug, self-righteous' (pp. 315–16) Brett and to the psychiatrist he ultimately brings to see her, and that we understand her sense of alarm at the male invasion of her house—of its interior, which is Edith's inner realm, containing physical evidence of her fantasies (pp. 294–5).

Highsmith leaves unresolved the question of how far Edith herself is responsible for her son's weakness. She is no monstrous mother responsible for the mental derangement of a psychopathic son. Nevertheless, Cliffie commits a murder and Edith carries a share of the guilt, not just in being overly protective or in having helped to shape his attitudes but in not trying to avert the murder of George. She has failed to 'say the words' ('criminal act [. . .] even possible murder') when she realizes Cliffie has been experimenting with over-dosing George (pp. 167–9). She goes out for a walk when she knows George might be in a dangerous condition, ultimately, on the day that Cliffie does murder him, lingering off-stage and deliberately suppressing her suspicions (pp. 192–9). Edith's silence about the fact of murder is in a sense just a further manifestation of her instinctive suppression of unpleasant realities. We have, however, been drawn so fully into her subjective experience that we do not morally judge her silent assent to the murder of George. The murdering son has, in effect, acted on Edith's unspoken wish; he has put an end to a crime (the abandonment to her care of an utterly disagreeable, incontinent old man) inflicted on her by the male world, and if anything our tendency is to share Edith's fleeting thought that

George's death represents 'great progress' (p. 209). Cliffie has served her interests in a way that her liberal conscience would never have allowed her to do. There is nothing romanticized or redemptive about his contempt for society's moral norms. But Cliffie's blackly comic maladjustment ultimately comes to seem less criminal than the behaviour of the normative male figures of Brett as detective and the psychiatrist he brings to see Edith—men who, between them, are responsible for Edith's death at the end of the novel, an ending which is, as the dust jacket proclaims, 'more terrifying than mere murder'.

Butch *v.* femme in the Reaganite 1980s

Sara Paretsky, *Bitter Medicine* (1987); Sue Grafton, '*C*' *is for Corpse* (1986); Mary Wings, *She Came Too Late* (1986)

By far the best-known kind of protagonist in contemporary feminist crime fiction is the hard-boiled female investigator, the gender-bending 'chick dick' who sprang into action at the end of the 1970s. The 'in-between locus' of the female dick is intended to undermine the essentialized masculine norms of hard-boiled fiction, and it is the implications of this oxymoronic phrase that have generated the most controversy amongst feminist critics themselves. How contradictory is the female performance of this macho role? How far can a female character carry such a role before she simply becomes the male private eye of whom she is a parody? Is she ultimately no more feminist than Mike Hammer in drag?[8]

One entertaining perspective on this question has been provided by the recent Liza Cody series featuring Eva Wylie, professionally known as the London Lassassin. Cody, whose earlier Anna Lee series (starting in 1980) introduced one of the first 'feisty' female detectives,

---

[8] Walton and Jones 1999: 99–103. Walton and Jones emphasize the destabilizing of gender categories as one important effect of the creation of 'the female dick': 'The female dick, in effect, signifies difference. This in-between locus can counter dominant constructions of gender and sexuality by placing in question the clear-cut and essentialized character of the norms established by previous practices of the hard-boiled mode. And mainstream formula fiction offers a controlled space that enables a wide audience to explore the borders of established categories and conventions.'

develops a much more parodic approach in the Eva Wylie novels (*Bucket Nut, Monkey Wrench,* and *Musclebound,* published between 1993 and 1997), using exaggeration and reversal to delineate in a splendidly extreme form a really thoroughgoing female performance of strong and aggressive masculinity. She takes the autobiographical voice that is so important a feature of the hard-boiled and turns up the volume, producing a confessional, hectoring, self-lacerating, balls-out monologue that makes a show of hiding nothing from its audience. The tough voice that is such a defining feature of American female private eye novels—particularly associated with Sue Grafton's crime fiction—here reaches a kind of *ne plus ultra* of hard-boiledness. Her protagonist is a woman who does not just adhere to keep-fit routines but builds herself up until she is 'so big and strong that when I'm there I'm really there. I *am*' (Cody 1993: 61). There is no danger of the muscle-bound, ironical, and self-centred London Lassassin being taken for part of a positive images strategy. Although she amply justi-fies her contempt for anyone who underrates a woman's abilities, Eva refuses to soften her character or become a liberal feminist role model: 'Maybe you think I'm pretending to be a cold-hearted bitch to protect my image ... Don't kid yourself. I do not give a wet fart for Dawn' (p. 10). The contradictions in the tough chick dick are expunged from the persona that Eva creates for herself: there is no sex with the enemy (she tried it once and didn't like it), there are no sentimental attachments to cute puppies, no communal support net-works, no liberal sentiments, no dead mother whose loss she mourns. She is not a professional investigator but a churlishly unwilling one, and her own sense of female independence is not founded on any-thing so fragile as a PI's licence. Where feminist crime fiction of the 1980s uses Hammett and Chandler as a point of reference, Cody plays against the character types and assumptions of feminist investigative fiction itself. Her 'London Lassassin' novels would be funny and effective on their own, but the teasingly abusive relationship estab-lished with the reader repeatedly tackles the assumptions that crime fiction readers might be expected, by the 'noughties' (the first decade of the twenty-first century), to have acquired during two decades of reading the series novels of Sara Paretsky, Sue Grafton, Marcia Muller, and others.

The Lassassin's comically exaggerated toughness gives us a satiric take on the complaints lodged against feminist detective fiction by

Klein and others—by the kind of criticism that sees this form of reverse discourse as a submission to male role models rather than as a form of resistance. In their article 'Tracking Down the Past', Rosalind Coward and Linda Semple describe the conventions of hard-boiled writing as inherently inhospitable to feminism. Like Klein, they praise some mystery novels written by women as explicitly feminist in their aims and effects, but regard the hard-boiled mode as particularly un-accommodating to feminist concerns: 'Given the extreme individual-ism, violence and outrageous social attitudes towards women and other minority groups which writers like Mickey Spillane, Dashiell Hammett and Raymond Chandler often display, it is hard to imagine a form less susceptible to a feminist interpretation' (Walton and Jones 1999: 88). Whereas Cody creates, in the Lassassin, a character who champions unapologetically the extreme individualism, the violence and the socially unacceptable, politically incorrect views stereotypic-ally associated with the male tradition, the butt-kicking feminist pri-vate eyes of the American 1980s want to muscle up without injecting testosterone.

It is a little like the well-known bumper sticker that reads 'Ginger Rogers did everything Fred Astaire did, but she did it backwards in high heels.' For characters like V. I. Warshawski, Kinsey Millhone, and Sharon McCone, the phrase 'female dick' signifies differences that they want to preserve. It is an awkward balancing act: the character aims to be as good as a man, but constrained by feminine attributes; she wishes to appropriate male agency without what are thought of as male attitudes. This tricky equilibrium is what leaves the female private eye open to the charge that, like Ginger Rogers, she is part of a routine in which, however competent the woman, the man still takes the lead. Writers like Paretsky and Grafton reject some of the key generic conventions governing 'feminine conduct', but the 'male' hard-boiled traits they lay claim to are assimilated to a cluster of other, more 'feminine' qualities functioning to disrupt the implicit norms as well as the gender codes associated with the genre. They signal their resistance to what they see as a masculine value system by vesting in their heroines such attributes as compassion, communal solidarity, and reluctance to act violently unless it is a matter of life and death. It can be argued that this strategy makes it possible for them to capitalize on the sense of empowerment that is available in the male hard-boiled tradition while still drawing attention to difference. In this reading, writers like Paretsky and Grafton are engaged in a form of subversive play, a tongue-in-cheek strategy that involves full awareness of the contradictions apparent in a female character's performative definition of herself as the 'dick' that she doesn't possess—'female dick' being 'a phrase that might also be read as a burlesquing of Freudian penis envy as it simultaneously draws attention to the performative body of the female detective' (Walton and Jones 1999: 122–5).

In contrast to victim- or transgressor-centred narratives, what the detective series has to offer its readers is obviously a subject-position with which they can identify, a marginal position (because not part of established power relationships and ruling hierarchies) but none the less one that is enabling. The great attraction of the hard-boiled model is the very direct, self-confident voice in which the narrator speaks, and the competence with which opposition is ultimately overcome. There is an opening out of the possibilities for an individual ability to effect change. In spite of the greater importance of community in female-authored detective fiction, this stress on individual agency often seems to carry all else before it. If we look, for example, at Paretsky's V. I. Warshawski, we see that one of her leading traits is her tolerant multiculturalism, but at the same time we recognize that her overriding obsession is her belief in effective action. In *Bitter Medicine*, when these qualities are weighed in the balance, V.I. struggles to feel any sympathy whatsoever for the stoical resignation to passive suffering of the archetypal Latino mother figure. She watches in extreme frustration as Consuelo's mother refuses to act: 'She lapsed into silence and sat waiting impassively for someone to come with news of her child. Her dignified quiet had an air of helplessness that got on my nerves'; she does not want, V.I. laments to herself, 'to do anything but sit with her sorrow wrapped around her, a sweater on top of her cafeteria uniform', and when V.I.'s doctor friend Lotty tells her of Mrs Alvarado's reproachful silence, V.I. responds, ' "Fucking victim" ' (Paretsky [1987] 2004: 33, 41).

The strength of Paretsky's own manifest aversion to female passivity is obviously part of what places her within the tradition of liberal feminist activism that has its roots in the Women's Liberation Movement. It is an ethos criticized, as we have seen, for being too stridently, too aggressively a replica of the tough guy, but at the same time, of course, and for much the same reason (its reliance on male models of action) is reproached for being too timid (that is, ultimately in collusion with the status quo). For a critic like Sally Munt, for example, it is a form of activism that fails because it is only 'mildly revisionist', assimilating difference into the dominant socio-cultural formations and hence never effecting any very radical change: Warshawski is the very type of a figure who, in Munt's argument, is complicit with the 'continuing hegemony' (1994: 41–8). One of the more persuasive arguments against Munt's position is that developed by Walton and Jones, who use Warshawski as an example of the female detective who *does* act individualistically but does so on behalf of an abjected 'other'. In contrast to the protagonists of the male tradition, this is action that is taken in defence of communal values and that in addition has 'representational value' (1999: 206–7). It signifies the wider potential of female agency, particularly with respect to women's issues but also more broadly, with respect to the many manifestations of political and financial corruption that can be investigated in a large American city like Chicago. Klein, as well, emphasizes Paretsky's preoccupation with the development of a sense of communal responsibility. Warshawski, then, is far from being the characteristic 'loner' of the male tradition. 'Active *v.* passive' is only one of several axes of comparison, and some of the other key con-trasts—for example, the creation of a protagonist who is involved rather than isolated, who adheres to an 'ethic of responsibility'[9] rather than the 'personal code' of a Sam Spade—suggest the importance for Paretsky of locating her heroine within a complex web of relation-ships. Warshawski, like most other female investigators, has acquired a kind of surrogate or 'chosen' family, and her work as a detective acts to strengthen these vital bonds. The non-patriarchal, surrogate family is established as a counter-image to the selfish, materialistic larger society that is the ultimate villain in Paretsky's novels.

At the same time, Warshawski is situated in a male world that provides some alliances but, more importantly, conflicts and con-trasts. In *Bitter Medicine*, the use of Consuelo's mother as an embodiment of the negative quality of female passivity is counterbal-anced by the inclusion of male characters whose thematic function is to signify corrupt activity—the thrusting, selfish male pursuit of

---

[9] Klein 1995a: 171–89 borrows this phrase from Carol Gilligan, *In a Different Voice*. Cambridge, Mass.: Harvard University Press, 1982.

power and privilege. By placing V. I. Warshawski between these extremes, Paretsky brings readers to reflect throughout on the active male–passive female binary, and on the distinction between the 'good feminist's' activity on behalf of others and her active male counterparts' dedication to serving themselves. We examined in *An Unsuitable Job for a Woman* the central importance of the juxtapositions signalled in James's title itself, and the definition of the protagonist via a network of relationships is even more pronounced in Paretsky's work.[10] Cordelia Gray's relationship with Miss Leaming was pivotal but distant, there being no personal bond between them. For V. I. Warshawski, on the other hand, both positive and negative pairings are intensely personal. Her female friendship with Lotty gives her a well-established context within which to act. On the other side of the equation, both the plot and the back story implicitly contrast her with male characters who themselves aim for effective agency, but in consequence betray communal ties.

Paretsky underscores the socially conscious attributes of her protagonist by giving her, as a PI, a semi-professional position from which to tackle corruption. Also, however, by making her an ex-lawyer, she sets up a contrasting sphere within which V.I. could have acted had she so wished. She has earned 'established' professional standing, but has also deliberately removed herself from this official position, and the contrast between the public role of the lawyer and the private role of the PI is significant. She has left her position as a defence lawyer because it produced too little by way of results. There is, in addition, a running contrast between V.I. and her fat-cat ex-husband. Indeed, she defines herself in distinction to him. He exemplifies the worst aspects of the upwardly mobile member of the masculine hierarchy, and defines by contrast all of V.I.'s own principles. The other man with whom she is paired is her lover during the course of the novel, Peter, who (though weak rather than simply loathsome) has also accepted the bribes of official position. When she finds his employment agreement with Friendship, offering him money and facilities that will 'not be equalled anywhere in the country', she reflects on the

---

[10] The male protagonist is, of course, also partly defined in this way (that is, we consider him in relation to the corrupt official forces of law and order, or he is paired with a villain who is both like and unlike the protagonist); but this kind of positioning tends to be much more complex in the case of a female protagonist.

contrast with her own situation, working 'for twenty or thirty thousand a year, plus no health insurance, plus getting your face cut open and your apartment burglarized every now and then' (pp. 255–6). Her position, as the amount of marginalization and physical knocks detailed here suggest, is also one in which she is constantly having to struggle against her own lack of an 'official' place to stand. It is a struggle in which she has nothing to sustain her other than her own toughness and determination.

The physical punishment V.I. is willing to take also makes the reader aware of her kinship with the victims of crime. Male hard-boiled protagonists, too, of course, tend to be physically damaged on a regular basis. But the female PI, as a woman, is more vulnerable and more likely to be represented as linked to those who are victims.[11] *Bitter Medicine*, for example, opens with the pairing of V.I. and a dead baby who is named after her: 'My stomach lurched. Some age-old superstition about names and souls made me shiver slightly. I knew it was absurd, but I felt uneasy, as though I'd been forced into an alliance with this dead infant because it bore my name.' When she dreams of the baby in conjunction with Peter, the image is of an almost hopeless uphill struggle to protect the innocent.[12] The identification of V.I. with the baby also, however, helps to establish from the outset her own comparative weakness in the face of the large-scale socio-economic forces that are her real antagonists. The powerless–powerful binary is one of the most important in the novel.

---

[11] It is worth pointing out that victimhood in Paretsky is a more serious business than it is, for example, in Chandler: Sinead Boyd has drawn to my attention the contrast between the description of V.I.'s vulnerability in *Toxic Shock* ('Alone in this dark cocoon, I was going to drown, black swamp water in my lungs, my heart, my brain. The blood roared in my head and I cried tears of utter helplessness.') and the black humour and self-irony with which Chandler presents an analogous scene in *Farewell, My Lovely* ('You've been sapped down twice, had your throat choked and been beaten half silly on the jaw with a gun barrel [. . .] Now let's see you do something really tough, like putting your pants on').

[12] In much female-authored crime fiction (not just that of Paretsky but also, for example, that of Grafton and Barbara Wilson), the main function of the female investigators is not just to solve the crime and punish the criminals 'but to attempt to heal those innocently involved in crimes. This derives from a recognition that both systems of justice and the concept of justice administered through patriarchal institutions and structures is deeply flawed and rarely recuperative for those people caught up in any criminal matter.' Delys Bird and Brenda Walker, Introduction to Delys Bird's *Killing Women: Rewriting Detective Fiction*. Sydney: Angus and Robertson, 1993: 37 (quoted by Walton and Jones 1999: 207).

Bitter Medicine (and this is characteristic of Paretsky's novels), having opened with a crisis that seems wholly personal (a dead baby and mother), then constructs an investigation that spirals outward. The apparently individual event turns out to be symptomatic of more wide-spread social ills. Again, it is misleading to argue that this kind of metonymic displacement is a distinctively feminist trait. From Hammett and Chandler on, a central element in hard-boiled plotting has been the discovery that what seems on the face of things to be personal is actually only a small corner of a scene of official wrong-doing so sprawling and intractable that the investigator is ultimately powerless to resolve things except within the most narrow limits. As Marlowe says in *The Big Sleep*, 'it all ties together' (Chandler [1959] 1993: 158–9), and, at the novel's end, the dead body of Rusty Regan and the private eye himself are 'part of the nastiness,' inseparable from the morass of corruption imaged by the 'dirty sump' that contains Regan's body (pp. 163–4). It is not only in feminist crime fiction, then, that an individual body ultimately comes to be seen as a political body. Paretsky's fiction, however, does undoubtedly accentuate this theme. In *Bitter Medicine* this is accomplished by making the 'murder' itself simply an accidental by-product of the demands of a remorselessly commercial society in which a profit motive stands behind both prejudices and pretences. As in much black crime fiction, the blame is placed on the whole system of oppression and the institutional discourses that hide the system's underlying brutality.

Paretsky is also like the hard-boiled writers of earlier decades in focusing on a single city. Frederic Jameson, in an often-cited essay,[13] criticizes Chandler for this tactic on the grounds that it was, in effect, an evasion of larger American realities, with its stress on local corruption rather than national politics. The same case might easily be lodged against Paretsky, and indeed, the Jameson case has some affinities with Sally Munt's accusation that the liberal critique is ultimately a form of acquiescence and compromise. On the other hand, following through the logic of the metonymic displacement argument, one might suggest that the very localness of Paretsky's focus, on Chicago, is what gives her critique of institutional corruption its focus and force. As the case nears its climax, there is the characteristic widening out to take in corruption at the highest state levels. The understanding

---

[13] Reprinted, for example, in VanDover 1995: 65 ff.

of how corrupt hierarchies function in Illinois is an important part of the movement of the narrative towards its end, and this is a resolution (or rather non-resolution) that ultimately broadens out to include the functioning of profit-driven, private-corporation America in the Reagan years: 'Every hospital department had separate sales and profit goals set by an administrative committee made up of Humphries and the department heads. The national parent set overall goals for each facility. It was hard to keep reminding myself that sales in this context referred to patient care' (pp. 253, 256–8).

A good deal has been written about the paradoxical nature of Paretsky's resolutions, with their implicit dichotomizing of knowledge and power, producing plots characterized by a duality of structure—what has been called, adapting Todorov's phrase, a 'double architecture'. That is, the novels move towards a traditional form of resolution: the reader comes to understand fully the pattern of events; there is the satisfaction of villainy exposed and, in one way or another, punished. This is combined, however, with an inability on the part of the protagonist to resolve any of the larger crimes in which society's established powers are implicated. The effect of this can be compared to what Thomas Schatz calls 'narrative rupture' in the cinema: the demand for happy endings produces 'narrative rupture' in films that appear to be confronting serious issues and ideological conflicts (1981: 32). In feminist detective fiction, the aim is to make readers conscious of this rupture rather than repressing it, and this awareness of the irresolvable nature of large issues becomes part of the formula. In terms of earlier forms of the genre, this is clearly a departure from the resolved endings of classic detective fiction in its 'pure' form (say, the country house whodunit), but an extension of the hard-boiled tendency to represent crimes as problems endemic in modern urban society rather than as mysteries that can be 'solved'.

In *Bitter Medicine*, this leaving intact of institutionalized power groups and of individuals too entrenched to be touched is imaged in terms of diagnosis and treatment. The causes of malaise extend beyond individual motivations to the ideological basis for systematic wrongdoing, and, where the disease has taken hold, the possibilities of cure are remote and incalculable: ' "Lotty, this is like—like a cholera epidemic. You wouldn't think you could cure that—you'd call in the state public-health people and leave it to them" '. Lotty responds by arguing that ' "if one friend I loved was dying in this epidemic, I would treat him, even if I couldn't stop the plague" ', and this is in effect what V.I. does. The 'treatment' requested, 'friend to friend, for a friend', is administered, but in terms of the wider malaise, she knows, at the end as at the beginning, that she cannot 'sit up nights waiting for the fever to break' (p. 56). The novel's disease imagery is used by Paretsky in relation to investigative methods and outcomes alike. It reinforces the contrasts she draws between V.I.'s investigative methods and those of, say, the 'scientific' Sherlock Holmes (she is, she says, ' "Not very scientific, I'm afraid." ' (119)). V.I.'s whole manner of proceeding (intuitive, compassionate, and acutely aware of her own limitations) is, implicitly, a more realistic response to a situation in which the scientifically treatable individual body has metamorphosed into the terminally ill political body.

In their structural departure from classic detective fiction, then, Paretsky's novels can be seen as elaborations of a characteristically hard-boiled narrative construction that both valorizes individual agency and demonstrates the limitations of that agency. If we are thinking in terms of a feminist agenda, then a novelist like Paretsky conveys to readers, particularly women readers, a simultaneous sense of potential agency and of actual oppression. At the end of the day, in *Bitter Medicine*, the cynical Murray speaks for the entrenched corruption that will continue to determine how the state and city are run: ' "I know. It's awful. It's shocking. A guy like that shouldn't be in a position to decide whether a hospital gets built or an obstetrics service gets licensed, but alas, this isn't Utopia or even Minneapolis—it's Illinois" ' (p. 271).

This diminished empowerment that stays in our minds at the end of the narrative is not altogether dissimilar to the mood of defeat that made Chester Himes's work, for example, unacceptable to many black radicals. It is presumably a part of what the more radical feminist critics perceive as a limitation of liberal feminism: that is, it is an exposure of the criminality of national power structures and institutional arrangements that terminates in ultimate acquiescence in these arrangements. Paretsky herself, in interview, has said,

In general, I think that you do not change or affect entrenched powerful institutions and my books make that clear, that I have no expectation that life is going to be made better in Chicago or America as the result of V.I.'s work. You know, the people who actually murder or do mayhem in my books are hired hands of the wealthy elite. The books make it clear that after the curtain falls these guys are going to be let off with fines or slaps on the hand or even nothing at all and that those systems will stay in place.[14]

This broadening out of the narrative to create a wide-ranging socio-political critique is particularly associated with Paretsky. In Sue Grafton's Kinsey Millhone novels, the tendency, though not entirely absent, is less pronounced, and this goes with a representation of Kinsey herself as a more isolated figure. She is an individual solving individual crimes, rather than part of a surrogate family that acts as a microcosm of a more caring, more right-thinking social organism. Kinsey is indeed so prickly and individualistic that she resists her own actual family as well. This characteristic of Grafton's novels arguably pulls in two rather different directions. Kinsey's hostility to the conventional pieties of familial affection can be viewed as a deconstructive move, a radical assault on the family values that were at the heart of the conservative ideology of the Thatcher–Reagan years (Munt 1994: 49). Following this line of argument, she could be said to assume the role of the hard-boiled male protagonist *in order* to expose the myth of the patriarchal family that sustains the male hierarchy. Alternatively, if this line of feminist defence is rejected, Kinsey can be seen as a figure who (in comparison to V. I. Warshawski) is very closely modelled on the hard-boiled male, with only minimal changes made to take account of her gender, and in many ways involved in quite a conventional relationship with the patriarchal system. Her association with established authority is evident, for example, in her personal links with individual police officers (having herself previously worked for the police). This quite different ethos can be seen if we compare Paretsky's *Bitter Medicine* with the third Kinsey Millhone novel, *'C' is for Corpse*, published in 1986 (the year before *Bitter Medicine*) and, like the Paretsky novel, centring on misconduct within the medical profession. In Grafton's novel, however, the murderous doctor is an isolable malefactor rather than a symptomatic part of an entirely corrupt system, and in its denouement the novel pits individual against individual in a way that much less equivocally allows the female private eye to achieve satisfying closure.

Kinsey's final confrontation with the villain brings to the fore her

---

[14] Paretsky in televised interview with Richler, quoted by Walton and Jones 1999: 210–11.

admirably hard-boiled traits of toughness and tenacity. This show-down is a chase through deserted hospital corridors after Kinsey has been injected with something that progressively paralyses her. The method of her attacker threatens to reduce her to stereotypical female helplessness, but in spite of this Kinsey is capable of effective violence: 'When he came around the corner, I stepped into the swing, the two-by-four aimed straight at his face [. . .] I felt the board connect with a sweet popping sound. It was out of the ball park and I went down with the roar of the crowd in my ears' (Grafton [1986] 1987: 212).

The satisfaction Kinsey finds in this climactic moment of physical violence goes with a considerable capacity for verbal aggression. Though mild-mannered and decidedly well-spoken in comparison, say, to Cody's London Lassassin, Kinsey is noted for her command of forceful vernacular speech. Such speech is generally taken to be an essential element in her self-definition, an act of enunciation that is both part of her performance of a 'tough guy' role and an instrument in achieving her ends (Walton and Jones 1999: 181–2). Particularly on the part of a female narrator, the violation of bourgeois codes of speech, together with the characteristic incorporation of wisecracks, makes this a style that is, like violence on the part of a female character, a form of resistance to establishment values. Whereas Cordelia Gray, say, is given a certain advantage by the register of voice she learned in the convent (her 'carefully modulated middle-class accent' (189)), Cordelia's transatlantic counterparts from the 1980s onward rely on a very different form of verbal one-upmanship: 'Against the good taste and breeding of hegemonic, dominant culture, the hard-boiled pri-vate eye is scandalous, indecorous, vulgar, offensive—and violent' (Christianson 1990: 146). It would have to be said that, with its sprink-ling of 'fucks' and 'shits', Kinsey's speech is really only mildly, indeed rather conventionally transgressive. With an eye on the commercial mainstream, perhaps (the Kinsey Millhone series is published by Bantam Books, a division of Random House), it makes a gesture in the direction of challenging patriarchal norms through its appropriation of tough talk, asserting some measure of equality and defending female autonomy by talking dirty and cracking wise. But the game is really more softball than 'hardball with the boys' (Irons 1995: p. xx). The claims made for Grafton and her 'gender-busting' reinvention of the 'rugged individual' as woman do perhaps have to be viewed in a larger generic context. Language is indeed central, given the importance of the tough style to the male tradition, but if we are thinking in terms of language as power and as a form of resistance, then Kinsey's speech, though certainly more potent than that of a stereotypical suburban housewife, would probably neither shock nor impress a contemporary hard man like Ellroy's Dave ('I will fucking kill them for free') Klein.[15]

Wherever one places her on the effective obscenity continuum, the tough-talking heroine's will to exercise verbal control in her dealings with opponents is closely related to her strength both as a character and as the narrator of her own subjective experience—her ability to bring the eye of the reader to focus on the world as perceived by the private eye. Grafton's *'C' is for Corpse* plays very explicitly with the idea of the empowered female gaze. In the gym scenes, for example, we have a strongly physical sense of Kinsey looking at men with the kind of appraising eye that in the hard-boiled tradition would be associated with male power: 'I was usually the only woman in the place at that hour and I tended to distract myself from the pain, sweat, and nausea by checking out men's bodies while they were checking out mine' (p. 2). Grafton also, however, explores other kinds of looking, and here again, we see the feminizing of the 'eye'. The compassionate looking of Kinsey herself at the terribly injured Bobby (her client, and the eponymous corpse) is juxtaposed with the ridiculing stares of those who just see him as freakish and unfortunate: 'We walked back to my car slowly and I was conscious of the stares of the curious [. . .] It made me want to punch somebody out' (p. 9). The last line here represents, of course, a reversion to the requisite hardness, but the compassion—though of course not a quality wholly absent from the male tradition—is so insistently present that it feminizes the entire narrative. Grafton's individual rather than communal ethos contains a maternal protectiveness that closely resembles the feeling that binds together Paretsky's alternative family. It is this quality that is explicitly brought to the fore in *'C' is for Corpse* to distinguish Kinsey from the archetypal male investigator. Grafton includes, for example, a scene comparing her methods to those of Fraker in Pathology: ' "I suspect this is a lot more scientific than what you do," he remarked. "Oh, no doubt about it," I said. "But I'll tell

---

[15] Ellroy [1992] 1993: 27. On Grafton's use of hard-boiled language, see Christianson 1995: 127–47.

you one advantage I have [. . .] I know the man whose death I'm dealing with and I have a personal stake in the outcome. I think he was murdered and it pisses me off. Disease is neutral. Homicide's not" ' (p. 192). Fraker, the 'objective scientist', is at the end, not too surprisingly, revealed as truly unbalanced. The extreme rationalist slides almost imperceptibly into the total lunatic, and it is significant that the contrasting of Kinsey's approach to that of the villain is also a move that associates her with the victim. It can be argued that Kinsey Millhone moves away from the hard-boiled tradition as her 'alphabet' series progresses, becoming more closely allied with the victims, but this tendency is to some degree there from the outset. Though only the third in the series, 'C' is in a sense structured around this kind of identification. Kinsey opens with her explanation of working for a dead man, and of the strange and not entirely explicable bond she felt with a character who is very familiar from male-authored noir. Bobby is a damaged and traumatized man, his masculine competence and memory both gone. He has survived one plunge off a precipice and is now headed for a second crash, its fatality clear from the first lines: 'I met Bobby Callahan on Monday of that week. By Thursday, he was dead' (p. 1). When Bobby is alive, she fears that he endangers her independence because of the sisterly affection he summons up; for all her pride in her independence, her commitment to the dead Bobby is a displacement of her feeling for her dead parents. Her connection with him takes her back to another car accident survived, when she was trapped in the wreck in which her parents died: 'I'd seen the miry pit into which he had been flung and I'd felt the bond between us strengthened', a bond explicitly contrasted with the meaning of death in the path lab, where it is scientifically 'measured, calibrated, and analyzed' (pp. 56; 65). Again, then, what we are seeing is the sense of an *essential* female weakness that the investigator has to overcome if she is to resist victimhood herself.

Authorial awareness of contradictions in feminist crime fiction is carried a stage further in lesbian detective fiction. Published in the same year as 'C' is for Corpse (1986), Mary Wings's She Came Too Late aims to offer, in Sally Munt's phrase, 'diversity without fragmentation' (1994: 142) in its highly self-conscious representation of the performance of a range of gender roles. For the lesbian critic, what might be said to differentiate lesbian detective fiction is a different conception of the contradictory nature of identity in the female private eye novel. Wings's protagonist, Emma Victor, it is argued, embodies and unifies the contradictions of gender. Combining butch and femme qualities, Emma narrates in a way that brings these shifts in subject position to the fore. One way of looking at this is as an assault on the 'unified subjectivity' that is seen as a characteristic of masculine form. Munt contends that simply to replace the male detective with, say, a strong, good lesbian heroine would smack of a 'positive images strategy' that, in its masculine/feminine binary, is as reductionist as the form you are resisting. The claim is that lesbian crime fiction, in contrast, eschews the liberal humanist sense of self (coherent, autonomous) and instead represents the 'self in relation', conceived as a kind of loose assembly of subject positions which need not be consistent. This 'displacement of selves across a range of diverse discourses' is, in contrast to the ideology of the autonomous, coherent self, fluid and dialectical (Munt 1994: 121, 135). Politically, this can be seen as a move that works to cut against the individualism and competitiveness of the Thatcher–Reagan years.

In *She Came Too Late*, the novel in which Wings creates her series protagonist, she introduces Emma Victor as a strong, capable woman who projects a fair amount of dominant sexuality, but whose dress and behaviour (in bed and out of it) are shifting, committed to neither a masculine nor a feminine polarity. She adjusts her performance to suit the occasion, whether this involves hitting 'the local dyke hangout', a submissive role in bed with the woman she falls for during the course of the story, or relieving her not infrequent anxiety and frustration by comic bouts of 'intensive ironing' (Wings [1986] 1995: 35, 73). She admires her lover for arriving at her house in 'an old four wheel drive jeep', given that 'a motor cycle would have pushed her tough style into affectation' (p. 65). This sense of making playful choices, of weighing forms of self-assertion against forms of affectation, is evident throughout. It is a performative strategy that can be regarded as a form of insubordination. Munt draws on Judith Butler's *Gender Trouble* (1990) for the argument that this parodic play with identity acts to destabilize the 'seriousness of heterosexuality'. As in the more general feminist construction of hard-boiled fiction as somewhat monologic and solemn, unaware of its own excess and unvarying in its binarism, this line of argument can be accused of oversimplifying the opposition. None the less, it is a persuasive explanation of an important element in the agenda of lesbian detective fiction. That is, a novel like *She Came Too Late* aims to help readers to explore alternative constructions of subjectivity and to resist the tendency of all discourses (in Foucault's terms) to 'constrain and construct us' as soon as we name ourselves, thus fixing meaning and prohibiting 'flow' (Munt 1994: 145).

In a detective novel, of course, this strategy has its problems. The representation of the strong, competent woman is, in this context, problematic, since the resolution of the crime-centred part of the plot generally requires some form of effective action on the part of the protagonist. This 'fantasy of agency' is, within lesbian crime fiction, most readily identified with the stereotypically butch detective, in comparison to whom a 'femme detective' is a figure less obviously empowered. Although the central character of Wings's novel is a strong woman, this strength does not take the form of the verbal aggression and physical prowess that we find in V. I. Warshawski or Kinsey Millhone. The novel opens with the difficulties of dealing over the phone with the silences of those calling the Women's Hotline in desperation, and with Emma's own role strictly circumscribed by hotline policies about what you are allowed to say and do to help people. One might in fact argue that this is the central tension of the novel: Emma is repeatedly involved in positions in which thoughtfulness and circumspection require some sort of reticence. At the outset she feels bound by words she has not said to meet a woman whose name she does not know for reasons that are equally obscure—simply because 'I didn't want her problems, but more than that I didn't want her walking up and down Lexington Street by herself' (p. 9). When she finds the woman dead, she cannot even cry out. She has had a public voice—for example, in anti-Vietnam and lesbian activism—and has been a 'revolutionary hero', but is now living in 'different times' (p. 16), when forthrightness about, say, one's sexual identity seems not to pay, and Emma seems irritated by idealism. This shift in the times is reflected in the shift in Emma's own role: 'I had been answering history; now I was answering phones' (p. 17). In keeping with this, we see, in the showdown at the end during which the murderer describes what precipitated the murder, that it was the victim's speaking out—coming out, in a sense—that led to her being killed; and we know her from the start to be the sort of woman who does speak out, who gets 'out there with her spray can' (p. 34).

One of the themes running through *She Came Too Late* is a suspicion of the 'strong woman'. Wings is explicit in the opening about those whose needs are ignored in the 1980s political climate: 'Our newly-elected female mayor [. . .] needed to be let off the hook; could we please slit our own throats for her? [. . .] The current administration had turned its back on minority groups, and women and children were the first to suffer in the land of plenty' (p. 3). The villain of the piece is the strongest of the novel's strong women, the key figure in running a prestigious clinic which, like the hospital in Paretsky's *Bitter Medicine*, is dependent on commercial investment: 'Biogenetics is a capital intensive high technology industry in a patriarchal world. Every eye will be on profit' (p. 58). The dilemma of being associated with their paymaster, Genocorp, is often to the fore, and it is only the alarmingly power-dressed woman, wholly involved in her PR role ('she gives good public relations' (p. 111)), who can, Thatcher-like, rise to the top in such a milieu: 'Stacy Weldemeer, head of the Black-stone Clinic, now receiving two hundred thousand dollars from the Glassman Foundation: I almost felt in awe of her [. . .] I shocked myself by feeling so inadequate with a fellow sister, a comrade, a media star, a woman in yellow satin jeans' (p. 99). Emma is accused of being jealous of Stacy, who is 'shaking up the world', who has 'energy, ambitions, plans and connections' (p. 112), and it is significant that it is Stacy, not Emma, who buys a gun and learns how to use it: ' "Well isn't that swell," ' Emma comments. ' "I haven't graduated to the bullet stage of fear yet. I don't want to live with a gun in my house" ' (p. 143).

The issue of female identity is much more to the fore in Wings's novel than in the novels of Paretsky and Grafton. *She Came Too Late* is a novel that can be read as a dialogue between agency and passivity. The title itself couples its mischievous sexual innuendo with a refer-ence not just to Emma's tardy arrival at the scene of the murder but to the wider issue of effective action. Emma may vacillate between butch and femme in her performance of gender roles, but she feels less at ease about hovering between active and passive roles in her approach to the crises that constitute the substance of a crime novel. One of the key choices she makes during the course of the narrative is between passive listening (motherly but desk-bound sympathy) and detective-style intervention (*responding* and *acting*): ' "Admit it, Emma. The Hotline job has you bored to tears and sitting at a desk all day long feeling helpless" ' (p. 112). It is in her character, she is told, to want action and drama. In a brief section near the end, Emma imagines the whole of the narrative as a painting. The painting of this dream vision is a *static* though 'busy' representation of the various sub-plots and competing forces, with individual characters enmeshed in a representation of a self-regarding male power structure, 'stern business people obeying Calvinism and capitalism with a twentieth-century public relations gloss' (p. 175). Within this world, it is Stacy who stands as the image of purposeful agency, ready for action with her 'glossy smile that was as hard as the shine on any publicity photo'.

When Emma herself finally acts, it is the antithesis of this display. There is obviously a generic commitment to the kind of reassuring, stabilizing closure that characterizes classic detective fiction. In this respect, *She Came Too Late* is actually fairly traditional, with a conventional climactic confrontation scene, though one in which the desperate physical exertions of, say, Kinsey Millhone, are replaced by explication and by reasoning the villain into a position in which suicide seems the only option. Emma's description of her exit from the house after Tracy's suicide is, in its direction and degree of self-effacement, the antithesis of Tracy's show of confident agency in the full glare of publicity: 'I backed across the room and wiped any object I might have touched. I backed out of the house. I left by a back porch doorway. I got in my car and drove away' (p. 196). This exit, and her concealment of her role, this effacing of her presence, is characteristic of Emma's means of involvement. She does not 'discover' herself to others, remaining in many senses closeted as the drama plays itself out. Like Ginger Rogers, she is performing the awkward task of accomplishing all that her male counterpart could whilst dancing backwards, a carefully executed performance in what will remain, it is implied, a routine controlled by the man, in this case the still-free Stanley Glassman. It is an ending resembling that of *Bitter Medicine*, leaving untouched the guilty man of power, who in this case has been instrumental in the suborning of the strong woman, though his male ego-giganticism has, of course, been exposed to us as readers.

The lesbian feminist detective novel, as Munt argues, plays very knowingly with the whole idea of 'discovery'. The generic emphasis on the discovery of wrongdoing runs parallel to the lesbian protagonist's self-discovery, with the detective herself as the 'other' who is revealed in the process of 'coming out'. The sense in Wings's novel, however, is that emergence as a *strong* woman is not in itself desirable.

The lesbian detective, in taking on what is easily perceived as a butch role, runs the risk of assuming too fixed an identity, and the ultimate limitation of this kind of female power is embodied in a form of closure from which the protagonist dissociates herself, perhaps lest she herself appear to have affinities with the corrupt, strong woman who is 'shaking up the world'. Emma avoids assuming the role of empowered female subjectivity, leaving herself room for the more fluid, playful, elusive identities possible at the margins but not in the glare of publicity.

Unsolved crimes of the 1990s

Susanna Moore, *In the Cut* (1995); Helen Zahavi, *Dirty Weekend* (1991); Vicki Hendricks, *Miami Purity* (1995)

The detective novel, as we have seen, moves towards at least some measure of comforting resolution, and this reassuring structure acts to contain such potentially destabilizing elements as impaired agency and contradictions in the investigator's identity. The 'respectable' criminals may still be free at the end, but at least some forms of individual wrongdoing are exposed and punished. Because it does not produce highly saleable series characters, non-investigative literary noir is on the whole a less visible kind of contemporary crime writing, and of course, because its female characters are not empowered role models, it does little to contribute 'positive images' of feminist self-assertion. The noir tradition of female-authored crime fiction has, however, continued to develop, from the mid-century novels of Margaret Millar and Patricia Highsmith through the non-investigative fiction of P. D. James and Ruth Rendell (as Barbara Vine) and the 1990s novels of, for example, Helen Zahavi, Susanna Moore, Vicki Hendricks, Charlotte Carter, Minette Walters, and Lesley Glaister. This is fiction in which gender stereotyping, the anxieties and contradictions of female experience, female desire, and identity are displayed and explored without the safety net of upbeat narrative closure.

In investigative crime fiction, we have examined the appropriation of 'male' qualities by female sleuths—the hard-boiled voice, the power of the gaze, the mental and physical qualities that go with confident agency. The same means of female empowerment are very much to the fore in the texts analysed in this section, but rather than being vested in the successful female private eye they are associated with the victim and the transgressor. In a conventional male-authored detective novel, it is more than likely that these stereotypical female roles will be part of a narrative which presents the repression of female discourse and subjectivity, and that legitimizes 'the ultimate control of the narrative by a male protagonist' (Kaplan 1990: 135). Such repression is only likely, however, in narratives that represent a male protagonist whose role is the restoration of normative order, the upholding of 'power and privilege in the name of law and justice as it validates readers' visions of a safe and ordered world' (Klein 1995*b*: 11). Literary noir, on the other hand, is an exploration of the condition of powerlessness in a world in which any dominant males are the antithesis of Chandler's knight of the mean streets. There is no just and confident detective figure and no plot resolution that acts to re-establish patriarchal orderings. The female crime novels discussed here are notable for the absence of any positive male characters functioning to restore order or to represent the Law of the Father.

In women's noir, what we see instead is the replacement of the impaired male characters of, say, Jim Thompson or David Goodis by female protagonists who are similarly entrapped and lacking in social power and effectivity. As in the female-authored investigative texts discussed, community is as important (or more important) than agency. By making very fully available to us the subjectivity of a central female figure, what these texts reveal are women who are suffering, in Jessica Benjamin's terms (1988: 215–18), from 'the loss of recognition' (of understanding, empathy, appreciation, love). The noir world is one of loss and dispossession, and when we hear their voices it becomes apparent how far their sense of deprivation or isolation has been due to their position within societies which deny them recognition as equal subjects. Although alienation is also suffered by the male noir protagonist—who is recurrently 'a stranger in a hostile world' (Silver and Ursini [1996] 1999: 85–6)—the impairment of social bonds and the absence of mutuality are more to the fore in the fractured world of female noir, in which protagonists must above all struggle with an absence of the 'integration and community' that is seen as a part of the positive trajectory of feminist detective novels (Munt 1994: 125). In contrast to the private eye novels, however, noir crime novels close off redemptive possibilities, and the female protagonist, who remains isolated, struggles simply to survive, to resist the binary opposition between male ascendancy (clean, whole, rational, and possessed of effective agency) and female debasement (reduction to the abject, the grotesque body, the corpse).

All three of the novels we are discussing here juxtapose images of female abjection with the male assumption of power and with male resistance to the contaminating effects of contact with a woman over whom they exercise ascendancy. The female protagonist, trying to resist the implications of her position, is alternately victim and transgressor. In feminist detective fiction we have seen the formation of identity (or at least of a range of playfully assumed identities) in the process of solving a crime; here, on the other hand, the female protagonist, deprived of the kind of intersubjective context within which she can receive a 'recognizing response', seems in constant danger of the complete effacement of her identity. The most unequivocally noir vision is to be found in Susanna Moore's *In the Cut* (1995). What is basically a very traditional noir plot is seen from a female perspective, raising in complex ways the question of how we understand the role of the central (and sexual) female character. As in much male-centred noir, the narrator's insecure identity finds self-preservation impossible. Along the way, there are glimpses of certain kinds of potential empowerment: Moore's protagonist, Frannie, in many respects occupies the role of the femme fatale, independent, sexually defined, courting danger, anything but domestic. The *femme fatale* is, of course, usually killed or otherwise defeated at the end of the male narrative, and the male protagonist who has desired her tends to be similarly fated, having throughout misjudged the motives and character of the woman at whom he gazes (Jeff Bailey, for example, in *Out of the Past* (directed by Jacques Tourneur, 1947), doomed from the moment he gazes at Kathie Moffett coming into the bar out of the sunlight). In a novel like Moore's, which leads us to enter so fully into the subjectivity of a female character, this inexorable movement from desire to death is more problematic. As Jane Campion's project of filming *In the Cut* took shape, the difficulties of putting a heroine who eventually succumbs at the centre of a film did not go away: as Campion said of the change of ending, 'Frannie lives, or the movie dies.' Campion says of Susanna Moore, who collaborated with her in scripting the 2003 film, 'Susanna was happy for me to change it [. . .] she was telling a story from an older generation's perspective about self-sacrifice, which is tragic.'[16]

It is not only the heroine's death, of course, but her motivation that presents problems for a modern feminist audience. When the project of filming *In the Cut* was first being considered some years ago, there was considerable debate about whether Frannie is to be seen as self-possessed or masochistic, a fighter against female powerlessness or a woman with a death wish. In Moore's novel, the ambiguities of Frannie's character are an important part of the narrative, and she herself reflects at some length on her own identity, motives, and, ultimately, her fate. Just as the male protagonist of traditional noir is entangled by desire and misjudges the motives and characters of the opposite sex, so Frannie is aware that she ultimately meets her end as a result of sundry such misjudgements. She becomes increasingly aware that potential sources of empowerment are also sources of danger. This is a novel in which the dangers of both gazing at others and displaying oneself are made more insistently evident. *In the Cut* begins with an act of voyeurism, when Frannie happens on a man who is being given a blow job by a red-headed woman who is later found murdered and 'disarticulated'. Frannie's voyeurism is a complex act of looking in which she reflects on her own difference from the girl ('oh, I don't do it that way, with a hitch of the chin like a dog nuzzling his master's hand' (Moore [1995] 1997: 9)) but also wants to come closer to the girl's own perspective. In the course of a narrative during which she takes much pleasure in looking—'curious to see if the performance of his dressing would make me want him again' (p. 88)—she traverses the distance between herself and the girl.

In the end, in spite of her boldness and resource, she is as helpless as the redhead, seen by her male attacker not as an individual but as the archetypally disgusting female: as she sits smelling her own blood, the killer finishes telling her his joke: ' "God was looking down, right? And he saw Eve go into the ocean for a swim and he yelled, oh no, how are we going to get the stink out of the fish?" ' (pp. 177–8). Like the male noir protagonist, Frannie herself has committed errors of

---

[16] Jane Campion interviewed by Anthony Quinn, 'Shadow Lands', *Telegraph*, 13/10/2003.

perception, 'looking' without really seeing until it is too late, and finds herself unable to remain a detached, safe observer. She cannot remain 'in the cut'—'A word used by gamblers for when you be peepin' [. . .] From vagina. A place to hide' (pp. 178–9). Forced to leave this female hiding place, she cannot even remain the narrating 'I'. Throughout the novel, it is Frannie's command of a confident voice, her articulateness, that has enabled her to distance herself from disturbing realities ('I was thinking that it was an interesting use of the word "on", as in "cutting on her body" (p. 137)). But she is ultimately herself "disarticulated" when she finds at the end that she can no longer speak of herself in the first person. She has heard, she reflects, that "the dying sometimes speak of themselves in the third person", and as death approaches her own subjectivity recedes, and the narrating "I" becomes impossible (p. 180).

Whereas Frannie's obsessive looking forces her out of her secure female place into victimization, other female voyeurs are led to abandon their female locations and roles in more radical ways. In assuming control of the gaze they also move towards male violence, creating revenge fantasies that much more directly constitute an assault on male-centred narratives. Both Helen Zahavi's *Dirty Weekend* and Vicki Hendrick's *Miami Purity* have the kind of extremity associated with satiric inversion; both novels construct quite savage critiques of contemporary society and of ingrained habits of gender stereotyping by parodying the conventions of the male thriller. Zahavi's novel begins with Bella 'in the cut', peeping out from her safe basement, only to realize that she herself is being observed by 'A man in black. Looking out of his window and down into hers' (Zahavi [1991] 1992: 16). From the perspective of the man, in his 'elevated' position, Bella is entirely given over to objecthood, inhabiting the repulsive 'female' space of her disgustingly impure hole of a flat. It might be said that *Dirty Weekend* starts where *In the Cut* leaves off, with a female protagonist as the archetypal victim, associated with images of abjection, condemned to utter helplessness. Zahavi, however, is creating a fantasy of revenge for such humiliation, a very elaborate turning of the tables.

Once she decides that she has 'had enough' of being in this sort of position, Bella's story 'really starts' (pp. 21–2). She takes control of the whole dynamic of seeing and being seen, presenting herself as a sexual object, reinventing herself until she becomes 'their most fertile fantasy', looking back at and evaluating the male gaze: 'She turned to look at him ... His piggy eyes were watching her' (pp. 94–5). In returning the gaze, she judges the men she encounters as grotesquely unappetizing physical objects. The narrative reversal involves not just Bella's appropriation of phallic weapons (knife, gun, car) but the recurrent association of male characters with the foul, oozing, slimy imagery of the Bakhtinian grotesque body. In Bella's increasingly savage vision of the world she moves through, men rather than women are the source of pollution: in her final encounter, with a serial killer on the beach, she can 'almost feel the filth that clung to him. He wanted to unclean her' (p. 172). Bella's 'dirty weekend' is actually a cleaning spree; as she tells Norman in the bar, she works in 'sanitation' and feels she has been called to 'clean up the mess' (p. 98).[17] Having appropriated purgative male violence, Bella survives in the end as a mythic figure. The victim has emerged as a triumphant aggressor, both a caricature (the exaggerated embodiment of sexual violence) and a warning to the male aggressor and the male voyeur: 'If you see a woman walking ... Just let her pass you by' (p. 185).

Vicki Hendricks's *Miami Purity*, another female rewriting of male thriller conventions, is also, as the title suggests, a novel that revolves around notions of purity and acts of purgation. Arguably, Hendricks creates more interesting ambiguities, in that her novel depends less for its effect simply on a heightening of either the victim or the aggressor roles. Her protagonist is neither satirically reduced to simple-mindedness (like Bella) nor knowingly introspective (like Frannie) but intermittently perceptive, often wayward and mistaken, admirable mainly for her temporary determination to lift herself out of a life that has no real narrative (since she can remember nothing of it) and ultimately to tell her own story. 'Sherri' is both victim and aggressor, wholeheartedly sexual, too often self-abasing, but also capable of redefining herself, as suggested by her changes of perception, of role, and of name. She is inclined to succumb to what she sees as her fate but also willing to work very hard at controlling her destiny. Like Cody's Bucket Nut, Sherri is a parodic figure—as Andrew Pepper says, 'deliciously politically incorrect' (2000: 61–2), the antithesis of a positive role model. Hendricks very deliberately rejects the

---

[17] Naomi King, 'The Noir Thriller: Male Identity and the Threat of the Feminine', *Online Publishing*, www.crimeculture.com.

'burden of representation', instead playing mischievously with the 'whiteness' and 'maleness' of hard-boiled fiction, subverting the conventions with a satirist's enjoyment of provocation. The man Sherri falls for, Payne, is created by Hendricks as a male version of the *femme fatale*—possessing, like Kathie in *Out of the Past*, an apparent purity that masks (along with his perfect white shirts) his depths of actual duplicity and corruption. Payne is constructed by Sherri herself as the antithesis of everything her life has made her: as a Catholic with rules and guilt about sex, Payne seems to her to be someone the whole world has been good to, 'pure and beautiful'. She sees him as youthful innocence to her jaded experience, and only towards the end Payne is finally revealed more fully, enabling Sherri to realize that there is no new life and that she never actually had any control (Hendricks [1995] 1997: 63, 197, 200–1). Once she has reconceived of herself as a victim, she determines to reverse her fate, a decision symbolized by the act of picking up Payne's gun. In contrast to the female private eye, she is not stepping into a heroic role, but she does, in seizing control of the gun, gain the strength that comes from refusing to fill an allotted role. She can now deconstruct the masochistic, self-deceiving role she has been playing. Her perceptions have been ironized throughout, but she has by the end begun to understand the irony herself: Payne is not a 'poor fuckin sweet lamb' but is 'the cat piss that contaminated everything'. Like Bella, Sherri arrives at the recognition that it is the man rather than the woman who has been the source of pollution, and she is now capable of inflicting on him the final irony of death by dry cleaning: 'He would soon be cleaner than any human ever got' (pp. 209, 221–3). The end of *Miami Purity* is left open, with Sherri (now the more forcefully named Cher) back in much the same life she fled at the outset, though now without the false blue promise of Miami and free of the masochistic female submission to a man who was all too aptly named Payne.

Zahavi, Moore, and Hendricks, placing their female protagonists in stereotypically negative roles (the sadistic, vengeful killer, the masochistic victim, the woman who was 'asking for it'), will not necessarily be seen by all feminists as producing effective feminist texts. Their explorations of female self-abasement and self-assertion, however, enlarge the possibilities for complex explorations of female identity within contemporary crime fiction. As Merja Makinen argues, one of the 'basic political requirements' of feminist fiction is the interrogation and destabilization of conservative discourses, a process concisely expressed by Anne Cranny-Francis:

In feminist fiction, including feminist genre fiction, feminist discourse operates to make visible within the text the practices by which conservative discourses such as sexism are seamlessly and invisibly stitched into the textual fabric, both into its structure and into its story, the weave and the print.[18]

This 'disarticulation' of conventions is at the heart not just of feminist critique but of all oppositional uses of crime fiction. For the better part of the twentieth century, writers who have wanted to subvert the conservative assumptions and practices of their society— whether with respect to class, race, or gender—have found a ready instrument in the crime novel, the narrative structure of which *requires* the disruption of apparently stable social arrangements. Just as the detective interrogates the guilty individual, the genre as a whole interrogates the collective guilts that society conceals under what looks like an orderly surface. At its best, it offers readers disturbing and unconventional perspectives on contemporary reality. 'Murder, and any other crime,' as Nicolas Freeling writes, 'is not a part of entertainment, but an integral part of life. We are all murderers, we are all spies, we are all criminals, and to choose a crime as the mainspring of a book's action is only to find one of the simplest ways of focusing eyes on our life and our world.'[19]

Into the twenty-first century

Most of the writers discussed in this chapter are still writing in the new millennium, as are the majority of writers included in earlier chapters. Looking through the lists of recent and forthcoming publications, one sees examples of all the various sub-genres of crime fiction discussed in this study. The 'whodunit'—the death–detection– explanation model of classic detective fiction—has continued to exert

---

[18] Anne Cranny-Francis, *Feminist-Fiction: Feminist Uses of Generic Fiction.* Cambridge, Polity Press, 1990: 2, quoted by Makinen 2001: 21.

[19] Nicolas Freeling, *Criminal Convictions: Errant Essays on Perpetrators of Literary Licence.* London: Peter Owen, 1994, quoted in Peter Guttridge's obituary for Freeling, *The Independent*, 23/7/2003.

a strong influence, and, though much modified to accommodate the form to contemporary issues and expectations, the basic structure is apparent in a range of twenty-first-century novels, from, say, BarbaraNeely's *Blanche Passes Go* (2000) to P. D. James's latest Dalgliesh novel, *The Murder Room*, out in paperback in 2004. The traditions of hard-boiled detection are still vigorously present in novels like James Lee Burke's *Last Car to Elysian Fields* (2003), George Pelecanos's *Soul Circus* (2003), and James Crumley, *The Right Madness* (2005). Long-running police procedural series continue to run—for example, Ed McBain's *The Frumious Bandersnatch* (2004) is another in his series of 87th Precinct police procedurals, and Patricia Cornwell published a new Kay Scarpetta novel, *Trace*, in 2004. A small sampling of the black crime writers publishing in recent years includes many of the most distinctive voices of the 1980s and 1990s: in addition to BarbaraNeely's fourth Blanche novel, for example, Gar Anthony Haywood's *All the Lucky Ones Are Dead* was published in 2000; Gary Phillips's *The Jook* in 2002; Charlotte Carter's *Jackson Park* in 2003; Walter Mosley's *Little Scarlet*, another in the Easy Rawlins series, in 2004; in Britain, Karline Smith, for example, published her second Moss Side Massive novel, *The Crew*, in 2002, and Victor Headley brought out *Seven Seals* in 2003. Feminist crime writing is equally vigorous: Sara Paretsky's *Blacklist* (2003) came out in paperback in 2004, dealing with such contemporary issues as 9/11 and the Patriot Act; other 2004 novels include Sue Grafton's *'R' is for Ricochet*, Katherine V. Forrest's *Hancock Park*, Val McDermid's *The Torment of Others*, and Stella Duffy's *State of Happiness*. Another of the strongest contemporary trends builds on the traditions of literary noir: for example, since 2000, we have had John Williams's *Cardiff Dead* (2000); the second and third novels in James Ellroy's Underworld USA series, *The Cold Six Thousand* (2001) and *Police Gazette* (2002); Carol Anne Davis's *Kiss It Away* (2003); Jason Starr's *Twisted City* (2004); Ken Bruen's fourth Jack Taylor novel, *The Dramatist* (2004); and David Peace's *Nineteen Eighty Three* (2004); and some of the most interesting offerings of independent press imprints such as Hard Case Crime and Wildside's Point Blank include the dark and twisted work of newly emerging novelists like Charlie Williams (*Deadfolk*, out 2004), Ray Banks (*The Big Blind*, 2004), and Allan Guthrie (*Two-Way Split* in 2004, *Kiss Her Goodbye* in 2005).

The aim of this book has been to provide readers with a historical and analytic context within which to enjoy the huge variety of twentieth- and twenty-first-century crime writing. It is hoped that the study will have contributed in some small measure to making readers as well-attuned to generic conventions, generic revision, rereading and rewriting—but still as involved in a good story—as are the two old ladies in Michael Dibdin's *The Dying of the Light*, who while away their time incorporating everyone at Eventide Lodge into their own impeccably plotted golden age detective story:

Dorothy's eyes narrowed. She gave her friend a suspicious look.
'Wait a minute,' she said. 'This has been used before, hasn't it?'
'Are you accusing me of plagiarism?' snapped Rosemary.
'Of course not, Rose. It's just that it has a familiar ring to it.'
'This is no time to discuss the finer points of genre, Dot!'[20]

[20] Michael Dibdin, *The Dying of the Light*. London: Faber and Faber, 1993: 38.

Select Bibliography

Primary texts

I have included here only those primary sources to which close references have been made. The original publication date is given in brackets, followed by the bibliographic details for the edition I have used. Page references in the body of this study refer to the editions identified here.

Allingham, Margery ([1952] 1992). *Tiger in the Smoke*. Harmondsworth, Middx.: Penguin.

Banks, Iain ([1993] 1995). *Complicity*. London: Abacus.

Burnett, W. R. ([1929] 1989). *Little Caesar*. Harpenden, Herts.: No Exit Press.

Carr, John Dickson ([1935] 2002). *The Hollow Man*. London: Orion.

Carter, Charlotte (2002). *Walking Bones*. London: Serpent's Tail.

Chandler, Raymond ([1939] 1993). *The Big Sleep*, in *Three Novels*. Harmondsworth, Middx.: Penguin.

—— ([1950] 1960). *Fingerman*. London: Ace.

—— ([1940] 1993). *Farewell, My Lovely*, in *Three Novels*. Harmondsworth, Middx.: Penguin.

Chesterton, G. K. ([1911] 1987). *The Innocence of Father Brown*. Harmondsworth, Middx.: Penguin.

Christie, Agatha ([1926] 1993). *The Murder of Roger Ackroyd*. London: HarperCollins.

—— ([1932] 1995). *Peril at End House*. London: HarperCollins.

Cody, Lisa (1993). *Bucket Nut*. London: Arrow.

Cornwell, Patricia ([1998] 2000). *Point of Origin*. London: Werner Books.

—— ([2000] 2001). *The Last Precinct*. London: Warner Books.

Doyle, Arthur Conan ([1892 and 1894] 2001). *The Adventures of Sherlock Holmes* and *The Memoirs of Sherlock Holmes*, ed. Iain Pears and Ed Glinert. Harmondsworth, Middx.: Penguin.

Ellis, Bret Easton (1991). *American Psycho*. London: Picador.

Ellroy, James ([1987] 1993). *The Black Dahlia*. London: Arrow.

—— ([1990] 1994). *LA Confidential*. London: Arrow.

—— ([1992] 1993). *White Jazz*. London: Arrow.

Freeman, R. Austin ([1912] 2001). *The Singing Bone*. Thirsk, Yorks.: House of Stratus.

Goodis, David ([1954] 1998). *The Blonde on the Street Corner*. London: Serpent's Tail.

Grafton, Sue ([1986] 1987). *'C' is for Corpse*. New York: Bantam.

Hammett, Dashiell ([1929] 1982). *Red Harvest*, in *The Four Great Novels*. London: Picador.

—— ([1931] 1982). *The Glass Key*, in *The Four Great Novels*. London: Picador.

Harris, Thomas ([1981] 1993). *Red Dragon*. London: Arrow.

—— ([1999] 2000). *Hannibal*. London: Arrow.

Headley, Victor ([1992] 1993). *Yardie*. London: Pan.

Hendricks, Vicki ([1995] 1997). *Miami Purity*. London: Minerva.

Hiaasen, Carl (1995). *Stormy Weather*. New York: Warner Books.

—— ([1999] 2001). *Kick Ass: Selected Columns of Carl Hiaasen*, ed. Diane Stevenson. New York: Berkley Publishing Group.

Highsmith, Patricia ([1977] 1980). *Edith's Diary*. Harmondsworth, Middx.: Penguin.

—— ([1955] 1992). *The Talented Mr Ripley*, in *Ripley*. Harmondsworth, Middx.: Penguin.

Himes, Chester ([1969] 1996). *Blind Man with a Pistol*, in *The Harlem Cycle*, vol. iii. Edinburgh: Payback Press.

James, P. D. ([1963] 1985). *A Mind to Murder*. London: Sphere.

—— ([1972] 2000). *An Unsuitable Job for a Woman*. London: Faber and Faber.

McBain, Ed, and Evan Hunter [both pseudonyms belonging to Salvatore A. Lombino] (2001). *Candyland*. London: Orion.

McCoy, Horace ([1935] 1995). *They Shoot Horses, Don't They?* London: Serpent's Tail.

MacDonald, John D. ([1962] 1983). *A Flash of Green*. New York: Fawcett Gold Medal.

Macdonald, Ross ([1958] 1990). *The Doomsters*. New York: Warner Books.

Moore, Susanna ([1995] 1997). *In the Cut*. London: Picador.

Morrison, Arthur ([1897] 2003). *The Dorrington Deed-Box*. Rockville, Md: James A. Rock.

Mosley, Walter ([1990] 1992). *Devil in a Blue Dress*. London: Pan.

Neely, Barbara ([1992] 1993). *Blanche on the Lam*. Harmondsworth, Middx.: Penguin.

Paretsky, Sara ([1987] 2004). *Bitter Medicine*. Harmondsworth, Middx.: Penguin.

Phillips, Mike ([1994] 1995). *Point of Darkness*. Harmondsworth, Middx.: Penguin.

Rendell, Ruth ([1967] 1990). *Wolf to the Slaughter*. Harmondsworth, Middx.: Arrow.

Ridley, John ([1998] 1999). *Love is a Racket*. London: Bantam.

Sallis, James ([1992] 1996). *The Long-Legged Fly*. Harpenden, Herts.: No Exit Press.

Sayers, Dorothy L. ([1930] 2004). *Strong Poison*. London: New English Library.

Spillane, Mickey ([1951] 1987). *One Lonely Night*. London: New English Library.

Starr, Jason (1997). *Cold Caller*. Harpenden, Herts.: No Exit Press.

Thompson, Jim ([1952] 1991). *The Killer Inside Me*. New York: Vintage Crime.

Trail, Armitage [Maurice Coons] ([1930] 1997). *Scarface*. London: Bloomsbury.

West, Nathaniel ([1939] 1991). *The Day of the Locust*. Harmondsworth, Middx.: Penguin.

Willeford, Charles ([1988] 1996). *The Way We Die Now*. New York: Dell.

Wings, Mary ([1986] 1995). *She Came Too Late*. London: Women's Press.

Zahavi, Helen ([1991] 1992). *Dirty Weekend*. London: Flamingo.

Secondary texts

Aisenberg, Nadya (1979). *A Common Spring: Crime Novel and Classic*. Bowling Green, Ohio: Popular Press.

Allen, Dick, and David Chacko, eds. (1974). *Detective Fiction: Crime and Compromise*. New York: Harcourt Brace Jovanovich.

Ashley, Bob (1989). *The Study of Popular Fiction: A Source Book*. London: Pinter Publishers.

Auden, W. H. ([1948] 1987). 'The Guilty Vicarage', in *The Dyer's Hand and Other Essays*. London: Faber and Faber, 146–58.

Bailey, Frankie Y. (1991). *Out of the Woodpile: Black Characters in Crime and Detective Fiction*. New York and Westport, Conn.: Greenwood Press.

Baldick, Chris, ed. (1992). *The Oxford Book of Gothic Tales*. Oxford: Oxford University Press.

Barson, Michael S. (1981). ' "There's No Sex in Crime": The Two-Fisted Homilies of Race Williams', *Clues: A Journal of Detection*, 2/2: 103–11.

Barthes, Roland (1974). *S/Z*. New York: Hill and Wang.

Bayard, Pierre ([1998] 2000). *Who Killed Roger Ackroyd? The Murderer who Eluded Hercule Poirot and Deceived Agatha Christie*. London: Fourth Estate.

Bell, Ian, and Graham Daldry, eds. (1990). *Watching the Detectives: Essays on Crime Fiction*. London: Macmillan.

Benjamin, Jessica (1988). *The Bonds of Love: Psychoanalysis, Feminism, and the Problem of Domination*. New York: Pantheon.

Bernstock, Bernard, ed. (1983), *Essays on Detective Fiction*. London: Macmillan.

Binyon, T. J. (1991). *Murder Will Out*. Oxford: Oxford University Press.

Bloom, Clive (1996). *Cult Fictions*. Basingstoke: Macmillan.

—— ed. (1990). *Twentieth-Century Suspense: The Thriller Comes of Age*. Basingstoke: Macmillan.

Botting, Fred (1996). *Gothic*. London: Routledge, New Critical Idiom.

Bradbury, Malcolm, and Howard Temperley ([1981] 1998). *Introduction to American Studies*. London: Longman.

Breen, Jon L., and Martin Harry Greenberg, eds. (1989). *Murder Off the Rack: Critical Studies of Ten Paperback Masters*. Metuchen, NJ: Scarecrow Press, 1989.

Browne, Ray B. (1990). 'Ross Macdonald: Revolutionary Author and Critic', *Journal of Popular Culture*, 24: 101–11.

Campbell, Neil, and Alasdair Kean (1997). *American Cultural Studies: An Introduction to American Culture*. London: Routledge.

Caputi, Jane (1993). 'American Psychos: The Serial Killer in Contemporary Fiction', *Journal of American Culture*, 16/4: 101–12.

Carr, Helen, ed. (1989). *From My Guy to Sci-Fi: Genre and Women's Writing in the Postmodern World*. London: Pandora Press.

Cawelti, John G. (1976). *Adventure, Mystery and Romance: Formula Stories as Art and Popular Culture*. Chicago: University of Chicago Press.

Chandler, Raymond ([1944] 1988). 'The Simple Art of Murder', in *The Simple Art of Murder*. New York, Vintage Crime.

—— (1984). *Raymond Chandler Speaking*, ed. Dorothy Gardiner and Kathrine Sorley Walker. London: Allison and Busby.

Chesterton, G. K. ([1902] 1974). 'A Defence of Detective Stories', in *The Defendant*. London: Johnson, reprinted in Haycraft [1946] 1974: 3–6.

Christian, Barbara (1985). *Black Feminist Criticism: Perspectives on Black Women Writers*. New York: Pergamon Press.

Christianson, Scott R. (1990). 'A Heap of Broken Images: Hard-boiled Detective Fiction and the Discourse(s) of Modernity', in Walker and Frazer 1990: 135–48.

—— (1995). 'Talkin' Trash and Kickin' Butt: Sue Grafton's Hard-Boiled Feminism', in Irons 1995: 127–47.

Cobley, Paul (2000). *The American Thriller: Generic Innovation and Social Change in the 1970s*. Basingstoke: Macmillan.

Cochran, David (2000). *American Noir: Underground Writers and Filmmakers of the Post-War Era*. Washington, DC: Smithsonian Books.

Cohen, Josh (1997). 'James Ellroy, Los Angeles and the Spectacular Crisis of Masculinity', in Messent 1997: 168–86.

Collins, Jim (1989). *Uncommon Cultures: Popular Culture and Postmodernism*. London: Routledge.

Collins, Max Allan, and James L. Traylor (1984). *One Lonely Knight: Mickey Spillane's Mike Hammer*. Bowling Green, Ohio: Popular Press.

Craig, Patricia, and Mary Cadogan ([1981] 1986). *The Lady Investigates: Women Detectives and Spies in Fiction*. Oxford: Oxford Paperback.

Cranny-Francis, Anne (1988). 'Gender and Genre: Feminist Rewritings of Detective Fiction', *Women's Studies International Forum*, 11/1: 69–84.

Cranny-Francis, Anne (1990). *Feminist Fiction: Feminnist Uses of Generic Fiction*. Cambridge: Polity Press.

Creed, Barbara (1993). *The Monstrous-Feminine*. London: Routledge.

Daly, Brenda O., and Maureen T. Reddy (1991). *Narrating Mothers: Theorizing Maternal Subjectivity*. Knoxville: University of Tennessee Press.

Davis, Mike (1990). *City of Quartz: Excavating the Future in Los Angeles*. London: Vintage.

De Jongh, James (1990). *Vicious Modernism: Black Harlem and the Literary Imagination*. Cambridge: Cambridge University Press.

Debord, Guy (1983). *Society of the Spectacle*. Detroit: Black and Red.

Denning, Michael (1987). *Mechanic Accents: Dime Novels and Working-Class Culture in America*. London: Verso.

Doane, Mary Ann (1991). *Femmes Fatales: Feminism, Film Theory, Psycho-analysis*. London: Routledge.

Docherty, Brian, ed. (1988). *American Crime Fiction: Studies in the Genre*. Basingstoke: Macmillan.

Dooley, Dennis (1984). *Dashiell Hammett*. New York: Frederick Ungar Publishing Co.

Douglas, John, and Mark Olshaker (1995). *Mindhunter: Inside the FBI's Elite Serial Crime Unit*. New York: Pocket Books.

Dove, George N. (1982). *The Police Procedural*. Bowling Green, Ohio: Popular Press.

Duncan, Paul, ed. (1997). *The Third Degree: Crime Writers in Conversation*. Harpenden, Herts.: No Exit Press and Crime Time Magazine.

Durham, Philip (1968). 'The "Black Mask" School', in Madden 1968: 51–79.

Eco, Umberto (1979). *The Role of the Reader: Explorations in the Semiotics of Texts*. Bloomington: Indiana University Press.

Eden, Rick A. (1983). 'Detective Fiction as Satire', *Genre*, 16: 279–95.

Elliott, Robert C. (1960). *The Power of Satire: Magic, Ritual, Art*. Princeton: Princeton University Press.

Fabre, Michel, and Robert E. Skinner, eds. (1995). *Conversations with Chester Himes*. Jackson: University Press of Mississippi.

—— —— and Lester Sullivan (1992). *Chester Himes: An Annotated Primary and Secondary Bibliography*. Westport, Conn.: Greenwood Press.

Farred, Grant (2001). 'The Postcolonial Chickens Come Home to Roost: How *Yardie* Has Created a New Postcolonial Subaltern', *South Atlantic Quarterly*, 100/1: 287–305.

Featherstone, Mike ([1991] 1998). *Consumer Culture and Postmodernism*. London: Sage Publications.

Fiedler, L. A. ([1960] 1998). *Love and Death in the American Novel*. Normal, Ill.: Dalkey Archives.

Fine, David, ed. (1984). *Los Angeles in Fiction*. Albuquerque: University of New Mexico Press.

Forter, Greg (2000). *Murdering Masculinities: Fantasies of Gender and Violence in the American Crime Novel*. New York: New York University Press.

Foster, Hal (1996). *The Return of the Real: The Avant-Garde at the End of the Century*. Cambridge, Mass.: MIT Press.

Foucault, Michel ([1975] 1991). *Discipline and Punish: The Birth of the Prison*. Harmondsworth, Middx.: Penguin.

Freccero, Carla (1997). 'Historical Violence, Censorship, and the Serial Killer: The Case of *American Psycho*', *Diacritics*, 27/2: 44–58.

Freeling, Nicolas (1994). *Criminal Conversations: Errant Essays on Perpetrators of Literary Licence*. Boston, Mass.: David R. Godine.

Freiburger, William (1996). 'James Ellroy, Walter Mosley, and the Politics of the Los Angeles Crime Novel', *Clues: A Journal of Detection*, 17/2: 87–104.

Gates, Henry Louis (1989). *The Signifying Monkey: A Theory of Afro-American Literary Criticism*. Oxford: Oxford University Press.

Geherin, David (1985). *The American Private Eye: The Image in Fiction*. New York: Frederick Ungar Publishing Co.

Glassman, Steve, and Maurice O'Sullivan, eds. (1997). *Crime Fiction and Film in the Sunshine State: Florida Noir*. Bowling Green, Ohio: Popular Press.

Gledhill, Christine (1988). 'Pleasurable Negotiations', in E. Deidre Pribram, ed. *Female Spectators: Looking at Film and Television*. London: Verso, 64–89.

Glover, David (2003). 'The Thriller', in Priestman 2003: 135–53.

Gosselin, Adrienne Johnson, ed. (1999) *Multicultural Detective Fiction: Murder from the "Other" Side*. New York: Garland Publishing.

Goulart, Ron (1972). *Cheap Thrills: An Informal History of the Pulp Magazines*. New Rochelle, NY: Arlington House.

Grimes, Larry E. (1983). 'Stepsons of Sam: Re-Visions of The Hard-Boiled Formula in Recent American Fiction', *Modern Fiction Studies*, 29/3: 535–44.

Grossvogel, David A. (1979). *Mystery and its Fictions: From Oedipus to Agatha Christie*. Baltimore: Johns Hopkins University Press.

Gruesser, John Cullen (1999). 'An Un-Easy Relationship: Walter Mosley's Signifyin(g) Detective and the Black Community', in Gosselin 1999: 325–49.

Hagemann, E. R. (1981). 'Cap Shaw and his "Great and Regular Fellows": The Making of *The Hard-Boiled Omnibus*, 1945–1946', *Clues: A Journal of Detection*, 2/2: 143–52.

Hantke, Steffen (1998). ' "The Kingdom of the Unimaginable": The Construction of Social Space and the Fantasy of Privacy in Serial Killer Narratives', *Literature/Film Quarterly*, 26/3: 178–95.

Haut, Woody (1995). *Pulp Culture and the Cold War*. London: Serpent's Tail.

Haut, Woody (1999). *Neon Noir: Contemporary American Crime Fiction.* London: Serpent's Tail.

Hawkins, Harriet (1990). *Classics and Trash: Traditions and Taboos in High Literature and Popular Modern Genres.* New York and London: Harvester Wheatsheaf.

Haycraft, Howard ([1942] 1984). *Murder for Pleasure: The Life and Times of the Detective Story.* New York, Carroll and Graf.

—— ed. ([1946] 1974). *The Art of the Mystery Story: A Collection of Critical Essays.* New York: Carroll and Graf.

Herbert, Rosemary, ed. (1999). *The Oxford Companion to Crime and Mystery.* New York: Oxford University Press.

Hilfer, Tony (1990). *The Crime Novel: A Deviant Genre.* Austin: University of Texas Press.

Hiney, Tom (1997). *Raymond Chandler: A Biography.* London: Vintage.

Hodgson, John A., ed. (1994). *Sir Arthur Conan Doyle, Sherlock Holmes: The Major Stories with Contemporary Critical Essays.* Boston: Bedford Books.

Horsley, Katharine, and Lee Horsley (1999). '*Mères Fatales*: Maternal Guilt in the Noir Crime Novel', *Modern Fiction Studies*, 45/2: 369–402.

—— —— (forthcoming). 'Body Language: Reading the Corpse in Forensic Crime Fiction', forthcoming in *Paradoxa.*

—— —— (forthcoming). 'Learning Italian: Serial Killers Abroad in the Novels of Highsmith and Harris', in *Murder and Mayhem in the Mare Nostrum.* (Newark: University of Delaware Press).

Horsley, Lee (1995). *Fictions of Power in English Literature: 1900–1950.* London: Longman.

—— (1998). 'Founding Fathers: "Genealogies of Violence" in James Ellroy's L.A. Quartet', *Clues: A Journal of Detection*, 19/2: 139–61.

—— (2001). *The Noir Thriller.* Basingstoke: Palgrave.

Hubly, Erlene (1983). 'The Formula Challenged: The Novels of P. D. James', *Modern Fiction Studies*, 29/3: 511–21.

Hutcheon, Linda (1989). *The Politics of Postmodernism.* London: Routledge.

Hutton, Will (1995). *The State We're In.* London: Vintage.

Inge, M. Thomas (1988). *Handbook of American Popular Literature.* New York and Westport, Conn.: Greenwood Press.

Irons, Glenwood, ed. (1992). *Gender, Language and Myth: Essays on Popular Narrative.* Toronto: University of Toronto Press.

—— ed. (1995). *Feminism in Women's Detective Fiction.* Toronto: University of Toronto Press.

Jaffe, Audrey ([1990] 1994). 'Detecting the Beggar: Arthur Conan Doyle, Henry Mayhew, and "The Man with the Twisted Lip" ', in Hodgson 1994: 402–27.

Kaplan, Cora (1986). 'An Unsuitable Genre for a Feminist?' *Feminist Review*, 8: 18–19.

Kaplan, E. Ann (1984). 'Is the Gaze Male?', in Ann Snitow *et al*, eds. *Desire: The Politics of Sexuality*. London: Virago Press, 321–38.

—— (1990). 'Motherhood and Representation: From Post-war Freudian Figurations to Postmodernism', in E. Ann Kaplan, ed. *Psychoanalysis and the Cinema*. New York: Routledge, 129–42.

—— ed. (1972). *Women in Film Noir*. London: British Film Institute.

Kernan, Alvin P. ([1959] 1971). 'A Theory of Satire', in Ronald Paulson, ed. *Satire: Modern Essays in Criticism*. Englewood Cliffs, NJ: Prentice-Hall, 249–77.

Klein, Kathleen Gregory (1988). *The Woman Detective: Gender and Genre*. Urbana and Chicago: University of Illinois Press.

—— (1995*a*). 'Habeas Corpus: Feminism and Detective Fiction', in Irons 1995: 171–89.

—— (1995*b*). *Women Times Three: Writers, Detectives, Readers*. Bowling Green, Ohio: Popular Press.

—— (1999). *Diversity and Detective Fiction*. Bowling Green, Ohio: Popular Press.

Knight, Stephen (1980). *Form and Ideology in Crime Fiction*. Basingstoke: Macmillan.

—— ([1981] 1994). 'The Case of the Great Detective', in Hodgson, *Holmes: The Major Stories*, 368–80.

—— (2003). 'The Golden Age', in Priestman 2003: 77–94.

—— (2004). *Crime Fiction, 1800–2000: Detection, Death, Diversity*. Basingstoke: Palgrave Macmillan.

Krutnik, Frank (1991). *In a Lonely Street: Film, Genre, Masculinity*. London: Routledge.

Landrum, Larry N., Pat Browne, and Ray B. Browne, eds. (1976). *Dimensions of Detective Fiction*. Bowling Green, Ohio: Popular Press.

Lee, A. Robert, ed. (1980). *Black Fiction: New Studies in the Afro-American Novel since 1945*. London: Vision Press.

Light, Alison (1991). *Forever England: Femininity, Literature and Conservatism between the Wars*. London: Routledge.

Lott, Rick (1997). 'John D. MacDonald: Puritan in Paradise', *Clues: A Journal of Detection*, 18/2: 19–30.

McCann, Sean (2000). *Gumshoe America: Hard-Boiled Crime Fiction and the Rise and Fall of New Deal Liberalism*. Durham, NC: Duke University Press.

McCauley, Michael J. (1991). *Jim Thompson: Sleep with the Devil*. New York: Mysterious Press.

McCracken, Scott (1998). *Pulp: Reading Popular Fiction*. Manchester: Manchester University Press.

McHale, Brian (1992). *Constructing Postmodernism*. London: Routledge.

Madden, David, ed. (1968). *Tough Guy Writers of the Thirties.* Carbondale, Ill.: Southern Illinois University Press.

Mahan, Jeffrey H. (1980). 'The Hard-Boiled Detective In the Fallen World', *Clues: A Journal of Detection,* 1/2: 90–9.

Makinen, Merja (2001). *Feminist Popular Fiction.* Basingstoke: Palgrave.

Malmgren, Carl D. (2001). *Anatomy of Murder: Mystery, Detective, and Crime Fiction.* Bowling Green, Ohio: Popular Press.

Mandel, Ernest (1984). *Delightful Murder: A Social History of the Crime Story.* London: Pluto Press.

Mann, Jessica (1981). *Deadlier than the Male: An Investigation into Feminine Crime Writing.* Newton Abbot: David and Charles.

Margolies, Edward (1970). 'The Thrillers of Chester Himes', *Studies in Black Literature,* 1/2: 1–11.

Marling, William (1995). *The American Roman Noir: Hammett, Chandler, Cain.* Athens, Ga.: University of Georgia Press.

Martin, Richard (1997). *Mean Streets and Raging Bulls: The Legacy of Film Noir in Contemporary American Cinema.* Lanham, Md.: Scarecrow Press.

Marwick, Arthur (1982). *British Society Since 1945.* Harmondsworth, Middx.: Penguin.

Messent, Peter, ed. (1997). *Criminal Proceedings: The Contemporary American Crime Novel.* London: Pluto Press.

Metress, Christopher, ed. (1994). *The Critical Response to Dashiell Hammett.* Westport, Conn.: Greenwood Press.

Milliken, Stephen E. (1976). *Chester Himes: A Critical Appraisal.* Columbia: University of Missouri Press.

Moi, Toril (1985). *Sexual/Textual Politics: Feminist Literary Theory.* London: Methuen.

Moore, Lewis D. (1994). *Meditations on America: John D. MacDonald's Travis McGee Series and Other Fiction.* Bowling Green, Ohio: Popular Press.

Moretti, Franco (1983). *Signs Taken for Wonders: Essays in the Sociology of Literary Forms.* London: Verso.

Most, Glenn W., and William W. Stowe, eds. (1983). *The Poetics of Murder: Detective Fiction and Literary Theory.* New York: Harcourt Brace Jovanovich.

Muller, Gilbert H. (1989). *Chester Himes.* Boston: Twayne Publishers.

Muller, John P., and William J. Richardson, eds. (1988). *Purloined Poe: Lacan, Derrida, and Psychoanalytic Reading.* Baltimore: Johns Hopkins University Press.

Munby, Jonathan (1999). *Public Enemies, Public Heroes: Screening the Gangster from Little Caesar to Touch of Evil.* Chicago: University of Chicago Press.

Munt, Sally R. (1994). *Murder by the Book? Feminism and the Crime Novel.* London: Routledge.

—— (1998). 'Grief, Doubt and Nostalgia in Detective Fiction, Or . . . Death and the Detective Novel: A Return', *College Literature*, 9/22: 133–45.

Naremore, James (1998). *More Than Night: Film Noir in its Contexts.* Berkeley: University of California Press.

Neale, Stephen (1980). *Genre.* London: British Film Institute.

Nelson, Raymond (1972). 'Domestic Harlem: The Detective Fiction of Chester Himes', *Virginia Quarterly Review*, 48/2: 260–76.

Nevins, Francis M., ed. (1970). *The Mystery Writer's Art.* Bowling Green, Ohio: Popular Press.

Nixon, Nicola (1995). 'Gray Areas: P. D. James's Unsuiting of Cordelia', in Irons 1995: 29–45.

Nolan, Tom (1999). *Ross Macdonald: A Biography.* New York: Scribner.

Nolan, William R. (1969). *Dashiell Hammett: A Casebook.* Santa Barbara: McNally and Loftin.

O'Brien, Geoffrey ([1981] 1997). *Hard-boiled America: Lurid Paperbacks and the Masters of Noir*, expanded edn. New York: Da Capo Press.

Ousby, Ian (1997). *The Crime and Mystery Book: A Reader's Companion.* London: Thames and Hudson.

Palmer, Jerry (1978). *Thrillers: Genesis and Structure of a Popular Genre.* London: Edward Arnold.

—— (1991). *Potboilers: Methods, Concepts and Case Studies in Popular Fiction.* London and New York: Routledge.

Panek, LeRoy Lad (1990). *Probable Cause: Crime Fiction in America.* Bowling Green, Ohio: Popular Press.

Paulson, Ronald ([1967] 1983). *The Fictions of Satire.* Baltimore: Johns Hopkins University Press.

Payne, Kenneth (1994). 'Pottsville, USA: Psychosis and the American "Emptiness" in Jim Thompson's *Pop. 1280*', *International Fiction Review*, 21: 51–7.

Pepper, Andrew (2000). *The Contemporary American Crime Novel: Race, Ethnicity, Gender, Class.* Edinburgh: Edinburgh University Press.

Plain, Gill (2001). *Twentieth-Century Crime Fiction: Gender, Sexuality and the Body.* Edinburgh: Edinburgh University Press.

Polito, Robert (1995). *Savage Art: A Biography of Jim Thompson.* New York: Alfred A. Knopf.

Porter, Dennis (1981). *The Pursuit of Crime: Art and Ideology in Detective Fiction.* New Haven: Yale University Press.

—— (2003). 'The Private Eye', in Priestman 2003: 95–113.

Powers, Richard Gid (1983). *G-Men: Hoover's FBI in American Popular Culture.* Carbondale, Ill.: Southern Illinois University Press.

Prassel, Frank Richard (1993). *The Great American Outlaw: A Legacy of Fact and Fiction.* Norman: University of Oklahoma Press.

Priestman, Martin (1990). *Detective Fiction and Literature: The Figure on the Carpet.* Basingstoke: Macmillan.

—— ([1990] 1994). 'Sherlock Holmes—The Series', in Hodgson 1994: 313–20.

—— (1998). *Crime Fiction from Poe to the Present.* Plymouth: Northcote House.

—— ed. (2003). *The Cambridge Companion to Crime Fiction.* Cambridge: Cambridge University Press.

Pronzini, Bill, and Jack Adrian, eds. (1995). *Hard-Boiled: An Anthology of American Crime Stories.* Oxford: Oxford University Press.

Punter, David (1980). *The Literature of Terror: A History of Gothic Fictions from 1765 to the Present Day.* London: Longman.

Pykett, Lyn (2003). 'The Newgate Novel and Sensation Fiction, 1830–1868', in Priestman 2003: 19–39.

Pyrhonen, Heta (1994). *Murder from an Academic Angle.* Columbia, SC: Camden House.

Raczkowski, Christopher T. (2003). 'From Modernity's Detection to Modernist Detectives: Narrative Vision in the Work of Allan Pinkerton and Dashiell Hammett', *Modern Fiction Studies* 49/4: 629–59.

Rader, Barbara A., and Howard G. Zettler, eds. (1988). *The Sleuth and the Scholar: Origins, Evolution and Current Trends in Detective Fiction.* New York and Westport, Conn.: Greenwood Press.

Raskin, Richard (1992). 'The Pleasures and Politics of Detective Fiction', *Clues: A Journal of Detection*, 13: 71–113.

Reddy, Maureen T. (1988). *Sisters in Crime: Feminism and the Crime Novel.* New York: Continuum Books.

—— (2003a). *Traces, Codes and Clues: Reading Race in Crime Fiction.* New Brunswick, NJ: Rutgers University Press.

—— (2003b). 'Women Detectives', in Priestman 2003: 191–207.

Reilly, John M. (1976). 'Chester Himes' Harlem Tough Guys', *Journal of Popular Culture*, 9/4: 935–47.

—— ed. ([1980] 1985). *Twentieth-Century Crime and Mystery Writers.* New York: St Martin's Press.

Rennison, Nick, and Richard Shephard, eds. (1997). *Waterstone's Guide to Crime Fiction.* Brentford, Middx.: Waterstone's Booksellers Ltd.

Ressler, Robert K., and Thomas Shachtman (1997). *I Have Lived in the Monster: Inside the Minds of the World's Most Notorious Serial Killers.* New York: St Martin's Press.

Reynolds, Quentin (1955). *The Fiction Factory: From Pulp Row to Quality Street.* New York: Random House.

Richmond, Lee (1971). 'A Time to Mourn and a Time to Dance: Horace Mc-Coy's *They Shoot Horses, Don't They?*', *Twentieth Century Literature*, 17: 91–9.

Roth, Marty (1995). *Foul & Fair Play: Reading Genre in Classic Detective Fiction*. Athens, Ga.: University of Georgia Press.

Routledge, Christopher (1997). 'A Matter of Disguise: Locating the Self in Raymond Chandler's *The Big Sleep* and *The Long Good-Bye*', *Studies in the Novel*, 29/1: 94–107.

Rowland, Susan (2001). *From Agatha Christie to Ruth Rendell: British Women Writers in Detective and Crime Fiction*. Basingstoke: Palgrave.

Rubin, Martin (1999). *Thrillers*. Cambridge: Cambridge University Press.

Ruehlmann, William (1974). *Saint with a Gun: The Unlawful American Private Eye*. Washington, DC: American University Press.

Ruhm, Herbert, ed. (1977). *The Hard-Boiled Detective: Stories from 'Black Mask' Magazine, 1920–1951*. New York: Random House.

Ruth, David E. (1996). *Inventing the Public Enemy: the Gangster in American Culture*. Chicago: University of Chicago Press.

Rzepka, Charles J. (2000). ' "I'm in the Business Too": Gothic Chivalry, Private Eyes, and Proxy Sex and Violence in Chandler's *The Big Sleep*', *Modern Fiction Studies*, 46/3: 695–724.

Sallis, James (1983). 'In America's Black Heartland: The Achievement of Chester Himes', *Western Humanities Review*, 37/3: 191–206.

—— (1993). *Difficult Lives: Jim Thompson, David Goodis, Chester Himes*. Brooklyn, NY: Gryphon Books.

—— (2000). *Chester Himes: A Life*. Edinburgh: Payback Press.

Sampson, Anthony (2004). *Who Runs This Place? The Anatomy of Britain in the 21st Century*. London: John Murray.

Sawday, Jonathan (1996). *The Body Emblazoned*. London: Routledge.

Schatz, Thomas (1981). *Hollywood Genres*. New York: McGraw-Hill.

Schmid, David (1999). 'Chester Himes and the Institutionalization of Multicultural Detective Fiction', in Gosselin 1999: 283–302.

Seltzer, Mark (1998). *Serial Killers: Death and Life in America's Wound Culture*. New York: Routledge.

Server, Lee (1993). *Danger is my Business: An Illustrated History of the Fabulous Pulp Magazines: 1896–1953*. San Francisco: Chronicle Books.

—— (1994). *Over my Dead Body: The Sensational Age of the American Paperback: 1945–1955*. San Francisco: Chronicle Books.

—— Ed Gorman, and Martin H. Greenberg, eds. (1998). *The Big Book of Noir*. New York: Carroll and Graf.

Shadoian, Jack (1977). *Dreams and Dead Ends: The American Gangster/Crime Film*. Cambridge, Mass.: MIT Press.

Shaw, Joseph T., ed. (1946). *The Hard-boiled Omnibus: Early Stories from 'Black Mask'*. New York: Simon and Schuster.

Silet, Charles L. P. (1994). 'The 87th Precinct and Beyond: Interview with Ed McBain', *Armchair Detective: A Quarterly Journal*, 27/4: 382–99.

Silver, Alain, and James Ursini, eds. ([1996] 1999). *Film Noir Reader*. New York: Limelight Editions.

Simpson, Philip L. (2000). *Psycho Paths: Tracking the Serial Killer through Contemporary American Film and Fiction*. Carbondale, Ill.: Southern Illinois University Press.

Skal, David J. (1993). *The Monster Show: A Cultural History of Horror*. New York: W. W. Norton.

Sklar, Robert (1975). *Movie-Made America: A Cultural History of the American Movies*. New York: Random House.

Skinner, Robert E. (1989). *Two Guns From Harlem: The Detective Fiction of Chester Himes*. Bowling Green, Ohio: Popular Press.

Snyder, Stephen (1983). 'Rescuing Chandler: Crime Fiction, Ideology and Criticism', *Canadian Review of American Studies*, 14/2: 185–94.

Soitos, Stephen F. (1996). *The Blues Detective: A Study of Afro-American Detective Fiction*. Amherst: University of Massachusetts Press.

Sturak, Thomas (1968). 'Horace McCoy's Objective Lyricism', in Madden 1968: 137–62.

Svoboda, Frederic (1983). 'The Snub-Nosed Mystique: Observations on the American Detective Hero', *Modern Fiction Studies*, 29/3: 557–68.

Symons, Julian ([1972] 1992). *Bloody Murder: From the Detective Story to the Crime Novel: A History*. London: Pan.

Tani, Stefano (1984). *The Doomed Detective: The Contribution of the Detective Novel to Postmodern American and Italian Fiction*. Carbondale, Ill.: Southern Illinois University Press.

Telotte, J. P. (1989). *Voices in the Dark: The Narrative Patterns of Film Noir*. Urbana and Chicago: University of Illinois Press.

Thomas, Ronald R. (1999). *Detective Fiction and the Rise of Forensic Science*. Cambridge: Cambridge University Press.

Todorov, Tzvetan (1977). *The Poetics of Prose*, trans. R. Howard. Oxford: Basil Blackwell.

Van Dine, S. S. (1928). 'Twenty Rules for Writing Detective Stories', *American Magazine*, September 1928, reprinted in Haycraft [1946] 1974: 189–93.

Vanacker, Sabine (1997). 'V. I. Warshawski, Kinsey Millhone and Kay Scarpetta: Creating a Feminist Detective Hero', in Messent 1997: 62–86.

VanDover, J. K., ed. (1995). *The Critical Response to Raymond Chandler*. Westport, Conn.: Greenwood Press.

Voss, Karen (1998). 'Replacing L.A.: *Mi Familia, Devil in a Blue Dress*, and Screening the Other Los Angeles', *Wide Angle*, 20/3: 157–181.

Walker, Ronald G., and June M. Frazer, eds. (1990). *The Cunning Craft: Original*

Essays on Detective Fiction and Contemporary Literary Theory. Macomb: Western Illinois University Press.

Walton, Priscilla L. (1999). 'Bubblegum Metaphysics: Feminist Paradigms and Racial Interventions in Mainstream Hard-boiled Women's Detective Fiction', in Gosselin 1999: 257–79.

—— and Manina Jones (1999). *Detective Agency: Women Rewriting the Hard-Boiled Tradition.* Berkeley: University of California Press.

Watson, Colin (1971). *Snobbery with Violence: English Crime Stories and their Audience.* London: Eyre and Spottiswoode.

Webster, Duncan (1988). *LookaYonder: The Imaginary America of Populist Culture.* London: Routledge.

Wells, Claire (1999). 'Writing Black: Crime Fiction's Other', in Klein 1999: 205–23.

West, Cornell (1993). *Race Matters.* Boston: Beacon Press.

Willett, Ralph (1996). *The Naked City: Urban Crime Fiction in the USA.* Manchester: Manchester University Press.

Williams, John ([1991] 1993). *Into the Badlands: Travels through Urban America.* London: Flamingo.

Wilson, Andrew (2003). *Beautiful Shadow: A Life of Patricia Highsmith.* London: Bloomsbury.

Winks, Robin W. (1982). *Modus Operandi: An Excursion into Detective Fiction.* Boston: D. R. Godine.

—— ed. ([1980] 1988). *Detective Fiction: A Collection of Critical Essays.* Woodstock, Vt.: Countryman Press.

Winston, Robert P., and Nancy C. Mellerski (1992). *The Public Eye: Ideology and the Police Procedural.* Basingstoke: Macmillan.

Wolfe, Peter (1983). 'The Critics Did It: An Essay-Review', *Modern Fiction Studies,* 29/3: 389–433.

Woods, Paula L. (1996). *Spooks, Spies and Private Eyes: An Anthology of Black Mystery, Crime, and Suspense Fiction of the 20th Century.* Edinburgh: Payback Press.

Worpole, Ken (1983). *Dockers and Detectives: Popular Reading: Popular Writing.* London: Verso.

York, Peter, and Charles Jennings (1995). *Peter York's Eighties.* London: BBC Books.

Zizek, Slavoj (1992). *Looking Awry: An Introduction to Jacques Lacan through Popular Culture.* Cambridge, Mass.: MIT Press.

Index